Gender and Reading
Essays on Readers, Texts, and Contexts

Edited by
Elizabeth A. Flynn and
Patrocinio P. Schweickart

The Johns Hopkins University Press

Baltimore and London

This book was brought to publication with the generous assistance of the
Andrew W. Mellon Foundation.

Originally published, hardcover and paperback, 1986
Third printing, paperback, 1992

The Johns Hopkins University Press, 701 West 40th Street, Baltimore, Maryland 21211-2190
The Johns Hopkins Press Ltd., London

Library of Congress Cataloging-in-Publication Data
Main entry under title:

Gender and reading.

Bibliography: p.
1. Women—Books and reading—Addresses, essays, lectures.   2. Feminism and
literature—Addresses, essays, lectures.   3. Reader-response criticism—Addresses,
essays, lectures.   4. Women in literature—Addresses, essays, lectures.   5. Sex role in
literature—Addresses, essays, lectures.   I. Flynn, Elizabeth A., 1944–
II. Schweickart, Patrocinio P.
Z1039.W65G46   1986   028'.9'088042   85-12611
ISBN 0-8018-2905-4 (alk. paper)
ISBN 0-8018-2907-0 (pbk.)

The following essays, some in altered form, were previously published. Grateful
acknowledgment is made to the publishers for permission to reprint.

Jean E. Kennard, "Ourself behind Ourself: A Theory for Lesbian Readers," *Signs* 9,
no. 4 (Summer 1984); Susan Rubin Suleiman, "Malraux's Women: A Re-vision,"
copyright © 1984. Reprinted from *Witnessing André Malraux* by permission of
Wesleyan University Press. Edited by Brian Thompson and Carl Viggiani; Elizabeth
Segel, "As the Twig Is Bent . . . : Gender and Childhood Reading," excerpted from
Children's Literature 8; Madonne M. Miner, "Guaranteed to Please: Twentieth-
Century American Women's Bestsellers," excerpted from "Introduction: Guaranteed
to Please the Female Reader" in Madonne M. Miner's *Insatiable Appetites: Twentieth-
Century Women's Bestsellers.* Copyright © 1984 by Madonne M. Miner. Used with
permission of the publisher, Greenwood Press; Norman N. Holland and Leona F.
Sherman, "Gothic Possibilities," *New Literary History* 8 (Winter 1977); Elizabeth A.
Flynn, "Gender and Reading," *College English* 45, no. 3 (March 1983).

Contents

Preface

Among the joys of collaboration are the stories that can be told about how it all came to be. Happily for us, the circumstances of our working together contain a curious enough mixture of the inevitable and the fortuitous to support some storytelling.

In retrospect, it seems we were fated to collaborate on this anthology. We both went to graduate school at Ohio State University, and our residency there overlapped by two years. In addition, we had two mentors in common, James Kincaid and Marlene Longenecker.

In graduate school we were both drawn to theory, and we both gradually realized the momentous significance of the issue of gender. It is not clear which interest came first—what is clear is that for us theory and gender intertwined. The need to comprehend the ramifications of gender deepened our passion for theoretical work, and the intense critical attitude and intellectual honesty demanded by the theoretical enterprise made the issue of gender inescapable. Many questions, we saw, cannot be fully answered without addressing the issue of gender.

Oddly enough, we did not meet at Ohio State. We often heard of each other—people kept advising each of us to look the other up. But our paths did not cross until a few years after we left graduate school. We met in 1981 at the National Women's Studies Association Convention in Connecticut. There, to our mutual amusement, we learned that we would both be attending the summer session of the School of Criticism and Theory at Northwestern University.

This book grew out of our work at the school. The topic was by no means on the official agenda, but discussions of the theoretical and political significance of gender rippled around the periphery and through the interstices of the dominant discourse. Beth's project at the school developed into the essay that is included here. A few months after the summer session, Beth asked Patsy to collaborate on a volume of essays on gender and reading. The essay Patsy wrote for the volume won the 1984 Florence Howe Award for Outstanding Feminist Scholarship.

This book has been a collective effort in many ways. The debt we owe to the scholarly contributions of our authors is clear. But equally indispensable were the spirit of cooperation and the patience they brought to a lengthy and sometimes frustrating endeavor.

We especially appreciate the advice and encouragement of Jean Kennard, Susan Schibanoff, David Bleich, and Judith Fetterley. We are also indebted to Jane Tompkins for reading the manuscript carefully and for offering invaluable comments and suggestions, and to Eric Halpern and Jane Warth of the Johns Hopkins University Press for administering the project so competently. We also thank Jackie Wehmueller for copyediting the manuscript so painstakingly.

The support of Art Young, head of the Department of Humanities at Michigan Technological University, and of Stuart Palmer, dean of the College of Liberal Arts at the University of New Hampshire, has been invaluable. Sandra Boschetto of MTU and Gary Lindberg of UNH provided useful feedback on two of the essays submitted to us. Jo Perkins, Lynn Foss, and Pam Kuivanen of MTU and Carol Demerit and Helen Brock of UNH helped with typing and manuscript preparation. Carol Brown, formerly of MTU, helped locate items for the Bibliography.

Finally, we could not have done without the intellectual and personal support of John Flynn and David Schweickart, and the help of Karen and Anita Schweickart, who took good care of themselves and each other and took over household responsibilities when it really counted.

Introduction

Patrocinio P. Schweickart
Elizabeth A. Flynn

Until recently, reading was thought to be a rather straightforward procedure. Whether one emphasized its cognitive aspects—reading as
apprehending the meaning of the text—or its affective aspects—reading as experiencing the effects intended by the text—the goal was to
respond *properly* to the stimulus provided by the text, that is, to an
object that remained the same at all times and for everyone. The cardinal rule for readers of literature in this era was: "Do not confuse what
you are doing to the text with what it is doing to you. The proper aim of
criticism is the apprehension of the text itself." The whole of schooling
in reading, from the most rudimentary to the most sophisticated, was
geared toward following this maxim.

However, in spite of the impressive institutions designed to preserve
this view of reading, it was in constant peril, especially in the field of
literary studies. Readers were continually producing counterexamples
in the form of irreducibly different and often contradictory readings of
the same text. The wealth of literary interpretations undermined the
doctrine of the objectivity of the text and threatened the integrity of
criticism as an academic discipline. The forcefulness of the measures
taken to uphold the doctrine of the-text-as-stable-object, for example,
Wimsatt and Beardsley's famous stigmatization of the "affective fallacy," and Hirsch's statistical procedure for adjudicating conflicting
interpretations, underscored the seriousness of the threat.[1]

Today, the "objectivist" model of reading is still powerful, but during
the last two decades, new "stories of reading" have begun to take root in
the field of literary criticism.[2] Reader-response criticism, the rubric
under which these stories have been classified, has promoted readers
from their previous role as "extra" to that of "co-star" with the text in a
new script—or, more accurately, scripts—thereby calling attention to
the problematical interaction between reader and text.

Periods of critical ferment attending the alteration of conceptual paradigms offer excellent occasions for renewing our acquaintance with concrete reality. An examination of two contrasting readings of Faulkner's "Spotted Horses," written by students enrolled in a course focusing on relationships between literature, reading theory, and writing theory, might bring the discussion down to earth. Because the discussions of the stories were initial impressions rather than polished essays, students were not expected to organize their responses carefully or to develop them fully. The first response reads:

> In my first reading I couldn't help but notice the strange Faulknerian mix of objects and dialect. Strange. We see the world of the story through an apparently objective and extremely insightful, though inarticulate (in a way) narrator. We see lusty, backward, ignorant people in an "old west" setting, yet there are "tennis shoes" and the horse runs "forty miles an hour"— details from the modern world.
>
> These backward people are swindled and controlled by Flem Snopes—a sort of low-class crook. Mrs. Armstid is not fooled by him in the end, but easily appeased. Like the rest of the people, there is no effort to make something good happen for yourself—except Flem. They don't make the effort to associate the man from Texas with Flem. This is truly a picture of the lazy southwest—where you just lazy around, get taken, and pass meaningless time (not unlike the people in the "Country Husband") chasing high strung horses around the "country."

The second response is different in style and tone:

> How could they all admire him? Mrs. Armstid in such poverty, serving all night to make nickels add to five dollars, spent on a worthless horse which they never get; her return for her labor is a sack of penny candy—and Flem is admired. Why do we admire a person's ability to outsmart and outmaneuver another—why do we admire someone's immorality? But we do— "Good for him, so clever he didn't get caught." I'm left feeling outraged and saddened.
>
> Enjoyed Faulkner's detail and description.

It is clear from their journal entries that both students took the assignment seriously but that this was a first reading for them; neither evidences a familiarity with Faulkner. Both students are critical of Flem Snopes, and both refer to Mrs. Armstid and to the people who allow Snopes to take advantage of them. The two students provide decidedly different emphases, however. The first reader focuses initially on the text as object, as created by Faulkner, as narrated, and begins the discussion by mentioning textual details. The second, in contrast, does not mention Faulkner until the end of the response; the reference to Faulkner's detail and description seems to be an afterthought. One concentrates on the ignorance of the townspeople; they are lazy and pass meaningless time. The other is "outraged" and "saddened" by the reaction of the townspeople to Snopes. The first response was written by a male, the second by a female.

Mike's response is Iserian. In *The Act of Reading*, Wolfgang Iser describes the reading process in terms of the reader's attempt to form consistent patterns of meaning as textual details are encountered.[3] Iser's reader is a serious student of literature, perhaps a trained critic, who is highly motivated to achieve textual meaning and who attends closely to textual cues. Reading, for Iser, is a cognitive activity, a process of selecting from among the multiplicity of strategies and structures that comprise the text.

In describing "Spotted Horses," Mike moves from part to whole, from textual detail to the formulation of a consistent pattern of meaning: "This is truly a picture of the lazy southwest—where you just lazy around, get taken, and pass meaningless time . . . chasing high strung horses around the 'country.'" And although his language is informal and his organizational pattern associative, a characteristic of writing meant to discover ideas rather than to communicate them to an audience, he nevertheless takes the stance of the critic-in-training. He seems to be rehearsing for a formal critical essay. He is also relatively detached from the characters in the story. The townspeople are ignorant fools, and Mrs. Armstid, who does protest Flem's behavior, is "easily appeased."

Ann's response, in contrast, more closely resembles Louise Rosenblatt's account of the reading process. In *The Reader, the Text, the Poem*, Rosenblatt emphasizes that reading has both a cognitive and an affective component.[4] Like Iser, she describes reading as an event in time, an experience. But unlike Iser, she allows that readers have different purposes for reading and read in different ways depending on those purposes. "Aesthetic" reading involves experiencing the text fully, living through the events of the text as they are encountered; "efferent" reading involves reading in order to take something away from the experience, to make some use of it. Rosenblatt's reader is the nonprofessional reader who should be encouraged, in initial encounters with texts, to read in order to experience the text fully rather than to analyze it. According to Rosenblatt, literary training sometimes interferes with a satisfying aesthetic engagement with a text.

Ann reacts emotionally as well as intellectually to the story. She also seems to be connected more directly to the characters and events of the story than was Mike; hers is an "aesthetic" response. She even seems to be connected to other readers of the story, seeing the townspeople's admiration of Flem as the equivalent of the reaction of a collective "we," readers like herself. Ann centers her discussion on a theme that she sees as being both within the text and outside it: the tendency to admire immoral behavior. She clearly identifies with Mrs. Armstid and is incensed at the treatment she receives by the men in the story.

Readings as different as Mike's and Ann's readings of Faulkner's story are an everyday fact of life for teachers of literature. How significant are the differences between readings? What prompts readers to read as they do? What do the differences between readings imply about the process of reading? The advent of reader-response criticism has brought these questions to the forefront of critical discussion. This book addresses these questions in light of an issue that is beginning to emerge from the periphery of reader-centered criticism and theory, namely, the issue of gender. If readers differ in their approaches to texts, how much of this difference can be attributed to gender?

While our principal concern is with literary criticism and theory, it is essential to recognize the interdisciplinary character of inquiry into the reading process. "The Reader's Construction of Meaning" by Mary Crawford and Roger Chaffin summarizes relevant work in linguistics, communication theory, and cognitive psychology. For the most part, research in these fields agrees with the emphasis placed by reader-response criticism on the activity and creativity of the reader in comprehending a text. While evidence is far from conclusive, important experiments indicate that comprehension is mediated by generalized knowledge structures, or schemata, that exist in the mind of the reader. The schemata that are activated in the process of understanding a text provide a framework for the construction of meaning. They allow the knower to process the given information and, importantly, go beyond what is actually given. In the final analysis, what one reads out of the text depends on what one reads into it. The similarity in terminology invites comparisons with Iser's position. However, since the emphasis in schema theory is on mental rather than textual schemata, it is closer to Stanley Fish's contention that the meaning of a text is a function of the interpretive strategies one employs.[5]

Crawford and Chaffin use schema theory as the framework for their discussion of gender as a factor in comprehension. There is strong evidence that a heterogeneous network of ideas, beliefs, and associations regarding the attributes, behavior, and roles natural or proper to women and men—in short, some kind of "gender schema"—is likely to be activated, more or less unconsciously, in the process of linguistic comprehension. Crawford and Chaffin underscore two distinctive characteristics of the gender schema: it is rich, diverse, and wide-ranging; and it is deeply ingrained—the process of introjection begins very early (around age three), and the gender schema is assimilated into the individual's sense of self. For all this, they are careful to point out that gender schemata and the sense of masculinity and feminity they induce are not biologically determined. Rather, they are internalized social constructs that are difficult but not impossible to change. In fact, the effect of the gender schema on ego formation is by no means uniform. People vary in the degree to which they are "sex-typed," and sex-typing appears to be as important as gender per se in determining how information is processed and remembered.

In all fields, the impetus for the examination of the ways in which gender shapes experience and behavior has come primarily from the feminist movement. The essays by Schweickart and Kennard explicitly situate the study of gender and reading in the context of feminist theory. In "Reading Ourselves," Patrocinio Schweickart identifies three distinctive features of a feminist theory of reading. First of all, it would attend to the issue of gender. But beyond this, a feminist theory would accord a privileged status to the experience and interests of women readers. They would be center stage in a feminist theory. Implicit in Schweickart's discussion is the recognition that in theories that overlook the issue of gender, the appearance of universality is almost always achieved through a concerted obliviousness to the female perspective. Finally, a feminist theory of reading would be conscious of the political dimensions of reading and writing, and of the political implications of the issue of gender. Schweickart stresses that the gender inscribed in the text is as crucial as the gender of the reader. She proposes a feminist "story" that has (at least) two chapters, the first concerned with women reading men's writing, the second with women reading women's writing.

Jean Kennard's "Ourself behind Ourself" supplies a necessary corrective to the impression unintentionally conveyed by Schweickart's essay, and by much feminist criticism, that gender is the only locus of difference. Kennard reminds us that the category "woman reader" glosses over crucial differences, among them race, class, and sexual orientation. To the extent that we leave this obliviousness unchecked, we risk falling into a "universal" that is as false and as repressive as the "generic masculine."

The exchange between Schweickart and Kennard illustrates a problem inherent in feminist theory. On the one hand, it is important to convey the multiplicity of interests and experiences that make up the female perspective and, more importantly, to avoid the repressive assimilation of the perspectives of more vulnerable groups. On the other hand, generalization is essential to theory formation: if we wish to examine the implications of gender, we must assume that there is some common ground in the experiences and perspectives of different kinds of women that sets women apart from men. The same is true if one is concerned with articulating the implications of race, class, or sexual orientation. Kennard, for example, is careful to note that, like the category "woman reader," the category "lesbian reader" is plural rather than singular. But eventually she must abstract out the differences within the category "lesbian"—in particular, those that are grounded in race and class—in order to place the distinguishing features of the lesbian orientation in the foreground. The play of difference presupposes and induces a play of identity. Every feminist theorist is faced with the challenge of devising a rhetoric that avoids the repressive exclusions that could ensue from theoretical constructs, a rhetoric of equivocal generalizations, if you will, that incorporates gestures pointing to the provisional and heuristic status of the categories in which her work is phrased.

According to Jonathan Culler, mainstream reader-response theory is torn between text-dominant and reader-dominant constructions of the reading process.[6] Schweickart points out that neither alternative is consonant with feminist concerns. Text-dominant models leave women readers at the mercy of androcentric texts, and reader-dominant models obscure the oppressive action of such texts. Similarly, neither model can form the basis for a feminist theory of women reading women's writings. They both confer authority on one woman at the cost of silencing another. What is needed, whether one is considering male or female writing, is a dialectical construction of the interaction between reader and text. In the case of the woman reading male texts, Schweickart proposes a story that is informed primarily by the dialectic of emancipatory struggle; in the case of the woman reading women's writing, by the dialectic of conversation.

Kennard's point of departure is the situation of the lesbian reader, who is surrounded, even within the feminist movement, by texts that are shaped by heterosexual perspectives. She proposes a model of "polar reading" adapted from Joseph Zinker's theory of gestalt therapy. Basic to the model is the conception of the individual as a composite of opposing characteristics, or "polarities." One "owns up" to certain traits and represses or hides their opposites. In the model proposed by Kennard, the lesbian reader faced with a heterosexual text would not adopt the strategy of resistance advocated by Judith Fetterley in *The Resisting Reader;* on the contrary, she would deliberately "lean into" the text, not to be absorbed or transformed by it, but to reinforce her own sense of self.[7] Polar reading calls for the full recognition and the heightened awareness of the other, and of those aspects of one's self that are normally projected on others. The reader deliberately allows polarities to coexist. To the extent that she conducts the process freely and consciously, the result will not be schizophrenic alienation but a deepening of and a consolidation of her sense of self: "I do not become heterosexual for allowing that part of myself to breathe, I become more fully, completely, lesbian."

Schweickart's and Kennard's models are by no means congruent. It could be argued that Kennard underestimates the alienating potential of self-negating texts. Surely, one could not subsist on a steady diet of such texts. Moreover, it would seem that the strategy of resistance advocated by Judith Fetterley must antedate, and perhaps coexist with, the strategy of polar reading. In any case, there is much here for critical reflection. For now, it is worth noting that, like Schweickart's models, Kennard's polar reading implies a dialectical conception of the relationship between text and reader.

The next four essays focus on particular works. Susan Schibanoff writes on the *Book of the City of Women* by Christine de Pisan, Kathryn Shevelow on Richard Steele's periodical, the *Tatler,* Susan Suleiman on the novels of André Malraux, and Judith Fetterley on stories by Susan Glaspell, Edgar Allan Poe, and Charlotte Perkins Gilman. Following custom, one might place these essays in the genre of "practical criticism." However, we must make two provisos: all four incorporate strong theoretical interests, and all construe the text as a story of reading. Foremost among the themes that recur in these stories is the theme of "immasculation" of the woman reader. The prominence of this theme testifies to the ground-breaking significance of Judith Fetterley's *The Resisting Reader* as well as to the reality of the phenomenon she names. Fetterley points out that everyone, men and women alike, learns to read like a man; that is, to adopt the androcentric perspective that pervades the most authoritative texts of the culture.

Crawford and Chaffin phrase the same observation in the idiom of schema theory. They observe that two factors influence the schemata that are activated during reading: "background" (education, upbringing, life experiences) determines the prior knowledge the reader brings to bear on the text; "viewpoint" (what she expects to learn from the text, what she believes about the author's intentions, and what she imagines to constitute proper reading and the language in which the reading is to be articulated, and so on) determines the reader's disposition toward the text and the activity of reading. Differences in viewpoint can override similarities in background, and differences in background can be masked by similarities in viewpoint. Crawford and Chaffin explain that one reason gender differences in comprehension are less apparent than we might expect is that women belong to a "muted group." In order to be heard they must learn the dominant idiom and express themselves within its parameters. This is especially so with regard to formal, public discourse. The adoption of the male viewpoint had been (and to a significant extent still is) a precondition, for example, to the participation of women in literary criticism and scholarship. Crawford and Chaffin add that because the standard male viewpoint is inscribed in "very high-level schemata," for example, the generic masculine, the dominant Western view of rationality, and the canons of critical discourse, neither men nor women can readily set it aside.

In "Taking the Gold Out of Egypt," Susan Schibanoff rereads Christine de Pisan's *Book of the City of Women* as a quasi-autobiographical story of the transformation of the narrator "Christine" from an immasculated reader into a woman reader intent on defying existing canons and on exercising her right to read texts according to her experiences and interests. The story opens, appropriately enough, in a library. Seeking to entertain herself, Christine happens on Matheolus's *Lamentations*. She decides to browse through it, and by the end of the first chapter of *Book of the City of Women,* we see her reduced to a self-doubting, self-hating woman, pathetically cursing her bad luck of being born female and desperately wishing she could be a man. The rest of the story describes Christine's recovery. The story follows along the general lines sketched by Schweickart. The key to the successful ending of Christine's story is her recognition that the strategies of reading learned in the course of acquiring literacy—in Christine's case, the "schema" of patristic exegesis—are themselves deeply implicated in the process of immasculation. Schibanoff suggests that the development of print media and increased female literacy has exacerbated the phenomenon of immasculation. Once they are set in print, texts become "fixed"—they acquire enough substance to support an official "objective" status, which in turn becomes the pretext for the notion of an official objective reading. Compared to Christine, who is highly literate, the "illiterate" wife of Bath appears to be less susceptible to the authority of patriarchal texts. Since she operates in an oral/aural culture that does not have a well-established concept of an official text, she remains relatively free to hear, remember, and repeat according to her own inclinations.

"Fathers and Daughters" by Kathryn Shevelow reinforces Schibanoff's idea that literacy for women is a mixed blessing. Steele's periodical was the most successful and influential of the early Augustan publications that recognized the commercial advantages that can be derived from female literacy. The distinctive and influential rhetoric of the *Tatler,* Shevelow argues, bears the traces of Steele's decision to "fair-sex it."

Shevelow distinguishes two levels of persuasion operating in the *Tatler:* overt and covert. Commentaries on didactic prose generally focus on the overt system, that is, on the rhetorical appeal that is consciously deployed and controlled by the author. However, a covert system of persuasion is generated by the interaction of the text with readers who come with certain predilections. This covert system exceeds authorial control and rests, finally, on the network of social and cultural conventions that surround the process of reading. The overt power of the much-admired prose of the *Tatler* is enhanced, with regard to women readers, by the covert system, which is set in motion by the paternal figure of Isaac Bickerstaff speaking to his younger sister, Jenny, in the accents of "father-to-daughter" advice books. The significance of the *Tatler* is therefore double-edged. It acknowledges the significance of women; by courting women readers, Steele's periodical pays tribute to their power and hints at the emancipatory potential of literacy. Unfortunately, the overt and covert rhetoric deployed in the *Tatler* work together to reinforce the concept of female subordination to patriarchal social structures, within the family and without. For the woman reader, the ability to read could be a liability. The more she reads, the more extensive her schooling in seeing it "his way."

In "Malraux's Women," Susan Suleiman exemplifies how the advent of a feminist perspective can radically alter a woman reader's perception of and attitude toward a male text. Suleiman opens with a personal, anecdotal introduction that owes much of its current acceptability to feminist criticism. Suleiman read Malraux in graduate school in the early sixties. Later, she reread him and wrote about his work, but this second reading did not occasion a rethinking, only an elaboration and an enhancement of the first reading. Malraux remained for her "a familiar and admired writer, exemplary in his concern for questions of the broadest human significance." His works, she concluded, were "definitely worth saving." Then, a few years ago, she read Annie Leclerc, who told her that Malraux is not worth saving, certainly not by or for women. Leclerc's angry denunciation induced a transmutation of the context of reading. It became clear that a re-reading from a new critical perspective was in order.

The story of reading told by Suleiman is familiar. For many of us, the man was D. H. Lawrence or Norman Mailer, the angry woman, Simone de Beauvoir or Kate Millett. Each of us was more or less susceptible to the woman writer's anger, but the heat freshened our eyes. Suleiman discovered on re-reading that the "broad" humanism she had admired in Malraux is really a male fiction, embodying a persistent male fantasy, the fantasy of a world without women.

It is striking to see how a shift in perspective could transform what was an admired text and an occasion for "historical nostalgia" into a "symptom" of a cultural malaise. Still, one cannot help thinking that since the discovery of Malraux's androcentricity is by now rather predictable, careful textual analysis seems hardly worth the effort. And yet, for women engaged in the literary profession, re-readings like Suleiman's represent a professional responsibility. Suleiman closes her essay with an anecdote about a lecture on *La Condition humaine* she presented to an undergraduate class in which she devoted a few minutes to the issue of woman's silence. The "nods of recognition" and "the almost grateful looks" with which the women students greeted her remarks prove that their import transcends the domain of academic questions. For these students and for others like them, it is essential (in the idiom of early feminist works, a matter of survival) that the derogatory attitudes toward women that mar the "broad humanism" of revered authors not be passed over in silence or with an offhand observation.

The emphasis in the three essays just discussed is on women reading androcentric texts. Judith Fetterley's "Reading about Reading" considers the reverse situation: men reading women's texts. The evidence indicates that men are resisting readers of women's texts, and that this resistance is deeply etched into our literary, critical, and educational establishments. The stories that Fetterley analyzes—"A Jury of Her Peers" by Susan Glaspell, "Murders in the Rue Morgue" by Edgar Allan Poe, and "The Yellow Wallpaper" by Charlotte Perkins Gilman—illustrate how far men will go to avoid reading women's texts and intimate the motivation for their resistance. If women could learn, and learn so well, to read men's texts, men should certainly be similarly educable. It is not that men can't read women's texts; it is, rather, that they *won't.*

What is at stake, according to Fetterley, is the control of textuality. In designing the literary curriculum, men have prepared a certain experience for themselves—that of seeing themselves reflected in and amplified in art—that they do not wish women to have, for in allowing women to have such an experience men risk provoking women into refusing their role of the "other without reciprocity." But beyond this, male control of textuality means men do not have to read women's texts. This, perhaps, points to the more intense psychological threat. Fetterley shows that to read women's texts, men must confront figures like John Wright ("A Jury of Her Peers") or John ("The Yellow Wallpaper"), both "good" men who gravely mistreat their wives. Male violence against women is a major theme, latent if not explicit, in women's stories. Moreover, unlike Poe, who projects the violence on a beast, women do not give men an easy "out." For men, reading women's stories means confronting themselves reflected in the eyes of women—they must endure the gaze of the other. Thus, it is not only a matter of depriving women of the self-enhancing readings men claim for themselves, but also of avoiding the alienating readings that they have allotted to women. With textuality firmly in male hands, men never have to face the risks inherent in genuine reciprocity.

The discussion thus far suggests the risks implicit in admitting the issue of gender in reader-response criticism. It is only fair to ask, What is to be gained? Fetterley states it strongly. Silence on the issue of gender leaves the control of textuality in male hands, and this entails madness for women. But beyond this, we can say what it would mean to us to be able to read and write as women, that is, without having to adopt the posture of the other.

It is significant that, unlike Christine de Pisan's contributions to the *Querelle de la Rose,* the *Book of the City of Women* is specifically addressed to a female audience. Here is the key to the paradox posed by Jonathan Culler in his essay "Reading as a Woman" in *On Deconstruction.*[8] The phrase "a woman reading as a woman" is abstract and subject to the dizzying deconstruction he demonstrates as long as we hold on to the singularity of the reading subject. A solitary woman reader cannot know what she is doing—her reflections, indeed, lead to an infinite regression: "a woman reading as a woman reading as a woman . . . " The impasse can only be thought through by admitting other women into the story. To know what it means to read as a woman, one must also know what it means to read women's writing and to write for women. This by no means implies that "reading as a woman" would thereby be rendered unproblematical, but it alters the nature of the problem. The production of the meaning of the phrase becomes a *task* that women collectively pose to themselves.

As we have said, the androcentric viewpoint that women, like men, have absorbed masks gender differences in reading. More to the point, it obscures women's perspective and distorts their mode of negotiating the subject/object interaction of reading. This is especially true when the text in question is male. Kathryn Shevelow's idea of a covert rhetoric set in motion by the social conventions that surround the activity of reading is germane here. The masculinity inscribed in the text—the male voice roused to life in the reading, in addition to any overt textual strategies—triggers the female reader's deep-seated inclination to adapt herself to the male viewpoint. The feminist reader consciously endeavors to disrupt this tendency. However, the posture of resistance and combat that perforce she adopts imposes its own distortions. In particular, the female viewpoint becomes defined negatively and thus remains a function of what it opposes. Without committing ourselves unequivocally to the existence of gender difference in reading, we could say that the female perspective, if there is such a thing, would most fully reveal itself in women's readings of women's writing, where both the pressure to adopt the male viewpoint and the pressure to negate it are relatively relaxed. Fetterley's discussion of Susan Glaspell's "A Jury of Her Peers" substantiates the judicial and dialogic components of Schweickart's model of feminist readings of women' writings.

Two women, Mrs. Hale and Mrs. Peters, are able to read the text—a disorderly kitchen, evidence of hastily abandoned tasks, crooked stitching in a quilt in progress, shabby clothes, an inadequate stove, a broken cage, a dead bird—that the men could/would not see. From the outset, Martha Hale has no trouble sensing the story written in the artifacts in Minnie's kitchen. But what qualifies her as a reader, finally, is her concern for the woman whose fate depends on a responsible reading of her story.

It is well to point out in this regard that *responsibility*, like many words in the lexicon, has a meaning that varies according to whether it is used in the context of male or female discourse. As Carol Gilligan points out in *In a Different Voice, responsibility*, in a male context, is strongly associated with liability.[9] To act responsibly is to exercise one's rights without impinging on the rights of others: to manage property, operate a car, practice a profession with the understanding that this may involve being held culpable of "mal-practice" and liable for damages. To accept responsibility is to accept both authority and the risk of liability. In the context of female discourse, *responsibility* is more closely associated with responsiveness to the needs of others. To act responsibly toward one's family, friends, and colleagues, and toward one's self, is to engage in a never-ending "juggling act," the governing principle of which is not the anticipation of blame, but the susceptibility to the feelings of others and the wish, whenever possible, to work out a compromise that minimizes pain and preserves relationships. This latter sense of responsibility defines Mrs. Hale's attitude toward the story she has been called on to read and to judge.

At the same time, Glaspell's story illustrates the ambiguity of the phrase "reading as a woman." Mrs. Peters, the sheriff's wife, reminds Mrs. Hale that "the law is the law." The dramatic action of Glaspell's story revolves around the conversion of this woman, who is "married to the law," into one who will interpret and judge Minnie according to a different sense of responsibility. The crucial moment is clearly marked by Glaspell's narration: "It was as if something within her [Mrs. Hale] had spoken, and it found in Mrs. Peters something she did not know as herself." At the end of the story, Martha Hale explicitly states the principles of empathetic understanding and tender solicitude that inform the two women's interpretations of Minnie's story: "We all go through the same things—it's all just a different kind of the same thing! If it weren't—why do you and I *understand?* Why do we *know*—what we know this minute?"

Reader-centered criticism and feminist criticism are alike in that they induce a heightened awareness of the way perspective conditions comprehension and interpretation. Perspective here signifies the capacity for certain insights as well as the limitation of vision. The essays that have been discussed so far define reading in relation to texts and readers that have privileged status for professional teachers and scholars of literature. They delineate the perspective of the trained reader confronting texts that have been sanctioned by other trained readers. The next two essays direct our attention to texts and readers that, for the most part, have been peripheral to academic literary studies.

"As the Twig Is Bent" by Elizabeth Segel discusses the development of segregated reading material for children. Young readers are especially vulnerable. Childhood reading is mediated by adult tastes, interests, and preconceptions at all stages of the production, distribution, procurement, and consumption of reading material. It is no exaggeration to say that gender identity is acquired hand-in-hand with literacy.

Segel shows that the wholesale segregation of childhood reading into girls' books and boys' books is a relatively recent development—she dates it no earlier than the 1850s. While several factors may account for the onset of differentiation, it is clear from the earliest examples of girls' books and boys' books that reading was perceived to be an excellent vehicle for sex-role socialization. Segel's research corroborates observations made earlier in this Introduction. The clear separation of books by gender did not deter girls from becoming avid readers of boys' books. This, as we have seen, represents a strength as well as a liability. Reading the adventure stories that were reserved for boys allowed girls imaginative relief from the strictures of the feminine role, and it gave them training in understanding and identifying with people who were unlike themselves. At the same time, this reading experience heightened their susceptibility to immasculation. Furthermore, Segel points out that adults generally assume that boys can not/will not read girls' books. This belief becomes especially consequential when those who hold it are in a position to regulate childhood reading. Boys who ventured to contradict this opinion did so with considerable trepidation. Male aversion for girls' books has been and is still considered a given, and this aversion has served as the pretext for a male-centered reading curriculum. Given the presumed inflexibility of boys' tastes, the apparently reasonable principle that "for reading in common, only materials well liked by both boys and girls should be used" translated in practice into exclusion of girls' books from the curriculum.

The women's movement has prompted a relaxation of the constraints on books written for girls, as well as a more balanced distribution of male and female protagonists in children's stories. Unfortunately, by and large, only girls reap the benefits of these enlightened texts. The taboo against boys reading girls' books is still very much in force. Segel's study of childhood reading bears out others that show that the negation of the female is a defining characteristic of traditional masculine gender identity. She concludes that although the boys' books–girls' books division depreciated female experience and extracted a heavy cost in feminine self-esteem, it was, paradoxically, more restrictive of boys' options.

Madonne Miner's "Guaranteed to Please" employs Norman Holland's psychoanalytic theory of reading to account for the tastes of a significant group of readers: the consumers of "women's bestsellers." According to Holland, whatever their conscious intentions, readers *unconsciously* read for the sake of the pleasurable transformation, in the course of reading, of "primitive wishes and fears into significance and coherence." Thus, the fictional text serves as a locus, a space for representing and reworking unresolved fantasies and fears. A reader will be most drawn to the text that maximizes the opportunity for this pleasurable transaction.

Miner's analysis of three exemplary twentieth-century bestsellers, *Gone with the Wind, Forever Amber,* and *The Valley of the Dolls,* reveals a basic white, middle-class American "woman's story." On the most obvious level, the story portrays a woman caught in the "web of desire" and appeals to women interested in heterosexual romance. On closer inspection, one sees that the story is really built on a bisexual triangle. Next to the heterosexual plot, and bearing much of the psychic tension, is the story of a daughter's relationship with her mother. Women's bestsellers support Nancy Chodorow's contention that although girls and women may seek refuge in the arms of male fathers/lovers, they retain their preoedipal attachment to their mothers.[10] Under the guise of the standard romance, women's bestsellers offer women texts that indulge their deepest preoccupations: the fantasies and the terrors, the joy and the pain, of the mother-daughter bond.

The study of gender and reading, of necessity, includes a consideration of both texts and readers. The text is construed in terms of the reaction of the reader, and, conversely, the reaction of the reader is realized and articulated with reference to a particular text. In the essays discussed above, the "reader" is no longer the abstract subject of mainstream theories of reading; instead, we have the "woman reader," the "lesbian reader," the "male reader," the "child reader." We also have accounts of certain exemplary fictional readers: "Christine," "Jenny Bickerstaff," Poe's Dupin, the women of Glaspell's story, "Adrienne Rich." But in spite of the gain in concreteness, the "reader" remains an ideal or fictional construct. Of course, it must be said that behind every mythic reader is a *real* reader, the author of the essay. The essay by Norman Holland and Leona Sherman, "Gothic Possibilities," reverses the distribution of particularity between text and reader. The text is the generalized gothic novel, the readers are particular persons—the authors of the essay.

Holland and Sherman begin by posing the general questions that have provoked them to examine their reactions to the gothic: "What, then, is the relation between the singularity and the regularity of literary response? How, for example, has a genre like the gothic maintained its popularity for two centuries? Why are the overwhelming majority of those who read gothics women?"

The discussion is framed in the psychoanalytic theory of reading developed by Holland. According to this theory, reading involves the recreation of the reader's "identity theme." This process is further articulated into four modalities: "We match inner defenses and expectations to outer realities [the text] in order to project fantasies into . . . significance." Defense, expectation, fantasy, transaction: DEFT. Each individual reader deploys characteristic strategies for achieving pleasure and avoiding distress. In keeping with its psychoanalytic base, Holland's model locates reading in the context of the ongoing process of managing desires and anxieties that are rooted in childhood experiences.

The choice of text—the gothic novel—places the issue of gender in the foreground. The gothic is immensely appealing to women, hardly at all to men. Holland and Sherman conform to this rule. To highlight the difference between them, it is useful to isolate their responses.

The structure Sherman reads out of the gothic matches that which Miner finds in women's bestsellers. The basic motif is that of a bisexual triangle: her (and the heroine's) interest in sexual relations with men is played against her intense, deep-seated preoccupation with the maternal bond. Sherman addresses the issue of gender forthrightly. She readily identifies herself as a female; her responses convey a lively interest in exploring the ramifications of this fact.

Holland's account of his response to the gothic, on the other hand, testifies to his uneasiness with the issue of gender and his unwillingness to thematize his maleness—to offer it up for discussion. The bulk of his response consists of strategies for deflecting discourse away from the issue of *his* gender: he tries to talk of everything else, it seems, so as to avoid examining the ramifications of his masculinity. Actually, although Holland is quite uneasy about the issue of gender, he makes no effort to mask this uneasiness and the psychic threat posed by gothic novels: "For me, both identifying with a female and imagining being penetrated call into question my male identity. Both raise the threat posed by the castle and the gothic machinery to a pitch where I no longer wish them relevant to me, the male me, and I sense myself relegating gothic to an alienating category, 'woman's fiction'."

In the end, it is clear that for Sherman, reading the gothic has been a pleasurable experience—the transaction proceeded successfully. For Holland, on the other hand, the transaction failed: "I find I can not shape from this heroine, this villain, this castle, or these descriptions satisfying structures (defenses) to cope with the theme or fantasy of penetration that I find intriguing but doubly threatening." Holland's thoughtful and frank analysis of this failure sheds light on the subjective dimension of the male aversion to female texts noted by Fetterley and Segel.

The discussion so far permits some speculation. It does not seem unreasonable to say that the theories of reading that currently dominate reader-response criticism—Holland's among them—embody characteristically male approaches to the interaction between self and other and so between reader and text. These approaches proceed from a subjectivity that is strongly invested in maintaining a firm ego boundary, hence the prominence of issues of partition and control, the strong interest in determining where the rights of the text end and those of the reader begin, the perception that what the reader gains in freedom, the text loses in authority. Moreover, although Holland's model of reading is hotly contested, it captures a characteristic feature of the masculine mode of reading, namely, the inability to entertain or play host to fundamental difference. This observation calls to mind Culler's argument that there is a radical ambiguity in the phrase "reading as a woman." The cogency of this argument rests on the fact—noted by feminists—that women often read as men. It would appear that the phrase "reading as a man" harbors no comparable ambiguity. A man (almost) always reads as a man—that is, (almost) never as a woman.

Miner and Sherman show that women readers are also inveterate self-replicators. They have an immense appetite for texts that allow them to play out their characteristic identity themes. At the same time, women do not necessarily turn their backs on texts that frustrate their drive toward self-replication. They can read and enjoy male texts, and they can do so without effacing the masculinity of the text. Their repertoire appears to include, in addition to a self-replicating mode, a mode that is akin to Kennard's polar reading. Women can cultivate and merge with fundamentally different—even hostile—texts, and often (given the prevailing gender hierarchy) they do so at great cost to themselves.

The last two essays, featuring studies of the responses of larger groups of real readers, essentially corroborate the difference suggested above. "Gender Interests in Reading and Language" by David Bleich reports the results of his analysis of two groups of responses. The first was provided by a graduate seminar on "Comparative Literary Response Patterns of Men and Women" which he taught at Indiana University. The members of the graduate seminar studied poetry and fiction by male and female authors, and each one (including the instructor) wrote "response statements" of the sort Bleich describes in *Subjective Criticism* and elsewhere. Analysis of these statements (collectively undertaken by the class) reveal significant gender-related difference with regard to literary genre. Men and women read lyric poetry similarly, narrative fiction differently. The salient parameter was the perception of "voice." Both men and women perceived a strong lyric voice, and usually attributed it to the author. With regard to narrative, however, men perceived a strong narrative voice, but women experienced the narrative as a "world" without a particularly strong sense that this world was narrated into existence. Bleich found that women enter the world of the novel and take it as something "there" for that purpose. Men, in contrast, see the novel as the result of someone's action and construe its meaning and logic in such terms.

The second group of responses (fifty by men, fifty by women) was collected from a large freshman class. The students were asked to retell Faulkner's "Barn Burning" as fully and as accurately as possible. Bleich found that men retold the story as if its purpose were to deliver a clear, simple structure or chain of information: these are the main characters; this is the main action; this is how it turned out. Their primary concern appeared to be getting the "facts" of the story "straight." Women, on the other hand, presented the narrative as if it were an atmosphere or an experience. They were also more inclined than men to make inferences and to respond affectively to the human relationships represented. Bleich concludes that abstractions emerge more readily when men retell a story because they are more "instinctively" distant from the text. Women, however, are more inclined to enter into the human relationships presented by the story, and, for this reason, they retell it in terms of interpersonal motives, allegiances, conflicts, rather than in terms of the perspective of a single character or the author.

Bleich's theoretical analysis of the difference revealed by these two stories calls attention, again, to the intimate link between language acquisition and gender-identity formation. Bleich notes that language acquisition in its earliest stages is linked with the voice of the mother and is part of the child's realization of the primary difference between self and other. At this early stage, neither self nor other is differentiated with respect to gender. The self-objectification of the poet/speaker of the lyric triggers a reciprocal self-objectification in the reader, and this self-reflexive convention recalls the psychological action associated with the onset of language acquisition. The reader—man or woman— focuses on the voice of the speaker of the lyric as the child focuses on the voice of the mother.

Although the narrative voice still recalls the voice of the mother, the characteristic trope of narrative is no longer "I speak" or "I speak of myself," but "I speak of this other item, this object, this 'third' person." Bleich associates this third, figuratively, with the father. Narrative, he says, recalls the acquisition of gender identity that follows the onset of language acquisition. The child now recognizes two kinds of otherness—masculine and feminine—and must objectify himself or herself into one of these categories. The gender difference in the perception of narrative voice is a function of the difference of gender-identity formation. Little girls have a greater tendency to sense that "My language is my mother's language," "My mother and I, because we are the same sex, speak the 'same' language." The little boy, on the other hand, seeing his gender affinity with the father, will have a greater tendency to feel that "My language is other than my mother's language." He has the psychological grounds for seeing an otherness in the mother's language (indeed, in the mother herself) that is more radical than the otherness the little girl sees. Thus, for the boy (and for the boy-in-the-man), both the content and the source of the narrative are experienced as other. Because female gender-identity formation does not require a radical differentiation from the mother, the narrator remains the "same" figure she was in the language acquisition stage, an other who is now somewhat *less* (rather than more) of an other by virtue of gender affinity. Women "blend in" readily with both teller and tale since for them neither is radically other.

Elizabeth Flynn's findings correspond to Bleich's in important respects. She, too, focuses on male detachment and on female participation in the events of the text. In "Gender and Reading" she analyzes freshman responses to Joyce's "Araby," Hemingway's "Hills Like White Elephants," and Woolf's "Kew Gardens." Flynn assumes that reading involves a confrontation between self and "other" and that the reading process necessitates the coexistence of self and other, reader and text, for a time. This coexistence can take a number of different forms, however. The reader can dominate the text by resisting it and so remain essentially unchanged by the encounter. Or the reader can submit to the text by allowing the text to become such a powerful presence that the self is replaced by the other and so is effaced. Or the reader can interact with the text by balancing empathetic involvement with critical detachment, thereby learning from the encounter.

Most of the responses by males and females were submissive; students became entangled in textual detail and so had difficulty creating a consistent pattern of meaning. On the periphery of these, however, were responses that revealed distinct patterns of response along gender lines. A pattern of dominance was evident in some of the male responses, especially in the statements based on "Araby" and "Hills Like White Elephants," but no such pattern was evident in responses by women. Also, more women than men were able to resolve the tensions in the stories and form a consistent pattern of meaning.

"Araby," perhaps because it deals directly with male fantasy, desire, and humiliation, seemed to provoke greater anxiety on the part of some male readers than did the other stories. Many male readers avoided the ending of the story or identified strongly with the male protagonist. The women were better able to respond with both empathy and judgment. "Hills Like White Elephants" centers more directly on female experience. Once again, though, the males tended either to reject the story because they found it to be difficult or else to be wholly uncritical of the situation it presents. More women than men related setting and theme in an effective way and recognized that the dialogue between the man and the girl revealed his dominance and her subordination. "Kew Gardens," a text in which gender is not overtly implicated, seemed to provoke androgynous responses. There was little evidence of resistance on the part of male readers. The women readers, however, interacted with the text more successfully than did the men in that they were, at one and the same time, more involved in its action and more critically alert than were their male classmates.

The tendency to dominate the text which Flynn detected in some male responses but not in female responses corresponds to the detachment that Bleich saw in his male subjects. (Incidentally, it also fits in with the resistance that characterized Holland's reaction to the gothic.) Furthermore, both Flynn and Bleich found in women a greater readiness to comment on the human relationships in the story and to enter into the experience offered by the narrative.

The essays in this volume support the thesis that gender is a significant determinant of the interaction between text and reader. Of course, work in this area is only beginning, and the exact nature of the role of gender is far from clear. What is apparent at this point is that gender-related differences are multifaceted and overdetermined. They are a function of the social, cultural, and political structures that form the context of reading and writing, and they interact with other differences, in particular, those grounded on class, race, and sexual orientation.

Consideration of gender inevitably ushers in the nature/nurture controversy. There is considerable evidence that gender roles and characteristics are learned. They are actively inculcated in the schools and in all levels of social and cultural life. "Gender," in other words, is a social construct, and its realization can be modified by deliberate concerted action. At the same time, the essays in this volume reflect research in other fields that indicates that gender-linked characteristics are deeply ingrained, are infinitely entwined with the individual's self-concept. This is so because gender-identity formation begins very early, when the individual is most vulnerable, and it occurs in the context of deeply charged parental bonds. In our culture, the child's relationship with its mother is especially important. As feminist theorists—most notably Nancy Chodorow and Dorothy Dinnerstein—have argued, the female monopoly of early childcare produces the psychological basis for the reproduction of the sexual division of labor.[11] But as powerful as these psychological structures may be, they do not amount to a biological or natural basis for the prevailing gender roles and characteristics. The female monopoly of early childcare is, after all, a social institution that is amenable to change. What part of gender identity is natural and what part is cultural remains to be seen. What has become clear during the last two decades is that the appeal to nature is often problematical.

The consideration of gender and reading presented in this book has two dimensions: an analytical dimension and a normative dimension. Gender has been the locus of oppression. Several essays in this volume emphasize the damage done to women by the prevailing gender hierarchy. One or two essays intimate the damage done to men. In any case, gender differences are not a matter merely of academic curiosity. Beyond the recognition of difference, there is the need to consider which differences are pernicious and which are salutary; which are to be modified and which are to be cultivated.

Focus on difference—in the case of this book, the result of deliberate editorial decision—involves certain risks. Foremost among these is that of reductiveness. It is possible to lose sight of the fact that categories obscure considerable individual variation. This is a serious risk, for it is likely that the people who hold the values we most wish to foster are precisely those who are overlooked by our categories. Another risk is the reification of difference. Concentrating on gender difference can lead us to slight the affinity of women and men. It is important that discussions of gender difference do not foreclose the recognition of individual variability and of the common ground shared by all humans. At the same time, the elaboration of difference is essential, given the false and damaging "universals" that saddle the major intellectual discourses.

Finally, we must note some important omissions. In this book, there is no essay representing black, Third World, or working-class perspectives. (This is *almost* accurate. Schweickart is a Filipino-American, and the perspective attending this fact is latent in her work.) Also, we do not offer an adequate consideration of the interaction of gender, race, and class. These omissions, which we regret, are a function of our limited angle of vision and our limited resources. Whenever possible, we have tried to leave space for the entry of these issues and perspectives into the conversation.

Notes

1. William K. Wimsatt and M. C. Beardsley, "Affective Fallacy," *Sewanee Review* 57 (1949):31–55. E. D. Hirsch, Jr., *Validity in Interpretation* (New Haven: Yale University Press, 1967), especially chap. 5 and app. 1.

2. Jonathan D. Culler uses the phrase "stories of reading" in *On Deconstruction: Theory and Criticism after Structuralism* (Ithaca: Cornell University Press, 1982).

3. Wolfgang Iser, *The Act of Reading: A Theory of Aesthetic Response* (Baltimore: Johns Hopkins University Press, 1978).

4. Louise Rosenblatt, *The Reader, the Text, the Poem: The Transactional Theory of the Literary Work* (Carbondale: Southern Illinois University Press, 1978).

5. Stanley E. Fish, *Is There a Text in This Class? The Authority of Interpretive Communities* (Cambridge: Harvard University Press, 1980); see especially the title essay.

6. Culler, *On Deconstruction,* p. 70.

7. Judith Fetterley, *The Resisting Reader: A Feminist Approach to American Fiction* (Bloomington: Indiana University Press, 1978).

8. Culler, "Reading as a Woman," in *On Deconstruction,* pp. 43–64.

9. Carol Gilligan, *In a Different Voice: Psychological Theory and Women's Development* (Cambridge: Harvard University Press, 1982).

10. Nancy Chodorow, *The Reproduction of Mothering: Psychoanalysis and the Sociology of Gender* (Berkeley and Los Angeles: University of California Press, 1978).

11. Chodorow, *Reproduction of Mothering;* Dorothy Dinnerstein, *The Mermaid and the Minotaur: Sexual Arrangements and Human Malaise* (New York: Harper and Row, 1977).

Part One
Research and Theory

Chapter 1
The Reader's Construction of Meaning: Cognitive Research on Gender and Comprehension

Mary Crawford
Roger Chaffin

What determines how a reader understands a text and what is remembered of it later? Just by asking this question we set ourselves apart from a long tradition in which the answer is simply: the text. This answer reflects a view of the mind as a passive recipient of information provided by the outside world, a view first expressed by Plato in the metaphor of the mind as a wax tablet: "When we wish to remember anything which we have seen, or heard, or thought in our own minds, we hold the wax to the perceptions and thoughts, and in that material receive the impression of them as from the seal of a ring."[1] Similarly, Locke wrote of the mind as a "white paper" to be "painted on" by experience.[2] Applied to reading, comprehension is seen as a process of simply extracting from a text the meaning the writer has put into it. This common-sense view is enshrined in the metaphors we use to talk about communication; we *put* our thoughts *into* words; all a reader must do is *get* our meaning.[3] This empiricist view of mind as passive allows the reader a minimal role; the possibility that different readers might legitimately extract different messages from the same words is not acknowledged.

A different, more rationalist, view of the mind has found expression in the young field of cognitive science and is leading to a new perspective on how readers understand texts. According to this account, understanding is a product of both the text and the prior knowledge and viewpoint that the reader brings to it. It thus allows the possibility of differences in comprehension between individuals or between groups due to differences in prior experience. Our purpose is to describe this cognitive view of comprehension and consider its implications for the hypothesis that men and women may read the same text differently.

In the first two sections we describe a theoretical framework called schema theory, and survey the empirical evidence that supports it. We show that comprehension is an active process of matching information in a text or utterance with the knowledge structures, or schemata, that the understander brings to the task. The research most relevant to gender differences in comprehension indicates that people with different backgrounds or viewpoints understand and remember the same information differently; this research is reviewed in the third section. The fourth section discusses gender as a social construction—a product of sex-role socialization which results in sex-role identification—and psychological measures of this identification. In the fifth section we review the limited evidence indicating that women and men interpret the same words and texts differently and that people who differ in degree of sex-role identification differ in the way that they organize information in memory. This evidence suggests that gender or gender-role identification should play a large part in determining how texts are understood. But effects of gender due to differences in background may be largely obscured if both female and male readers read from a male viewpoint. The issue of the connection between gender and viewpoint is considered in the last two sections.

The Nature of Understanding: Schema Theory

One of the main achievements of cognitive science in the past fifteen years has been to make us aware of the extent to which even the simplest understanding and recollection depend on knowledge that the reader brings to the task. To understand, in an ordinary way, the sentence

1. The little girl heard the ice cream man and rushed upstairs to get her piggy bank.

the reader is required to bring to bear knowledge about ice cream vending systems, taste preferences of children, conventions governing purchasing, and the financial resources of children. Note that the sentence itself says nothing about selling, liking ice cream, getting money, or buying; this is all provided by you, the reader. According to schema theory, your experience of ice cream buying is summarized in an organizing structure, called a schema, which provides the framework necessary to understand the sentence. The schema provides a general outline of the main events (going to the van, choosing, buying, and eating) and of the acts that make up each event (paying, getting the ice cream). The schema also specifies entry conditions (having money, liking ice cream), roles (vendor, customer), props (money, popsicles), and results (satisfaction, having less money). Understanding sentence (1) involves mapping the information provided in the sentence onto the schema: the little girl is the customer and the piggy bank is a source of money.

A schema is activated when part of the incoming information matches part of the schema in memory. Slots in the schema (e.g., vendor, money) are then instantiated by filling them with the details provided. If particular slots are not filled by information from the text, the schema will provide the necessary information, since it includes default values for the normal ways of filling each slot (e.g., that the ice cream vendor is usually male). In a similar way the schema fills in gaps in the narrative. Any events not explicitly mentioned are assumed to have occurred in the normal way. So, if sentence (1) is followed by

2. Later she was sorry she would not have any money to buy her mother a birthday present until next week.

we assume that the ice cream–buying sequence has been completed and that the little girl has spent her money.

Memory and comprehension are based on the same structures. What is recalled, according to schema theory, is not usually the actual sentences presented but a reconstruction based on what was understood. Memory for sentence (1) is likely to be based on the schemata for ice cream vending and pocket money. At this point the reader might be unsure whether sentence (1) actually said that the little girl went to get her pocket money or her piggy bank, and whether she ran upstairs or to her room.[4] The schema fills in missing information, and later the memory trace may not distinguish between information provided by the sentence and information "read into" it.

An important property of schemata is their hierarchical organization, which allows one schema to embed within another. For example, the ice cream–buying schema consists of actions (e.g., buying) which are made up of other actions (e.g., paying) which involve props (e.g., money) which are in turn represented by schemata. For sentence (1), the ice cream–buying schema would need to call the pocket money schema in order to instantiate the money slot. Moving up the hierarchy of embedded schemata, for most readers the use of the ice cream–buying schema for sentence (1) would be in the service of a linguistic example schema, which would in turn be embedded in a schema that might be labelled *academic treatise*.[5]

The schema approach to understanding can be expressed by three tenets. First, the structures that represent understanding and memory are abstract representations of the original events or statements; our mental representations are not "copies" of the original information, as the passive view of the mind suggests. Second, schemata are generalized knowledge structures that provide the framework for and determine the nature of understanding. Third, schemata allow the understander to go beyond the information actually given in a situation.

We refer to the approach represented by these three tenets as *schema theory*, although the theory is more a promise than an actuality. The tenets are preliminary assumptions rather than explanations. They will serve, however, to organize our review of the literature and to make the case that gender differences in comprehension and memory are to be expected.

The Evidence for Schema Theory

Rather than duplicate recent reviews of the experimental literature on schema theory, we describe in this section representative experiments for the main types of evidence supporting each of the three tenets.[6]

Tenet 1: Mental Representations Are Abstract, Not Literal, Copies

There is direct evidence that memory for meaning is better than memory for syntax or for particular wording in sentences.[7] Further, information in memory undergoes various forms of systematic change due to the organizing effect of the schemata by which it is represented. We describe two types of change that occur. First, people tend to remember stories in a canonical form. Second, information already in memory can be altered by new information, which is integrated with the old.

Bower, Black, and Turner asked students to read ten short passages about common activities and events for which people would be expected to have scripts available.[8] For five of the scripts there was a canonical order (e.g., birthday party, shopping for a coat), and for five there was not (e.g., cleaning house, Veterans' Day parade). Each passage was presented on a set of cards, with one action on each card. After reading all the passages, the students were asked to put the cards for each passage in the order in which they had read them. For the ordered scripts, activities tended to be recalled in their canonical order: actions that originally had been presented "out of order" were displaced toward their "normal" position and were located less accurately than corresponding actions from the unordered scripts.

One example of how memories for events can be altered by information obtained after the events have occurred comes from the work of Loftus on eyewitness testimony.[9] She showed people a film of a collision between two cars and then questioned them about what they had seen. Memory of the accident was found to have been affected by the questions that had been asked immediately after the film. People who had been asked, "About how fast were the cars going when they smashed into each other?" were more likely, one week later, to answer "Yes" to the question "Did you see any broken glass?" than were people who were asked, "About how fast were the cars going when they hit each other?" The people who were asked the "smashed into" question also gave higher estimates of the speed of the car. Information presupposed by the question was incorporated into the memory of the accident. The memory was thus seen to be a dynamic structure subject to change.[10]

Tenet 2: Comprehension and Memory Are Based on Schemata

Comprehension occurs when a schema is activated and its variables or slots are matched against features of the input. Relevant evidence comes, first, from studies that show that comprehension and memory are poor in the absence of an activated schema. Evidence also comes from studies showing that the particular information remembered from any situation, as well as the general interpretation, are determined by the match between the information to be recalled and the schema used to encode or recall it.

Bransford and Johnson asked people to read the following passage and then recall it.

> The procedure is actually quite simple. First you arrange things into different groups. Of course, one pile may be sufficient depending on how much there is to do. If you have to go somewhere else due to lack of facilities that is the next step, otherwise you are pretty well set. It is important not to overdo things. That is, it is better to do too few things at once than too many. In the short run this may not seem important but complications can easily arise. A mistake can be expensive as well. At first the whole procedure will seem complicated. Soon, however, it will become just another facet of life. It is difficult to foresee any end to the necessity for this task in the immediate future, but then one never can tell. After the procedure is completed one arranges the materials into different groups again. Then they can be put into their appropriate places. Eventually they will be used once more and the whole cycle will then have to be repeated. However, that is part of life.[11]

People who read the passage without any further context found it hard to understand and were not able to recall many of the ideas in it. Others were given a title, "Washing Clothes." These people found the passage quite easy to understand, and their memory of it was much better. If you now look back at the passage, you will find that you read it with a "new understanding." The clothes-washing schema provides the structure that interrelates and explains all of the previously obscure details. Without the schema, the individual sentences are quite straightforward, but their relationship cannot be grasped; comprehension and memory are poor.

When a passage is ambiguous, comprehension and memory will be determined by the schema that is more readily invoked. Bransford and Johnson asked people to read and then recall the following passage. Some people were given the title, "Watching a Peace March from the Fortieth Floor."

> The view was breathtaking. From the window one could see the crowd below. Everything looked extremely small from such a distance but the colorful costumes could still be seen. Everyone seemed to be moving in one direction in an orderly fashion, and there seemed to be little children as well as adults. The landing was gentle, and luckily the atmosphere was such that no special suits had to be worn. A first there was a great deal of activity. Later, when the speeches started, the crowd quieted down. The man with the television camera took many shots of the setting and the crowd. Everyone was very friendly and seemed glad when the music started.[12]

For the people who had been given the "Peace March" title, recall for the passage was good, except for the sentence, "The landing was gentle, and luckily the atmosphere was such that no special suits had to be worn." This sentence, however, was recalled by people who had been given the title "Space Trip to an Inhabited Planet." All the information in the passage can be matched against slots in either schema, except that the peace march schema has no slot for information about a landing. People using this schema, therefore, did not recall this information.

We have seen evidence that, in the absence of an appropriate schema, comprehension and memory are poor. Furthermore, the schema activated determines the particular details that will be recalled, and, in the case of ambiguous passages, the nature of what is understood and remembered.

Tenet 3: Schemata Allow Inferences to Be Made

Perhaps the most important insight of recent work on comprehension is the recognition of the degree to which even the most mundane communication requires the understander to go beyond the information given. First, individual concepts that are directly mentioned in a text are endowed with detailed properties that are consistent with the context but that were not explicitly mentioned. Second, information not explicitly mentioned is inferred as part of the process of understanding even individual sentences. Third, information necessary to interrelate parts of the text is inferred.

Here is a riddle.

> A big Indian and a little Indian are sitting on a log. The big Indian points to the little Indian and says, "That Indian is my son." The little Indian points to the big Indian and says "That Indian is not my father." Both are telling the truth. How is this possible?

The difficulty that some people have with this riddle is caused by the instantiation of the word *Indian*. Since the gender of the Indians is not specified, the default value is assumed. For most of us the default value for the gender of *Indian,* based on stories of the Wild West, is "male." The solution to the "problem" created by this is to see that the big Indian is the little one's mother. Puzzles like this make us notice the operation of default values we are normally unaware of in everyday comprehension.

The effect of instantiation on memory is demonstrated by an experiment by Anderson and Ortony.[13] Students read a list of sentences which included one of the following.

The container held the apples.
The container held the cola.

Later the students were given a cued recall test; a word was given to remind them of each sentence. The cue *basket* produced better recall for people who had seen the sentence about apples than for those who saw the sentence about cola; the cue *bottle* produced the opposite result. Neither cue had been seen as part of the original sentence. When the sentences were read, *container* was instantiated as a basket or a bottle, depending on what it was holding; it was the instantiation that was stored in memory. In understanding the sentence, the students thus made use of pragmatic knowledge about containers and the sorts of things they can be used for.

The process of going beyond the information given in a sentence does not by any means stop with the instantiation of the concepts that are explicitly mentioned. Inferences are also made about motives, consequences, enabling conditions, instruments used, and numerous other matters. Brewer read lists of sentences to students.[14] After all the lists had been read, a cued recall test was given in which the initial noun phrase of each sentence was the cue and the students were to recall the rest of the sentence. The sentences invited a variety of inferences, and these inferences appeared frequently in the recalled sentences. The sentence "The hungry python caught the mouse." was recalled accurately by only two students, whereas eleven "recalled" the implication of the original sentence: "The hungry python ate the mouse." This involves an inference about the motives of hungry pythons and is based on some rather esoteric knowledge about their eating habits. Similarly, the sentence "The absent-minded professor did not have his car keys." was accurately recalled by only four students, while sixteen recalled an inference about how the situation had arisen: "The absent-minded professor forgot his car keys."[15]

The inferences that we have examined so far in this section have occurred during the recall of isolated objects, situations, and events. Similar processes occur for larger sequences. Consider the following account of going to a doctor, from an experiment by Bower, Black and Turner:

> John was feeling bad today so he decided to go see the family doctor. He checked in with the doctor's receptionist, and then looked through several medical magazines that were on the table by his chair. Finally the nurse came and asked him to take off his clothes. The doctor was very nice to him. He eventually prescribed some pills for John. Then John left the doctor's office and headed home.[16]

When we read this account, the actions mentioned are matched against our knowledge of the "visit to the doctor" script. The script allows us to infer that many other actions not explicitly mentioned in the script also occurred, for example, "John entered the doctor's office," "The doctor examined John." Evidence that such inferences are made comes from the intrusion in recall of script actions that were not mentioned, and from incorrect recognition of script actions on recognition tests. The above passage was presented to students together with other stories similarly based on common scripts. When the stories were recalled, approximately 20 percent of the actions recalled were appropriate script actions that were not in the original story, such as "The doctor examined John."

The evidence reviewed here leads us to conclude that readers go beyond the information given in a text in instantiating particular objects and actions mentioned and in drawing inferences about such things as motives, causes, and consequences. Inferences are a normal part of understanding and remembering. They are necessary because no text can explicitly state all the information required by the reader to understand it. The gaps in what is explicitly stated are filled by inferences.

The studies described in this section reveal that comprehension and memory are active processes in which the external message and the internal knowledge structures of the understander interact in complex ways. Understanding a text is not simply a matter of unpacking a parcel and taking out a fixed set of information; memory is not a wax tablet on which experiences stamp their impressions. The mental representations of comprehension and memory are abstractions of the meaning of the message. The process of building a meaning, a representation, is frequently accompanied by alterations and distortions that are imposed by the nature of the schemata used to encode the information. Such alterations are not a sad failing to which humans are prone in moments of weakness, they are the essence of comprehension; they reflect the operation of schemata. Furthermore, it is schemata that allow the understander to go beyond the ideas overtly expressed by providing the elaboration, explanation, and interconnections that we call *understanding*.

Effects of Background and Viewpoint on Comprehension and Memory

Differences in the schemata that people bring to bear on a text may result from differences in background or from differences in viewpoint. Differences in background—upbringing, education, and life experiences—cause differences between people in what they know. Differences in viewpoint, on the other hand, may occur even when people share similar knowledge. A reader's viewpoint on a text is determined by factors such as what she wants to learn from it, what she thinks the author is trying to do, and her opinion of the author. Differences in background knowledge are relatively enduring; they can be altered only by the acquisition of new knowledge. Differences in viewpoint may be more transient; as we shall see, receiving a simple instruction to look at things differently can cause a reader to shift her viewpoint.

Effects of Background

Studies of the effect of background on comprehension and memory are few, but their conclusions are unequivocal and unsurprising: background does make a difference. Anderson and his colleagues presented two passages to students. One was:

> Rocky slowly got up from the mat, planning his escape. He hesitated a moment and thought. Things were not going well. What bothered him the most was being held, especially since the charge against him had been weak. He considered his present situation. The lock that held him was strong but he thought he could break it. He knew, however, that his timing would have to be perfect. Rocky was aware that it was because of his earlier roughness that he had been penalized so severely—much too severely from his point of view. The situation was becoming frustrating; the pressure had been grinding on him for too long. He was being ridden unmercifully. Rocky was getting angry now. He felt he was ready to make his move. He knew that his success or failure would depend on what he did in the next few seconds.[17]

The students, who were from classes in music education and in wrestling, interpreted the passage in different ways. The music students placed Rocky in jail; the wrestling students put him in a wrestling bout. For example, students recalled that "Rocky sat in his cell," or that "Rocky was penalized early in the match for roughness." The passage was carefully constructed so that it could activate either the schema for prisons or the schema for wrestling matches. The schema that was activated was determined by the background and interests of the individual.

Another way of investigating effects of background on comprehension is to compare the comprehension of experts and nonexperts. Chiesi, Spilich, and their colleagues studied the effects of knowledge of baseball on comprehension and memory for passages about baseball.[18] People were classified as high or low in knowledge of the terminology and principles of baseball; high-knowledge individuals were more able than low-knowledge individuals to identify small changes in short descriptions of episodes in a game. Moreover, the superiority of the high-knowledge people was greater for changes that were more important— for example, the runner was on third rather than first base—than for changes that were less important, such as the ball was hit over the 420-foot, rather than the 400-foot, mark. These differences can be attributed to the greater ability of high-knowledge people to understand the detailed information they are given in terms of its relation to the larger goal structure of the game, the schema. The schemata activated in high-knowledge people result in a more complete record of the information presented; this advantage is greater for information that is stored most effectively by the schema, such as more important facts and better-organized sequences.

Effects of Viewpoint

Comprehension and memory are affected not only by long-term differences in knowledge due to background, but also by temporary differences, as in Bransford and Johnson's "Washing Clothes" experiment (described earlier), in which the presence or absence of a title affected the reader's viewpoint.[19] Pichert and Anderson directly instructed people to read stories from a particular viewpoint.[20] Students read a story in which two boys play hooky from school and one takes the other on a tour of his well-appointed house. Some of the students were asked to read the story from the perspective of a potential homebuyer, and some from the perspective of a burglar. These instructions led the students to activate either a homebuying schema or a burglary schema. As they read the passage they matched the information provided with slots provided by the schema they were using. The students recalled best the ideas that were most important from the perspective they had adopted. Those who read from the perspective of a homebuyer most often recalled facts about the soundness and desirability of the house—for example, that the basement was damp and musty. Those who read from the burglary perspective recalled facts that were relevant to ease of entry, danger of getting caught, and the location of valuables—for example, that the side door was kept unlocked.

We have already seen that the schema that a reader brings to a passage profoundly affects what is understood and remembered of it. This study suggests, in addition, that almost any passage, not just deliberately ambiguous ones, may be understood and remembered differently depending on the viewpoint of the reader. Thus gender might affect comprehension by influencing either background or viewpoint. To the extent that gender is the source of important differences in knowledge and interests, it should affect comprehension at both points. However, no studies in the literature that we have reviewed directly measure the effect of gender on reading; such studies are clearly needed.

Gender and Gender Typing: Female and Male, Masculine and Feminine

We expect gender-related schemata to affect comprehension and memory. By *gender,* we do not mean chromosomal sex, with which it is usually—but not always—congruent. Chromosomal sex is merely one influence on gender, which is best defined as one's psychological sense of one's self as female or male. At least two other forces help determine gender. These are the hormonal climate of the body and the gender label given the individual. Although chromosomes and hormones are biological variables, the gender label can override them when the three are not completely congruent.[21] It is the gender label that begins the process of elaboration and mythification of the biological. Gender is thus socially defined and constructed, becoming "the means through which we attempt to apprehend sex."[22]

Gender identity usually develops unambiguously and early in life. Individuals then develop various degrees of gender-typing, or acceptance of the culture's views of masculinity/feminity as appropriate for and characteristic of themselves. We use the terms *gender-typing* and *sex-typing* interchangeably to refer to one's degree of acceptance of sex-role norms for one's self. Thus, an individual at birth is given a gender label (female or male); develops a gender identity (e.g., "I am a male"); is exposed from birth onward to prescriptions and proscriptions consistent with that label and identity (sex-role or gender-role norms); and comes to behave and evaluate himself or herself in terms of those norms (sex-typing).

Traditionally, masculinity and feminity have been viewed as opposite poles of a single dimension and, thus, as mutually exclusive and incompatible; a person could no more be both masculine and feminine than both short and tall.[23] Psychological assessment measures were therefore constructed in which the test taker was obliged to choose between "masculine" and "feminine" alternatives. Underlying this approach was the belief that a high degree of gender-typing is necessary to and associated with psychological well-being: the "well-adjusted person" should be either a "masculine" man or a "feminine" woman.

In contrast to the bipolar opposites model, Bem proposed that femininity and masculinity are independent dimensions, and she designed a scale, the Bem Sex Role Inventory (BSRI), to measure them separately.[24] A person completes the BSRI by rating himself or herself on a series of personality traits that are stereotyped "masculine" (e.g., analytical, ambitious) or "feminine" (e.g., yielding, cheerful), or that are neutral with respect to gender roles (e.g., sincere, truthful). Thus, an individual might view himself or herself as being high in masculine- and low in feminine-stereotyped traits; as low in masculine- and high in feminine-stereotyped traits; as high in both sets of traits; or as high in neither set of traits. These four orientations toward gender roles may be labeled masculine sex-typed, feminine sex-typed, androgynous, and undifferentiated, respectively. Bem has suggested that psychologically androgynous people, who view themselves as having a wider range of personality strengths than do sex-typed people, should be capable of more flexible behavior in a variety of situations.[25] She has demonstrated, albeit in contrived laboratory tasks, that androgynous people of both genders behave adaptively, whether the task is one stereotyped as appropriate for females or for males, while sex-typed people perform well only in appropriately sex-typed situations. Bem also suggests that psychological androgyny should be positively related to adjustment, partly as a consequence of the behavioral flexibility it engenders. Current research supports this view rather than the traditional one, which identifies adjustment with a high degree of sex-typing.[26]

The obvious approach to the study of gender effects on comprehension is to look for effects of gender per se by comparing women and men. But the BSRI and similar measures also allow us to look for effects of gender-typing by comparing sex-typed and non-sex-typed people. In the following section we examine both approaches.

Effects of Gender and Gender-Typing on Comprehension

Gender and gender-typing are among the most powerful influences channeling the experiences of individuals. We should therefore expect the reading process to be affected by gender-specific schemata.

Effects of Gender

Differences in reading due to gender have been demonstrated with two types of stimuli, interpersonal verbs and "generic" masculine pronouns. In one study men and women were asked to rate a series of interpersonal verbs on two dimensions, reflecting power and emotional tone.[27] Interpersonal verbs describe actions or attitudes of one person with respect to another (e.g., *likes, challenges, tolerates*) in the sentence frame "Person A *verbs* person B." Women rated the words as more extreme in emotional tone, and men rated them as more extreme in power. This finding—that interpersonal verbs have different meanings for women and men—has intriguing implications both for the interpretation of prose by female and male readers and for the potential for misunderstanding between female and male speakers.

Gender also affects the interpretation of "generic" masculine language. Traditionally, linguists and grammarians have maintained that the pronoun *he* and the noun *man* have a "generic" meaning that includes both sexes. Recently, critics have argued that the use of masculine terms to refer to women results in women being invisibile and constitutes sexism in language.[28] The argument is supported by evidence indicating that people of both genders tend to interpret "generic" terms literally rather than generically.[29] Thus, women readers must make a particular effort to maintain a "generic" interpretation of *he* and *man* in order not to exclude themselves from what they read. The interpretation that men and women give to these "generic" terms is, therefore, likely to be different. Evidence for this conclusion comes from a study by Martyna exploring gender differences in imagery elicited by "generic" pronouns. Men reported a high incidence of male imagery when completing neutral sentences with "generic" pronouns, while women reported virtually no imagery. To men, the word *he* referred to males only; to women, *he* was an "automatic" choice[30] that led to neither male nor female images.

Another reason that "generic" masculine language may be understood differently by men and women is its ambiguity. Since the words *he* and *man* are often used interchangeably in their generic and their literal sense within the same text, the reader may have to depend on the context to decide which interpretation is intended. For example, consider sentence (3):

3. Man is by nature a rational being.

It could reasonably be followed by either sentence (4) or sentence (5):

4. A good teacher can help to foster that rationality.
5. Woman, on the other hand, is intuitive by nature.

Sentence (4) permits a generic interpretation of sentence (3), while sentence (5) requires a literal interpretation. In the absence of the context provided by (4) or (5), readers are free to interpret (3) generically or literally. Several studies show that the ambiguity inherent in the two meanings of masculine forms is resolved differently by male and female readers. Martyna, for example, asked students to complete sentence fragments that referred to people in male-stereotyped (e.g., engineer), female-stereotyped (e.g., secretary) or neutral (e.g., teenager) roles.[31] Women used the "generic" *he* much less often than men did in this task, though they were not aware they were avoiding its use and did not view their pronoun choices as reflecting feminist values.

In summary, there is empirical evidence to support the claim that "generic" masculine language is ambiguous and is interpreted differently by men and women. When both men and women read the word *he,* a male interpretation (the default value) initially predominates. But if women are not to exclude themselves from what they read, they must do additional mental processing to transform the initial literal interpretation into one that includes them. Thus, they suppress male imagery associated with *he* and avoid its generic use (and the necessity for the transformation process) when writing.

These gender differences in the use and interpretation of "generic" masculine language are also reflected in memory. In recent research in our laboratory, college students read a brief factual essay on psychology as an occupation.[32] Half the students were given an essay titled "The Psychologist and His Work," which was written in "generic" style ("the psychologist . . . he"). The other half received an essay titled "Psychologists and Their Work," which used language that either avoided masculine pronouns ("psychologists . . . they") or specifically referred to both sexes ("the psychologist . . . he or she"). Other than in the use of "generic" or specific language, the essays were identical. When they were tested for memory of the factual content of the essay, men who had read the "generic" essay recalled more than those who had read the specific version. Exactly the opposite occurred for women, who recalled better the essay form that specifically included them.

This effect does not occur at the conscious level. Our subjects rarely could remember which essay form they had read, and not one student was aware that pronoun type was the focus of the study. If we had asked them, both the male and the female students would probably have replied that psychologists are sometimes female, and, reflecting their schooling in grammar, that "The Psychologist and His Work" can refer to both female and male psychologists. Yet their recall of the essay's content was powerfully affected by an aspect of language of which they were unaware. And, most importantly in the present context, the effects were opposite for men and women readers.

Effects of Sex-Typing

A finer-grained analysis should theoretically be possible if, rather than simply comparing males and females, the researcher compares people who differ in their degree of gender-typing. Bem proposed that gender-typing is best understood as the development of a gender schema.[33]

Like the other schemata we have discussed, the gender schema is a heterogeneous network of associations representing general knowledge rather than specific incidents, and it is used by the individual as an aid in assimilating new information. Learning of the gender schema begins very early. By the time they are three years old, children can accurately state their own gender and identify the gender of others from photographs. They show that they are aware of sex-role stereotypes, and they pattern their own behavior in conformity with these stereotypes.[34] Bem has delineated the relationship between the gender schema and the development of gender-typing:

> the phenomenon of sex-typing derives, in part, from gender-based schematic processing, from a generalized readiness to process information on the basis of the sex-linked associations that constitute the gender schema. In particular, [gender schema] theory proposes that sex-typing results, in part, from the fact that the self-concept itself gets assimilated into the gender schema. As children learn the contents of the society's gender schema, they learn which attributes are to be linked with their own sex and, hence, with themselves. This does not simply entail learning where each sex is supposed to stand on each dimension or attribute—that boys are to be strong and girls weak, for example—but involves the deeper lesson that the dimensions themselves are differentially applicable to the two sexes.[35]

According to Bem's gender schema theory, people who are more highly sex-typed are those who not only conform to their culture's definition of masculinity or femininity, but also readily process information in terms of the gender schema. In other words, sex-typed and non-sex-typed people differ in the extent to which they spontaneously rely on the gender schema in understanding. Thus the theory predicts that schema effects on memory should occur differentially for sex-typed and non-sex-typed people when memory for gender-relevant material is measured.

Bem reported a study in which male and female students first were classified as sex-typed or non-sex-typed using the BSRI, and then were

17

compared on a memory task involving gender-related stimuli. The task was to recall as many words from a list as possible, in any order. The words were from four different semantic categories. Within each category, one-third of the words had been previously judged to be masculine, one-third feminine, and one-third neutral in gender connotation. For example, in the "animal" category, *gorilla* had been judged to be connotatively "masculine," *butterfly* to be "feminine," and *ant* to be "neutral." The words were presented in random order. The extent to which an individual recalls the words clustered by semantic category or by gender connotation when instructed to recall them "in any order" is an indication of how that individual has organized the words for storage in memory. Here, of course, Bem was interested in whether sex-typed people would cluster words by gender connotation. She found that sex-typed people tended to recall gender-related words in same-gender clusters more than did non-sex-typed people, indicating a reliance on gender-based schematic processing.[36]

In another experiment, Bem measured the speed with which sex-typed and non-sex-typed people were able to decide whether gender-stereotyped traits applied to themselves (a "me/not me" judgment).[37] She found that sex-typed people were faster than others at making schema-consistent judgments (e.g., deciding that a trait stereotyped for their gender was "me" or that an opposite-sex-typed trait was "not me"), and slower than non-sex-typed people in making schema-inconsistent judgments. Bem interpreted this result to mean that the self-concepts of sex-typed people are organized by means of the gender schema. They can make gender-schema-consistent judgments quickly because, in deciding whether a sex-stereotyped trait is "me" or "not me," they do not introspect deeply but simply rely on the readily available gender schema; non-sex-typed people are slower because they presumably have less well developed and less accessible gender schemata.

Cynthia Jones, working in our laboratory, designed an experiment that allowed subjects to choose either the gender schema or the self schema in processing information.[38] The subjects' task was, on the surface, a simple one; they were to insert the word *and* or the word *but* in sentence frames such as these:

6a. Mary is gentle _____ affectionate.
6b. Mary is gentle _____ self-reliant.
7a. John is forceful _____ self-reliant.
7b. John is forceful _____ gentle.

Concepts that are congruent, that is, concepts that would be expected to go together, are conjoined by *and*. For example, most people would put *and* in sentences (6a) and (7a). Concepts that are incongruent, or not expected to go together, are conjoined by *but*. Most people would put *but* in sentences (6b) and (7b). This congruity effect is very general. It is triggered by any kind of expectation about what sorts of things go together, as (8a) and (8b) indicate.

8a. Joan went to the store _____ bought bread.
8b. Joan went to the store _____ did not buy bread.

The selection of *and* indicates that two ideas are seen as congruent; choosing *but* indicates that they are seen as incongruent. The choice of *and* or *but* may, therefore, serve as a covert classification measure.[39]

The congruity principle just described would lead us to expect that traits that are stereotyped as appropriate for one gender would be viewed as congruent and conjoined by *and,* as in (6a) and (7a), while traits that are stereotyped as appropriate for people of different genders would be viewed as incongruent and conjoined by *but.* Gender schema theory would lead us to suspect, in addition, that this congruity effect would be stronger for sex-typed than for non-sex-typed people. That is, sex-typed people would be more likely than non-sex-typed people to conjoin "same-sex" adjectives with *and* and "different-sex" adjectives with *but.*

The results showed a strong effect of gender congruity: there were many more *and* responses to "same-sex" than to "different-sex" pairs. Also, as predicted by gender schema theory, the effect of gender-stereotype congruity was larger for sex-typed than for non-sex-typed subjects. In other words, sex-typed people were more likely to select *and* for "same-sex" adjectives and *but* for "different-sex" adjectives than were non-sex-typed people.

This experiment supports the claim of gender schema theory that sex-typed people are more likely than non-sex-typed people to use the gender schema in processing information. It shows that individual differences in gender typing can affect grammatical decisions, in this case the choice of *and* or *but.*

In summary, the experiments described in this section indicate that both gender and gender-typing can affect the organization of information in memory. In some situations, such as comprehension of "generic" masculine pronouns, differences emerge when we simply compare the behavior of males and females. In other situations, the important differences are not between males and females, but between sex-typed and non-sex-typed people. In Bem's memory research and in Jones's study of grammatical choice, sex-typed men and women behaved similarly to each other and differently from non-sex-typed men and women. Gender and degree of gender-typing affect memory, comprehension, and even grammatical choices, presumably by influencing the availability of the gender schema.

Sex-typing seems to be as important as gender in determining how information is interpreted and remembered. Currently, however, agreement among different measures of sex-typing is lower than we would like, and it is not clear whether different measures in fact measure the same thing.[40] It is troubling that most of the effects of sex-typing seem to be due to masculinity, while femininity, as currently measured, has little effect.[41] Furthermore, sex-typed and non-sex-typed people do not always behave as personality theorists would expect them to.[42]

The discrepancies between expected and observed behavior have led several critics to suggest that the BSRI and similar scales are at best weak and imperfect measures of sex-typing, and at worst are not measuring sex-typing at all.[43] Before the role of gender-typing in comprehension can be fully explored, better measures of gender-typing must be developed.

Another, more general, difficulty in observing the effect of the gender schema on comprehension is that the gender schema may have unique properties that make it difficult to apprehend with the techniques used for other schemata. Unlike the limited and relatively well-defined burglar and homeowner schemata studied by Pichert and Anderson,[44] the gender schema is enormously rich and diverse:

> [A] sprawling network of associations encompassing not only those features directly related to male and female persons, such as anatomy, reproductive function, division of labor, and personality attributes, but also features more remotely or metaphorically related to sex, such as the angularity or roundedness of an abstract shape and the periodicity of the moon. Indeed, there appears to be no other dichotomy in human experience with as many entities assimilated to it as the distinction between male and female.[45]

Richness and diversity are not the only qualities unique to the gender schema. The gender schema becomes assimilated to the self schema. Inevitably, our gender is part of our self-concept. Thus the very sense of self comes to depend, to some degree, on conformity with gender stereotypes:

> The child also learns to evaluate his or her adequacy as a person in terms of the gender schema, to match his or her preferences, attitudes, behaviors, and personal attributes against the prototypes stored within it. The gender schema becomes a prescriptive standard or guide . . . and self-esteem becomes its hostage.[46]

When we consider that the gender schema is learned beginning in earliest childhood, is extremely rich in its associations, and is intimately connected with the sense of self, it seems that the backgrounds and viewpoints of men and women should be very different. We should find large and reliable differences in reading when we simply compare the understanding of women and men. Effects of gender should be much more powerful than the effects of instructing people to adopt a burglar schema or a homeowner schema. Intuition tells us, however, that men and women, given a text to read, will not always generate radically different interpretations. Differences may be subtle, if they exist at all. In the studies described above, the effects of gender and gender-typing, while reliable, are small. They are not the kind of robust differences we would expect from so salient a factor as gender and so pervasive a process as sex-role socialization.

The missing factor in our analysis so far may be that the asymmetrical power relationship between women and men in our culture affects the viewpoints of women and men differently. We now turn to social anthropology for a theory of the behavior of dominant and subordinate groups, a theory that proposes that gender differences caused by differences in background may be obscured by similarities in viewpoint. After describing and evaluating the theory, we relate its constructs to their representations in the schemata of individuals.

Women as a Muted Group

Because women and men in our culture are exposed to systematically different experiences from earliest childhood, we would expect systematic differences in the way women and men understand some kinds of texts. One reason that such differences are not readily apparent may be that women learn to read and understand from a male point of view. This possibility is suggested by muted group theory.[47]

The theory of muted groups was developed to describe situations in which groups of people exist in asymmetrical power relationships (e.g., blacks and whites; colonizers and the colonized). The theory proposes that language and the norms for its use are controlled by the dominant group. Members of the muted group are disadvantaged in articulating their experience, since the language they must use is derived largely from the perceptions of the dominant group. To some extent, the perceptions of the muted group are unstatable in the idiom of the dominant group. In order to be heard, muted group members must learn the dominant idiom and attempt to articulate within it, even though this attempt will inevitably lead to some loss of meaning. The experiences "lost in the translation" to the dominant idiom remain unvoiced, and perhaps unthought, even within the muted group.

Muted group theory provides a framework within which the pervasiveness of linguistic, semantic, and social distinctions based on gender can be seen as a product of the dominance of male perceptions of the world. Gender distinctions beyond those necessary for biological purposes are built into the language because a focus on the supposed differences between dominant and muted groups serves the interests of the dominant group.

Kramarae has applied muted group theory to male and female language. Her analysis begins by stating the basic assumptions of the theory as they apply to women and men:

1. Women perceive the world differently from men because of women's and men's different experiences and activities rooted in the division of labor.
2. Because of their political dominance, the men's system of perception is dominant, impeding the free expression of the women's alternative models of the world.
3. In order to participate in society women must transform their own models in terms of the received male models of expression.

Kramarae then draws from these assumptions seven specific hypotheses about male and female expression and analyzes the empirical evidence bearing on each. Two hypotheses illustrate the approach:

Hypothesis A: Females are likely to find ways to express themselves outside the dominant public modes of expression used by males. . . .
Hypothesis B: Females are more likely to state dissatisfaction with the dominant public modes of expression.[48]

Evidence that women seek to express themselves by writing in other than the dominant (public) modes of expression comes from an analysis of diaries and letters written by women and from collective writing as practiced in feminist groups.[49] Women's letters and diaries have often been ignored or destroyed for two closely related reasons: they have not been considered to be literary genres, and their subjects have not been considered to be important. We can only speculate as to whether more women than men keep diaries, though Kramarae believes that available evidence suggests that there is a difference in the audience and purpose of female and male writing. Although women may have resorted to diary and letter writing partly because their work in "male" genres would have been ignored, it is also possible that they have found diary and letter writing to be less constricting to the articulation of their own experience.

Writing collectives, emerging from feminist consciousness-raising groups of the late 1960s and early 1970s, are another alternative mode of expression, one that questions the individualistic view of writing that predominates in Western culture. Rather than viewing ideas as the property of individuals, they

are using unconventional forms and forums of expression, unconventional in the sense that they do not pay tribute to the form and forums set by men. Members exchange rough drafts and suggestions, sometimes writing the papers during group sessions. The papers are considered either as the product of the group rather than of individuals or as essays that explicitly acknowledge the aid of others. The approach combines writing and speaking interaction.[50]

Kramarae points out that male-controlled institutions do not value such communality. University tenure committess, for example, may demand that authors specify the percentage of work done by each author on multi-authored papers.

In evaluating hypothesis (B), which states that women will be dissatisfied with the dominant modes of expression, Kramarae draws on the analyses by women writers of the difficulties they experience in finding their own voices, in "trying to speak about their own experiences, through or around the *literary* language and form accepted by men."[51] Because writers are more attuned to difficulties in expressing perceptions of the world than are most people, their insights may be particularly relevant. However, even women who are writers cannot always clearly define their problems of articulation. And muted group theory suggests why such problems should be difficult to express. "The dominant structure does not provide clear, neat labels for the ideas the women are discussing."[52]

Although some women writers have recognized that the masculine idiom limits their vision, there seem to be many who adopt it without recognizing a loss. Heilbrun argues persuasively that women writers have failed to articulate the female search for identity in female characters, but have instead projected the ideal of autonomy onto their male characters.[53] In other words, many women writers have adopted the dominant group's perceptions that selfhood, love of adventure, strength, and autonomy are embodied only in males. The result is that only their male characters can symbolize the whole range of human experience.

Heilbrun believes that this abandonment or rejection of the autonomous female character by women writers, this "inability to imagine for other women, fictional or real, the self they have in fact achieved," occurs because the woman writer "is as lost in her creative imagination as she is in life for a knowledge of the process by which a woman could achieve identity, or of what the result might be if she did. Her creative imagination will fail her even when life, in her own case, does not."[54]

Conclusion

Differences in background between women and men in our society should, by themselves, lead to differences in the way women and men understand a wide variety of texts. The primacy and centrality of the gender schema should ensure differential encoding of experiences by women and men. Working to counteract these differences is the need of women to adapt to the idiom of the dominant group, men, and to read and write like men. To the extent that women use the dominant idiom in reading, the comprehension of men and women will be similar; the expected effects of background will not appear.

Is reading from the viewpoint of the dominant, male, world the same process as reading from the viewpoints studied in memory experiments? The effects of reading from the viewpoint of a homebuyer or a burglar can be attributed to the use of a suitable schema that encodes some types of information more readily than others; the burglar schema, for example, would have slots for such things as safe entries and loot. The burglar schema is fairly well defined and circumscribed. This makes it possible to list its characteristics and to recognize when a person is or is not using it. The dominant viewpoint, in contrast, is much more diffuse, touching every aspect of our knowledge. Its properties cannot be so easily enumerated. It is difficult to recognize the operation of the schema representing the male world view because it is so pervasive.

Understanding always involves the operation of many levels of hierarchically organized schemata. Most experimental studies have dealt with specific, low-level schemata (e.g., for clothes washing), although the studies of the effect of viewpoint and background by Anderson and by Chiesi and Spilich are exceptions. An example of the operation of higher level schemata is provided by the study of Tannen, who showed a film to American and Greek female students and asked each student to describe it.[55] She inferred the use of particular schemata from comments that referred to expectations based on those schemata. The presence of an experiment schema was indicated by expressions of anxiety about the role of subject (e.g., "How picky do you want?"). The use of a story-telling schema was indicated by the expectation that events should be told in order ("Let's see, is it while he's up in the ladder, or . . . before?"). Tannen found that her American women used the experiment schema and a film schema, whereas the Greek women were more likely simply to report what happened as though they had witnessed it directly. Lower in the hierarchy, below all of these schemata, the women's descriptions made use of schemata relevant to the specific content of the film. The schemata invoked can thus be seen as a hierarchy, with higher level schemata operating at the same time as lower level ones. A theft was part of the story; the story was part of the film; the film was part of the experience of viewing a film; viewing the film was part of the experience of being in the experiment.

The standard, male, viewpoint on an experience might be viewed as a very high-level schema or set of schemata. Because the male viewpoint is diffuse and pervasive, neither men nor women can readily step in and out of it as they attempt to apprehend their experiences. To discard it entirely would require an alternative schema, such as a woman's viewpoint. But alternative viewpoints, according to muted group theory, are less well articulated, or they may not exist.

The development of a uniquely female viewpoint has been a major part of the work of the women's movement. To have a "raised consciousness" is to have schemata for a woman's viewpoint. The experience of having one's consciousness raised is explained very well as the acquisition of a new schema that fits the experience. Old objects and relationships are suddenly "understood" in new ways, just as the passage on washing clothes was "understood" in a new way when the title was given.

One place where the female viewpoint has been expressed is in feminist literature. It is to feminist literature that we should turn first in our search for gender differences in reading. Literature written from the male point of view, whether by men or women writers, will presumably be understood most readily from that point of view by men and women. Some women may also be able to read it from a female point of view; that is a question worth exploring, and one that Heilbrun has begun to analyze. But differences should be found most readily with regard to literature written from a female viewpoint. These texts will be understood best by those who have appropriate schemata and differently by those who read from the traditional, male, point of view.

One of the first questions to explore will be whether gender or gender-typing is the most important determinant of how such texts are understood. Will the understanding of women readers be most different from that of men readers, or will the biggest difference be between people with "raised consciousnesses" and those with traditional views of sex roles? Related to this question is the extent to which a female viewpoint is expressed in more traditional women's literature. If there is a female viewpoint expressed, then these texts, too, should be understood differently by men and women or by sex-typed and non-sex-typed people.

The exploration of these questions will require a variety of methods, those of literary critics and linguists as well as the experimental methods typically used in studies of schematic processing. The results should be a better understanding of gender as a high-level schema and a better understanding of the relation between gender and comprehension.

Notes

We thank the following people for their comments on earlier versions of this chapter: Jim Esposito, Madelyn Gutwirth, Lynn Waterhouse, Mike Weiss, and Morton Winston. This work was supported in part by a Faculty Development Award from West Chester University to Mary Crawford and by a similar grant from Trenton State College to Roger Chaffin.

1. *The Dialogues of Plato,* trans. B. Jowett (Oxford: Oxford University Press, 1953), "Theatatus," p. 191d.

2. John Locke, *An Essay Concerning Human Understanding* (New York: Dutton, 1965), vol. 1, bk. 2, chap. 1, para. 2.

3. Richard C. Anderson et al., "Frameworks for Comprehending Discourse," *American Educational Research Journal* 14 (1977): 367–81.

4. This type of memory for inferences is described by William F. Brewer, "Memory for the Pragmatic Implications of Sentences," *Memory and Cognition* 5 (1977): 673–78.

5. This use of *schema* was introduced by Fredrick Bartlett, *Remembering* (Cambridge: Cambridge University Press, 1932). The term was adopted more recently for a similar idea by David E. Rumelhart and Andrew Ortony, "The Representation of Knowledge in Memory," in *Schooling and the Acquisition of Knowledge,* ed. Richard C. Anderson, Rand J. Spiro, and William E. Montague (Hillsdale, N.J.: Erlbaum, 1977), p. 101. Their discussion develops ideas of Marvin Minsky, who uses the term *frame* in "A Framework for Representing Knowledge," in *The Psychology of Computer Vision,* ed. P. H. Winston (New York: McGraw-Hill, 1975). The most complete Artificial Intelligence implementation of the concept is by R. C. Schank and R. P. Abelson, *Scripts, Plans, Goals, and Understanding: An Inquiry into Human Knowledge Structures* (Hillsdale, N.J.: Erlbaum, 1977), who use the term *script.* A history of "schema" and related concepts is given by Deborah Tannen, "What's in a Frame? Surface Evidence for Underlying Expectations," in *New Directions in Discourse Processing,* ed. R. O. Freedle (Norwood, N.J.: Ablex, 1979); and Perry W. Thorndyke and Frank R. Yekovitch, "A Critique of Schema-Based Theories of Human Story Memory," *Poetics* 9 (1980): 23–49. The latter reviews the application of the schema approach to the structure of discourse, particularly stories. Sources for this work include Perry W. Thorndyke, "Cognitive Structures in Comprehension and Memory of Narrative Discourse," *Cognitive Psychology* 9 (1977): 77–110; J. M. Mandler and N. S. Johnson, "Remembrance of Things Parsed: Story Structure and Recall," *Cognitive Psychology* 9 (1977): 111–51; W. Kintsch and T. A. Van Dijk, "Toward a Model of Text Comprehension and Production," *Psychological Review* 85 (1978): 363–94; and Arthur C. Graesser, *Prose Comprehension beyond the Word* (New York: Springer-Verlag, 1981).

6. Thorndyke and Yekovitch, "Critique of Schema-Based Theories of Human Story Memory"; Joseph W. Alba and Lynn Hasher, "Is Memory Schematic?" *Psychological Bulletin* 93 (1983): 203–31; Reid Hastie, "Schematic Principles in Human Memory," in *The Ontario Symposium on Personality and Psychology,* vol. 1, ed. E. T. Higgins, P. Hermann, and M. P. Zanna (Hillsdale, N.J.: Erlbaum, 1981); Richard Harris, "Inferences in Information Processing," in *The Psychol-*

ogy of Learning and Motivation, vol. 14, ed. G. H. Bower (New York: Academic Press, 1981); Shelley E. Taylor and Jennifer Crocker, "Schematic Bases of Social Information Processing," in Higgins, Hermann, and Zanna, *The Ontario Symposium on Personality and Psychology,* vol. 1.

7. J. S. Sachs, "Recognition Memory for Syntactic and Semantic Aspects of Connected Discourse," *Perception and Psychophysics* 2 (1967): 437–42. Several studies show that the gist of prose is remembered better than its exact wording. See William F. Brewer, "Memory for Ideas: Synonym Substitution," *Memory and Cognition* 4 (1975): 458–64; J. S. Sachs, "Memory in Reading and Listening to Discourse," *Memory and Cognition* 2 (1974): 95–100; J. R. Anderson, "Verbatim and Propositional Representation of Sentences in Immediate and Long-Term Memory," *Journal of Verbal Learning and Verbal Behavior* 13 (1974): 149–62; I. Begg and W. A. Wickelgren, "Retention Functions for Syntactic and Lexical vs. Semantic Information in Sentence Recognition Memory," *Memory and Cognition* 2 (1974): 353–59; William F. Brewer and E. H. Lichtenstein, "Memory for Marked Semantic Features versus Memory for Meaning," *Journal of Verbal Learning and Verbal Behavior* 13 (1974): 172–80.

8. An event schema is often referred to as a script. See G. H. Bower, J. B. Black, and T. J. Turner, "Scripts in Memory for Text," *Cognitive Psychology* 11 (1979): 177–220, experiment 5.

9. E. F. Loftus and J. C. Palmer, "Reconstruction of Automobile Destruction: An Example of the Interaction between Language and Memory," *Journal of Verbal Learning and Verbal Behavior* 13 (1974): 585–89.

10. Similar distortions can be caused by social stereotypes. See M. Snyder and S. W. Uranowitz, "Reconstructing the Past: Some Cognitive Consequences of Person Perception," *Journal of Personality and Social Psychology* 36 (1978): 941–50.

11. J. D. Bransford and M. K. Johnson, "Contextual Prerequisites for Understanding: Some Investigation of Comprehension and Recall," *Journal of Verbal Learning and Verbal Behavior* 11 (1972): 717–26; p. 722.

12. J. D. Bransford and M. K. Johnson, "Considerations of Some Problems of Comprehension," in *Visual Information Processing,* ed. W. G. Chase (New York: Academic Press, 1973), p. 412.

13. Richard C. Anderson and A. Ortony, "On Putting Apples into Bottles: A Problem of Polysemy," *Cognitive Psychology* 7 (1975): 167–80.

14. Brewer, "Memory for the Pragmatic Implications of Sentences." See also Ken G. Schweller, William F. Brewer, and D. A. Dahl, "Memory for Illocutionary Forces and Perlocutionary Effects of Utterances," *Journal of Verbal Learning and Verbal Behavior* 15 (1976): 325–37; M. K. Johnson, J. D. Bransford, and S. K. Solomon, "Memory for Tacit Implications of Sentences," *Journal of Experimental Psychology* 98 (1973): 203–5.

15. These are pragmatic inferences requiring the use of factual knowledge that goes beyond the literal meaning of the sentence. Harris, "Inferences in Information Processing"; Brewer, "Memory for the Pragmatic Implications of Sentences"; and Roger Chaffin, "Knowledge of Language and Knowledge about the World: A Reaction Time Study of Invited and Necessary Inferences," *Cognitive Science* 3 (1979): 311–28.

16. Bower, Black, and Turner, "Scripts in Memory for Text," p. 190.

17. Anderson et al., "Frameworks for Comprehending Discourse," p. 372.

18. H. L. Chiesi, G. J. Spilich, and J. F. Voss, "Acquisition of Domain-Related Information in Relation to High and Low Domain Knowledge," *Journal of Verbal Learning and Verbal Behavior* 18 (1979): 257–73; G. J. Spilich, G. T. Vesonder, H. L. Cheisi, and J. F. Voss, "Text Processing of Domain-Related Information for Individuals with High and Low Domain Knowledge," *Journal of Verbal Learning and Verbal Behavior* 18 (1979): 275–90. In addition, interesting work has been done comparing the perception and memory of chess players of different levels of expertise by W. G. Chase and H. A. Simon, "The Mind's Eye in Chess," in Chase, *Visual Information Processing.*

19. Bransford and Johnson, "Contextual Prerequisites for Understanding"; idem, "Considerations of Some Problems of Comprehension."

20. J. W. Pichert and Richard C. Anderson, "Taking Different Perspectives on a Story," *Journal of Educational Psychology* 69 (1977): 309–15; Richard C. Anderson and J. W. Pichert, "Recall of Previously Unrecallable Information following a Shift in Perspective," *Journal of Verbal Learning and Verbal Behavior* 17 (1978): 1–12.

21. Juanita H. Williams, *Psychology of Women: Behavior in a Biosocial Context* (New York: W. W. Norton, 1977), pp. 90–108.

22. Clara Mayo and Nancy M. Henley, "Nonverbal Behavior: Barrier or Agent for Sex Role Change?" in *Gender and Nonverbal Behavior,* ed. Clara Mayo and Nancy M. Henley (New York: Springer-Verlag, 1981), p. 3.

23. A. Constantinople, "Masculinity-Feminity: An Exception to the Famous Dictum?" *Psychological Bulletin* 80 (1973): 389–407.

24. Sandra L. Bem, "The Measurement of Psychological Androgyny," *Journal of Consulting and Clinical Psychology* 42 (1974): 155–62.

25. Sandra L. Bem, "Probing the Promise of Androgyny," in *Beyond Sex-Role Stereotypes,* ed. A. Kaplan and J. Bean (Boston: Little, Brown, 1976).

26. F. Cosentino and A. B. Heilbrun, "Anxiety Correlates of Sex-Role Identity in College Students," *Psychological Reports* 14 (1964): 729–30. Barbara L. Forisha, *Sex Roles and Personal Awareness* (New York: Scott, Foresman, 1978), provides a good review of the literature (pp. 82–109). See also Bernard E. Whitely, "Sex-Role Orientation and Self-Esteem: A Critical Meta-Analytic Review," *Journal of Personality and Social Psychology* 44 (1983): 765–78.

27. E. G. Thompson, P. Hatchett, and J. L. Phillips, "Sex Differences in the Judgment of Interpersonal Verbs," *Psychology of Women Quarterly* 5 (1981): 523–31.

28. Robin Lakoff, *Language and Woman's Place* (New York: Harper and Row, 1975); Wendy Martyna, "Beyond the 'He/Man' Approach: The Case for Nonsexist Language," *Signs* 5 (1980): 482–93.

29. Joseph W. Schneider and Sally L. Hacker, "Sex-Role Imagery and Use of the Generic Man in Introductory Texts: A Case in the Sociology of Sociology," *American Sociologist* 8 (1973): 12–18; Donald G. MacKay and David C. Fulkerson, "On the Comprehension and Production of Pronouns," *Journal of Verbal Learning and Verbal Behavior* 18 (1979): 661–73.

30. Wendy Martyna, "The Psychology of the Generic Masculine," in *Women and Language in Literature and Society*, ed. Sally McConnell-Ginet, Ruth Borker, and Nelly Furman (New York: Praeger, 1980).

31. Martyna, "Psychology of the Generic Masculine."

32. Mary Crawford and Linda English, "Generic versus Specific Inclusion of Women in Language: Effects on Recall," *Journal of Psycholinguistic Research* 13 (1984): 373–81.

33. Sandra L. Bem, "Gender Schema Theory: A Cognitive Account of Sex Typing," *Psychological Review* 88 (1981): 354–64.

34. S. K. Thompson, "Gender Labels and Early Sex-Role Development," *Child Development* 46 (1975): 339–47.

35. Bem, "Gender Schema Theory."

36. This experiment is described in Bem, "Gender Schema Theory." K. Deaux and B. Major, "Sex-Related Patterns in the Unit of Perception," *Personality and Social Psychology Bulletin* 3 (1977): 297–300, also showed that sex-typed people differentiated between the behavior of male and female stimulus persons more than did non-sex-typed people when they segmented a videotape into "natural, meaningful" units.

37. Cited in Bem, "Gender Schema Theory." Similar results have been obtained by H. Markus et al., "Self-Schemas and Gender," *Journal of Personality and Social Psychology* 42 (1982): 38–50; C. J. Mills, "Sex-Typing and Self-Schemata Effects on Memory and Response Latency," *Journal of Personality and Social Psychology* 45 (1983): 163–72; T. E. Moore and J. Hood, "Schematic Processing of Sex Stereotypes" (Paper presented at the Eastern Psychological Association, Philadelphia, Apr. 7, 1983).

38. Cynthia Jones, "Self-Schema versus Sex-Role-Schema Utilization in Linguistic Judgments" (Master's thesis, West Chester State College, 1983). Also see Roger Chaffin, Mary Crawford, and Cynthia Jones, "The Effect of the Gender Schema on Linguistic Judgments," Educational Resources Information Center (ERIC) document ED 242 198.

39. Rumjahn Hoosain, "The Processing of Negation," *Journal of Verbal Learning and Verbal Behavior* 12 (1973): 618–26.

40. Faye Crosby, Paul Jose, and William Wong-McCarthy, "Gender, Androgyny, and Conversational Assertiveness," in Mayo and Henley, *Gender and Nonverbal Behavior*.

41. Whiteley, "Sex-Role Orientation and Self-Esteem."

42. Crosby, Jose, and Wong-McCarthy, "Gender, Androgyny, and Conversational Assertiveness."

43. Ibid; Bernice Lott, "A Feminist Critique of Androgyny: Toward the Elimination of Gender Attributions for Learned Behavior," in Mayo and Henley, *Gender and Nonverbal Behavior*.

44. Pichert and Anderson, "Taking Different Perspectives on a Story."

45. Bem, "Gender Schema Theory," p. 354.

46. Ibid., p. 355.

47. Shirley Ardener, ed., *Perceiving Women* (London: Malaby Press, 1975).

48. Cheris Kramarae, *Women and Men Speaking* (Rowley, Mass.: Newbury House, 1981), pp. 1–63; pp. 3, 4.

49. Kramarae (*Women and Men Speaking,* p. 16) also provides a fascinating analysis of women's interactions in feminist consciousness-raising groups, and of women's art forms (e.g., quilting and embroidery) as alternative means of expression. Both are devalued by males: women's interaction styles are derided as "hen parties" or "gossip"; women's art forms are "domestic crafts" or "decorating." Both exist outside the "mainstream."

50. Ibid., p. 13.

51. Ibid., p. 19.

52. Ibid., p. 20.

53. Carolyn G. Heilbrun, *Reinventing Womanhood* (New York: W. W. Norton, 1979).

54. Ibid., p. 73.

55. Tannen, "What's in a Frame?"

Chapter 2
Reading Ourselves: Toward a Feminist Theory of Reading
Patrocinio P. Schweickart

Three Stories of Reading

A. Wayne Booth begins his Presidential Address to the 1982 MLA Convention by considering and rejecting several plausible myths that might enable us "to dramatize not just our inescapable plurality but the validity of our sense that [as teachers and scholars of literature and composition] we belong together, somehow working on common ground." At last he settles on one story that is "perhaps close enough to our shared experience to justify the telling."[1]

Once upon a time there was a boy who fell in love with books. When he was very young he heard over and over the legend of his great-grandfather, a hard-working weaver who so desired knowledge that he figured out a way of working the loom with one hand, his legs, and his feet, leaving the other hand free to hold a book, and worked so steadily in that crooked position that he became permanently crippled. The boy heard other stories about the importance of reading. Salvation, he came to believe, was to be found in books. When he was six years old, he read *The Wizard of Oz*—his first *real* book—and was rewarded by his Great-Aunt Manda with a dollar.

When the boy grew up, he decided to become a teacher of "litcomp." His intiation into the profession was rigorous, and there were moments when he nearly gave up. But gradually, "there emerged from the trudging a new and surprising love, a love that with all my previous reading I had not dreamed of: the love of skill, of craft, of getting clear in my mind and then in my writing what a great writer had got right in his work" (Booth, p. 315). Eventually, the boy, now grown, got his doctorate, and after teaching for thirteen years in small colleges, he returned to his graduate institution to become one of its eminent professors.

Booth caps his narration by quoting from *The Autobiography of Malcolm X*. It was in prison that Malcolm learned to read:

> For the first time I could pick up a book and now begin to understand what
> the book was saying. Anyone who has read a great deal can imagine the new
> world that opened. Let me tell you something: from then until I left that
> prison, in every free moment I had, if I was not reading in the library, I was
> reading on my bunk. . . . [M]onths passed without my even thinking about
> being imprisoned. In fact, up to then, I never had been so truly free in my life.
> (As quoted by Booth, p. 317)

"Perhaps," says Booth, "when you think back now on my family's
story about great-grandfather Booth, you will understand why reading
about Malcolm X's awakening speaks to the question of where I got my
'insane love' [for books]" (p. 317).

B. When I read the Malcolm X passage quoted in Booth's address,
the ellipsis roused my curiosity. What, exactly, I wondered, had been
deleted? What in the original exceeded the requirements of a Presidential Address to the MLA? Checking, I found the complete sentence to
read: "Between Mr. Muhammad's teachings, my correspondence, my
visitors—usually Ella and Reginald—and my reading, months passed
without my even thinking about being imprisoned."[2] Clearly, the first
phrase is the dissonant one. The reference to the leader of the notorious
Black Muslims suggests a story of reading very different from Booth's.
Here is how Malcolm X tells it. While serving time in the Norfolk
Prison Colony, he hit on the idea of teaching himself to read by copying
the dictionary.

> In my slow, painstaking, ragged handwriting, I copied into my tablet every
> thing on that first page, down to the punctuation marks. . . . Then, aloud, to
> myself, I read back everything I'd written on the tablet. . . . I woke up the
> next morning thinking about these words—immensely proud to realize that
> not only had I written so much at one time, but I'd written words that I never
> knew were in the world. . . . That was the way I started copying what
> eventually became the entire dictionary. (P. 172)

After copying the dictionary, Malcolm X began reading the books in
the prison library. "No university would ask any student to devour
literature as I did when this new world opened to me, of being able to
read and *understand*" (p. 173). Reading had changed the course of his
life. Years later, he would reflect on how "the ability to read awoke
inside me some long dormant craving to be mentally alive" (p. 179).

What did he read? What did he understand? He read Gregor Mendel's *Findings in Genetics* and it helped him to understand "that if you
started with a black man, a white man could be produced; but starting
with a white man, you never could produce a black man—because the
white chromosome is recessive. And since no one disputes that there

was but one Original Man, the conclusion is clear" (p. 175). He read histories, books by Will Durant and Arnold Toynbee, by W. E. B. du Bois and Carter G. Woodson, and he saw how "the glorious history of the black man" had been "bleached" out of the history books written by white men.

> [His] eyes opened gradually, then wider and wider, to how the world's white men had indeed acted like devils, pillaging and raping and bleeding and draining the whole world's non-white people. . . . I will never forget how shocked I was when I began reading about slavery's total horror. . . . The world's most monstrous crime, the sin and the blood on the white man's hands, are almost impossible to believe. (P. 175)

He read philosophy—the works of Schopenhauer, Kant, Nietzsche, and Spinoza—and he concluded that the "whole stream of Western Philosophy was now wound up in a cul-de-sac" as a result of the white man's "elaborate, neurotic necessity to hide the black man's true role in history" (p. 180). Malcolm X read voraciously, and book after book confirmed the truth of Elijah Muhammad's teachings. "It's a crime, the lie that has been told to generations of black men and white both. . . . Innocent black children growing up, living out their lives, dying of old age—and all of their lives ashamed of being black. But the truth is pouring out of the bag now" (p. 181).

Wayne Booth's story leads to the Crystal Ballroom of the Biltmore Hotel in Los Angeles, where we attend the protagonist as he delivers his Presidential Address to the members of the Modern Language Association. Malcolm X's love of books took him in a different direction, to the stage of the Audubon Ballroom in Harlem, where, as he was about to address a mass meeting of the Organization of Afro-American Unity, he was murdered.

C. As we have seen, an ellipsis links Wayne Booth's story of reading to Malcolm X's. Another ellipsis, this time not graphically marked, signals the existence of a third story. Malcolm X's startling reading of Mendel's genetics overlooks the most rudimentary fact of human reproduction: whether you start with a black man or a white man, without a woman, you get *nothing*. An excerpt from Virginia Woolf's *A Room of One's Own* restores this deleted perspective.[3]

The heroine, call her Mary, says Woolf, goes to the British Museum in search of information about women. There she discovers to her chagrin that woman is, "perhaps, the most discussed animal in the universe?"

> Why does Samuel Butler say, "Wise men never say what they think of women"? Wise men never say anything else apparently. . . . Are they capa-

ble of education? Napoleon thought them incapable. Dr. Johnson thought the opposite. Have they souls or have they not souls? Some savages say they have none. Others, on the contrary, say women are half divine and worship them on that account. Some sages hold that they are shallower in the brain; others that they are deeper in consciousness. Goethe honoured them; Mussolini despises them. Wherever one looked men thought about women and thought differently. (Pp. 29–30)

Distressed and confused, Mary notices that she has unconsciously drawn a picture in her notebook, the face and figure of Professor von X. engaged in writing his monumental work, *The Mental, Moral, and Physical Inferiority of the Female Sex.* "His expression suggested that he was labouring under some emotion that made him jab his pen on the paper as if he were killing some noxious insect as he wrote, but even when he had killed it that did not satisfy him; he must go on killing it. . . . A very elementary excercise in psychology . . . showed me . . . that the sketch had been made in anger" (pp. 31–32).

Nothing remarkable in that, she reflects, given the provocation. But "How explain the anger of the professor? . . . For when it came to analysing the impression left by these books, . . . there was [an] element which was often present and could not be immediately identified. Anger, I called it. . . . To judge from its effects, it was anger disguised and complex, not anger simple and open" (p. 32).

Disappointed with essayists and professors, Mary turns to historians. But apparently women played no significant role in history. What little information Mary finds is disturbing: "Wife-beating, I read, was a recognized right of a man, and was practiced without shame by high as well as low" (p. 44). Oddly enough, literature presents a contradictory picture.

> If women had not existence save in fiction written by men, we would imagine her to be a person of utmost importance; very various; heroic and mean; splendid and sordid; infinitely beautiful and hideous in the extreme; as great as a man, some think even greater. But this is women in fiction. In fact, as Professor Trevelyan points out, she was locked up, beaten and flung about the room. (P. 45)

At last, Mary can draw but one conclusion from her reading. Male professors, male historians, and male poets can not be relied on for the truth about women. Woman herself must undertake the study of woman. Of course, to do so, she must secure enough money to live on and a room of her own.

Booth's story, we recall, is told within the framework of a professional ritual. It is intended to remind us of "the loves and fears that inform our daily work" and of "what we do when we are at our best," to show, if not a unity, then enough of a "center" "to shame us whenever we violate it." The principal motif of the myth is the hero's insane love for books, and the way this develops with education and maturity into "critical under-standing," which Booth defines as that synthesis of thought and passion which should replace, "on the one hand, sentimental and uncritical identifications that leave minds undisturbed, and on the other, hyper-critical negations that freeze or alienate" (pp. 317–18). Booth is confi-dent that the experience celebrated by the myth is archetypal. "What-ever our terms for it, whatever our theories about how it happens or why it fails to happen more often, can we reasonably doubt the impor-tance of the moment, at any level of study, when any of us—you, me, Malcolm X, my great-grandfather—succeeds in entering other minds, or 'taking them in,' as nourishment for our own?" (p. 318).

Now, while it is certainly true that something one might call "critical understanding" informs the stories told by Malcolm X and Virginia Woolf, these authors fill this term with thoughts and passions that one would never suspect from Booth's definition. From the standpoint of the second and third stories of reading, Booth's story is utopian. The powers and resources of his hero are equal to the challenges he encoun-ters. At each stage he finds suitable mentors. He is assured by the people around him, by the books he reads, by the entire culture, that he is right for the part. His talents and accomplishments are acknowledged and justly rewarded. In short, from the perspective of Malcolm X's and Woolf's stories, Booth's hero is fantastically privileged.

Utopian has a second meaning, one that is by no means pejorative, and Booth's story is utopian in this sense as well. In overlooking the realities highlighted by the stories of Malcolm X and Virginia Woolf, Booth's story anticipates what might be possible, what "critical under-standing" might mean for *everyone,* if only we could overcome the pervasive systemic injustices of our time.

Reader-Response Theory and Feminist Criticism

Reader-response criticism, as currently constituted, is utopian in the same two senses. The different accounts of the reading experience that have been put forth overlook the issues of race, class, and sex, and give no hint of the conflicts, sufferings, and passions that attend these real-ities. The relative tranquility of the tone of these theories testifies to the privileged position of the theorists. Perhaps, someday, when privileges have withered away or at least become more equitably distributed, some of these theories will ring true. Surely we ought to be able to talk about reading without worrying about injustice. But for now, reader-response criticism must confront the disturbing implications of our historical reality. Paradoxically, utopian theories that elide these realities betray the utopian impulses that inform them.

To put the matter plainly, reader-response criticism needs feminist criticism. The two have yet to engage each other in a sustained and serious way, but if the promise of the former is to be fulfilled, such an encounter must soon occur. Interestingly, the obvious question of the significance of gender has already been explicitly raised, and—this testifies to the increasing impact of feminist criticism as well as to the direct ideological bearing of the issue of gender on reader-response criticism—not by a feminist critic, but by Jonathan Culler, a leading theorist of reading: "If the experience of literature depends upon the qualities of a reading self, one can ask what difference it would make to the experience of literature and thus to the meaning of literature if this self were, for example, female rather than male. If the meaning of a work is the experience of a reader, what difference does it make if the reader is a woman?"[4]

Until very recently this question has not occurred to reader-response critics. They have been preoccupied with other issues. Culler's survey of the field is instructive here, for it enables us to anticipate the direction reader-response theory might take when it is shaken from its slumber by feminist criticism. According to Culler, the different models (or "stories") of reading that have been proposed are all organized around three problems. The first is the issue of control: Does the text control the reader, or vice versa? For David Bleich, Normal Holland, and Stanley Fish, the reader holds controlling interest. Readers read the poems they have made. Bleich asserts this point most strongly: the constraints imposed by the words on the page are "trivial," since their meaning can always be altered by "subjective action." To claim that the text supports this or that reading is only to "moralistically claim . . . that one's own objectification is more authoritative than someone else's."[5]

At the other pole are Michael Riffaterre, Georges Poulet, and Wolfgang Iser, who acknowledge the creative role of the reader, but ultimately take the text to be the dominant force. To read, from this point of view, is to create the text according to *its* own promptings. As Poulet puts it, a text, when invested with a reader's subjectivity, becomes a "subjectified object," a "second self" that depends on the reader, but is not, strictly speaking, identical with him. Thus, reading "is a way of giving way not only to a host of alien words, images and ideas, but also to the very alien principle which utters and shelters them. . . . I am on loan to another, and this other thinks, feels, suffers and acts within me."[6]

Culler argues persuasively that, regardless of their ostensible theoretical commitments, the prevailing stories of reading generally vacillate between these reader-dominant and text-dominant poles. In fact, those who stress the subjectivity of the reader as against the objectivity of the text ultimately portray the text as determining the responses of the reader. "The more active, projective, or creative the reader is, the more she is manipulated by the sentence or by the author" (p. 71).

The second question prominent in theories of reading is closely related to the first. Reading always involves a subject and an object, a reader and a text. But what constitutes the objectivity of the text? What is "in" the text? What is supplied by the reader? Again, the answers have been equivocal. On the face of it, the situation seems to call for a dualistic theory that credits the contributions of both text and reader. However, Culler argues, a dualistic theory eventually gives way to a monistic theory, in which one or the other pole supplies everything. One might say, for instance, that Iser's theory ultimately implies the determinacy of the text and the authority of the author: "The author guarantees the unity of the work, requires the reader's creative participation, and through his text, prestructures the shape of the aesthetic object to be produced by the reader."[7] At the same time, one can also argue that the "gaps" that structure the reader's response are not built into the text, but appear (or not) as a result of the particular interpretive strategy employed by the reader. Thus, "there is no distinction between what the text gives and what the reader supplies; he supplies *everything*."[8] Depending on which aspects of the theory one takes seriously, Iser's theory collapses either into a monism of the text or a monism of the reader.

The third problem identified by Culler concerns the ending of the story. Most of the time stories of reading end happily. "Readers may be manipulated and misled, but when they finish the book their experience turns into knowledge . . . as though finishing the book took them outside the experience of reading and gave them mastery of it" (p. 79). However, some critics—Harold Bloom, Paul de Man, and Culler himself—find these optimistic endings questionable, and prefer instead stories that stress the impossibility of reading. If, as de Man says, rhetoric puts "an insurmountable obstacle in the way of any reading or understanding," then the reader "may be placed in impossible situations where there is no happy issue, but only the possibility of playing out the roles dramatized in the text" (Culler, p. 81).

Such have been the predominant preoccupations of reader-response criticism during the past decade and a half. Before indicating how feminist critics could affect the conversation, let me consider an objection. A recent and influential essay by Elaine Showalter suggests that we should not enter the conversation at all. She observes that during its early phases, the principal mode of feminist criticism was "feminist critique," which was counter-ideological in intent and concerned with the feminist as *reader.* Happily, we have outgrown this necessary but theoretically unpromising approach. Today, the dominant mode of feminist criticism is "gynocritics," the study of woman as *writer,* of the "history, styles, themes, genres, and structures of writing by women; the psychodynamics of female creativity; the trajectory of the individual or collective female career; and the evolution and laws of a female literary tradition." The shift from "feminist critique" to "gynocritics"—from emphasis on woman as reader to emphasis on woman as writer—has put us in the position of developing a feminist criticism that is "genuinely woman-centered, independent, and intellectually coherent."

> To see women's writing as our primary subject forces us to make the leap to a new conceptual vantage point and to redefine the nature of the theoretical problem before us. It is no longer the ideological dilemma of reconciling revisionary pluralisms but the essential question of difference. How can we constitute women as a distinct literary group? What is the *difference* of women's writing?[9]

But why should the activity of the woman writer be more conducive to theory than the activity of the woman reader is? If it is possible to formulate a basic conceptual framework for disclosing the "difference" of women's writing, surely it is no less possible to do so for women's reading. The same difference, be it linguistic, biological, psychological, or cultural, should apply in either case. In addition, what Showalter calls "gynocritics" is in fact constituted by feminist *criticism*—that is, *readings*—of female texts. Thus, the relevant distinction is not between woman as reader and woman as writer, but between feminist readings of male texts and feminist readings of female texts, and there is no reason why the former could not be as theoretically coherent (or irreducibly pluralistic) as the latter.

On the other hand, there are good reasons for feminist criticism to engage reader-response criticism. Both dispute the fetishized art object, the "Verbal Icon," of New Criticism, and both seek to dispel the objectivist illusion that buttresses the authority of the dominant critical tradition. Feminist criticism can have considerable impact on reader-response criticism, since, as Culler has noticed, it is but a small step from the thesis that the reader is an active producer of meaning to the recognition that there are many different kinds of readers, and that women—because of their numbers if because of nothing else—constitute an essential class. Reader-response critics cannot take refuge in the objectivity of the text, or even in the idea that a gender-neutral criticism is possible. Today they can continue to ignore the implications of feminist criticism only at the cost of incoherence or intellectual dishonesty.

It is equally true that feminist critics need to question their allegiance to text- and author-centered paradigms of criticism. Feminist criticism, we should remember, is a mode of *praxis*. The point is not merely to interpret literature in various ways; the point is to *change the world*. We cannot afford to ignore the activity of reading, for it is here that literature is realized as *praxis*. Literature acts on the world by acting on its readers.

To return to our earlier question: What will happen to reader-response criticism if feminists enter the conversation? It is useful to recall the contrast between Booth's story and those of Malcolm X and Virginia Woolf. Like Booth's story, the "stories of reading" that currently make up reader-response theory are mythically abstract, and appear, from a different vantage point, to be by and about readers who are fantastically privileged. Booth's story had a happy ending; Malcolm's and Mary's did not. For Mary, reading meant encountering a tissue of lies and silences; for Malcolm it meant the verification of Elijah Muhammad's shocking doctrines.

Two factors—gender and politics—which are suppressed in the dominant models of reading gain prominence with the advent of a feminist perspective. The feminist story will have *at least* two chapters: one concerned with feminist readings of male texts, and another with feminist readings of female texts. In addition, in this story, gender will have a prominent role as the locus of political struggle. The story will speak of the difference between men and women, of the way the experience and perspective of women have been systematically and fallaciously assimilated into the generic masculine, and of the need to correct this error. Finally, it will identify literature—the activities of reading and writing—as an important arena of political struggle, a crucial component of the project of interpreting the world in order to change it.

Feminist criticism does not approach reader-response criticism without preconceptions. Actually, feminist criticism has always included substantial reader-centered interests. In the next two sections of this paper, I will review these interests, first with respect to male texts, then with respect to female texts. In the process, I will uncover some of the issues that might be addressed and clarified by a feminist theory of reading.

The Female Reader and the Literary Canon

Although reader-response critics propose different and often conflicting models, by and large the emphasis is on features of the process of reading that do not vary with the nature of the reading material. The feminist entry into the conversation brings the nature of the text back into the foreground. For feminists, the question of *how* we read is inextricably linked with the question of *what* we read. More specifically, the feminist inquiry into the activity of reading begins with the realization that the literary canon is androcentric, and that this has a profoundly damaging effect on women readers. The documentation of this realization was one of the earliest tasks undertaken by feminist critics. Elaine Showalter's 1971 critique of the literary curriculum is exemplary of this work.

> [In her freshman year a female student] . . . might be assigned an anthology of essays, perhaps such as *The Responsible Man, . . .* or *Conditions of Man,* or *Man in Crisis,* or again, *Representative Man: Cult Heroes of Our Time,* in which thirty-three men represent such categories of heroism as the writer, the poet, the dramatist, the artist, and the guru, and the only two women included are the actress Elizabeth Taylor, and the existential Heroine Jacqueline Onassis.
>
> Perhaps the student would read a collection of stories like *The Young Man in American Literature: The Initiation Theme,* or sociological literature like *The Black Man and the Promise of America.* In a more orthodox literary program she might study eternally relevant classics, such as *Oedipus;* as a professor remarked in a recent issue of *College English,* all of us want to kill our fathers and marry our mothers. And whatever else she might read, she would inevitably arrive at the favorite book of all Freshman English courses, the classic of adolescent rebellion, *The Portrait of the Artist as a Young Man.*
>
> By the end of her freshman year, a woman student would have learned something about intellectual neutrality; she would be learning, in fact, how to think like a man. And so she would go on, increasingly with male professors to guide her.[10]

The more personal accounts of other critics reinforce Showalter's critique.

> The first result of my reading was a feeling that male characters were at the very least more interesting than women to the authors who invented them. Thus if, reading their books as it seemed their authors intended them, I naively identified with a character, I repeatedly chose men; I would rather have been Hamlet than Ophelia, Tom Jones instead of Sophia Western, and, perhaps, despite Dostoevsky's intention, Raskolnikov not Sonia.
>
> More peculiar perhaps, but sadly unsurprising, were the assessments I accepted about fictional women. For example, I quickly learned that power was unfeminine and powerful women were, quite literally, monstrous. . . . Bitches all, they must be eliminated, reformed, or at the very least, condemned. . . . Those rare women who are shown in fiction as both powerful and, in some sense, admirable are such because their power is based, if not on beauty, then at least on sexuality.[11]

For a woman, then, books do not necessarily spell salvation. In fact, a literary education may very well cause her grave psychic damage: schizophrenia "is the bizarre but logical conclusion of our education. Imagining myself male, I attempted to create myself male. Although I knew the case was otherwise, it seemed I could do nothing to make this other critically real."[12]

To put the matter theoretically, androcentric literature structures the reading experience differently depending on the gender of the reader. For the male reader, the text serves as the meeting ground of the personal and the universal. Whether or not the text approximates the particularities of his own experience, he is invited to validate the equation of maleness with humanity. The male reader feels his affinity with the universal, with the paradigmatic human being, precisely because he is male. Consider the famous scene of Stephen's epiphany in *The Portrait of the Artist as a Young Man.*

> A girl stood before him in midstream, alone and still, gazing out to sea. She seemed like one whom magic had changed into the likeness of a strange and beautiful seabird. Her long slender bare legs were delicate as a crane's and pure save where an emerald trail of seaweed had fashioned itself as a sign upon the flesh. Her thighs, fuller and softhued as ivory, were bared almost to the hips, where the white fringes of her drawers were like feathering of soft white down. Her slateblue skirts were kilted boldly about her waist and dovetailed behind her. Her bosom was a bird's, soft and slight, slight and soft, as the breast of some dark plummaged dove. But her long fair hair was girlish: and touched with the wonder of mortal beauty, her face.[13]

A man reading this passage is invited to identify with Stephen, to feel "the riot in his blood," and, thus, to ratify the alleged universality of the experience. Whether or not the sight of a girl on the beach has ever provoked similar emotions in him, the male reader is invited to feel his *difference* (concretely, *from the girl*) and to equate that with the universal. Relevant here is Lévi-Strauss's theory that woman functions as currency exchanged between men. The woman in the text converts the text into a woman, and the circulation of this text/woman becomes the central ritual that establishes the bond between the author and his male readers.[14]

The same text affects a woman reader differently. Judith Fetterley gives the most explicit theory to date about the dynamics of the woman reader's encounter with androcentric literature. According to Fetterley, notwithstanding the prevalence of the castrating bitch stereotype, "the cultural reality is not the emasculation of men by women, but the *immasculation* of women by men. As readers and teachers and scholars, women are taught to think as men, to identify with a male point of view, and to accept as normal and legitimate a male system of values, one of whose central principles is misogyny."[15]

The process of immasculation does not impart virile power to the woman reader. On the contrary, it doubles her oppression. She suffers "not simply the powerlessness which derives from not seeing one's experience articulated, clarified, and legitimized in art, but more significantly, the powerlessness which results from the endless division of self against self, the consequence of the invocation to identify as male while being reminded that to be male—to be universal— . . . is to be *not female*."[16]

A woman reading Joyce's novel of artistic awakening, and in particular the passage quoted above, will, like her male counterpart, be invited to identify with Stephen and therefore to ratify the equation of maleness with the universal. Androcentric literature is all the more efficient as an instrument of sexual politics because it does not allow the woman reader to seek refuge in her difference. Instead, it draws her into a process that uses her against herself. It solicits her complicity in the elevation of male difference into universality and, accordingly, the denigration of female difference into otherness without reciprocity. To be sure, misogyny is abundant in the literary canon.[17] It is important, however, that Fetterley's argument can stand on a weaker premise. Androcentricity is a sufficient condition for the process of immasculation.

Feminist critics of male texts, from Kate Millett to Judith Fetterley, have worked under the sign of the "Resisting Reader." Their goal is to disrupt the process of immasculation by exposing it to consciousness, by disclosing the androcentricity of what has customarily passed for the universal. However, feminist criticism written under the aegis of the resisting reader leaves certain questions unanswered, questions that are becoming ripe for feminist analysis: Where does the text get its power to draw us into its designs? Why do some (not all) demonstrably sexist texts remain appealing even after they have been subjected to thorough feminist critique? The usual answer—that the power of male texts is the power of the false consciousness into which women as well as men have been socialized—oversimplifies the problem and prevents us from comprehending both the force of literature and the complexity of our responses to it.

Fredric Jameson advances a thesis that seems to me to be a good starting point for the feminist reconsideration of male texts: "The effectively ideological is also at the same time necessarily utopian."[18] This thesis implies that the male text draws its power over the female reader from authentic desires, which it rouses and then harnesses to the process of immasculation.

A concrete example is in order. Consider Lawrence's *Women in Love,* and for the sake of simplicity, concentrate on Birkin and Ursula. Simone de Beauvoir and Kate Millet have convinced me that this novel is sexist. Why does it remain appealing to me? Jameson's thesis prompts me to answer this question by examining how the text plays not only on my false consciousness but also on my authentic liberatory aspirations—that is to say, on the very impulses that drew me to the feminist movement.

The trick of role reversal comes in handy here. If we reverse the roles of Birkin and Ursula, the ideological components (or at least the most egregious of these, e.g., the analogy between women and horses) stand out as absurdities. Now, if we delete these absurd components while keeping the roles reversed, we have left the story of a woman struggling to combine her passionate desire for autonomous conscious being with an equally passionate desire for love and for other human bonds. This residual story is not far from one we would welcome as expressive of a feminist sensibility. Interestingly enough, it also intimates a novel Lawrence might have written, namely, the proper sequel to *The Rainbow.*

My affective response to the novel Lawrence did write is bifurcated. On the one hand, because I am a woman, I am implicated in the representation of Ursula and in the destiny Lawrence has prepared for her: man is the son of god, but woman is the daughter of man. Her vocation is to witness his transcendence in rapt silence. On the other hand, Fetterley is correct that I am also induced to identify with Birkin, and in so doing, I am drawn into complicity with the reduction of Ursula, and therefore of myself, to the role of the other.

However, the process of immasculation is more complicated than Fetterley allows. When I identify with Birkin, I unconsciously perform the two-stage rereading described above. I reverse the roles of Birkin and Ursula and I suppress the obviously ideological components that in the process show up as absurdities. The identification with Birkin is emotionally effective because, stripped of its patriarchal trappings, Birkin's struggle and his utopian vision conform to my own. To the extent that I perform this feminist rereading *unconsciously,* I am captivated by the text. The stronger my desire for autonomous selfhood and for love, the stronger my identification with Birkin, and the more intense the experience of bifurcation characteristic of the process of immasculation.

The full argument is beyond the scope of this essay. My point is that *certain* (not all) male texts merit a dual hermeneutic: a negative hermeneutic that discloses their complicity with patriarchal ideology, and a positive hermeneutic that recuperates the utopian moment—the authentic kernel—from which they draw a significant portion of their emotional power.[19]

Reading Women's Writing

Showalter is correct that feminist criticism has shifted emphasis in recent years from "critique" (primarily) of male texts to "gynocritics," or the study of women's writing. Of course, it is worth remembering that the latter has always been on the feminist agenda. *Sexual Politics,* for example, contains not only the critique of Lawrence, Miller, and Mailer that won Millett such notoriety, but also her memorable rereading of *Villette*.[20] It is equally true that interest in women's writing has not entirely supplanted the critical study of patriarchal texts. In a sense "critique" has provided the bridge from the study of male texts to the study of female texts. As feminist criticism shifted from the first to the second, "feminist critique" turned its attention from androcentric texts per se to the androcentric critical strategies that pushed women's writing to the margins of the literary canon. The earliest examples of this genre (for instance, Showalter's "The Double Critical Standard," and Carol Ohmann's "Emily Brontë in the Hands of Male Critics") were concerned primarily with describing and documenting the prejudice against women writers that clouded the judgment of well-placed readers, that is, reviewers and critics.[21] Today we have more sophisticated and more comprehensive analyses of the androcentric critical tradition.

One of the most cogent of these is Nina Baym's analysis of American literature.[22] Baym observes that, as late as 1977, the American canon of major writers did not include a single woman novelist. And yet, in terms of numbers and commercial success, women novelists have probably dominated American literature since the middle of the nineteenth century. How to explain this anomaly?

One explanation is simple bias of the sort documented by Showalter, Ohmann, and others. A second is that women writers lived and worked under social conditions that were not particularly conducive to the production of "excellent" literature: "There tended to be a sort of immediacy in the ambitions of literary women leading them to professionalism rather than artistry, by choice as well as by social pressure and opportunity."[23] Baym adduces a third, more subtle, and perhaps more important reason. There are, she argues, "gender-related restrictions that do not arise out of the cultural realities contemporary with the writing woman, but out of later critical theories . . . which impose their concerns anachronistically, after the fact, on an earlier period."[24] If one reads the critics most instrumental in forming the current theories about American literature (Matthiessen, Chase, Feidelson, Trilling, etc.), one finds that the theoretical model for the canonical American novel is the "melodrama of beset manhood." To accept this model is also to accept as a consequence the exclusion from the canon of "melodramas of beset womanhood," as well as virtually all fiction centering on the experience of women.[25]

The deep symbiotic relationship between the androcentric canon and androcentric modes of reading is well summarized by Kolodny.

> *Insofar as we are taught to read, what we engage are not texts, but paradigms.* . . . Insofar as literature is itself a social institution, so, too, reading is a highly socialized—or learned—activity. . . . We read well, and with pleasure, what we already know how to read; and what we know how to read is to a large extent dependent on what we have already read [works from which we have developed our expectations and learned our interpretive strategies]. What we then choose to read—and, by extension, teach and thereby "canonize"—usually follows upon our previous reading.[26]

We are caught, in other words, in a rather vicious circle. An androcentric canon generates androcentric interpretive strategies, which in turn favor the canonization of androcentric texts and the marginalization of gynocentric ones. To break this circle, feminist critics must fight on two fronts: for the revision of the canon to include a significant body of works by women, and for the development of the reading strategies consonant with the concerns, experiences, and formal devices that constitute these tets. Of course, to succeed, we also need a community of women readers who are qualified by experience, commitment, and training, and who will enlist the personal and institutional resources at their disposal in the struggle.[27]

The critique of androcentric reading strategies is essential, for it opens up some ideological space for the recuperation of women's writing. Turning now to this project, we observe, first, that a large volume of work has been done, and, second, that this endeavor is coming to look even more complicated and more diverse than the criticism of male texts. Certainly, it is impossible in the space of a few pages to do justice to the wide range of concerns, strategies, and positions associated with feminist readings of female texts. Nevertheless, certain things can be said. For the remainder of this section, I focus on an exemplary essay: "Vesuvius at Home: The Power of Emily Dickinson," by Adrienne Rich.[28] My commentary anticipates the articulation of a paradigm that illuminates certain features of feminist readings of women's writing.

I am principally interested in the rhetoric of Rich's essay, for it represents an implicit commentary on the process of reading women's writing. Feminist readings of male texts are, as we have seen, primarily resisting. The reader assumes an adversarial or at least a detached attitude toward the material at hand. In the opening pages of her essay, Rich introduces three metaphors that proclaim a very different attitude toward her subject.

> The methods, the exclusions, of Emily Dickinson's existence could not have been my own; yet more and more, as a woman poet finding my own methods, I have come to understand her necessities, could have served as witness in her defense. (P. 158)

> I am traveling at the speed of time, along the Massachusetts Turnpike. . . . "Home is not where the heart is," she wrote in a letter, "but the house and adjacent buildings." . . . I am traveling at the speed of time, in the direction of the house and buildings. . . . For years, I have been not so much envisioning Emily Dickinson as trying to visit, to enter her mind through her poems and letters, and through my own intimations of what it could have meant to be one of the two mid-nineteenth century American geniuses, and a woman, living in Amherst, Massachusetts. (Pp. 158–59)

> For months, for most of my life, I have been hovering like an insect against the screens of an existence which inhabited Amherst, Massachusetts between 1830 and 1886. (P. 158) . . . Here [in Dickinson's bedroom] I become again, an insect, vibrating at the frames of windows, clinging to the panes of glass, trying to connect. (P. 161)

A commentary on the process of reading is carried on silently and unobtrusively through the use of these metaphors. The first is a judicial metaphor: the feminist reader speaks as a witness in defense of the woman writer. Here we see clearly that gender is crucial. The feminist reader takes the part of the woman writer against patriarchal misreadings that trivialize or distort her work.[29] The second metaphor refers to a principal tenet of feminist criticism: a literary work cannot be understood apart from the social, historical, and cultural context within which it was written. As if to acquiesce to the condition Dickinson had imposed on her friends, Rich travels through space and time to visit the poet on her own *premises*. She goes to Amherst, to the house where Dickinson lived. She rings the bell, she goes in, then upstairs, then into the bedroom that had been "freedom" for the poet. Her destination, ultimately, is Dickinson's mind. But it is not enough to read the poet's poems and letters. To reach her heart and mind, one must take a detour through "the house and adjacent buildings."

Why did Dickinson go into seclusion? Why did she write poems she would not publish? What mean these poems about queens, volcanoes, deserts, eternity, passion, suicide, wild beasts, rape, power, madness, the daemon, the grave? For Rich, these are related questions. The revisionary re-reading of Dickinson's work is of a piece with the revisionary re-reading of her life. "I have a notion genius knows itself; that Dickinson chose her seclusion, knowing what she needed. . . . She carefully selected her society and controlled the disposal of her time. . . . Given her vocation, she was neither eccentric nor quaint; she was determined to survive, to use her powers, to practice necessary economies" (p. 160).

> To write [the poetry that she needed to write] she had to enter chambers of the self in which
>> Ourself, concealed—
>> Should startle most—
> and to relinquish control there, to take those risks, she had to create a relationship to the outer world where she could feel in control. (P. 175)

The metaphor of visiting points to another feature of feminist readings of women's writing, namely, the tendency to construe the text not as an object, but as the manifestation of the subjectivity of the absent author—the "voice" of another woman. Rich is not content to revel in the textuality of Dickinson's poems and letters. For her, these are doorways to the "mind" of a "woman of genius." Rich deploys her imagination and her considerable rhetorical skill to evoke "the figure of powerful will" who lives at the heart of the text. To read Dickinson, then, is to try to visit with her, to hear her voice, to make her live *in* oneself, and to feel her impressive "personal dimensions."[30]

At the same time, Rich is keenly aware that visiting with Dickinson is *only* a metaphor for reading her poetry, and an inaccurate one at that. She signals this awareness with the third metaphor. It is no longer possible to visit with Dickinson; one can only enter her mind through her poems and letters as one can enter her house—through the backdoor out of which her coffin was carried. In reading, one encounters only a text, the trail of an absent author. Upstairs, at last, in the very room where Dickinson exercised her astonishing craft, Rich finds herself again "an insect, vibrating at the frames of windows, clinging to panes of glass, trying to connect." But though "the scent is very powerful," Dickinson herself is absent.

Perhaps the most obvious rhetorical device employed by Rich in this essay, more obvious even than her striking metaphors, is her use of the personal voice. Her approach to Dickinson is self-consciously and unabashedly subjective. She clearly describes her point of view—what she saw as she drove across the Connecticut Valley toward Amherst (ARCO stations, MacDonald's, shopping plazas, as well as "light-green spring softening the hills, dogwood and wild fruit trees blossoming in the hollows"), and what she thought about (the history of the valley, "scene of Indian uprisings, religious revivals, spiritual confrontations, the blazing-up of the lunatic fringe of the Puritan coal," and her memories of college weekends in Amherst). Some elements of her perspective—ARCO and MacDonald's—would have been alien to Dickinson; others—the sight of dogwood and wild fruit trees in the spring, and most of all, the experience of being a woman poet in a patriarchal culture—would establish their affinity.

Rich's metaphors together with her use of the personal voice indicate some key issues underlying feminist readings of female texts. On the one hand, reading is necessarily subjective. On the other hand, it must not be wholly so. One must respect the autonomy of the text. The reader is a visitor and, as such, must observe the necessary courtesies. She must avoid unwarranted intrusions—she must be careful not to appropriate what belongs to her host, not to impose herself on the other woman. Furthermore, reading is at once an intersubjective encounter and something less than that. In reading Dickinson, Rich seeks to enter her mind, to feel her presence. But the text is a screen, an inanimate object. Its subjectivity is only a projection of the subjectivity of the reader.

Rich suggests the central motivation, the regulative ideal, that shapes the feminist reader's approach to these issues. If feminist readings of male texts are motivated by the need to disrupt the process of immasculation, feminist readings of female texts are motivated by the need "to connect," to recuperate, or to formulate—they come to the same thing—the context, the tradition, that would link women writers to one another, to women readers and critics, and to the larger community of women. Of course, the recuperation of such a context is a necessary basis for the nonrepressive integration of women's point of view and culture into the study of a Humanities that is worthy of its name.[31]

Feminist Models of Reading: A Summary

As I noted in the second section, mainstream reader-response theory is preoccupied with two closely related questions: (1) Does the text manipulate the reader, or does the reader manipulate the text to produce the meaning that suits her own interests? and (2) What is "in" the text? How can we distinguish what it supplies from what the reader supplies? Both of these questions refer to the subject-object relation that is established between reader and text during the process of reading. A feminist theory of reading also elaborates this relationship, but for feminists, gender—the gender inscribed in the text as well as the gender of the reader—is crucial. Hence, the feminist story has two chapters, one concerned with male texts and the other with female texts.

The focus of the first chapter is the experience of the woman reader. What do male texts *do* to her? The feminist story takes the subject-object relation of reading through three moments. The phrasing of the basic question signals the first moment. Control is conferred on the text: the woman reader is immasculated by the text. The feminist story fits well at this point in Iser's framework. Feminists insist that the androcentricity of the text and its damaging effects on women readers are not figments of their imagination. These are implicit in the "schematized aspects" of the text. The second moment, which is similarly consonant with the plot of Iser's story, involves the recognition of the crucial role played by the subjectivity of the woman reader. Without her, the text is *no-thing*. The process of immasculation is latent in the text, but it finds its actualization only through the reader's activity. In effect, the woman reader is the agent of her own immasculation.[32]

Here we seem to have a corroboration of Culler's contention that dualistic models of reading inevitably disintegrate into one of two monisms. Either the text (and, by implication, the author) or the woman reader is responsible for the process of immasculation. The third moment of the subject-object relation—ushered in by the transfiguration of the heroine into a feminist—breaks through this dilemma. The woman reader, now a feminist, embarks on a critical analysis of the reading process, and she realizes that the text has power to structure her experience. Without androcentric texts she will not suffer immasculation. However, her recognition of the power of the text is matched by her awareness of her essential role in the process of reading. Without her, the text is nothing—it is inert and harmless. The advent of feminist consciousness and the accompanying commitment to emancipatory *praxis* reconstitutes the subject-object relationship within a dialectical rather than a dualistic framework, thus averting the impasse described by Culler between the "dualism of narrative" and the "monism of theory." In the feminist story, the breakdown of Iser's dualism does not indicate a mistake or an irreducible impasse, but the necessity of *choosing* between two modes of reading. The reader can submit to the power of the text, or she can take control of the reading experience. The recognition of the existence of a choice suddenly makes visible the normative dimension of the feminist story: She *should* choose the second alternative.

But what does it mean for a reader to take control of the reading experience? First of all, she must do so without forgetting the androcentricity of the text or its power to structure her experience. In addition, the reader taking control of the text is not, as in Iser's model, simply a matter of selecting among the concretizations allowed by the text. Recall that a crucial feature of the process of immasculation is the woman reader's bifurcated response. She reads the text both as a man and as a woman. But in either case, the result is the same: she confirms her position as other. Taking control of the reading experience means reading the text as it was *not* meant to be read, in fact, reading it against itself. Specifically, one must identify the nature of the choices proffered by the text and, equally important, what the text precludes—namely, the possibility of reading as a woman *without* putting one's self in the position of the other, of reading so as to affirm womanhood as another, equally valid, paradigm of human existence.

All this is easier said than done. It is important to realize that reading a male text, no matter how virulently misogynous, could do little damage if it were an isolated event. The problem is that within patriarchal culture, the experience of immasculation is paradigmatic of women's encounters with the dominant literary and critical traditions. A feminist cannot simply refuse to read patriarchal texts, for they are everywhere, and they condition her participation in the literary and critical enterprise. In fact, by the time she becomes a feminist critic, a woman has already read numerous male texts—in particular, the most authoritative texts of the literary and critical canons. She has introjected not only androcentric texts, but also androcentric reading strategies and values. By the time she becomes a feminist, the bifurcated response characteristic of immasculation has become second nature to her. The feminist story stresses that patriarchal constructs have objective as well as subjective reality; they are inside and outside the text, inside and outside the reader.

The pervasiveness of androcentricity drives feminist theory beyond the individualistic models of Iser and of most reader-response critics. The feminist reader agrees with Stanley Fish that the production of the meaning of a text is mediated by the interpretive community in which the activity of reading is situated: the meaning of the text depends on the interpretive strategy one applies to it, and the choice of strategy is regulated (explicitly or implicitly) by the canons of acceptability that govern the interpretive community.[33] However, unlike Fish, the feminist reader is also aware that the ruling interpretive communities are androcentric, and that this androcentricity is deeply etched in the strategies and modes of thought that have been introjected by all readers, women as well as men.

Because patriarchal constructs have psychological correlates, taking control of the reading process means taking control of one's reactions and inclinations. Thus, a feminist reading—actually a re-reading—is a kind of therapeutic analysis. The reader recalls and examines how she would "naturally" read a male text in order to understand and therefore undermine the subjective predispositions that had rendered her vulnerable to its designs. Beyond this, the pervasiveness of immasculation necessitates a collective remedy. The feminist reader hopes that other women will recognize themselves in her story, and join her in her struggle to transform the culture.[34]

"Feminism affirms women's point of view by revealing, criticizing and examining its impossibility."[35] Had we nothing but male texts, this sentence from Catherine MacKinnon's brilliant essay on jurisprudence could serve as the definition of the project of the feminist reader. The significant body of literature written by women presents feminist critics with another, more heartwarming, task: that of recovering, articulating, and elaborating positive expressions of women's point of view, of celebrating the survival of this point of view in spite of the formidable forces that have been ranged against it.

The shift to women's writing brings with it a shift in emphasis from the negative hermeneutic of ideological unmasking to a positive hermeneutic whose aim is the recovery and cultivation of women's culture. As Showalter has noted, feminist criticism of women's writing proposes to articulate woman's difference: What does it mean for a woman to express herself in writing? How does a woman write as a woman? It is a central contention of this essay that feminist criticism should also inquire into the correlative process of *reading:* What does it mean for a woman to read without condemning herself to the position of other? What does it mean for a woman, reading as a woman, to read literature written by a woman writing as a woman?[36]

The Adrienne Rich essay discussed in the preceding section illustrates a contrast between feminist readings of male texts and feminist readings of female texts. In the former, the object of the critique, whether it is regarded as an enemy or as symptom of a malignant condition, is the text itself, *not* the reputation or the character of the author.[37] This impersonal approach contrasts sharply with the strong personal interest in Dickinson exhibited by Rich. Furthermore, it is not merely a question of friendliness toward the text. Rich's reading aims beyond "the unfolding of the text as a living event," the goal of aesthetic reading set by Iser. Much of the rhetorical energy of Rich's essay is directed toward evoking the personality of Dickinson, toward making *her* live as the substantial, palpable presence animating her works.

Unlike the first chapter of the feminist story of reading, which is centered around a single heroine—the woman reader battling her way out of a maze of patriarchal constructs—the second chapter features two protagonists—the woman reader and the woman writer—in the context of two settings. The first setting is judicial: one woman is standing witness in defense of the other; the second is dialogic: the two women are engaged in intimate conversation. The judicial setting points to the larger political and cultural dimension of the project of the feminist reader. Feminist critics may well say with Harold Bloom that reading always involves the "art of defensive warfare."[38] What they mean by this, however, would not be Bloom's individualistic, agonistic encounter between "strong poet" and "strong reader," but something more akin to "class struggle." Whether concerned with male or female texts, feminist criticism is situated in the larger struggle against patriarchy.

The importance of this battle cannot be overestimated. However, feminist readings of women's writing opens up space for another, equally important, critical project, namely, the articulation of a model of reading that is centered on a female paradigm. While it is still too early to present a full-blown theory, the dialogic aspect of the relationship between the feminist reader and the woman writer suggests the direction that such a theory might take. As in all stories of reading, the drama revolves around the subject-object relationship between text and reader. The feminist story—exemplified by the Adrienne Rich essay discussed earlier—features an intersubjective construction of this relationship. The reader encounters not simply a text, but a "subjectified object": the "heart and mind" of another woman. She comes into close contact with an interiority—a power, a creativity, a suffering, a vision— that is *not* identical with her own. The feminist interest in construing reading as an intersubjective encounter suggests an affinity with Poulet's (rather than Iser's) theory, and, as in Poulet's model, the subject of the literary work is its author, *not* the reader: "A book is not only a book; it is a means by which an author actually preserves [her] ideas, [her] feelings, [her] modes of dreaming and living. It is a means of saving [her] identity from death. . . . To understand a literary work, then, is to let the individual who wrote it reveal [herself] to us *in* us."[39]

For all this initial agreement, however, the dialogic relationship the feminist reader establishes with the female subjectivity brought to life in the process of reading is finally at odds with Poulet's model. For the interiorized author is "alien" to Poulet's reader. When he reads, he delivers himself "bound hand and foot, to the omnipotence of fiction." He becomes the "prey" of what he reads. "There is no escaping this takeover." His consciousness is "invaded," "annexed," "usurped." He is "dispossessed" of his rightful place on the "center stage" of his own mind. In the final analysis, the process of reading leaves room for only one subjectivity. The work becomes "a sort of human being" at "the expense of the reader whose life it suspends."[40] It is significant that the metaphors of mastery and submission, of violation and control, so prominent in Poulet's essay, are entirely absent in Rich's essay on Dickinson. In the paradigm of reading implicit in her essay, the dialectic of control (which shapes feminist readings of male texts) gives way to the dialectic of communication. For Rich, reading is a matter of "trying to connect" with the existence behind the text.

This dialectic also has three moments. The first involves the recognition that genuine intersubjective communication demands the duality of reader and author (the subject of the work). Because reading removes the barrier between subject and object, the division takes place *within* the reader. Reading induces a doubling of the reader's subjectivity, so that one can be placed at the disposal of the text while the other remains with the reader. Now, this doubling presents a problem, for in fact there is only one subject present—the reader. The text—the words on the page—has been written by the writer, but meaning is always a matter of interpretation. The subjectivity roused to life by reading, while it may be attributed to the author, is nevertheless not a separate subjectivity but a projection of the subjectivity of the reader. How can the duality of subjects be maintained in the absence of the author? In an actual conversation, the presence of another person preserves the duality. Because each party must assimilate and interpret the utterances of the other, we still have the introjection of the subject-object division, as well as the possibility of hearing only what one wants to hear. But in a real conversation, the other person can interrupt, object to an erroneous interpretation, provide further explanations, change her mind, change the topic, or cut off conversation altogether. In reading, there are no comparable safeguards against the appropriation of the text by the reader. This is the second moment of the dialectic—the recognition that reading is necessarily subjective. The need to keep it from being *totally* subjective ushers in the third moment of the dialectic.

In the feminist story, the key to the problem is the awareness of the double context of reading and writing. Rich's essay is wonderfully illustrative. To avoid imposing an alien perspective on Dickinson's poetry, Rich informs her reading with the knowledge of the circumstances in which Dickinson lived and worked. She repeatedly reminds herself and her readers that Dickinson must be read in light of her *own* premises, that the "exclusions" and "necessities" she endured, and, therefore, her choices, were conditioned by her own world. At the same time, Rich's sensitivity to the context of writing is matched by her sensitivity to the context of reading. She makes it clear throughout the essay that her reading of Dickinson is necessarily shaped by her experience and interests as a feminist poet living in the twentieth-century United States. The reader also has her own premises. To forget these is to run the risk of imposing them surreptitiously on the author.

To recapitulate, the first moment of the dialectic of reading is marked by the recognition of the necessary duality of subjects; the second, by the realization that this duality is threatened by the author's absence. In the third moment, the duality of subjects is referred to the duality of contexts. Reading becomes a mediation between author and reader, between the context of writings and the context of reading.

Although feminists have always believed that objectivity is an illusion, Rich's essay is the only one, as far as I know, to exhibit through its rhetoric the necessary subjectivity of reading coupled with the equally necessary commitment to reading the text as it was meant to be read.[41] The third moment of the dialectic is apparent in Rich's weaving—not blending—of the context of writing and the context of reading, the perspective of the author and that of the reader. The central rhetorical device effecting this mediation is her use of the personal voice. As in most critical essays, Rich alternates quotes from the texts in question with her own commentary, but her use of the personal voice makes a difference. In her hands, this rhetorical strategy serves two purposes. First, it serves as a reminder that her interpretation is informed by her own perspective. Second, it signifies her tactful approach to Dickinson; the personal voice serves as a gesture warding off any inclination to appropriate the authority of the text as a warrant for the validity of the interpretation. Because the interpretation is presented as an *interpretation,* its claim to validity rests on the cogency of the supporting arguments, *not* on the authorization of the text.

Rich accomplishes even more than this. She reaches out to Dickinson not by identifying with her, but by establishing their affinity. Both are American, both are women poets in a patriarchal culture. By playing this affinity against the differences, she produces a context that incorporates both reader and writer. In turn, this common ground becomes the basis for drawing the connections that, in her view, constitute the proper goal of reading.

One might ask: Is there something distinctively female (rather than "merely feminist") in this dialogic model? While it is difficult to specify what "distinctively female" might mean, there are currently very interesting speculations about differences in the way males and females conceive of themselves and of their relations with others. The works of Jean Baker Miller, Nancy Chodorow, and Carol Gilligan suggest that men define themselves through individuation and separation from others, while women have more flexible ego boundaries and define and experience themselves in terms of their affiliations and relationships with others.[42] Men value autonomy, and they think of their interactions with others principally in terms of procedures for arbitrating conflicts between individual rights. Women, on the other hand, value relationships, and they are most concerned in their dealings with others to negotiate between opposing needs so that the relationship can be maintained. This difference is consistent with the difference between mainstream models of reading and the dialogic model I am proposing for feminist readings of women's writing. Mainstream reader-response theories are preoccupied with issues of control and partition—how to distinguish the contribution of the author/text from the contribution of the reader. In the dialectic of communication informing the relationship between the feminist reader and the female author/text, the central issue is not of control or partition, but of managing the contradictory implications of the desire for relationship (one must maintain a minimal distance from the other) and the desire for intimacy, up to and including a symbiotic merger with the other. The problematic is defined by the drive "to connect," rather than that which is implicit in the mainstream preoccupation with partition and control—namely, the drive to get it right. It could also be argued that Poulet's model represents reading as an intimate, intersubjective encounter. However, it is significant that in his model, the prospect of close rapport with another provokes both excitement and anxiety. Intimacy, while desired, is also viewed as a threat to one's integrity. For Rich, on the other hand, the prospect of merging with another is problematical, but not threatening.

Let me end with a word about endings. Dialectical stories look forward to optimistic endings. Mine is no exception. In the first chapter the woman reader becomes a feminist, and in the end she succeeds in extricating herself from the androcentric logic of the literary and critical canons. In the second chapter the feminist reader succeeds in effecting a mediation between her perspective and that of the writer. These "victories" are part of the project of producing women's culture and literary tradition, which in turn is part of the project of overcoming patriarchy. It is in the nature of people working for revolutionary change to be optimistic about the prospect of redirecting the future.

Culler observes that optimistic endings have been challenged (successfully, he thinks) by deconstruction, a method radically at odds with the dialectic. It is worth noting that there is a deconstructive moment in Rich's reading of Dickinson. Recall her third metaphor: the reader is an insect "vibrating the frames of windows, clinging to the panes of glass, trying to connect." The suggestion of futility is unmistakable. At best,

Rich's interpretion of Dickinson might be considered as a "strong mis-reading" whose value is in its capacity to provoke other misreadings.

We might say this—but must we? To answer this question, we must ask another: What is at stake in the proposition that reading is impossible? For one thing, if reading is impossible, then there is no way of deciding the validity of an interpretation—the very notion of validity becomes problematical. Certainly it is useful to be reminded that the validity of an interpretation cannot be decided by appealing to what the author "intended," to what is "in" the text, or to what is "in" the experience of the reader. However, there is another approach to the problem of validation, one that is consonant with the dialogic model of reading described above. We can think of validity not as a property inherent in an interpretation, but rather as a *claim* implicit in the *act* of propounding an interpretation. An interpretation, then, is not valid or invalid in itself. Its validity is contingent on the agreement of others. In this view, Rich's interpretation of Dickinson, which is frankly acknowl-edged as conditioned by her own experience as a twentieth-century feminist poet, is not necessarily a misreading. In advancing her in-terpretation, Rich implicitly claims its validity. That is to say, to read a text and then to write about it is to seek to connect not only with the author of the original text, but also with a community of readers. To the extent that she succeeds and to the extent that the community is poten-tially all-embracing, her interpretation has that degree of validity.[43]

Feminist reading and writing alike are grounded in the interest of producing a community of feminist readers and writers, and in the hope that ultimately this community will expand to include everyone. Of course, this project may fail. The feminist story may yet end with the recognition of the impossibility of reading. But this remains to be seen. At this stage I think it behooves us to *choose* the dialectical over the deconstructive plot. It is dangerous for feminists to be overly enamored with the theme of impossibility. Instead, we should strive to redeem the claim that it is possible for a woman, reading as a woman, to read literature written by women, for this is essential if we are to make the literary enterprise into a means for building and maintaining connec-tions among women.

Notes

I would like to acknowledge my debt to David Schweickart for the substantial editorial work he did on this chapter.

1. Wayne Booth, Presidential Address, "Arts and Scandals 1982," *PMLA* 98 (1983): 313. Subsequent references to this essay are cited parenthetically in the text.

2. *The Autobiography of Malcolm X,* written with Alex Haley (New York: Grove Press, 1964), p. 173. Subsequent references are cited parenthetically in the text.

3. Virginia Woolf, *A Room of One's Own* (New York: Harcourt Brace Jovanovich, 1981). Subsequent references are cited parenthetically in the text.

4. Jonathan D. Culler, *On Deconstruction: Theory and Criticism after Structuralism* (Ithaca: Cornell University Press, 1982), p. 42. (Subsequent references are cited parenthetically in the text.) Wayne Booth's essay "Freedom of Interpretation: Bakhtin and the Challenge of Feminist Criticism," *Critical Inquiry* 9 (1982): 45–76, is another good omen of the impact of feminist thought on literary criticism.

5. David Bleich, *Subjective Criticism* (Baltimore: Johns Hopkins University Press, 1978), p. 112.

6. Georges Poulet, "Criticism and the Experience of Interiority," trans. Catherine and Richard Macksey, in *Reader-Response Criticism: From Formalism to Structuralism,* ed. Jane Tompkins (Baltimore: Johns Hopkins University Press, 1980), p. 43. Poulet's theory is not among those discussed by Culler. However, since he will be useful to us later, I mention him here.

7. This argument was advanced by Samuel Weber in "The Struggle for Control: Wolfgang Iser's Third Dimension," cited by Culler in *On Deconstruction,* p. 75.

8. Stanley E. Fish, "Why No One's Afraid of Wolfgang Iser," *Diacritics* 11 (1981): 7. Quoted by Culler in *On Deconstruction,* p. 75.

9. Elaine Showalter, "Feminist Criticism in the Wilderness," *Critical Inquiry* 8 (1981): 182–85. Showalter argues that if we see feminist critique (focused on the reader) as our primary critical project, we must be content with the "playful pluralism" proposed by Annette Kolodny: first because no single conceptual model can comprehend so eclectic and wide-ranging an enterprise, and second because "in the free play of the interpretive field, feminist critique can only compete with alternative readings, all of which have the built-in obsolescence of Buicks, cast away as newer readings take their place" (p. 182). Although Showalter does not support Wimsatt and Beardsley's proscription of the "affective fallacy," she nevertheless subscribes to the logic of their argument. Kolodny's "playful pluralism" is more benign than Wimsatt and Beardsley's dreaded "relativism," but no less fatal, in Showalter's view, to theoretical coherence.

10. Elaine Showalter, "Women and the Literary Curriculum," *College English* 32 (1971): 855. For an excellent example of recent work following in the spirit of Showalter's critique, see Paul Lauter, *Reconstructing American Literature* (Old Westbury, N.Y.: Feminist Press, 1983).

11. Lee Edwards, "Women, Energy, and *Middlemarch,*" *Massachusetts Review* 13 (1972): 226.

12. Ibid.

13. James Joyce, *The Portrait of the Artist as a Young Man* (London: Jonathan Cape, 1916), p. 195.

14. See also Florence Howe's analysis of the same passage, "Feminism and Literature," in *Images of Women in Fiction: Feminist Perspectives,* ed. Susan

Koppelman Cornillon (Bowling Green, Ohio: Bowling Green State University Press, 1972), pp. 262–63.

15. Judith Fetterley, *The Resisting Reader: A Feminist Approach to American Fiction* (Bloomington: Indiana University Press, 1978), p. xx. Although Fetterley's remarks refer specifically to American Literature, they apply generally to the entire traditional canon.

16. Fetterley, *Resisting Reader,* p. xiii.

17. See Katharine M. Rogers, *The Troublesome Helpmate: A History of Misogyny in Literature* (Seattle: University of Washington Press, 1966).

18. Fredric Jameson, *The Political Unconscious: Narrative as a Socially Symbolic Act* (Ithaca: Cornell University Press, 1981), p. 286.

19. In *Woman and the Demon: The Life of a Victorian Myth* (Cambridge: Harvard University Press, 1982), Nina Auerbach employs a similar—though not identical—positive hermeneutic. She reviews the myths and images of women (as angels, demons, victims, whores, etc.) that feminist critics have "gleefully" unmasked as reflections and instruments of sexist ideology, and discovers in them an "unexpectedly empowering" mythos. Auerbach argues that the "most powerful, if least acknowledged creation [of the Victorian cultural imagination] is an explosively mobile, magic woman, who breaks the boundaries of family within which her society restricts her. The triumph of this overweening creature is a celebration of the corporate imagination that believed in her" (p. 1). See also idem, "Magi and Maidens: The Romance of the Victorian Freud," *Critical Inquiry* 8 (1981): 281–300. The tension between the positive and negative feminist hermeneutics is perhaps most apparent when one is dealing with the "classics." See, for example, Carol Thomas Neely, "Feminist Modes of Shakespeare Criticism: Compensatory, Justificatory, Transformational," *Women's Studies* 9 (1981): 3–15.

20. Kate Millett, *Sexual Politics* (New York: Avon Books, 1970).

21. Elaine Showalter, "The Double Critical Standard and the Feminine Novel," chap. 3 in *A Literature of Their Own: British Women Novelists from Brontë to Lessing* (Princeton: Princeton University Press, 1977), pp. 73–99; Carol Ohmann, "Emily Brontë in the Hands of Male Critics," *College English* 32 (1971): 906–13.

22. Nina Baym, "Melodramas of Beset Manhood: How Theories of American Fiction Exclude Women Authors," *American Quarterly* 33 (1981): 123–39.

23. Ibid., p. 125.

24. Ibid., p. 130. One of the founding works of American Literature is "The Legend of Sleepy Hollow," about which Leslie Fiedler writes: "It is fitting that our first successful homegrown legend would memorialize, however playfully, the flight of the dreamer from the shrew" (*Love and Death in the American Novel* [New York: Criterion, 1960] p. xx).

25. Nina Baym's *Women's Fiction: A Guide to Novels by and about Women in America, 1820–1870* (Ithaca: Cornell University Press, 1978) provides a good survey of what has been excluded from the canon.

26. Annette Kolodny, "Dancing through the Minefield: Some Observations on the Theory, Practice, and Politics of a Feminist Literary Criticism," *Feminist*

Studies 6 (1980): 10–12. Kolodny elaborates the same theme in "A Map for Rereading: Or, Gender and the Interpretation of Literary Texts," *New Literary History* 11 (1980): 451–67.

27. For an excellent account of the way in which the feminist "interpretive community" has changed literary and critical conventions, see Jean E. Kennard, "Convention Coverage, or How to Read Your Own Life," *New Literary History* 8(1981): 69–88. The programs of the MLA Convention during the last twenty-five years offer more concrete evidence of the changes in the literary and critical canons, and of the ideological and political struggles effecting these changes.

28. In Adrienne Rich, *On Lies, Secrets, and Silence: Selected Prose, 1966–1978* (New York: W. W. Norton, 1979). Subsequent references are cited parenthetically in the text.

29. Susan Glaspell's story "A Jury of Her Peers" revolves around a variation of this judicial metaphor. The parable of reading implicit in this story has not been lost on feminist critics. Annette Kolodny, for example, discusses how it "explores the necessary gender marking which *must* constitute any definition of 'peers' in the complex process of unraveling truth or meaning." Although the story does not exclude male readers, it alerts us to the fact that "symbolic representations depend on a fund of shared recognitions and potential references," and in general, "female meaning" is inaccessible to "male interpretation." "However inadvertently, [the male reader] is a *different kind* of reader and, . . . where women are concerned, he is often an inadequate reader" ("Map for Rereading," pp. 460–63).

30. There is a strong counter-tendency, inspired by French poststructuralism, which privileges the appreciation of textuality over the imaginative recovery of the woman writer as subject of the work. See, for example, Mary Jacobus, "Is There a Woman in This Text?" *New Literary History* 14 (1982): 117–41, especially the concluding paragraph. The last sentence of the essay underscores the controversy: "Perhaps the question that feminist critics should be asking is not 'Is there a woman in this text?' but rather: 'Is there a text in this woman?' "

31. I must stress that although Rich's essay presents a significant paradigm of feminist readings of women's writing, it is not the only such paradigm. An alternative is proposed by Caren Greenberg, "Reading Reading: Echo's Abduction of Language," in *Women and Language in Literature and Society,* ed. Sally McConnell-Ginet, Ruth Borker, and Nelly Furman (New York: Praeger, 1980), pp. 304–9.

Furthermore, there are many important issues that have been left out of my discussion. For example:

a. The relationship of her career as reader to the artistic development of the woman writer. In *Madwoman in the Attic* (New Haven: Yale University Press, 1980) Sandra Gilbert and Susan Gubar show that women writers had to struggle to overcome the "anxiety of authorship" which they contracted from the "sentences" of their predecessors, male as well as female. They also argue that the relationship women writers form with their female predecessors does not fit the model of oedipal combat proposed by Bloom. Rich's attitude toward Dickinson (as someone who "has been there," as a "foremother" to be recovered) corroborates Gilbert and Gubar's claim.

b. The relationship between women writers and their readers. We need actual reception studies as well as studies of the way women writers conceived of their readers and the way they inscribed them in their texts.

c. The relationship between the positive and the negative hermeneutic in feminist readings of women's writing. Rich's reading of Dickinson emphasizes the positive hermeneutic. One might ask, however, if this approach is applicable to *all* women's writing. Specifically, is this appropriate to the popular fiction written by women, e.g., Harlequin Romances? To what extent is women's writing itself a bearer of patriarchal ideology? Janice Radway addresses these issues in "Utopian Impulse in Popular Literature: Gothic Romances and 'Feminist Protest,'" *American Quarterly* 33 (1981): 140–62, and "Women Read the Romance: The Interaction of Text and Context," *Feminist Studies* 9 (1983): 53–78. See also Tania Modleski, *Loving with a Vengeance: Mass-Produced Fantasies for Women* (New York: Methuen, 1982).

32. Iser writes:

> Text and reader no longer confront each other as object and subject, but instead the "division" takes place within the reader [herself]. . . . As we read, there occurs an artificial division of our personality, because we take as a theme for ourselves something we are not. Thus, in reading there are two levels—the alien "me" and the real, virtual "me"—which are never completely cut off from each other. Indeed, we can only make someone else's thoughts into an absorbing theme for ourselves provided the virtual background of our personality can adapt to it. ("The Reading Process: A Phenomenological Approach," in Tompkins, *Reader-Response Criticism,* p. 67)

Add the stipulation that the alien "me" is a male who has appropriated the universal into his maleness, and we have the process of immasculation described in the third section.

33. Stanley E. Fish, *Is There a Text in This Class? The Authority of Interpretive Communities* (Cambridge: Harvard University Press, 1980), especially pt. 2.

34. Although the woman reader is the "star" of the feminist story of reading, this does not mean that men are excluded from the audience. On the contrary, it is hoped that on hearing the feminist story they will be encouraged to revise their own stories to reflect the fact that they, too, are gendered beings, and that, ultimately, they will take control of their inclination to appropriate the universal at the expense of women.

35. Catherine A. MacKinnon, "Feminism, Marxism, Method, and the State: Toward Feminist Jurisprudence," *Signs* 8 (1981): 637.

36. There is lively debate among feminists about whether it is better to emphasize the essential similarity of women and men, or their difference. There is much to be said intellectually and politically for both sides. However, in one sense, the argument centers on a false issue. It assumes that concern about women's "difference" is incompatible with concern about the essential humanity shared by the sexes. Surely, "difference" may be interpreted to refer to what is distinctive in women's lives and works, *including* what makes them essentially human; unless, of course, we remain captivated by the notion that the standard model for humanity is male.

37. Although opponents of feminist criticism often find it convenient to characterize such works as a personal attack on authors, for feminist critics

themselves, the primary consideration is the function of the text as a carrier of patriarchal ideology, and its effect as such especially (but not exclusively) on women readers. The personal culpability of the author is a relatively minor issue.

38. Harold Bloom, *Kabbalah and Criticism* (New York: Seabury, 1975), p. 126.

39. Poulet, "Criticism and the Experience of Interiority," p. 46.

40. Ibid., p. 47. As Culler has pointed out, the theme of control is prominent in mainstream reader-response criticism. Poulet's story is no exception. The issue of control is important in another way. Behind the question of whether the text controls the reader or vice versa is the question of how to regulate literary criticism. If the text is controlling, then there is no problem. The text itself will regulate the process of reading. But if the text is not necessarily controlling, then, how do we constrain the activities of readers and critics? How can we rule out "off-the-wall" interpretations? Fish's answer is of interest to feminist critics. The constraints, he says, are exercised not by the text, but by the institutions within which literary criticism is situated. It is but a small step from this idea to the realization of the necessarily political character of literature and criticism.

41. The use of the personal conversational tone has been regarded as a hallmark of feminist criticism. However, as Jean E. Kennard has pointed out ("Personally Speaking: Feminist Critics and the Community of Readers," *College English* 43 [1981]: 140–45), this theoretical commitment is not apparent in the overwhelming majority of feminist critical essays. Kennard found only five articles in which the critic "overtly locates herself on the page." (To the five she found, I would add three works cited in this essay: "Women, Energy, and *Middlemarch,*" by Lee Edwards; "Feminism and Literature," by Florence Howe; and "Vesuvius at Home," by Adrienne Rich.) Kennard observes further that, even in the handful of essays she found, the personal tone is confined to a few introductory paragraphs. She asks: "If feminist criticism has on the whole remained faithful to familiar methods and tone, why have the few articles with an overt personal voice loomed so large in our minds?" Kennard suggests that these personal introductions are invitations "to share a critical response which depends upon unstated, shared beliefs and, to a large extent, experience; that of being a female educated in a male tradition in which she is no longer comfortable." Thus, these introductory paragraphs do not indicate a "transformed critical methodology; they are devices for transforming the reader. I read the later portions of these essays—and by extension other feminist criticsim—in a different way because I have been invited to participate in the underground. . . . I am part of a community of feminist readers" (pp. 143–44).

I would offer another explanation, one that is not necessarily inconsistent with Kennard's. I think the use of a personal and conversational tone represents an overt gesture indicating the dialogic mode of discourse as the "regulative ideal" for all feminist discourse. The few essays—indeed, the few introductory paragraphs—that assert this regulative ideal are memorable because they strike a chord in a significant segment of the community of feminist critics. To the extent that we have been touched or transformed by this idea, it will be implicit in the way we read the works of others, in particular, the works of other women.

Although the ideal must be overtly affirmed periodically, it is not necessary to do so in all of our essays. It remains potent as long as it is assumed by a significant portion of the community. I would argue with Kennard's distinction between indicators of a transformed critical methodology and devices for transforming the reader. To the extent that critical methodology is a function of the conventions implicitly or explicitly operating in an interpretive community—that is, of the way members of the community conceive of their work and of the way they read each other—devices for transforming readers are also devices for transforming critical methodology.

42. Jean Baker Miller, *Toward a New Psychology of Women* (Boston: Beacon Press, 1976); and Nancy Chodorow, *The Reproduction of Mothering: Psychoanalysis and the Sociology of Gender* (Berkeley and Los Angeles: University of California Press, 1978); and Carol Gilligan, *In a Different Voice: Psychological Theory and Women's Development* (Cambridge: Harvard University Press, 1982).

43. I am using here Jurgen Habermas's definition of truth or validity as a claim (implicit in the act of making assertions) that is redeemable through discourse—specifically, through the domination-free discourse of an "ideal speech situation." For Habermas, consensus attained through domination-free discourse is the warrant for truth. See "Wahrheitstheorien," in *Wirklichkeit und Reflexion: Walter Schulz zum 60. Geburtstag* (Pfullingen: Nesge, 1973), pp. 211–65. I am indebted to Alan Soble's unpublished translation of this essay.

Chapter 3
Ourself behind Ourself:
A Theory for Lesbian Readers
Jean E. Kennard

> Ourself behind ourself, concealed—
> should startle most.
> Emily Dickinson

If feminist criticism has demonstrated anything, it has surely demonstrated the importance of the reader to what is read. The connections between reader-response criticism and feminist criticism are becoming more widely acknowledged, most frequently but not exclusively by feminist critics. As reader-response critics, feminists face the primary problem of all theorists using this approach, that of defining their reader.[1] In what sense is it meaningful to talk about the *woman reader?*

Most feminist scholars have assumed a definition of *woman* based on biology, even though this has inevitably led to some questionable generalizations. What does the term *woman reader* signify if it is presumed to include Third World women, Caucasian women, upper-middle-class women, women living below the poverty level, and, my chief concern here, both heterosexual and lesbian women? Can we safely assume that there are no innate differences between the lesbian and the heterosexual woman? If there are, then surely they must be considered in studies of gender and reading. Even if there were no social or political evils in a denial of lesbian experience, there would still remain the question of the validity of feminist research that operates from a limited or inaccurate definition of its terms.

This essay assumes that at least we need to ask whether the lesbian reader is not a different reader from the heterosexual woman reader, and what it means to her and to the reading enterprise if she is. It assumes also that, despite an increased awareness of available lesbian material, for the foreseeable future, lesbian students, both inside and outside classrooms, will be faced with the familiar heterosexually biased literature. If as lesbian readers we can only appreciate literature that reflects our own experience, we are likely to be very limited in our reading pleasure.[2] In the background of my discussion, then, are three questions: How do we define *lesbian reader?* Can we reread/rewrite the old canon so that it no longer denies the lesbian reader? Can we do it in such a way that we do not in the process deny other readers?

Jean E. Kennard

Much of the new lesbian scholarship focuses on the definition of *lesbian*.[3] In a recent review article on the history of sexuality, Martha Vicinus summarized the work of current participants in this discussion.[4] The question of definition has become a debate between those who insist that lesbianism must imply an erotic component and those who wish to broaden the definition to include all women whose primary emotional bonds are to other women. Rightly, I think, Martha Vicinus links self-definition to periodization. Those historians interested in the period before 1910 are more likely than modernists to call romantic friendship lesbianism.

This discussion has importance to a definition of the lesbian reader, since only if we insist on the erotic nature of a lesbian bond can we consider the possibility that lesbianism is an innate aspect of sexual identity. Also relevant to a definition of the lesbian reader is the related question of nature versus nurture, which Lillian Faderman outlines in *Surpassing the Love of Men*.[5] Is lesbianism a congenital defect (Krafft-Ebing)? Is it congenital but not necessarily a defect (Hirschfeld)? Is it the result of childhood trauma, that is, an environmental hazard (Freud)?

One of the problems in current writing about lesbianism is that the debate between nature and nurture has been treated as synonymous with a debate between choice and no choice. Given the historical reasons for resisting the biological argument and the modern predilection for a loosely defined existentialist world view, it is not surprising that most lesbians have opted for choice. Women, Coletta Reid claims, "could choose to be lesbians, lesbians weren't born, they were made." Similarly, Barbara Soloman states: "Lesbians are not born. We have made a conscious choice to be lesbians."[6] Faderman talks of lesbianism as "a natural impulse and a choice made in a healthy response to one's environment."[7]

But lesbian literature also contains an apparently contradictory theme of discovering "one's true self," often in work by the same lesbians who talk about choice. Many of the women Deborah Wolf interviews in *The Lesbian Community* talk of lesbian experience as fulfilling a need they had always had, as "just seeming right."[8]

Certainly choice is involved. Even if lesbians are born rather than made, one can choose to deny one's lesbianism, something one cannot yet do so easily with one's gender. Therefore, acceptance of a lesbian identity involves choice. But does one choose to *be* a lesbian? What do Faderman's words *natural impulse* imply? Certainly lesbianism is to be found in nature, that is, in female human beings. Then are all women potentially lesbians? Have some more potential than others? What is the lesbian discovering when she feels she is discovering her true self?

64

Despite the attractiveness of the idea that a lesbian lifestyle is a viable option for all women, we put future lesbian scholarship at risk if we ignore the evidence of those who feel as if they, more than others, have lesbian tendencies. We should at least be willing to consider the possibility of a biological predisposition. As Sara Ruddick says: "Neither our own ambivalence to our women's bodies nor the bigoted, repressive uses which many men, colonizers, and racists have made of biology, should blind us to our body's possibilities."[9] Nor should we feel that to accept the idea of a predisposition toward lesbianism in some women negates the political validity of a choice to *accept* a lesbian identity.

Further research may one day clarify these questions. In the meantime, a useful compromise between the two positions is Ethel Spector Person's theory of sex printing. Arguing for nurture over nature, she nevertheless describes a gradual narrowing of sexual potential—sex printing—which happens to all human beings as they mature and over which they have no control. "From the subjective point of view the sex print is experienced as sexual 'preference.' Because it is revealed rather than chosen, sexual preference is felt as deep rooted and deriving from one's nature." Apparently seeing no possibility of or value in determining causation—thus avoiding the resurrection of possessive mothers and absent fathers—she stresses the "relative irreversibility of the sex print," which is nevertheless "learned" behavior.[10]

Person's theory seems to me valuable partly because it appears to describe my own experience. It is useful, because it accounts for the most usual descriptions of lesbian self-awareness and for the difficulties experienced by those who attempt to change a homosexual orientation[11] but does not require the demonstration of biological determinism. It is the theory behind my use of the term *lesbian* in this discussion. I shall assume, too, that, although we bring to our reading other aspects of our identities, sexual identity is, as Ethel Person claims, uniquely central.

The conflicting views on the nature of lesbianism could mean significant differences to a theory of the lesbian reader. If the lesbian reader has chosen a lesbian identity but has no innate predisposition toward lesbianism, she may respond positively to lesbian characters or experience either overtly presented or encoded in the text;[12] she may respond negatively to negative portrayals of lesbianism or to the assumption of exclusive heterosexuality. However, if the lesbian reader has an innate predisposition toward lesbianism, or if her sexual preference has become mentally coded during her maturation, we may be looking at a different set of questions. Does the lesbian reader read or the lesbian writer write in ways that are characteristic of her lesbianism but that she does not necessarily choose to employ or that she does not even become aware of? Does the lesbian mind produce styles and structures that are in any way different from those of the heterosexual female mind? Will we eventually be able to define lesbian thinking as, for example, Sara Ruddick has defined maternal thinking?[13]

Judith Gardiner's article "On Female Identity," which defines the relationship between the female writer/reader and fictional characters, offers a useful approach to a theory of the lesbian reader. One advantage of Gardiner's work is that Gardiner does not accept a simple notion of reader identification with literary texts or characters. She points out the shifting nature of this process: "Both writer and reader can relate to the text as though it were a person with whom one might alternatively be merged empathically or from whom one might be separated and individuated."[14] It is, of course, important that there are works that present lesbian characters and experience positively, but the call for positive role models too often assumes a simple notion of identification in the reading process, which in the end, as Bertha Harris says, may prevent "a deeper look into the nature of lesbianism."[15] As Wolfgang Iser points out: "A response that depends upon the reader finding a reflection of himself [*sic*] could scarcely bring the reader anything *new* . . . (and literature would be barren indeed if it led only to a recognition of the already familiar)."[16]

What I wish to suggest here is a theory of reading which will not oversimplify the concept of identification, which will not subsume lesbian difference under a universal female, and which will be applicable to all texts, including those written by men, heterosexual women, and self-hating lesbians. It is an attempt to suggest a way in which lesbians could reread and write about texts (in-scribe them, if you will) rather than a description of how we do, though for demonstration purposes I shall draw on what has been done. Though when it is consciously employed as a critical method, the theory is applicable to any of the definitions of *lesbian* I have discussed so far, if we accept the idea of an innate or imprinted lesbianism, the reading process may not be entirely volitional. As will become apparent, it is a method of reading which necessarily includes the lesbian reader, rather than a theory of lesbian reading. Although it can be used by any reader, it is particularly valuable to those readers whose experiences are not frequently reflected in literature.

I am particularly interested in the question of lesbian re-reading of the dominant heterosexual tradition, of finding something else to do than substitute *woman* where the word *man* appears.[17] Although it is true that readers understand texts that describe their own experience differently from the way they understand other texts, as I have argued elsewhere, it is also true that most reading is of texts that have a very limited relationship to the reader's own experience.[18] How can we read alien texts and avoid the schizophrenia (often more severe for a lesbian than for a heterosexual woman) that so many feminists have described as a result of their education in the male tradition?[19]

Psychological theories of identity formation which underlie the work of Gardiner and Iser, and implicitly that of all reader-response critics, can be helpful here, at least as paradigms. As Norman Holland says, "To go from the text as an object to our experience of it calls for a psychology of some kind."[20] Catherine Stimpson's objection to the narrowness of a psychological approach to literature on the grounds that "psychology hardly defines the totality of our lives"[21] misses the point, I think. Psychology does aim to define the totality of our lives; it is, though, only one of the languages that do so.

The question of what kind of psychology is very important, for, as feminist scholars have demonstrated, the male bias on which some psychological theory rests essentially invalidates it. Since reading is a process, and a process that we invariably describe as beneficial to the reader, it seems sensible to look at a form of therapy that stresses process. Since many psychological theories make generalizations about human nature which often fail to distinguish female from male, let alone lesbian from heterosexual female, we also need a theory that at least does not distort lesbian experience by accepting too many premises about "human" or even "female" reactions. We need a theory, then, that is client (reader) centered.

I am using Joseph Zinker's views as outlined in *Creative Process in Gestalt Therapy* because, first, they meet these conditions. Second, I am comfortable with the language in which he talks about therapy because it is frequently the language of literary criticism: "each therapy session has an intrinsic flow and structure"; "the theme is then elaborated"; "a simple translation of a person's metaphor."[22] My third reason for turning to Zinker is that what he says about the therapeutic process can so often be transferred verbatim to the reading process: "We must take the risk of projecting the most idiosyncratic, personal imagery upon objects, words and other symbols" (p. 9). However, in borrowing Zinker's ideas, I do not imply that other theories might not work as well.

The aspect of Zinker's theory that is most useful to a discussion of the reading process begins with his concept of the individual as a composite of "polarities," or opposing characterisics. "In an oversimplified example, we might say that a person has within him [*sic*] the characteristic of kindness and also its polarity of cruelty, the characteristic of hardness and its polarity, softness" (p. 197). Zinker recognizes that all these qualities may, in a given case, generate different opposing characteristics; the polarities are not fixed. On different occasions the opposite of lesbian emotions may be those of a heterosexual female, a homosexual male, or even a heterosexual male. In this way the concept of polarities incorporates any differences that, under specific circumstances, can be defined as each other's opposite.

One's inner reality consists of both those qualities in one's self that one finds acceptable and those that are unacceptable and therefore often hidden or denied. Zinker explains, "We often identify ourselves with one characteristic and not its counterpart, e.g. I see myself as peaceful and not aggressive, or stingy and not generous, or honest and not devious" (p. 33). The aspects of ourselves we do not own he calls "dark polarities"; those we see as part of ourselves, "light polarities."

The concept of polarities is one of the few premises about human nature that Zinker asks us to accept. It is, perhaps surprisingly, compatible with Ethel Person's theory of sex printing, in which there is a narrowing of sexual potential until the individual's sense of her/his own sexual identity finally does not acknowledge the polarity from which it became differentiated. It is often true, I think, when an aspect of our identity is claimed in the face of societal opposition, lesbianism, for example, that we stifle our doubts (deny the polarities) all the more forcefully in order to maintain the tabooed aspect. Jane Rule, talking about her younger self, says: "I was sexually so hungry, humanly so isolated, psychically so traumatized by social judgement that I required of myself a purity of motive so self-sacrificing, a vision of love so redeeming that to be a lover was an annihilation of all the healthy instincts of self-preservation I had."[23] This perhaps explains why apparently clearly defined personalities so often acknowledge or reveal a chink in the armor of their self-concepts. Who has not known (or been) the intellectual who watches soap operas, the vegetarian who makes an exception of hamburgers, the pacifist who enjoys war movies? The chink acts as a safety valve, but it also indicates the pressure of the so-called dark polarities.

Of course, Zinker is not saying that we are not what we claim to be, that all kind people are really cruel, all lesbians are really heterosexuals. He merely claims that even if we are primarily kind, the impulse toward unkindness is still within us. Indeed, his aim in therapy is to strengthen, deepen the original self-concept and to change only those forms of behavior that disturb the client. Health, for Zinker as for many therapists, lies in self-awareness, in letting the light in on the "dark polarities." Healthy people may not approve of all their tendencies, but their acknowledgment of them indicates "inner strength" (p. 200).

At the center of gestalt methodology is the experiment, an often playful acting out of new behavior, none of which is necessarily to be incorporated into "real" behavior. "The experiment," says Zinker, "gives us permission to be priest, whore, faggot, holy man, wise witch, magician—all things, beings, notions hidden within us" (p. 18). (He could have added, of course, "heterosexual.") Particularly relevant to an application to the reading process is the word *notions;* the "things hidden within us" are qualities as much of the imagination as of the self, or, rather, what we are capable of imagining is given equal weight with our actions. The experiment may involve dramatizing, drawing, writing, and talking, and it is clearly adaptable to reading if this is seen as incorporating projections of the reader.

What we become, for a time, during the experiment is an extreme form of an aspect of ourselves, often a denied one; the experiment is basically a means of differentiation for the purposes of self-awareness. The particular experiment that is important here is a classic gestalt one called "around the world." It is based on two premises (the final ones Zinker asks us to accept): one, when we exaggerate ("lean into" is the gestalt jargon) one side of a polarity/aspect of the self, the other side gets "attracted" toward it, pulled as if in a magnetic field; two, the side that gets pulled is deepened and solidified in the process. "My theory of polarities dictates that if I do not allow myself to be unkind, I will never be genuinely kind," explains Zinker. "If I am in touch with my own unkindness and stretch that part of myself, when my kindness emerges it will be richer, fuller, more complete . . . I call this the 'around the world' phenomenon: If you keep flying north long enough, you'll eventually be heading south" (p. 202). I do not become heterosexual for allowing that part of me to breathe, I become more fully, completely lesbian.

In order to begin the experiment it is obviously necessary to have at least an indication of the hidden characteristic one will "lean into." "I have to teach myself to invade that part of me which I do not approve of." In the therapeutic process, clients may reach part of the hidden side of themselves through unstructured activity with an observant therapist who will spot the chinks in the armor. But the process of reading, "of losing one's self in a book," as it was once innocently called, can serve the same purpose.

To read Zinker's ideas as a methodology of reading takes remarkably little translation. If the experiment is an experiment in reading—a lesbian reading a heterosexual male work, for example—the process might take the following form. Rather than resist the text, the reader grasps one familiar or shared aspect of the male protagonist,[24] for "we *can* only bring another person's thoughts into our foreground if they are in some way related to the virtual background of our own orienta-tions."[25] She "leans into" the character, identifies with him as fully as possible, in a sort of willing suspension of belief. She uses the strategies she was probably taught so well; she reads like a man, but with a new awareness. Rather than experiencing schizophrenia, she allows the po-larities to coexist. She forces the concentration on the heterosexual until the lesbian in her is pulled forward to the surface of her consciousness. The text or the character is made to signify also what it is not. For example, to be Stephen Dedalus—as most of us educated in British and American English departments have had to be—is to be a heterosexual. The lesbian reader, identifying initially perhaps with Stephen's aliena-tion from his family or with his guilty adolescent sexuality, must finally experience his heterosexual maleness, his sense of the female as other, as symbol. By fully examining this aspect of his character (and its implications), the lesbian reader can make apparent its opposite. Ste-phen Dedalus is not a homosexual female.

Wolfgang Iser provides an interesting gloss on Zinker as a reading theorist: "Thus there occurs a kind of artificial division as the reader brings into his [*sic*] own foreground something which he is not. This does not mean that his own orientations disappear completely. . . . In reading, then, there are also two levels, and despite the multifarious ways in which they can be related they can never be totally kept apart." Iser claims that "a layer of the reader's personality is brought to light which had hitherto remained hidden in the shadows." The result of the reading process is therapeutic to the reader, for "it enables us to formu-late ourselves."[26]

Although Iser acknowledges the necessity of some projection from the reader's past experience in order to enter the text, he puts more emphasis on the effect of text on reader than I intend here. Although he sees the reading process as a transaction, he nevertheless stresses the capacity of the text to open up an inner world in the reader of which s/he had not previously been conscious, rather than the reader's capaci-ty to deepen the self-concept. As readers we do more than simply repeat ourselves, more than recognize "the already familiar," but I suggest the process is closer to reinforcing than to transforming. We redefine as-pects of ourselves through contrast with the opposite aspects in a fic-tional other which we have temporarily experienced.[27]

It is, I realize, one thing to take the study of literature into the world of psychoanalysis and another to leave it there. The reading process certainly involves more than providing low-cost therapy for the indi-vidual reader, though it may serve that function. What are the implica-tions of the theory of polar reading to critical methodology? How does a polar reader write about literature? Polar reading/writing is primarily a question of contrast. Just as with a black and white photograph, in which the intensification of the black means the inevitable intensification of the white, so the polar reader intensifies the attitude of character or author, embodies it so fully, that the contrasting aspects of the reader's own attitudes come into the picture. (The implications of negatives, of backgrounds and foregrounds, and, considering the earlier discussion, of prints, could obviously be developed here. But it is primarily, to deconstruct my own image, a question of overexposure.)

While the work of many critics might no doubt furnish examples of polar reading, two essays, by Virginia Woolf and Adrienne Rich, provide unusually clear illustrations. As writers of established reputation both within and without the lesbian feminist community, they also seem particularly relevant here. I shall look at Woolf reading *Robinson Crusoe* and Rich reading Emily Dickinson. Woolf reads a male character by a male novelist of a different century and temperament than her own and thus provides an illustration of a lesbian reader responding to the traditional heterosexual canon. Rich reads a woman poet much closer to her in temperament than Defoe is to Woolf, but a poet of a different century and set of circumstances.

These two essays illustrate a distinction that must be made in any discussion of reading theory. Just as "reading as a woman is not necessarily what occurs when a woman reads,"[28] so reading as a lesbian is not necessarily what happens when a lesbian reads. Woolf is in one sense a lesbian reader, but she is not reading as a lesbian in this essay. Nevertheless, Woolf's lesbianism is not denied by this reading; the emotions summoned by the reading do not exclude those characteristic of lesbian experience. Rich, on the other hand, provides us with a lesbian reading. She is concerned, to adapt Elaine Showalter's comment of the *female* reader, "with the way in which the hypothesis of a *lesbian* reader changes our apprehension of a given text."[29]

Much of Woolf's criticism is marked by an awareness of readers' responses. Indeed, it provides a link between the affective criticism of the nineteenth century and contemporary reader-response theory. She talks frequently of the influence of the reader on the reading,[30] and, like Wolfgang Iser, she recognizes two "selves" involved in the process: that other self, which the text elicits, and the reader's predefined self, which can never be entirely subsumed by the other: "We may stress the value of sympathy; we may try to sink our identity as we read. But we know that we cannot sympathise wholly or immerse ourselves wholly."[31] Although for Woolf both the text and the author are less insubstantial artifacts than they are for many a contemporary critic, she nevertheless talks, perhaps playfully, of readers who "know without a word to guide them precisely what he [a character] thought and felt."[32]

The texture of *Orlando* alone, woven as it is from the opposing tension of male and female selves, from contrasted scenes, from reversed mirror images, invites a consideration of polarities in Woolf's other work. A comment by T. S. Eliot suggests Woolf's interest in what is not stated in the text: "Instead of looking for the primitive, she looks rather for the civilized, the highly civilized, where nevertheless something is found to be *left out*. And this something is deliberately left out, by what could be called a moral effort of the will. And, being left out, this something is, in a sense, in a melancholy sense, present."[33] It is precisely this characteristic (one typical of her own work) that she observes in *Robinson Crusoe*.

The essay begins with a discussion of two possible critical approaches to the text, the historical and the biographical. Her consideration of the historical recognizes the relationship of reader to text: "A middle class had come into existence, able to read and anxious to read . . . about themselves."[34] Her consideration of the biographical deals with the relationship of the author's "self" to his [Defoe's] text. Woolf dismisses both the historical and the biographical approaches as unlikely to make reading either more pleasurable or more intelligent.

The "book itself remains," (p. 52) says Woolf, and the contemporary critic awaits an argument for a "new critical" reading. But Woolf continues in language that suggests Iser or Holland: "There is a piece of business to be transacted between writer and reader before any further dealings are possible" (p. 52). Thus at the outset she establishes the reading process as an interchange between two entities, the reader and an "other"; the other, in the case of Woolf's essay, is variably the writer, Defoe, represented by the "perspective" implied in his text and the protagonist of his novel. The first task of the reader is to see the world from Defoe's point of view, to look at things from his perspective: "All alone we must climb upon the novelist's shoulders and gaze through his eyes until we, too, understand in what order he ranges the large common objects upon which novelists are fated to gaze" (p. 52). This is a familiar direction from Woolf: elsewhere she instructs us "to go back three or four hundred years and become in fancy at least an Elizabethan"; she cautions us, "Do not dictate to your author; try to become him."[35] She is not, however, talking loosely of "losing one's self in a book," of escaping. She is fully aware of the difficulties of identification, of participating in the alien world of the "other," difficulties perhaps suggested by the impossibility of seeing through the eyes while standing on the shoulders.

If readers could fully participate in the world of a novel, that is, completely lose all sense of self while reading, "the battle" between reader and text would be over. But "we have our own vision of the world," Woolf explains, and we are afraid and angry when that is challenged. This "vision of the world" is more than merely a set of opinions, though it may be manifested in that fashion; it is basic to our sense of our selves, "our private harmony" (p. 53). When the perspective of the novel differs from our own, "we are afraid because the old supports are being wrenched from us" (p. 54). So we resist the text. She describes two letter writers to the newspapers: Major Gibbs, who objects to Hardy's pessimism, and Miss Wiggs, who "must protest that though Proust's art is wonderful, the real world, she thanks God, has nothing in common with the distortions of a perverted Frenchman." Both, Woolf explains, "are trying to control the novelist's perspective so that it shall resemble and reinforce their own" (p. 53). Unlike the polar reader, they seek to affirm themselves by a denial of "the other" rather than through a full recognition of it.

Reading begins with our own expectations as readers. We come to *Robinson Crusoe* knowing it is the story of a man shipwrecked on a desert island. We thus expect, says Woolf, sunsets, sunrises, solitude, and soul—in other words, an intense spirituality, an awareness of the mind in isolation. But who is the reader who expects these things? She is Woolf herself. The expectations she describes are those she satisfies in readers of her own fiction. Isolation, the life of the mind, solitude, and soul, are among the most obvious of her own preoccupations, noted and documented by every critic from Winifred Holtby on.

Robinson Crusoe initially resists Woolf the reader, who is "rudely contradicted on every page" (p. 54). Everything is "fact," "substance." "Each sortie of ours in pursuit of information upon these cardinal points of perspecitve—God, Man, Nature—is snubbed back with ruthless common sense." Reflecting her own attempt to "control the novelist's perspective," she repeats each of her three terms, "God," "man," "nature," three times within one paragraph. Each is furled, reduced, shriveled, and finally "does not exist." "Nothing exists except an earthenware pot. Finally that is to say, we are forced to drop our own preconceptions and to accept what Defoe himself wishes to give us" (p. 55).

Woolf makes the journey from York to the island sitting on Crusoe's shoulders. She does not tell us exactly what enables her to gain access to his perspective, but she is "drawn on" by a consideration, a shared knowledge, of the virtues of British middle-class life. Those rarely acknowledged aspects of Woolf, "temperance, moderation, quietness and health," (p. 55) come to the foreground. She "leans into" Crusoe, "his shrewdness, his caution, his love of order and comfort and respectability" until "everything appears as it would appear to that naturally cautious, apprehensive, conventional and solidly matter-of-fact intelligence" (p. 56).

Woolf marks this change in her position as reader by beginning to write from Crusoe's point of view:

> He is so busy and has such an eye to the main chance that he notices only a tenth part of what is going on around him. Everything is capable of a rational explanation, he is sure, if only he had time to attend to it. We are much more alarmed by "the vast creatures" that swim out in the night and surround his boat than he is. . . . He is forever counting his barrels, and making sensible provisions for his water supply . . . the pressure of life when one is fending entirely for oneself alone on a desert island is really no laughing matter. It is no crying one either. A man must have an eye to everything; it is no time for raptures about Nature when the lightning may explode one's gunpowder. (Pp. 56–57)

Woolf has come as close to participating in Crusoe's emotions as she can. But there is another voice here. She is, after all, on his shoulders, and not in his head; she also sees "what is going on around him." There are two selves present. The reader's own self can play at matter-of-factness, but barrel counting will, in time, come to feel inadequate. Her imaginative pole is drawn forward; she is alarmed where he explains. She knows him well enough to know what he is not and can only know this because of what she is: a woman capable of laughter and tears and raptures about nature.

Woolf attributes to Defoe the capacity to suggest great emotion by describing fact: "Thus Defoe, by reiterating that nothing but a plain earthenware pot stands in the foreground, persuades us to see remote islands and the solitudes of the human soul" (p. 58). But is it Defoe who has done this, or is it Woolf, who has revealed to us that pole in herself which this novel with all its matter-of-factness has attracted? By the end of the essay Woolf has found in *Robinson Crusoe* those best aspects of "God," "man," and "nature" she initially thought the novel denied. The text has allowed her to affirm herself.

Has Woolf's "self"—at least the aspect of it attracted to this subject—been affected at all? Has Woolf's capacity for the sublime been changed, reinforced, by reading *Robinson Crusoe?* Perhaps. She now describes the beauty of common objects and actions as revelation and asks in a tone of discovery, "Why," after all, "the perspective that a plain earthenware pot exacts should not satisfy us as completely" as "a background of broken mountains and tumbling oceans with stars flaming in the sky?" (p. 58). She remarks how by mentioning the absence of his companions, visible now only in "three of their hats, one cap, and two shoes that were not fellows," Defoe suggests "a sense of desolation and the deaths of many men" (pp. 57–58). And I remember the end of *Jacob's Room,* where Jacob's death in war is suggested so powerfully by his empty shoes.

In her preface to the reprinted version of her 1975 essay "Vesuvius at Home: The Power of Emily Dickinson," Adrienne Rich provides a context for it within lesbian feminist scholarship. Quoting Toni McNaron's call for a lesbian feminist reading of Dickinson, Rich gives us her view of what that might be: "To 'prove' that a woman of the nineteenth century did or did not sleep with another woman, or women, is beside the point. . . . Such a criticism will ask questions hitherto passed over; will not search obsessively for heterosexual romance as the key to a woman artist's life and work."[36] A lesbian reading, then, will allow for different answers to the questions about Dickinson's life and work, will create "a context in which the importance, and validity, of Dickinson's attachments to women may now, at last, be seen in full" (p. 162).

Unlike Virginia Woolf reading *Robinson Crusoe,* Rich is a self-defined lesbian reader. Her subject, the "other" of her essay, is also on the surface much more similar to her than Defoe is to Woolf; in "Vesuvius at Home" a lesbian poet reads another woman poet she sees as woman-identified. The major difference between Rich's essay and Woolf's is this initial distance between reader and text. Woolf had to gain a foothold across barriers of gender, personality, and time; Rich is distanced from Dickinson primarily by time and, therefore, circumstances.

Nevertheless, Rich's essay as much as Woolf's is an illustration of polar reading. In an earlier essay, "When We Dead Awaken: Writing as Re-Vision," Rich defines the imagination in terms of polarities in a way surprisingly reminiscent of Zinker: "You have to be free to play around with the notion that day might be night, love might be hate; nothing can be too sacred for the imagination to turn into its opposite or to call experimentally by another name. For writing is renaming" (p. 43). Rich "renames" Dickinson, herself defined as composite of polarities: a practical woman rather than "partially cracked," a strong woman who emphasized her "littleness," "a creative and powerful" self hidden within a "publicly acceptable persona," in other words, "Vesuvius at home." The Massachusetts from which Rich writes is composed of polarities also; both "peaceful" and "threatened," it is hills and fruit trees contrasted with ARCO, MacDonald's, shopping plazas.

The structure of Rich's essay, however, is different from the structure of Woolf's. Rather than moving gradually into identification with a protagonist against whom she finally defines herself, Rich moves backward and forward from Dickinson, "leaning into" a point of identification, then clarifying its opposite. The difference of method is, perhaps, the difference between a polar reading of a novel and the polar reading of individual poems.

Rich begins with a Woolfian image, describing herself as an insect hovering for most of her life against the screens of Emily Dickinson's existence. At once she acknowledges their differences: "The methods, the exclusions, of Emily Dickinson's existence could not have been my own." To recapture the time that separates them, Rich, like Woolf, begins with a journey, "traveling at the speed of time along the Massachusetts Turnpike" (p. 158). But as she drives through Northampton, Hadley, Amherst, it is her own past, "college weekends" of her undergraduate days, which are polarized with an unstated present: a heterosexual past with a lesbian present.

In order to broaden her own and our understanding of a Dickinson "reduced to quaintness of spinsterish oddity by many of her commentators," Rich has been "trying to visit, to enter her mind, through her poems and letters" (p. 159). The tone of Rich's commentary is that of someone who has a special understanding of Dickinson's poetry. She simply tells us what the poems are without arguing for her reading or demonstrating its validity. Again like Woolf, this "inside" position is alternated with a polar position in Rich herself. There are two voices here, too. "I do not pretend to have—I don't even wish to have— explained this poem," Rich says at one point (p. 174).

In fully experiencing the reasons for Dickinson's seclusion, Rich finally understands it as creative freedom. She describes Dickinson deliberately intensifying "the confined space in which the genius of the nineteenth-century mind in America moved" in order to create a language for poetry "more varied, more compressed, more dense with implications, more complete of syntax, than any American poetic language to date" (p. 163). But it is not freedom as Rich defines it in her own life and work. Objecting to the pointless hunt for a secret male lover in Dickinson's life, Rich offers as one possible definition of the masculine element, the "he" of Dickinson's poems, her own power externalized as a daemon. But, Rich points out, "the archetype of the daemon as masculine is beginning to change" (p. 173). Her discussion of Dickinson "slanting" the truth in order to voice it in her poetry reminds us of the contrasting directness of Rich's own work, of a named lesbianism, of the title of the book in which this essay is reprinted, *On Lies, Secrets, and Silence.* But, Rich reminds us, "the nineteenth-century woman had much to repress" (p. 175). In almost every way the twentieth-century woman has less. In one important respect, however, that is not so: Dickinson's deeply charged relationships with women could be experienced in greater freedom than that available to contemporary women, for "none of this was perceived or condemned as 'lesbianism' " (p. 163).

So Rich's insight into Dickinson allows her to affirm her own values through polarizing aspects of her "real" self. It is not coincidental that Dickinson finally teaches Rich what Rich has taught us: "More than any other poet Emily Dickinson seemed to tell me that the intense inner event, the personal and the psychological, was inseparable from the universal; that there was a range for psychological poetry beyond mere self-expression" (p. 168).

Polar reading permits the participation of any reader in any text and thus opens up the possibility of enjoying the widest range of literary experience. It does not, however, involve the reader in denying herself. The reader redefines herself in opposition to the text; if that self-definition includes lesbianism, this becomes apparent in any commentary she may make on her reading.

Polar reading, then, is not a theory of lesbian reading, but a method particularly appropriate to lesbian readers and others whose experience is not frequently reflected in literature. Of course there is much work to do on whether lesbians read/write differently from heterosexual women, on encoding lesbian experience, on specifically lesbian literature. But we also need a way of reading/writing about any literature that does not reconfirm the universality of heterosexual experience. Because it is based in readers' individual differences, the theory of polar reading must necessarily include us. As individual lesbian readers, our critical work can expose the assumption of universal heterosexuality for what it is, a false assumption.

Notes

1. For discussions of the relationship between reader-response theory and feminist criticism see, for example, Annette Kolodny, "A Map for Rereading: Or, Gender and the Interpretation of Literary Texts," *New Literary History* 11 (1980): 451–67; Jonathan D. Culler, *On Deconstruction: Theory and Criticism after Structuralism* (Ithaca: Cornell University Press, 1982), pp. 43–64; Judith Fetterley, *The Resisting Reader: A Feminist Approach to American Fiction* (Bloomington: Indiana University Press, 1978); Jean E. Kennard, "Convention Coverage, or How to Read Your Own Life," *New Literary History* 8 (1981): 69–88; Elizabeth A. Flynn, "Gender and Reading," *College English* 45 (1983): 236–521. I am aware that in contemporary critical theory, feminist and nonfeminist,

the existence of the reader as a "self" is as problematic as the existence of the text. For the purposes of my discussion here I assume with Elizabeth Flynn that "reading involves a confrontation between self and 'other,' the text, and the nature of that confrontation depends upon the background of the reader as well as upon the text" (p. 236).

2. Although the situation is likely to be worse for the lesbian reader, enjoying literature seemingly antithetical to her beliefs is a problem for any feminist reader. For comments on this problem see Annette Kolodny, "Dancing through the Minefield: Some Observations on the Theory, Practice, and Politics of a Feminist Literary Criticism," *Feminist Studies* 6 (1980): 1–25.

3. Such early studies as Del Martin and Phyllis Lyon's *Lesbian/Woman* (San Francisco: Glide Publications, 1972), Jill Johnston's *Lesbian Nation: The Feminist Solution* (New York: Simon and Schuster, 1973), Charlotte Wolff's *Love Between Women* (New York: Harper and Row, 1971), assume that a lesbian is a woman whose sexual relationships are primarily with members of her own sex, though that assumption is frequently implied rather than stated. The "new" scholarship insists on the necessity of defining *lesbian*. It seems to me to date from Carroll Smith Rosenberg's essay "The Female World of Love and Ritual," *Signs* 1 (1975): 1–30; it includes the work of Adrienne Rich, "Compulsory Heterosexuality and Lesbian Existence," *Signs* 5 (1980): 631–60; Blanche Wiesen Cook, " 'Women Alone Stir My Imagination': Lesbianism and the Cultural Tradition," *Signs* 4 (1979): 718–39; Catherine R. Stimpson, "Zero Degrees Deviancy: The Lesbian Novel in English," *Critical Inquiry* 8 (1981): 363–79.

4. Martha Vicinus, "Sexuality and Power: A Review of Current Work in the History of Sexuality," *Feminist Studies* 8 (1982): 134–56.

5. Lillian Faderman, *Surpassing the Love of Men: Romantic Friendship and Love between Women from the Renaissance to the Present* (New York: William Morrow, 1981). Kinsey researchers concluded recently that since there is insufficient evidence for any of the suggested "causes" of homosexuality, we should look again at "possible biological bases for homosexuality." See Alan P. Bell, Martin S. Weinberg, and Sue Kiefer Hammersmith, *Sexual Preference: Its Development in Men and Women* (Bloomington: Indiana University Press, 1981), p. 213. For a discussion of a medical research on this topic, see Susan W. Baker, "Biological Influences on Human Sex and Gender," *Signs* 6 (1980): 80–96.

6. Coletta Reid, "Coming Out in the Women's Movement," and Barbara Solomon, "Taking the Bullshit by the Horns," in *Lesbianism and the Women's Movement,* ed. Nancy Myron and Charlotte Bunch (Baltimore: Diana Press, 1975), pp. 91–103 and 39–48, esp. pp. 97, 40.

7. Faderman, *Surpassing the Love of Men,* p. 323, points out the connections between supporting "choice" and opposing the patriarchal definition of lesbianism in entirely sexual terms.

8. Deborah Goleman Wolf, *The Lesbian Community* (Berkeley and Los Angeles: University of California Press, 1980) p. 35.

9. Sarah Ruddick, "Maternal Thinking," *Feminist Studies* 6 (1980): 342–67.

10. Ethel Spector Person, "Sexuality as the Mainstay of Identity: Psychoanalytic Perspectives," *Signs* 5 (1980): 605–30.

11. Ibid., p. 621: "In therapy, change in sexual orientation . . . is achieved only with great difficulty and sometimes not at all."

12. See Stimpson, "Zero Degrees Deviancy," p. 366 ff., and Faderman, *Surpassing the Love of Men,* p. 400 ff., on encoding lesbian texts as a strategy for survival.

13. Much of the recent work on mothers and daughters is also relevant here. See Marianne Hirsch's review essay "Mothers and Daughters," *Signs* 7 (1981): 200–222.

14. Judith Kegan Gardiner, "On Female Identity and Writing by Women," *Critical Inquiry* 8 (1981): 347–61.

15. Quoted by Stimpson, "Zero Degrees Deviancy," p. 378.

16. Wolfgang Iser, *The Act of Reading: A Theory of Aesthetic Response* (Baltimore: Johns Hopkins University Press, 1978), pp. 42–43.

17. Faderman, *Surpassing the Love of Men,* p. 357.

18. Jean E. Kennard, "Personally Speaking: Feminist Critics and the Community of Readers," *College English* 43 (1981): 140–45.

19. See Fetterley, *Resisting Reader,* pp. xx–xxiv, for a good overview of these statements.

20. Norman N. Holland, *The Dynamics of Literary Response* (New York: Oxford University Press, 1968), p. xv. Cf. Iser, *Act of Reading,* p. 28: "Recourse to psychology, as a basis for a particular category of reader in whom the responses to literature may be observed, has come about not least because of the desire to escape from the limitations of other categories." Cf. Culler, *On Deconstruction,* p. 225, for a discussion of the possible complexities in the relationship between literature and psychoanalysis.

21. Stimpson, "Zero Degrees Deviancy," p. 377.

22. Joseph Zinker, *Creative Process in Gestalt Therapy* (New York: Random House, 1977), p. 18. Subsequent references are cited parenthetically in the text.

23. Jane Rule, *Outlander* (Tallahassee: Naiad Press, 1981), p. 182.

24. What I am explaining here is perhaps more readily understood if I talk about fictional characters, but it can be applied equally to aspects of texts'/authors' attitudes.

25. Iser, *Act of Reading,* p. 155.

26. Ibid.

27. Cf. Holland, *Dynamics of Literary Response,* p. 101: "One of literature's adaptive functions, then, is that it allows us to loosen boundaries—between self and not self, inner and outer." Iser quotes Husserl on this subject: "We might say that the ego as ego continually develops itself through its original decisions, and at any given time is a pole of multifarious and actual determinations, and a pole of an habitual, radiating system of realizable potentials for positive and negative attitudes" (p. 157). This does not have to mean, as David Bleich suggests in his objections to Holland's description of reading as a reiterative process, that "the idea of novelty loses its meaning altogether" (*Subjective Criticism* [Baltimore: Johns Hopkins University Press, 1978], p. 111). Each new text calls on slightly different aspects of ourselves and thus strengthens different parts of our identity.

28. Culler, *On Deconstruction,* p. 49.

29. Quoted by Culler, *On Deconstruction,* p. 50. This, of course, raises the question of the definition of *lesbian.* Recent biographical work on Woolf indicates that she had lesbian sexual experiences. I would argue, too, that her primary emotional bonds were with women.

30. In *Virginia Woolf: The Inward Voyage* (Princeton: Princeton University Press, 1970), Harvena Richter points out that Woolf's "Vision of the novel . . . implies an unusually close relationship between the reader and the work" (p. 234).

31. Virginia Woolf, "How Should One Read a Book?" in *The Common Reader, Second Series* (London: Hogarth Press, 1932), p. 268.

32. Virginia Woolf, *Orlando* (London: Hogarth Press, 1928), p. 69.

33. T. S. Eliot in *Virginia Woolf: The Critical Heritage,* ed. Robin Majumdar and Allen McLaurin (London: Routledge and Kegan Paul, 1975), p. 192.

34. Virginia Woolf, "Robinson Crusoe," in *The Common Reader, Second Series,* p. 51. Subsequent references are cited parenthetically in the text.

35. Virginia Woolf, "The Strange Elizabethans," in *The Common Reader, Second Series,* p. 9. Woolf, "How Should One Read a Book?" p. 259. Woolf's own intensity of identification with the characters she creates is a relevant parallel here. In "An Unwritten Novel," in *A Haunted House* (London: Hogarth Press, 1944), pp. 22–23, she talks of a desire "to lodge myself somewhere in the firm flesh . . . or find a foothold on the person, in the soul," in order to feel "the suck and regurgitation of the heart."

36. Adrienne Rich, *On Lies, Secrets, and Silence: Selected Prose, 1966–1978* (New York: W. W. Norton, 1979), p. 158. Subsequent references are cited parenthetically in the text.

Part Two
Texts

Chapter 4
Taking the Gold Out of Egypt:
The Art of Reading as a Woman
Susan Schibanoff

> The only phenomenon which, in
> all parts of the world, seems to be
> linked with the appearance of
> writing . . . is the establishment of
> hierarchical societies, consisting of
> masters and slaves and where one
> part of the population is made to
> work for the other part. . . . And
> when we consider the first uses to
> which writing was put, it would
> seem clear that it was connected
> first and foremost with power . . .
> exercised by some men over other
> men [*sic*] and over worldly
> possessions.
>
> Claude Lévi-Strauss

In 1473, Anthony Woodville, Earl Rivers, came across a French version of the *Liber Philosophorum Moralium Antiquorum* and decided to translate it into English for the edification of his royal charge, the Prince of Wales. When he completed his anglicized version, entitled *The Dictes and Sayengs of the Philosophres*, Rivers asked another translator, the early printer and publisher William Caxton, for a professional opinion of his work. No doubt Caxton was pleased to review the Earl's *Dictes*. He was familiar with its French original and was aware that thus far it had not been made available to English-speaking readers, and Rivers—brother-in-law of Richard III—was potentially an important patron and client of Caxton's new press at Westminster. Not surprisingly, Caxton found Rivers's efforts a "meritory dede," his work "right wel and connyngly made and translated into ryght good and fayr englissh."[1] Despite his obvious reluctance to criticize Rivers's work, Caxton did identify one flaw in the translation.

This flaw was in the form of an omission: Rivers had failed to translate a passage of several pages from his French manuscript which Caxton described as "certayn and diuerce conclusions towchyng women" (p. 20). These "conclusions" were, in fact, a conventional set of antifeminist proverbs and *exempla* attributed to the classical philosopher Socrates.[2] Actually, Rivers had acknowledged the omitted passage in a brief statement: "the said Socrates had many seyings ayenst women whiche is not translated."[3] But Caxton chose to overlook this notice in order to try his hand first at a bit of witticism and then at a well-worn convention. Humorously, Caxton wondered whether the Earl's French manuscript lacked the passage in question or whether the "wynde had blowe ouer the leef / at the tyme of translacion of his booke" (p. 24). Or, perhaps, Caxton next employed a traditional theme, a female reader had directly or indirectly influenced Rivers's version of the *Liber Philosophorum:* either "some fayr lady" had objected to the antifeminist passage and prevailed on Rivers to strike it, or Rivers's own amorous designs on some "noble lady" had led to the same outcome.

Caxton was too androcentric and conventional to toy with the possibility that Rivers himself found misogyny reprehenisble or tedious.[4] Instead, he followed the well-established *topos* of manuscript literature that women readers alone are offended by antifeminist texts. When men were the fictional audience of antifeminist material, the author assumed that misogyny neither troubled nor offended them. Instead, the author presented antifeminist material as a useful encouragement to men to avoid the entrapments of marriage, or as a sympathetic consolation to assuage their grief that resulted from unrequited love.[5] But when women were the fictional audience, the author conceived of misogyny as offending them and in need of apology. Thus, for example, in his address to the audience of the thirteenth-century *Roman de la Rose* (part 2, 11.15135–15302), Jean de Meun apologized to his female readers for anything he said against women, just as Chaucer begged forgiveness from his female readers for his depiction of the false Criseyde in *Troilus and Criseyde* (5.1772 ff.).

Authorial apologies do not, however, relieve the problems that the antifeminist text causes the female reader. Instead, they intensify them, for the *topos* commonly includes a justification of the offensive text. In apologizing for his malicious words against womankind, Jean de Meun excused himself by noting that he did not invent these words, but nevertheless defended them by explaining that ancient and reputable writers, wise men who never lied, created them. Caxton did likewise. He could not believe that so true a man and noble a philosopher as "Socrates" "shold wryte other wyse than trouthe," even if contemporary English women were far more virtuous than the Greek women of "Socrates'" time. As regrettable as his task might have been, good scholarship demanded that Caxton restore the philosopher's opinions about women to Rivers's text. And Chaucer pleaded with his female readers not to blame him for inventing Criseyde's guilt; "other bokes" before him record it, and he must follow his written sources. Implicit in this self-excuse by source is the threat that the written texts of anti-feminism are "fixed": they are autonomous entities that may be neither altered nor discontinued. The female reader is to understand, then, that when writers must choose between pleasing her and venerating the written traditions of antifeminism created by wise men of the past and noble ancient philosophers, patriarchy has first claim on their loyalty.

Faced with this choice, Caxton honored patriarchal tradition by restoring the antifeminist passages from "Socrates" which Rivers had deleted. Following the restored passage, Caxton again engaged in uncharacteristic badinage with his audience. He advised anyone who was offended by the reinstated antifeminist material to delete it physically: "wyth a penne race [scratch] it out or ellys rente [tear] the leef oute of the booke" (p. 30). (To minimize damage to the text, Caxton facetiously located the passage in a conveniently detachable appendix at the end of the book.) In the context of both the written manuscript and the printed book, Caxton's suggested solution to the problem of a hostile text is, of course, ironic. As Rivers or the "fayr lady" had attempted, a reader could resist offensive material by literally deleting it—but only in his or her own copy or memory, not in the "work" itself. Caxton and others before him perceived the work as a multiple entity that, thanks to the numerous copies made possible by the technology of writing and printing, possessed a permanence no individual reader could easily undo.[6] One reader could attempt to alter a text; but another, such as Caxton, could restore it to its original form and content by consulting the written exemplar, in this case, a French manuscript, and then producing hundreds of printed copies which would further insure the fixity of the text.[7]

Authorial apologies to the female reader for antifeminist texts are, clearly enough, something other than heartfelt laments. They are attempts both to intimidate her and, borrowing Judith Fetterley's term, to immasculate her.[8] They warn her that the written traditions of antifeminism have contemporary guardians and custodians who will not allow these texts to disappear. If the text is "fixed"[9] in this fashion, then the only solution to the otherwise irremediable problem of the hostile text is for the female reader to change herself: she must read not as a woman, but as a man, for male readers, according to the *topos,* are neither offended nor troubled by literary misogyny.

In the first chapter of her *Book of the City of Women* (ca. 1405), Christine de Pisan depicts the immasculation of a woman reader, the narrator "Christine."[10] The work opens with the narrator sitting by herself in her library, hard at work on her literary studies. She decides to relax by reading some light poetry and begins to search among her many volumes for "some small book" of verse. Instead, into "Christine's" hands comes a "strange" book, not one, she assures us, that she has acquired by choice, but one that has been given to her. She opens the volume to find that it contains Matheolus's *Lamentations,* a well-known thirteenth-century antifeminist diatribe that "Christine" has heard of but has never been anxious to read. This time, however, she determines to amuse herself by browsing through Matheolus's tirade. Soon, her mother calls her to supper, and "Christine" puts the book down. When "Christine" returns to her library the next morning, Matheolus is waiting for her. Again, she starts to read the work and continues for a little while. But despite her resolution to "enjoy" Matheolus—to read the work with detachment and irony—"Christine" finds herself increasingly annoyed by its mendacity, immorality, and lack of integrity on the subject of women. She browses a bit more, reads the end, and then puts the book down in order to turn her attention to "more elevated and useful study."

Physically distancing the text from herself, however, does not halt the negative effects this work has on "Christine." The mere sight of the volume sends her memory reeling back over all the other books she has read which present a similarly vicious opinion of women. "Christine" recalls that she "could hardly find a book on morals where, even before I had read it in its entirety, I did not find several chapters or certain sections attacking women, no matter who the author was." Matheolus's text, in other words, is "fixed"—in "Christine's" mentality and memory and in the written traditions of Western literature and philosophy. And so "transfixed in this line of thinking" is this female reader that she feels as if she has fallen into a stupor. "Christine" is utterly unable to close the floodgates of her reading memories of antifeminist writers: "Like a gushing fountain, a series of authorities, whom I recalled one after another, came to mind, along with their opinions on this topic."

"Christine" is, in Adrienne Rich's phrase, "drenched" with male assumptions and prejudices about women.[11] Her survival—her self-identity and self-confidence—is at stake, and, at least temporarily, "Christine" succumbs to the ultimate immasculation, the most extreme form of self-hatred and self-doubt: she agrees with her written authorities that God made an "abominable work" in creating woman, curses her fate of having been born female, and wishes that she had been born male. The first chapter of Christine de Pisan's *City of Women* ends with its reader-narrator sunk in despair, unable to resolve the problem her hostile and fixed texts have caused her other than through the self-eradicating fantasy of wishing she were a man. She has failed to resist the palpable design the written traditions of patriarchal authority have on her.

Yet, as we know, "Christine" does survive. By the end of the *Book of the City of Women* she has reclaimed both her self-identity and her self-confidence and has constructed one of the earliest histories of women and critiques of patriarchal society.[12] What I wish to examine more closely here is how Christine does survive, how she "emasculates" herself as a reader. But first it is useful to look at the case of another fictional female reader contemporary with "Christine." She is exposed to the same antifeminist readings "Christine" is, but she neither succumbs to them nor loses her sense of self and confidence. Instinctively she knows how to resist an offensive text, and the way in which she automatically reads is the way that "Christine" must and does teach herself to read in order to survive. It is also the way every female reader since "Christine" has had to learn to read in order to avoid immasculation. The female reader I refer to here is Chaucer's Wife of Bath.

Most of us will recall that the Wife is a book-burner, and that the text she makes her fifth husband pitch into the flames is his beloved "book of wicked wives," a manuscript anthology of classic antifeminist treatises.[13] Night after night Jankyn delights in reading this work to Alysoun, until her anger erupts into a physical assault on the text—she tears three pages from it—and finally to its destruction. As violent as this response is, it is not Alysoun's most radical challenge to the written traditions of patriarchy. Caxton reminds us that written texts are replaceable, hence autonomous, and Chaucer does, too. Soon after the Wife of Bath destroys the book of wicked wives, another Canterbury pilgrim, the Merchant, restores the text that offended her so: to his character Justinus, "the just one," the Merchant assigns an attack on matrimony which makes use of the same antifeminist *exempla* Alysoun had consigned to the flames. The technology of writing has made books of wicked wives indestructible, permanently available to merchants and others who, in turn, perpetuate them. In short space, patriarchal tradition thus reasserts and reestablishes itself in the microcosm of experience the *Canterbury Tales* represents. On this score, we hear no further protest from the Wife of Bath. None is possible.

More radical than the Wife's attempt to censor and destroy offensive texts in her appropriation of them, which she demonstrates in her scriptural quotations at the opening of her Prologue. When she quotes scriptural passages, she instinctively and automatically adjusts or interprets them to serve her own needs. To support her argument for female supremacy in marriage, for instance, the Wife repeats Paul's command that husbands love their wives (1 Corinthians 7:3), but she selectively forgets the remainder of Paul's command that wives obey their husbands. And to justify her own multiple marriages, she cites the examples of Abraham and Jacob, both Old Testament patriarchs who were married more than once. More importantly, the Wife chooses to interpret these examples as literal mandates for her own marital conduct rather than, for instance, to read them allegorically as Jerome had, as examples of conduct sanctioned under the Old Law but not under the New.[14] In these and other uses of Scripture, the Wife implicitly calls attention to the existence of two "texts": the fixed one, which consists of words on manuscript and printed pages, and the variable one, which consists of the meaning or significances readers assign to these words. In claiming her right to produce her own variable text, the Wife is at her most radical, for she demonstrates that Jerome's text, no matter how sanctified by tradition and authority, is in fact exactly that, *Jerome's* text, not the Wife of Bath's. And in selectively forgetting Paul's command about wifely obedience, the Wife is no more and no less biased and self-serving than Paul was in issuing the command. The Wife survives— welcome ever the sixth husband!—not because she burns books, but because she rereads old texts in new ways. And on this score, none of Alysoun's Canterbury companions, clerical or secular, wishes to confront her directly; her re-readings go unchallenged. Only the Pardoner manages the oblique criticism of dubbing her a "noble prechour."

What accounts for the Wife's ability to survive in this fashion? It does not proceed, I suggest, from a conscious analysis of the situation of the female reader in a patriarchal society. Nor does it proceed, as one modern critic suggests, from the Wife's "perverse" inclination to mis-quote, misunderstand, and misinterpret holy writ.[15] Rather, the Wife's survival skills as a reader are, at least in part, a function of the *way* in which she reads. As we often fail to distinguish, Alysoun is an aural reader, not a visual reader—an ear-reader, not an eye-reader.[16] In modern terms, she must be classified pejoratively as "illiterate"; her texts are read to her by her priests, her husbands, and others. Her choice of texts is largely controlled by the men who read to her, and, as her Prologue witnesses, she is probably as well versed in antifeminist traditions as is "Christine," her contemporary.

Although aural readers such as the Wife of Bath live in a world of written records—a manuscript culture—in at least one important respect they behave as if they exist in a totally oral culture, one altogether devoid of written records. Oral cultures preserve their literary and other "texts" through continual recitation and repetition, but neither ancient nor modern oral cultures display anything near a *verbatim* recollection of their verbal works.[17] Instead, as these works are repeated over the years, they change form and content, and the alterations proceed according to the demands of relevance and utility. Oral cultures, in other words, constantly "reread" their "texts"; each retelling of a narrative is slightly different from the previous one, and there is a built-in, unconscious procedure of updating oral traditions over the years. Anthropologists term this phenomenon *structural amnesia,* and numerous modern examples exist in which that "part of the past with no immediately discernible relevance to the present ha[s] simply fallen away" in oral tradition.[18] The implication is that orally composed, aurally perceived, narratives reflect a society's present cultural values; what fails to harmonize with these values is forgotten or altered. In Walter Ong's words, "Oral societies live very much in a present which keeps itself in equilibrium or homeostasis by sloughing off memories which no longer have present relevance."[19] Authority and tradition are readily and naturally altered, sometimes deleted altogether, to serve the needs of present experience.

As an aural reader, the Wife of Bath utilizes "methodology" and procedures that resemble those of oral tradition. She has no concept of the "fixed" text of written tradition; unconsciously, she alters or destroys those authorities that conflict with her values or experiences. Her much-noted self-confidence, vitality, and eagerness for yet more marital adventure are not due merely, as she would hold, to her astrological inheritance; they are also due to her ability to keep the world around her in equilibrium with her concept of self. To be sure, she achieves a precarious homeostasis that demands constant vigilance, but unlike her literate counterpart "Christine," the Wife never succumbs and subscribes to antifeminist views of woman. She resists immasculation because she instinctively rereads authority and tradition, a survival skill that does not come easily to the literate reader burdened by the immobile written records of the past.

Written cultures do, of course, update or modernize the texts they receive from the past, but the process by which they do so is both more cumbersome and more restricted than that of oral society. A case in point here is the method by which early Christian writers of the fourth and fifth centuries attempted to harmonize the Old Testament with their own values. In many instances, the Old Testament appeared immoral or contrary to new Christian doctrines and ethics. What to do, for instance, with a scriptural passage such as the Wife quotes, in which an Old Testament patriarch practices bigamy? To the literate reader, the written text itself was fixed; it was the word of God transcribed, and both its literal and its historical form had to be preserved. Nor could one simply "forget" troublesome passages. Instead, the past could be brought into equilibrium with the present only by creating an interpretation or meaning for the fixed text which complemented contemporary values. As Augustine phrased it, hermeneutics or exegesis allowed Christians to take the gold out of pagan cultures and convert it to their own use:

> Just as the Egyptians had not only idols and grave burdens which the people of Israel detested and avoided, so also they had vases and ornaments of gold and silver which the Israelites took with them secretly when they fled, as if to put them to a better use. They did not do this on their own authority but at God's commandment, while the Egyptians unwittingly supplied them with things which they themselves did not use well. . . . When the Christian separates himself in spirit from their miserable society, he should take this treasure with him for the just use of teaching the gospel. And their clothing . . . should be seized and held to be converted to Christian uses.[20]

With written texts such as the Old Testament, the method of converting the past and putting it to better use often took the form of allegorical interpretation. Thus, the patristic exegete explained, many passages in the Old Testament were to be understood by Christians as containing an *allegoria,* literally, a "something other," beneath their literal surface. In some cases, the *allegoria* or inner significance was the direct opposite of what the literal surface suggested. While the Old Testament patriarch is, on the surface, an immoral bigamist, allegorically he may be understood as Christ, his wives as faithful Christian souls, and the intimacies between husband and wives as the loving relationship between divine and human in the Christian religion. The rationale patristic exegetes offered for such ironic interpretation *per antiphrasim,* "by opposites," was complex. They maintained that immoral surfaces or literal meanings acted as a protective shroud over inner and true meanings. The unworthy, the scornful, or the ignorant, as was appropriate in the opinion of the church fathers, would be distracted by the glitter of the literal surface and thus denied access to the inner kernel of Christian truth, while the worthy and the faithful would know how to penetrate surfaces to reach essences.[21]

Although patristic exegesis is the literate equivalent of homeostasis and structural amnesia in oral culture, a method of preserving and harmonizing the traditions of the past with those of the present, it suffered from the same problem it attempted to remedy: by recording its interpretations of scriptural texts in writing, it gave to its reading a fixed character that became no less authoritative and ineradicable than sacred writing itself. What began as a method of revitalizing earlier texts became inert and unchangeable.[22] In Christine de Pisan's era, almost a thousand years after Augustine wrote *De doctrina,* Augustine's "modernizations" of scriptural texts were still being cited, despite the fact that both Christian culture and Western society had obviously undergone enormous changes. For an aural reader, such as Alysoun of Bath, this petrification of an earlier point of view and set of values causes little problem; she freely adapts the opinions and readings of church fathers to reflect her own times and experiences. But for literate readers, such as Christine de Pisan, these earlier endeavors to update the past become in themselves part of the burden of the past which oppresses her fictional reader, "Christine," as well as herself. What she must learn and practice is what the Wife unconsciously knows: in order to survive, to read as woman, she must, in fact, reread, enter old texts from new critical directions.

As reflected in the fictional experiences of the narrator of the *City of Women,* Christine de Pisan herself learned this survival skill slowly and somewhat painfully. Her progress from immasculated reader to woman reader can be traced over a series of her works, including *Epistle of the Goddess Othea to Hector* (ca. 1399–1400); *Epistle to the God of Love* (1399); her letters, which form a part of the debate over the *Romance of the Rose* called the *Querelle de la Rose* (ca. 1400–1402); and, finally, the *City of Women* (ca. 1405). In the *Othea,* Christine schooled herself in the art of reading as a man or, more accurately, a patristic exegete. The work consists of one hundred chapters, each divided into three sections: "texte," "glose," and "allegorie." The "texte" is a short narrative, usually no longer than a quatrain, from classical mythology, the story of Troy, or another source. Following the "texte," the "glose" explains or elaborates the passage, frequently employing illustrative or edifying quotations from the ancient moralists and philosophers (Aristotle, Socrates, Hermes, Diogenes, Pythagoras, and others). Each chapter concludes with an "allegorie," an interpretation or re-reading of the text according to patristic—and patriarchal—tradition. The "allegorie," or what I have earlier termed the "variable text," is studied with appropriate quotations from the church fathers and other clerical authorities— Jerome, Gregory, Origen, Bernard, Augustine, Ambrose, and others— and Scripture.

Christine's chapter on Briseyde (the English "Criseyde") demonstrates her ability to read the text as a patristic exegete would. The "glose" provides a brief summary of the love affair between Troilus and Criseyde, of Calchas's removal of his daughter to the Greek camp, and of Criseyde's affair with the Greek warrior Diomede. It closes with an indictment of Criseyde for having so "light a corage" and warnings to good men to avoid "such a lady as Criseyde was."[23] In Hermes' words, she represents "evil fellowship." The "allegorie" then interprets the text, the significance of which is made unequivocally clear: "Criseyde . . . is vainglory, with which the good soul should not acquaint himself, but flee it with all his power, for it is quick and overtakes too suddenly." Augustine is called on to witness the dangers of vainglory, the hardest of sins to overcome, and the re-reading ends with Paul's admonishment in *Corinthians* to take one's glory in God.

Christine's allegorization of the story of Troilus and Criseyde is anything but original, for this text had often been reread to yield an *exemplum* against the female vices of duplicity, pride, and fickleness which seduce and ruin good men such as Troilus.[24] It is still reread in this fashion by modern patristic exegetical critics.[25] In fact, Christine's allegorization is so conventional it appears that she is unaware that any other interpretation is possible; the "allegorie" or variable text is fixed for her, and she shows no inclination here, or elsewhere in the *Othea,* to assign her own significances to the texts she reads. Perhaps because of its very traditional and patriarchal re-readings, the *Othea* was extraordinarily successful; more contemporary manuscripts (forty-three) of this work can be verified than of any of Christine's other numerous writings. Within a hundred years, it had been translated into English at least three times, and early publishers, such as Caxton, frequently printed and reprinted the *Othea.*

At almost the same time, however, that Christine was perfecting the art of patriarchal reading in the *Othea,* she was beginning to detect and criticize the antifeminist bias of two important literary works of her day, Ovid's *Art of Love* and Jean de Meun's *Romance of the Rose.* In her *Epistle to the God of Love,* she briefly attacked both works for their vicious and illogical slanders against women. By modern standards, her critique of Ovid and Jean might appear tame and attenuated, and in itself her analysis did not confront the central question of who is privileged to determine the variable meaning of a text, each individual reader or the dominant set of readers in a culture. Despite its mildness, Christine's *Epistle to Love* provoked an immediate, strong, and hostile response. By 1402, Thomas Hoccleve had turned out a smutty anglicized parody of it,[26] and three erudite French men—Pierre and Gontier Col and Jean de Montreuil—rose to Jean de Meun's defense and engaged Christine in a lengthy debate known as the *Querelle de la Rose*. Although Christine's opponents wished to reform her errant, that is, feminine, reading of the *Romance of the Rose,* in fact they enlightened her and motivated her to read as a woman.

The central portion of the debate took the form of a series of letters written by and circulated among Jean de Meun's defenders, the Cols and de Montreuil, and his opponents, Christine and her semi-ally, Jean Gerson. At the heart of the debate was the question of how different readers respond to the *Romance.* Jean's defenders maintained that all readers should interpret the work as they did, as an ironic discouragement of vice and a promotion of virtue. When, they argued, Jean narrates an assault on the castle—rape—it is not because he wishes to condone immorality; rather, his purpose is of the highest morality, for he describes the assault "in order to teach more effectively how gatekeepers should guard the castle." When Jean invents speeches of vicious antifeminism for his character the Jealous Husband, it is not because the author wishes to promote misogyny, but because he wishes to "demonstrate and correct the enormous irrationality and disordered passion of jealous men."[27] In the opinion of Jean's admirers, the *Romance*'s literal scurrility and antifeminism must be interpreted allegorically as "something other" in their purpose and intent, and readers must interpret its surface *fabula* or narrative *per antiphrasim* ("by opposites") in order to detect its true meaning.[28]

Christine did not concern herself with the question of how the *Romance* ought to be read, but with how, in her opinion, the work *would* be read by different readers. Basically, she argued that readers would interpret the *Romance* according to their own lights. The virtuous, she conceded to her opponents, might well find in the *Romance* a powerful and persuasive praise of virtue (p. 63). But, by the same token, the vicious would easily find in the work an endorsement of vice. To Pierre Col's defense of the Jealous Husband's misogyny, Christine responded that a reader who was actually a jealous husband would recognize only the poem's misogyny and read it literally as a justification rather than a condemnation of his vice:

> Not long ago, I heard one of your familiar companions and colleagues, a man of authority, say that he knew a married man who believed in the *Roman de la Rose* as in the gospel. This was an extremely jealous man, who, whenever in the grip of passion, would go and find the book and read it to his wife; then he would become violent and strike her and say such horrible things as, "These are the kinds of tricks you pull on me. This good, wise man Master Jean de Meun knew well what women are capable of." And at every word appropriate, he gives her a couple of kicks or slaps. Thus it seems clear to me

that whatever other people think of this book, this poor woman pays too high a price for it. (P. 136)

If, Christine continued logically and pragmatically, only the erudite or the pure were able to pierce through the *Romance*'s scurrilous surface to its inner moral message, then its message or meaning was wasted on those who most needed to hear it, the foolish and the vicious. Again and again Christine argued the point that an ironic discrepancy between a poem's immoral *fabula* or narrative surface and its moral *sententia* or inner meaning ran the risk of inculcating the superficial values, for readers read—and create texts—in their own images. On this score, Jean Gerson agreed with Christine; he wished that the *Romance* inculcated virtue in the way that Scripture did:

> That is, to reprove evil in such a way that every man might perceive that condemnation of evil and that approbation of good, and (what is most important) that all those things could have been done without excessive frivolity. But no. . . . Everything [in the *Romance*] seems as true as the Gospel, particularly to those foolish and vicious lovers to whom [Jean] speaks. (P. 81)

Christine phrased it more succinctly: "There is no point in reminding human nature, which is naturally inclined to evil, that it limps on one foot, in the hope that it will then walk straighter" (p. 55).

Inadvertently, Jean's defenders proved Christine's point. Although they continued to justify the morality of the *Romance* on the basis of an ideal reading—*their* reading—increasing frustration with Christine's attack led them to admit that other readers were, in fact, understanding the work differently, or, in their terms, misreading it. Among these misreaders, of course, was Christine de Pisan. Jean de Montreuil complained that Christine and other detractors of the *Romance* lacked the intelligence and sophistication necessary to perceive the moral purpose of Jean's work: "They do not understand how that teacher has fulfilled the function of a satirist and is therefore permitted many things prohibited to other writers" (p. 154). In Christine's case, he charged more specifically, the misreading proceeded from the regrettable fact that she was reading (just) like a woman; to him, she sounded like "Leontium the Greek whore, as Cicero says, who dared to criticize the great philosopher Theophrastus" (p. 153). Similarly, Gontier Col identified female pride as the source of Christine's misreading of the *Romance*. He exhorted and begged her to correct the "manifest error, folly, or excessive willfulness which has risen in [her], a woman impassioned in this matter, out of presumption or arrogance" (p. 60). Pierre Col also charged that Christine read—that is, misread—like a woman, and prescribed a hundred readings of the *Romance* to rid Christine of this unfortunate point of view:

> Oh excessively foolish pride! Oh opinion uttered too quickly and thoughtlessly by the mouth of a woman! A woman who condemns a man of high understanding and dedicated study, a man who, by great labor and deliberation, has made the very noble book of the *Rose,* which surpasses all others that ever were written in French. When you have read this book a hundred times, provided you have understood the greater part of it, you will discover that you could never have put your time and intellect to better use. (P. 103)

Christine's male ally, Jean Gerson, was also accused of reading like a woman, even though he possessed sufficient "manly" intellect to arrive at a proper understanding of the *Romance*'s worth:

> And granted that the book was more attentively read by one of these detractors [i.e., Gerson] and, that brooding over the processes and nuances of the work, it was given to him to understand, still he was led to speak and feel differently because of his religious vocation and vows, or perhaps he is simply the kind of man who is rendered useless for the propagation of the species, which is, after all, the purpose of this book. (P. 154)

In the course of the debate, Christine replied often to the accusation that she read the *Romance* like a woman—that envy, pride, or foolishness led her to misunderstand the work. Her responses range from ironic comment on the double standard to outright denial and, finally, to a redefinition of the charge: she was not reading *like* a woman, she was reading *as* a woman. To Jean de Montreuil she argued that if she were reading like a woman, then Jean de Meun deserved even more censure for writing like a man: "And may it not be imputed to me as folly, arrogance, or presumption, that I, a woman, should dare to reproach and call into question so subtle an author, and to diminish the stature of his work, when he alone, a man, has dared to undertake to defame and blame without exception an entire sex" (p. 56). To de Montreuil, she denied that her reading proceeded from "feminine bias" (p. 53); to Pierre Col, that pride, envy, or indignation produced her reading (pp. 142–43); and to Gontier Col, that folly and presumption motivated her attack on the *Romance* (pp. 62–63).

Christine's denials of the charge that she read like a woman were futile, judging from the number of times such pejorative comments recur in the debate. But in the course of defending herself, Christine gradually began to develop a positive view of the way in which she was reading. In a letter to Gontier Col, she redefined his insult about her sex into a compliment:

> And if you despise my reasons so much because of the inadequacy of my faculties, which you criticize by your words, "a woman impassioned," etc., rest assured that I do not feel any sting in such criticism, thanks to the comfort I find in the knowledge that there are, and have been vast numbers of excellent, praiseworthy women, schooled in all the virtues—whom *I* would rather resemble than to be enriched with all the goods of fortune. (P. 63)

To Jean de Montreuil, she defended her reading of the *Romance* as an antifeminist work not on the basis that she had arrived at a universal interpretation of the work, but on the basis that as a woman she possessed a more authoritative understanding of women than did Jean de Meun: "And it is precisely because I am a woman that I can speak better in this matter than one who has not had the experience, since he speaks only by conjecture and chance" (p. 53). As Christine phrased this new understanding in her final entry in the debate, "Nothing gives one so much authority as one's own experience" (p. 143). In part, Christine's experience as the only female participant in the *Querelle de la Rose* taught her to read authoritatively, to read, that is, as a woman.

Christine also learned from the debate the art of deconstructing a text, of recognizing and examining the means by which readers construct the variable meanings of a text. It appears she never convinced her opponents that readers inevitably recreate the texts they read in their own images, even though she herself was charged with reading in precisely that way. Nor did she convince them specifically that the *Romance* was morally ineffective because it was especially vulnerable to being re-created in diverse, often opposite, ways. Jean de Meun's defenders held fast to their conviction that there was only one correct reading of the *Romance,* that the variable text was in fact fixed, and that the goal of each reader should be to arrive at this same reading. As Christine left the debate, in 1402, she remarked with evident weariness and frustration on the futility of arguing the issue further:

> You know that it happens with the reading of this book as with the books of the alchemists. Some people read them and understand them in one way; others read them and understand them in a totally opposite way. And each thinks he understands very well indeed. . . . So it is with you and me and many others. You understand the book in one way, and I, quite the opposite. You quote; I reply. And when we have worked and worked, it is all worth nothing. (P. 125)

I do not know why we are debating these questions so fully, for I do not believe we will be able to change each other's opinions. You say that [Jean de Meun] is good; I say that he is evil. Now show me which of the two is right. (P. 140)

As her *Book of the City of Women* witnesses, however, the debate was worth much to Christine de Pisan, for it had transformed her from being the immasculated reader who composed the *Othea* into the woman reader, one who claimed her right to reread texts according to her own experiences and knowledge. She would not again subscribe to a patristic "allegorie" or interpretaion of a "texte"; instead, she created her own readings of standard texts which, in many cases, were startling in their divergence from other readings. As I have suggested, the *City of Women* may be read as a quasi-autobiographical work, and the extreme immasculation of the fictional reader, "Christine," reflects in part its author's early experiences. The narrator's subsequent transformation into a woman reader also, I think, reflects Christine de Pisan's experience in the *Querelle de la Rose*. The turning point in "Christine's" reader identity occurs shortly after she experiences the depths of self-hatred and self-doubt. The allegorical personification, Reason, appears to her, determined to rescue her from the blind ignorance that so clouds her intellect that she "shun[s] what [she] know[s] for a certainty and believe[s] what [she does] not know or see or recognize except by virtue of many strange opinions" (p. 6). "Christine's" wish that she were male strikes Reason as utter folly: "You resemble the fool in the prank who was dressed in women's clothes while he slept; because those who were making fun of him repeatedly told him he was a woman, he believed their false testimony more readily than the certainty of his own identity. Fair daughter, have you lost all sense?" (p. 6).

Reason then proceeds to show "Christine" how to read as a woman, specifically, how to reread both Matheolus's *Lamentations* and Jean's *Romance* in a way that does not immasculate her, and she does so in a completely irrational fashion:

As far as the poets of whom you speak are concerned, do you not know that they spoke on many subjects in a fictional way and that often they mean the contrary of what they say? One can interpret them according to the grammatical figure of *antiphrasis,* which means, as you know, that if you call something bad, in fact, it is good and vice versa. Thus I advise you to profit from their works and to interpret them in the manner in which they are intended in those passages where they attack women. (P. 7)

In a patently outrageous conclusion, Reason demonstrates that both the *Lamentations* and the *Romance* actually praise women. Despite the facetious tone in Reason's instructions on the art of reading as a woman, there is a serious dimension to her observations. She has taken the methodology used by both patristic exegetes and the defenders of the *Romance*—interpretation "by opposites"—and turned it to women's advantage. In doing so, she points squarely at the issue of how readers create texts in their own images and claims the same privilege for female readers that male readers have always enjoyed, even though the latter have often claimed that their readings are the "correct" and universal ones sanctioned by God and Reason.

"Christine's" instruction in the art of reading as a woman serves her well, and much of the remainder of the *City of Women* contains her re-readings of women's history as presented by male writers. She does not continue in the outrageous and comic mode of her instructor, Reason, although many of her re-readings are unusual for their boldness and originality. Two examples from the *City* must suffice here to indicate the extent to which "Christine"—and her creator, Christine de Pisan— learned to enter old critical texts from new directions, to take the gold from Egypt and convert it to better use. The first is the story of Circe, a figure Christine de Pisan had earlier treated in her *Othea* and "Christine" discusses in the *City of Women.* To the *Othea* author, Circe may be read either as a woman full of wantonness and idleness who led Ulysses' knights astray (p. 118), or as the female deceiver and enchant- ress whom the good knight should avoid (p. 51). Christine's reading of Circe as the "wicked woman" who leads men astray is traditional enough; Boccaccio, for instance, had interpreted her meaning in pre- cisely the same way in *Concerning Famous Women* (ca. 1355–1359).[29] In the *City of Women,* however, "Christine" completely rereads the signifi- cance of Circe; she is no longer the wicked woman par excellence, but a historical example of a woman of great learning who proves that women were not naturally inept in the much-respected ancient art of divination. Circe excelled so in this art "that there was nothing which she might want to do that she could not accomplish by virtue of the strength of her spells" (p. 70). As an example of Circe's art, "Christine" briefly narrates the Ulysses episode, as Christine earlier had in the *Othea.* But again, she rereads the meaning of Circe's transformation of Ulysses' men into swine. In the *Othea,* Circe's spell is capricious and unmotivated, the action of a fickle and malicious woman. But in the *City of Woman,* "Christine's" Circe behaves as a woman might when she is suddenly confronted by ten strange men: "Ulysses . . . sent his knights to her in order to find out whether it would please her for them to land. But this lady, *thinking they were her enemies,* gave the ten knights a drink of her concoction, which immediately changed them into swine. *Ulysses quickly went to her, and the men were subsequently changed back to their proper form*" (p. 70; italics mine).

The second example is brief, but striking: Leontium. To Boccaccio, she was a scholar who, "moved either by envy or womanly temerity," dared "write against and criticize Theophrastus, a famous philosopher of that period." Although Leontium was "brilliant," Boccaccio admits, she ruined her reputation because she "threw away womanly shame and was a courtesan, or rather a harlot": "We must certainly bewail the fact that so brilliant a mind, given by heaven as a sacred gift, could be subjected to such filthy practices."[30] And to Jean de Montreuil (as well as Cicero), Leontium was nothing more than "the Greek whore . . . who dared to criticize the great philosopher Theophrastus"; Leontium also reminded him of his opponent in the *Querelle de la Rose,* Christine de Pisan. In her *City,* Christine de Pisan, however, detected an entirely different woman: "I could tell you a great deal about women of great learning. Leontium was a Greek woman and also such a great philosopher that she dared, *for impartial and serious reasons,* to correct and attack the philosopher Theophrastus, who was quite famous *in her time*" (p. 68; italics mine). As Christine had earlier turned the insult, reading like a woman, into a beneficial methodology, reading as a woman, so here she transformed a woman reviled by male readers into a woman both admired and understood. Her gold from Egypt—women's experience as presented by men—was converted to better use.

Unlike the earlier *Othea,* Christine's *City of Women* was allowed to fall into obscurity. To date, no critical edition of the original French text has been published, and the first modern English translation of it did not appear until 1982. Modern readers have frequently labelled it an "imitation" of Boccaccio's *Concerning Famous Women,* which it decidedly is not.[31] Not only does it contain straightforward analyses and critiques of patriarchal culture that are altogether absent in Boccaccio's work, but, as I hope the two examples above may indicate, it also entirely rereads Boccaccio and other male authorities who had, until Christine's time, controlled the production of the written records of women's history. Her achievement is, I think, stunning, but still undervalued. Almost single-handedly, Christine came to the realization that in order to read as a woman, she would have to reread almost the entire corpus of men's writings about women; the *City of Women* rereads the written narratives of more than one hundred and twenty women, ranging from the ancient poet, Sappho, to the modern queen, Isabella of Bavaria. From her experiences in the *Querelle,* Christine must also have realized that she would again be accused of reading like a woman in the *City;* perhaps for that reason, the *City* is a work about women for women readers. She addressed the work specifically to women and presented the dedication copy to the queen. No *Querelle de la Cité* ensued. Instead, Christine went on to write a continuation of the *City, The Book of Three Virtues.*

Christine de Pisan's transformation from immasculated reader to woman reader occurred at a critical point in the history of Western women: as Christine herself witnesses, more and more women, secular as well as religious, were gaining the formerly male prerogative of literacy.[32] In many cases, women were doing so with the aid rather than the opposition of those who controlled their access to learning. Although Christine's mother opposed her academic pursuits, her father encouraged them and made them possible.[33] Even such conservative moralists as Geoffrey La Tour Landry—who argued, for instance, that bad husbands deserve good wives in order to remedy their faults— advised other parents to teach their daughters how to read.[34] And the so-called Renaissance increased women's access to literacy and learning. As always, when considering such apparent progress, we must reread, by, in this case, asking the question *"Cui bono?"* If Christine's experiences tell us anything, it is that we must be cautious in assuming that women were necessarily the primary beneficiaries of their own literacy. As my two paradigms, "Christine" and the Wife of Bath, suggest, female literacy brought women into a more submissive relationship to men's texts.[35] (There was, of course, little else to read.) Even women's courtesy books—on the art of being a good woman—were largely male authored and contain male views of ideal female behavior: modesty, obedience, chastity, humility.[36] Renaissance educational writers frequently remarked that women should be taught to read in order not to be learned, but to be good. Literacy was and remains an effective and efficient means of indoctrination, of immasculation. When we ask why, between Christine and the Wife of Bath's time and the sixteenth and seventeenth centuries, women's status declined and roles narrowed, increased female literacy may, in fact, provide part of the answer.[37]

At the same time, however, literacy provided some women the opportunity to take the gold from Egypt, to reread and thus reclaim their own history from antifeminist texts. That relatively few women developed the feminist exegetical methodology of a Christine de Pisan until recently is perhaps less significant than the fact that a few did so in the face of opposition and hostility. What is still crucial for us to examine now is how and why some female readers resist immasculation and others succumb to it, for our literary texts and traditions remain largely male-made. In Christine's case, literacy and learning were crucial factors in her development of a feminist exegesis. But, as I have noted earlier, Christine also credits personal experience for her new-found authority. And one dimension of that experience was evidently in the oral rather than the literate mode. "Christine" recounts that she frequently talked with other women, "princesses, great ladies, women of the middle and lower classes, who . . . graciously told me of their most private and intimate thoughts" (p. 4).[38] Presumably, Christine de Pisan did likewise and found it just as hard to reconcile what she heard from them with the written opinions of male authorities on women's base and immoral character. If one of the mainsprings which motivated Christine's re-readings was the conflict between what she heard from women and what she read by men, then perhaps it is well for us to remember that modern feminist oral traditions—such popular forms of feminism as the consciousness-raising sessions, the discussion group, the work-shop—have a vital role to play in the otherwise intellectual and literate act of re-reading, reading as women. We must, I believe, continue to honor the methods and mentalities of both the garrulous Alysoun of Bath and the scholarly Christine de Pisan if we are to succeed in re-possessing all of our gold.

Notes

1. W. J. B. Crotch, ed., *The Prologues and Epilogues of William Caxton,* Early English Text Society, o.s. 176 (1928; reprint, London: Oxford University Press, 1956), p. 19. Subsequent references are cited parenthetically in the text. N. F. Blake (*Caxton and His World* [London: Andre Deutsch, 1969], p. 86) speculates that Rivers had already granted financial assistance to Caxton.

2. E. g., "And [Socrates] saw a long mayde that lerned to wryte / of whom he sayde that me[n] multiplied euyl upon euyll" (Caxton, *Prologues and Epilogues,* p. 26).

3. Curt F. Bühler, ed., *The Dicts and Sayings of the Philosophers,* Early English Text Society, o.s. 211 (London: Oxford University Press, 1941), p. 345, note on 100.24–102.29.

4. Rivers's family library did include a copy of Christine de Pisan's *The Book of the City of Women*; from this manuscript, Harley 4431, evidently the first translation was made for English readers.

5. Thus, Ruffinus in Walter Map's *De nugis curialium* (ca. 1181–1193), Walter in the third book of Andreas Capellanus's *De arte honeste amadi* (ca. 1185), and January in Chaucer's *Merchant's Tale* (1380s) listen to antifeminist material in order to dissuade themselves from matrimony or devotion to women, while the anonymous dreamer in Boccaccio's *Corbaccio* (ca. 1355) is consoled for his unsuccessful love affair by the same means. Another version of the *topos* that

employs men as the fictional audience of misogyny does so by encoding anti-feminist statements in Latin. See, for example, Chauntecleer's "mulier est hominis confusio" in Chaucer's *Nun's Priest's Tale;* and the destroying burden, "cuius contrarium verum est," in poems that otherwise praise women. In his *Philobiblon* (1345), Richard de Bury comments that "biped beasts" (i.e., women) would be even more opposed to the clergy if they "could see our inmost hearts, . . . had listened to our secret counsels, . . . had read the book of Theophrastus or Valerius, or only heard the twenty-fifth chapter of Ecclesiasticus with understanding ears" (ed. E. C. Thomas [New York: Barnes and Noble, 1970], pp. 43–45). The "book of Valerius," or Walter Map's *De nugis curialium;* Theophrastus's *Liber aureolus de nuptiis;* and the *Philobiblon* are, of course, all in Latin. In "Latin Language Study as a Renaissance Puberty Rite," *Studies in Philology* 56 (1959): 103–24; *The Presence of the Word: Some Prolegomena for Cultural and Religious History* (New Haven: Yale University Press, 1967), pp. 249–52; and *Orality and Literacy: The Technologizing of the Word* (New York: Methuen, 1982), pp. 112–15, Walter J. Ong discusses Latin as a sex-linked language written and spoken only by males. Josephine Donovan ("The Silence Is Broken," in *Women and Language in Literature and Society,* ed. Sally McConnell-Ginet, Ruth Borker, and Nelly Furman [New York: Praeger, 1980], pp. 205–18) examines the effects of the masculinizing of Latin on early women writers.

6. Ong (*Orality and Literacy,* p. 82) argues that "writing is in a way the most drastic of the three technologies. It initiated what print and computers only continue, the reduction of dynamic sound to quiescent space, the separation of the word from the living present, where alone spoken words can exist." M. T. Clanchy (*From Memory to Written Record: England, 1066–1307* [Cambridge: Harvard University Press, 1979], pp. 88–115) characterizes writing as a "special skill in the Middle Ages which was not automatically coupled with the ability to read," and discusses the tools of this technology. While I do not wish to sweep aside the often cogent distinctions between chirographic (or script) and print cultures made by such recent writers as Elizabeth L. Eisenstein (*The Printing Press as an Agent of Change,* 2 vols. [Cambridge: Cambridge University Press, 1979]), I do take the point of view here that script and print cultures are similar in that they use their respective technologies to achieve a uniformity and permanence among texts which would be impossible in an oral culture. The ancient maxim "vox audita perit, littera scripta manet" ("the heard voice perishes, the written word endures") was used by scribe and early printer alike to justify the production of written and printed books, e.g., de Bury, *Philobiblon,* pp. 19–21, and Caxton, *Prologues and Epilogues,* p. 50. For a complementary view of similarities between script and print cultures, see Donald R. Howard, *The Idea of the Canterbury Tales* (Berkeley and Los Angeles: University of California Press, 1976), pp. 60–67.

7. The number of copies Caxton printed is not known, but H. S. Bennett (*English Books and Readers, 1475 to 1557,* 2d ed. [Cambridge: Cambridge

University Press, 1969], pp. 224–25) speculates that "between four and five hundred copies would be a fair average for a book published" between 1480 and 1490 on the Continent.

8. Judith Fetterley, *The Resisting Reader: A Feminist Approach to American Fiction* (Bloomington: Indiana University Press, 1978), p. xx: "Though one of the most persistent of literary stereotypes is the castrating bitch, the cultural reality is not the emasculation of men by women but the *immasculation* of women by men."

9. I use the term *fixed* as does Franz H. Baüml, "Varieties and Consequences of Medieval Literacy and Illiteracy," *Speculum* 55 (1980): 248, n. 31: "The fixity of the written word, of course, does not necessarily imply 'stability' of a written text in its transmission. It merely means that, in contrast to the spoken word, the written word does not change or disappear without being made to change or disappear—unless the written symbol changes."

10. Christine de Pisan, *Book of the City of Women,* trans. Earl Jeffrey Richards (New York: Persea Books, 1982), pp. 3–5. Subsequent references are cited parenthetically in the text.

11. Adrienne Rich, "When We Dead Awaken: Writing as Re-Vision," *College English* 34 (1972): 18. Also cited by Fetterley, *Resisting Reader,* p. xix.

12. Joan Kelly ("Early Feminist Theory and the *Querelle des Femmes,* 1400–1789," *Signs* 8 [1982]: 20) characterizes the *City* as one of the "first attempts" at women's studies.

13. Included are Walter Map's *Valerius to Ruffinus* (or *De nugis curialium*), Theophrastus's Golden Book of Marriage, Jerome's *Epistle against Jovinian,* Ovid's *Art of Love,* etc.

14. Graham D. Caie, ("The Significance of the Early Chaucer Manuscript Glosses [with Special Reference to the *Wife of Bath's Prologue*]," *Chaucer Review* 10 [1976]: 354) notes that early fifteenth-century glossators of the *Canterbury Tales* cite Jerome's reading from the *Epistola adversus Jovinianum* (Migne, *Patrologia Latina,* XXIII, 211 ff.).

15. Caie, "Significance of the Early Chaucer Manuscript Glosses," p. 353.

16. An exception is Paula Neuss ("Images of Writing and the Book in Chaucer's Poetry," *Review of English Studies,* n.s. 32 [1981], p. 394), who recognizes that Alysoun cannot write or read, but assumes that she wishes to emulate men "and so the only way that she can take a leaf out of Jankin's book is *literally.*" For some of the distinctions between hearing and seeing, illiterate and literate, see Clanchy, *From Memory to Written Record,* pp. 175–91. Franz H. Baüml ("Transformations of the Heroine: From Epic Heard to Epic Read," in *The Role of Woman in the Middle Ages,* ed. Rosmarie Thee Morewedge [Albany: State University of New York Press, 1975], pp. 23–40) compares aural and visual reception of literature about women.

17. Ong, *Orality and Literacy,* pp. 46–49.

18. *Structural amnesia* is a phrase coined by J. A. Barnes in "The Collection of Genealogies," *Rhodes-Livingston Journal: Human Problems in British Central*

Africa 5 (1947): 48–56. The quotation is from Ong, *Orality and Literacy,* p. 48. For discussion, examples, and bibliography, see Ong, pp. 46–49, and Jack Goody and Ian Watt, "The Consequences of Literacy," in *Literacy in Traditional Societies,* ed. Jack Goody (Cambridge: Cambridge University Press, 1968), pp. 1–27.

19. Ong, *Orality and Literacy,* p. 46.

20. Augustine, *De doctrina Christiana,* II, 40, trans. D. W. Robertson, Jr., *On Christian Doctrine* (New York: Liberal Arts Press, 1958), p. 75.

21. E.g., Augustine, *De doctrina Christiana,* III, 12 (Robertson, *On Christian Doctrine,* p. 83). Macrobius, *Commentary on the Dream of Scipio,* I, ii, similarly maintains that a "modest veil of allegory" insures that "only eminent men of superior intelligence gain a revelation of [Nature's] truths" (trans. William Harris Stahl [New York: Columbia University Press, 1952], p. 85).

22. Jack Goody and Ian Watt ("Literate Culture: Some General Considerations," in *The Future of Literacy,* ed., Robert Disch [Englewood Cliffs, N.J.: Prentice Hall, 1973], pp. 51–52) term this phenomenon *culture lag* and maintain that it was surely "this lack of social amnesia in alphabetic cultures which led Nietzsche to describe 'we moderns' as 'wandering encyclopaedias,' unable to live and act in the present and obsessed by a 'historical sense that injures and finally destroys the living thing, be it man or a people or a system of culture'."

23. Christine de Pisan, *Epistle of the Goddess Othea to Hector,* trans. Stephen Scrope, ed. Curt F. Bühler, *The Epistle of Othea,* Early English Text Society, o.s. 264 (London: Oxford University Press, 1970), p. 102. Subsequent references are cited parenthetically in the text.

24. Gretchen Mieszkowski (*The Reputation of Criseyde: 1155–1500* [Hamden, Conn.: Archon Books, 1971], pp. 71–153) documents the widespread reading of Criseyde as a "type of the fickle woman." For exceptions, see Susan Schibanoff, "Argus and Argyve: Etymology and Characterization in Chaucer's *Troilus,*" *Speculum* 51 (1976): 647–58, and idem, "Criseyde's 'Impossible' *Aubes,*" *Journal of English and Germanic Philology* 76 (1977): 326–33. For innovative aspects of Christine's work, see Mary Ann Ignatius, "Christine de Pizan's *Epistre Othea:* An Experiment in Literary Form," *Medievalia et Humanistica,* n.s. 9 (1979), pp. 127–42.

25. E.g., D. W. Robertson, Jr. ("Chaucerian Tragedy," in *Chaucer Criticism: Troilus and Criseyde and The Minor Poems,* ed. Richard J. Schoeck and Jerome Taylor [Notre Dame, Ind.: University of Notre Dame Press, 1961], pp. 86–121) interprets Chaucer's work as an "echo" of the Adam and Eve story.

26. *The Letter of Cupid,* in *Hoccleve's Works: The Minor Poems,* vol. 1, ed. F. J. Furnivall, Early English Text Society, e.s. 61 (1892), rev. by Jerome Mitchell and A. I. Doyle (reprint, London: Oxford University Press, 1970). Diane Bornstein ("Antifeminism in Thomas Hoccleve's Translation of Christine de Pisan's *Epistre au dieu d'amours,*" *English Language Notes* 19 [1981]: 7–14) finds the *Letter of Cupid* subtler in its methods of undermining feminism than I do.

27. Joseph L. Baird and John R. Kane, trans., *"La Querelle de la Rose": Letters and Documents,* North Carolina Studies in the Romance Languages and Liter-

atures, no. 199 (Chapel Hill: University of North Carolina Press, 1978), p. 104. Subsequent references are cited parenthetically in the text.

28. E.g., Pierre Col argues that one must not take the *Romance* literally, "but rather according to what was previously said and the intention of the author" (*"La Querelle de la Rose,"* p. 102).

29. Boccaccio, *De Claris Mulieribus,* trans. Guido A. Guarino (New Brunswick, N.J.: Rutgers University Press, 1963), pp. 77–78. Subsequent references are cited parenthetically in the text.

30. Ibid., p. 132.

31. E.g., Francis Lee Utley, *The Crooked Rib: An Analytical Index to the Argument about Women in English and Scots Literature to the End of the Year 1568* (New York: Octagon Books, 1970), p. 120.

32. Reliable statistics on the literacy rate for men or women in the fourteenth and fifteenth centuries are hard to come by, but M. B. Parkes ("The Literacy of the Laity," in *The Medieval World,* ed. David Daiches and Anthony Thorlby [London: Aldus Books, 1973], p. 557) notes that from the twelfth century on there were didactic treatises addressed to women. "One of them, written in the early 14th century, discusses whether it is proper that a woman should learn to read. Such a discussion would be pointless if by that time reading had not already become something of a habit. This evidence is supported in the literature itself." See also Joan M. Ferrante, "The Education of Women in the Middle Ages in Theory, Fact, and Fantasy," in *Beyond Their Sex: Learned Women of the European Past,* ed. Patricia H. Labalme (New York: New York University Press, 1980), pp. 9–42.

33. de Pisan, *Book of the City of Women,* pp. 154–55.

34. William Caxton, trans. *The Book of the Knight of the Tower,* ed. M. Y. Offord, Early English Text Society, s.s. 2 (London: Oxford University Press, 1971), p. 122. Geoffrey argues that women should learn to read in order to recognize better perils to the soul; there is no use, however, in teaching women to write. (Cf. n. 2 above.)

35. Another aural reader of the early fifteenth century, Margery Kempe, readily accommodated the written lives of the women saints to her own secular life and aroused both suspicion and hostility by practicing celibacy in marriage. *The Book of Margery Kempe,* ed. Sanford Brown Meech and Hope Emily Allen, Early English Text Society, o.s. 212 (1940 [for 1939]; reprint, London: Oxford University Press, 1961).

36. Diane Bornstein, *The Lady in the Tower: Medieval Courtesy Literature for Women* (Hamden, Conn.: Archon Books, 1983), p. 120.

37. Both Joan Kelly-Gadol ("Did Women Have a Renaissance?" in *Becoming Visible: Women in European History,* ed. Renate Bridenthal and Claudia Koonz [Boston: Houghton Mifflin, 1977], pp. 139–152) and Ruth Kelso (*Doctrine for the Lady of the Renaissance* [Urbana: University of Illinois Press, 1956]) have considered this question. Jane Tibbetts Schulenburg ("Clio's European Daughters: Myopic Modes of Perception," in *The Prism of Sex: Essays in the Sociology of Knowledge,* ed. Judith A. Sherman and Evelyn Torton Beck

[Madison: University of Wisconsin Press, 1977], p. 37) remarks that both the Wife of Bath and Christine de Pisan "coincide with a period in which women's experiential realm had become substantially circumscribed; in general, their previous options in political, religious, and economic spheres had sharply contracted." See also idem, "Sexism and the Celestial Gynaceum: From 500 to 1200," *Journal of Medieval History* 4 (1978): 177–33.

38. Garrulous and frequently "illiterate" women are often viewed as threatening androcentric values and institutions; the satirical caricature of these women as "gossips" is an attempt to silence them.

Chapter 5
Fathers and Daughters:
Women as Readers of the *Tatler*

Kathryn Shevelow

Isaac Bickerstaff announced in the first issue of the *Tatler* (April 12, 1709) that he had "also resolved to have something which [might] be of entertainment to the fair sex, in honour of whom [he had] taken the title of this paper." Thus, Richard Steele specified an intended audience of women as well as men, and targeted female behavior as an appropriate subject for satire. The mocking flattery of the paper's title is characteristic of the language the *Tatler* adopted to address women, mingling compliment and chastisement in the service of a didactic intent. Steele's editorial decision to court women readers placed his journal among a company of early Augustan publications—John Dunton's *Athenian Mercury,* Peter Motteux's *Gentlemen's Journal,* and, initially, Daniel Defoe's *Review*—which tacitly acknowledged the commercial potential of female consumers of popular literature. The *Tatler* was the best and most influential of these early publications to (in Swift's sarcastic witticism) "fair-sex it"—an activity that rapidly became a Grub Street trademark—and, equaled only by its successor, the *Spectator,* the paper attained a unique literary status.

The *Tatler* achieved that compromise between moral edification and literary merit which Ian Watt cites as the most significant development in eighteenth-century literature,[1] and which was particularly appropriate to its less-educated readers, many of whom were women. Though Rae Blanchard has thoroughly demonstrated that behind Steele's much-touted deference to "the fair sex" lay the typically conservative attitudes of the Augustan moralist—the *Tatler* adhered firmly to the status quo when addressing women[2]—Steele's recognition of the importance of a female audience marks the full-scale emergence of women into the mainstream of literary history as consumers of literature, several decades before they fully emerged as its producers. The *Tatler* was one of the first major literary works systematically to acknowledge women as readers, an acknowledgment that became a characteristic feature of its distinctive and influential rhetoric.

Traditionally, much of the literary fame of the *Tatler* (and the *Spectator*) has rested on the deftness of Steele and Addison's didactic prose, a prose that directly solicits audience response. However, recent audience-oriented criticism has largely ignored didactic nonfiction in favor of nondidactic fiction, probably because the strong authorial voice in the former seems to place meaning entirely in control of the author. This notion assumes that the only message of the didactic text is its overt one. Yet, though the response actively sought by the didacticism (i.e., that which can be marked by changes in behavior) is manifestly the intended response, frequently a didactic text like the *Tatler* elicits another kind of response which, in a sense, *readies* the reader to receive and, presumably, act on the text's teaching. That is, the text may interact with its readers' predilections to create a receptivity that strengthens and supplements the paper's didactic message.

Not all rhetorical appeal in a text is the direct result of conscious authorial intention. We must distinguish between a rhetoric consciously exercised by the author—the direct address that we usually consider to be characteristic of a didactic text—and that generated only by the interaction between the text and the reader. In order to characterize this distinction, I differentiate between two separate, though complementary, levels of persuasion, which I call, simply, overt and covert.[3] The overt is the didactic message that comprises the content of the text; the covert is the rhetorical power surrounding the text, which is entirely dependent on the way in which the intended readers read the text (which is in turn dependent on their social and psychological backgrounds). The covert rhetoric lies outside the realm of authorial control, though its results do, in the case of the *Tatler*, support the overt, consciously intended results, and are, in fact, inseparable from them. But the covert rhetorical effect can not be controlled by the author; at best, s/he can set it in motion, since it finally rests on what the reader brings to the text. Steele as author can begin to tap this level of response based on his understanding of and participation in the values of his reading community, but the actual response passes through a sociological and psychological filter constructed by the emotions and attitudes that the reader engages in the act of reading.

The *Tatler*'s didacticism is thus double-edged: the overt rhetorical effect, which we can ascribe completely to Steele or one of his contributors, comprises only part of the journal's persuasive power. The *Tatler* contains another, covert, system of persuasion which, though it is thoroughly intertwined with the overt, relies on the interaction of text with readers who had internalized a network of social conventions based on historically relative phenomena such as family structure, psychological constitution, and learned response to literary traditions. This specific network was shared by all early eighteenth-century readers, male and female alike, for it was a social and historical construct that informed all of the *Tatler*'s rhetoric. But as a means of handling its relatively large and diversified audience, the *Tatler*'s rhetorical operations (on both the overt and the covert level) fragmented that general readership into subaudiences, which were constituted in accordance with such frequently overlapping categories as gender, age, occupation, and class.[4] Thus, at different moments the *Tatler* might project as its primary audience one or another of its subaudiences without, however, focusing so narrowly as to exclude, alienate, or bore other readers. A discussion of courtship, for example, might offer direct advice to young, unmarried female readers while providing information and entertainment, in the form of social commentary, for the entire readership. In all cases, the *Tatler*'s overt rhetoric is covertly reinforced by the conscious and unconscious assumptions that guide its audience's reading of the text.

The *Tatler* addresses its women readers in the form of several intended subaudiences, each of which corresponds to a different role adopted by Isaac Bickerstaff, the paper's protean eidolon. At various points throughout the *Tatler*'s run, Bickerstaff assumed the guise of the sentimental lover, the sympathetic correspondent, and the father, each role embodying a rhetorical strategy. Bickerstaff's assumption of the parental role—which primarily concerns me here—is particularly powerful, for it calls forth from female readers a response based on an elaborate process of cultural conditioning, and to some degree it underlies all of the voices Bickerstaff adopts when he addresses women. Though Steele was obviously aware of the authority exercised by the paternal figure (the overt rhetoric) in 1709, when he created the role, the full extent of its power depends on a complex of culturally and psychologically determined responses brought to the text by women readers (the covert rhetoric).[5] As covert influences on reading, these social determinants interact in the text with artistic determinants, most importantly for this argument, the incorporation of the language and techniques of "courtesy literature." Although Richmond Bond is quite correct in maintaining that the *Tatler* "was at no time a serialized courtesy book," its echoes of conduct writing, particularly the "paternal advice" books of the previous century, are pronounced.[6] The invocation of a powerful literary tradition that was aimed at shaping behavior exerts a rhetorical effect based not only on the conduct book's didactic content but also on readers' internalization of the terms of that content: the authority of the paternal voice. The pattern of references to conduct literature is an overt gesture that places the *Tatler* within a tradition of didactic literature and at the same time releases the operations of the covert rhetoric which emanate from the structural, unconscious, social, and psychological conditions that informed the way in which early eighteenth-century Englishwomen read.

Bickerstaff's "paternal voice" has direct literary antecedents in the English courtesy literature of the sixteenth and seventeenth centuries, particularly the type that John E. Mason calls the "parental advice book," which were influenced heavily by James I's *Basilikon Doron* (1599).[7] Directed almost exclusively at men, these books, Polonius-like, advise a son or heir on his course through life with varying degrees of courtly cynicism or Puritan admonition; the usual format includes a dedicatory epistle followed by a collection of maxims or subject headings based on conventional wisdom or scriptural authority. Despite their familial, affectionate dedications, these books resemble handbooks in their impersonal presentation of guidelines and avoidance of intimacy. The bond of identification which does remain assumes a "man-to-man" businesslike tone. No doubt this accounts for the relative scarcity of seventeenth-century advice books written for daughters: the books always assume that the son is created in his father's image and will grow to inherit his estate or responsibilities. The formal tone renders the book suitable for use by the adult, for whom the address to the child would no longer be appropriate.

When, in the eighteenth century, women like Hester Chapone and Sarah Pennington began to write conduct books to daughters, they created a similar identification based on a shared social role. However, the smaller but extremely popular and influential genre, the "father to daughter" advice book, operates under different principles. These books reflect, not only in content but in form as well, societal realities of relationships between men and women. The books are conservative; they extol obedience and the other "female" virtues of piety, chastity, and patience. A significant feature of these books is their lack of that identification characteristic of father-son books: writing for a daughter, a father wrote for an audience that would *never* grow to be his equal, for, even as an adult, a woman's subordinate status in a patriarchal society replicates that of the daughter. Thus, in a book intended for adult use, the address to a child is maintained. Even the unusually liberal Dr. Gregory demonstrates awareness of relative status in his *A Father's Legacy to His Daughters* (1774); Swift, in *Letter to a Very Young Lady* (1723), more typically adopts a consistently condescending tone. The reinforcement of unequal status seems to have been one of the major concerns of these books. *The Ladies Library* (1714), published under Steele's auspices, provides a large selection of such writings, including a lengthy borrowing from the most famous, *The Lady's New-*

Year's-Gift: Or Advice to a Daughter, by George Savile, first marquis of Halifax. Extremely influential, Halifax's *Advice* (1688) went through at least six editions before 1700 and at least eleven more in the eighteenth century; it was translated into French and Italian. Not only did it exert a strong influence on the development of female-oriented conduct books, but it also helped establish a language of address to women which was echoed countless times in the eighteenth century.

Halifax wrote *Advice to a Daughter* for his daughter Elizabeth (later, wife of the third earl of Chesterfield; mother of the letter-writer) as a present. The book's tone is familiar, personal, parental, and affectionate, and its advice was immediately referential to her. Yet, because the major subjects broached—social behavior, religion, and, especially, marriage—were of nearly universal interest to women, and were appropriate not only for the aristocracy but also for the middle class (as its continued popularity in the eighteenth century seems to indicate), the book transcended its specific context and appealed to a general readership.

The transference of an essentially private genre to the public domain exercises a rhetorical power that, along with the multifaceted appeal of the paternal voice, explains the effectiveness of Halifax's work. For the book establishes a dynamic between author and reader based on familial ties. *Advice to a Daughter* projects a strong fatherly voice, transferring both the familiarity and the authority vested in the patriarchal role into the interaction between the text and the intended reader. The reader, in order to "read" the book (i.e., to absorb Halifax's advice), endows the fatherly voice with power. The voice draws the reader in, casting her into a new mold as reader which is at the same time an ancient one as woman. The book, acting in loco parentis, elicits a response based on the reader's experience. The reader becomes, in effect, a surrogate daughter.

Elizabeth, who was the actual recipient of the book and who is repeatedly addressed within it, is a "characterized reader"—a reader who explicitly exists in the text.[8] Unlike the typical characterized reader in fiction, however, she is not a foil or a caricature of the reader, but, rather, the focus around which the book's address to its intended readers revolves. Here, the intended reader is required to identify with the characterized reader.

Halifax's dedication, following the standard format, presents a personal address to Elizabeth in a tone of fatherly intimacy:

Dear Daughter,

I Find, that even our most pleasing Thoughts *will* be unquiet; they *will* be in motion; and the *Mind* can have no rest whilst it is possess'd by a darling Passion. *You* are at present the Chief Object of my *Care,* as well as of my

Kindness, which sometimes throweth me into *Visions* of your being happy in the World, that are better suited to my partial *Wishes,* than to my reasonable *Hopes* for you. At other times, when my *Fears* prevail, I shrink as if I was struck, at the Prospect of *Danger,* to which a young Woman must be expos'd. But how much the more *Lively,* so much the more *Liable* you are to be hurt; as the finest Plants are the soonest nipped by the *Frost.* Whilst you are playing full of Innocence, the spitefull World will bite, except you are guarded by your *Caution.* Want of *Care* therefore, my dear Child, is never to be excus'd; since, as to *this* World, it has the same effect as want of *Vertue.* Such an early sprouting Wit requireth so much the more to be sheltered by some *Rules,* like something strew'd on tender Flowers to preserve them from being blasted. You must take it well to be prun'd by so kind a Hand as that of a *Father.* There may be some bitterness in meer Obedience: The natural Love of *Liberty* may help to make the Commands of a Parent harder to go down: Some inward resistance there will be, where *Power* and not *Choice* maketh us move. But when a *Father* layeth aside his Authority, and persuadeth only by his kindness, you will never answer it to Good Nature, if it hath not weight with you.[9]

Through this familiar paternal voice, tender in concern for his daughter and stern in his parental authority (however he repudiates it), Halifax establishes an ethos. Like the *bonus orator* of classical rhetoric, the voice brings to the book a weight of already established authority; speaking as father and referring to the characterized reader, the voice invokes a specific relationship between individuals. Because it possesses correlates outside of the text (that is, a real father and a real daughter), the initial speaker-audience relationship is embodied entirely within the text. On a secondary level, though, a level with which I am most concerned, the speaker speaks through the characterized audience to address the intended audience.

The ethos constructed by the voice of *Advice to a Daughter* elicits a complementary audience pathos through the cumulative, authority-building process of pronouncing on behavior, and through elicitation of response based on the personal situations of readers. Halifax's book creates an ethos/pathos interaction based on three factors: the didactic message of the speech itself; the speaker's assumption of fatherly authority, which is directed toward a characterized reader and transferred to the intended readers; and the audience's own experience of the father-daughter relationship, which is reenacted as the text is read. The three are, of course, thoroughly interconnected. Thus, the parental advice conduct book is both particular to an individual relationship (characterized inside the text) and transferable to a public one (intended for those outside the text). In order to respond to the text's didactic message, the intended readers must image themselves as daughters, a process to which they bring extensive social and psychological conditioning.

In a significant departure from the tradition of "advice to sons," Halifax maintained the personal voice of the dedication in the body of the book. Insistently his prose invokes *you* (the reader) and apostrophizes *my Dear*. These signals construct the characterized reader, Elizabeth, but also, in a complementary way, the intended reader. The following passage, drawn from a chapter concerned with marriage and husbands, follows the familiar pattern and is characteristic of the entire book; here the familiarity is further reinforced by references to the parental home and all that it, ideally, represents:

> The tenderness we have had for you, *My Dear,* is of another nature, peculiar to kind Parents, and differing from that which you will meet with first in any Family into which you shall be transplanted. . . . You must not be frightened with the first Appearance of a *differing scene;* for when you are used to it, you may like the House you go to, better than that you left; and your *Husband*'s Kindness will have so much the advantage of ours, that we shall yield up all *Competition,* and as well as we love you, be very well contented to Surrender to such a *Rival.*[10]

With the first-person plural, Halifax, the head of the household, here speaks for its inhabitants; his expressions of concern and affection when alluding to the arrangements that he will make for his daughter's marriage establish that combination of love and absolute authority which, without contradiction, constitute the parental role.

The tone and pronoun construction of *Advice to a Daughter* combines specificity with general applicability, filtered through a familiar and idiosyncratic voice speaking in reference to a personal relationship. Halifax creates in this book both a simulacrum of the parent-child relationship and a monument to himself, a fixed piece of his personality and authority. His voice is concrete, interjecting endearments, alluding to personal matters, rendering this document a lasting testimony of fatherly love and advice: the power of his authority depends to a large extent on the convincing overtones of genuine paternal affection. The effect on the reader is that of being admitted to a private world that is enhanced by referentiality to a larger world. The interchange between characterized reader and intended reader and the evocation of paternal authority result in a text whose didactic message is underscored, and transcended, by elements beyond its overt content. The ostensibly reasoned tone and arguments take their real force not from the logic of the reasoning process and the presentation of irrefutable facts, but from the voice that presents those arguments. It is not the argumentation that commands, but rather the relationship behind it: the weight of paternal authority. Resting heavily on the social structure, the book appears to convince, but in reality it asserts, and it does so effectively because the paternal role itself, however kindly presented, is an assertive one.

The parental voice in the *Tatler* is transformed, of course, to suit the requirements of a different genre, a multifaceted audience, and an eidolon. For instance, the *Tatler* lacks the second-person direct address, and Isaac Bickerstaff, a confirmed (and moral) bachelor, has no off-spring. Yet Bickerstaff possesses a highly developed paternal voice that, though intertwined with a variety of other Bickerstaffian roles, intends an audience of pseudo-daughters and endows the paper with one of its most characteristic tones. In his role of censor, Bickerstaff comments directly on female behavior—satire on petticoats or beauty spots, for example—but, more subtly, he appeals to female readers by assuming the fatherly stance, which he uses for the conduct book purpose of influencing behavior. As in *Advice to a Daughter,* the paternal voice here carries a rhetorical weight that extends beyond the overt content of the advice itself and elicits responses based on female readers' experience of the father-daughter or male-female social dynamic.

Halifax's conduct book constructs a reading situation in which Eliz-abeth, addressed directly throughout, constitutes the characterized au-dience, and other "daughters," the public, constitute the intended au-dience. The *Tatler* adapts this situation to its own conditions, creating a characterized figure of the speaker (father) as well. Avoiding the inap-propriate directness of second-person address, Steele constructs a fic-tionalized version of the father-daughter relationship in the figures of Isaac Bickerstaff and his young half-sister, Jenny Distaff. Carrying on a dialogue throughout a number of issues, this pair *enact* the author-reader relationship of the conduct book. And just as, in Halifax, the characterized reader is a channel of communication to the intended reader, so, too, does this fictionalized enactment of paternal advice–filial response imply an audience of women readers who respond by identifying with Jenny, both as recipient of, and responder to, paternal authority. (This fictionalizing of the author-reader relationship conceiv-ably could allow a variety of reading responses from very different intended audiences, but it does possess as a *primary* intended audience those readers whose behavior the overt content seeks to affect: in other words, women.)

Though Jenny Distaff appears early in the periodical, Isaac Bick-erstaff does not adopt the paternal voice in regard to her until issue 75. Before that, Jenny (who is about twenty) is characterized primarily as a younger, female extension of Bickerstaff and, as author of several

Tatlers, she provides valuable commentary about him and about women's issues, in a tone virtually indistinguishable from that of Isaac himself. Bond explains that Steele, who wrote nearly all of the Jenny Distaff papers, "used her to create a light tone for serious comment, to illustrate a domestic theme, and to picture feminine winsomeness. She could say things about her sex (in Steele's own style) with better grace and better credibility than the aging bachelor."[11]

But in paper number 40, Jenny becomes the subject of a Bickerstaff essay, and in number 75, which presents the issue of marriage, she is the topic of discussion and the occasion for Bickerstaff's adoption of a fatherly perspective: "The girl is a girl of great merit, and pleasing conversation; but I being born of my father's first wife, and she of his third, she converses with me rather like a daughter than a sister."[12] When Isaac assumes the paternal duty of providing Jenny with a husband and, correspondingly, with advice about marriage, the *Tatler* enters the conduct book realm. Since Jenny at this point prefers taking snuff and reading romances to considering the arts of feminine propriety, Isaac must teach her the rudiments of appropriate female behavior: "She is so very a wit, that she understands no ordinary thing in the world. For this reason I have disposed of her to a man of business, who will soon let her see, that to be well dressed, in good humour, and cheerful in the command of a family, are the arts and sciences of female life." Though ostensibly her new husband will instruct her in these attributes, Isaac in several subsequent issues takes the task on himself, imitating the conduct books' emphasis on subordination and good domestic management. As he begins to mold Jenny into an exemplary woman, he molds himself into an illustration of appropriate paternal behavior.

In the dialogue that occurs just before Jenny's marriage to the pointedly named Tranquillus, Isaac and Jenny enact the conduct book interaction between author and reader. Jenny, as the reader characterized within the text, provides a model of proper response to the conduct book "father," a model that, of course, solicits a corresponding response from the intended female reader.[13] The dialogue between the characters requires the reader to identify with Jenny so that it can instruct. The tone assumed by Bickerstaff on this occasion invokes the culturally conditioned apparatus of father-daughter interaction, underscoring that identification.

"Sister," said I, "you are now going from me; and be contented, that you leave the company of a talkative old man, for that of a sober young one: but take this along with you, that there is no mean in the state you are entering into, but you are to be exquisitely happy or miserable, and your fortune in this way of life will be wholly of your own making. In all the marriages I have ever seen (most of which have been unhappy ones), the great cause of evil has proceeded from slight occasions; and I take it to be the first maxim in a married condition, that you are to be above trifles. When two persons have so good an opinion of each other as to come together for life, they will not differ in matters of importance, because they think of each other with respect in regard to all things of consideration that may affect them, and are pre- pared for mutual assistance and relief in such occurrences; but for less occasions, they have formed no resolutions but leave their minds un- prepared. (No. 79)

The conventional substance of this advice and, even more, the inti- mate, proprietary tone assumed by Bickerstaff as a continuing reference to the family relationship, follow the same principles of persuasion— both to the characterized reader (auditor) and to the intended au- dience—which are present in *Advice to a Daughter.* This fictional enact- ment of the advice-giving familial relationship creates a model of the author-reader relationship. Jenny is the representative, within the text, of the reader that the text intends but does not characterize. And that reader responds to Jenny through identification, not with Jenny as a distinct person, but with Jenny as that reader's representation. As with Halifax, such representation is based on the endowment of the father's voice with authority, though here the characterized reader, who is not the more easily translatable *you* or *my Dear daughter,* constitutes a third- person medium through which the rhetorical intention is channeled. In one sense, this medium distances the intended reader from the text by the interposition of a more fully realized (fictionalized) personality, but in another, by creating a model of the intended *response* (though ob- viously a more limited one than the complex response that is based on the implied reader's internalization of social determinants), such inter- position provides a stronger basis for identification.

In issue 85, Isaac intervenes in a marital quarrel to remind Jenny of her husband's better sense, and in issue 104, he returns to his concern with preservation of martial happiness. Jenny, now Mrs. Tranquillus, provides a complete representation of conduct book standards, receiv- ing from Isaac fatherly approbation of her adherence to his counsel:

She showed a little dislike at my raillery; and by her bridling up, I perceived she expected to be treated hereafter not as Jenny Distaff, but Mrs. Tran- quillus. I was very well pleased with this change in her humour; and upon talking with her on several subjects, I could not but fancy that I saw a great deal of her husband's way and manner in her remarks, her phrases, the tone of her voice, and the very air of her countenance. This gave me an unspeaka- ble satisfaction, not only because I had found her a husband, from whom she could learn many things that were laudable, but also because I looked upon her imitation of him as an infallible sign that she entirely loved him. . . . The natural shyness of her sex hindered her from telling me the greatness of her own passion; but I easily collected it, from the representation she gave me of his. "I have everything," says she, "in Tranquillus that I can wish for; and enjoy in him (what indeed you have told me were to be met with in a good husband) the fondness of a lover, the tenderness of a parent, and the intimacy of a friend." It transported me to see her eyes swimming in tears of affection when she spoke. "And is there not, dear sister," said I, "more pleasure in the possession of such a man than in all the little impertinences of balls, assemblies, and equipage which it cost me so much pains to make you contemn?"

Through dialogue, Isaac and Jenny act out the parent/child conduct book dynamic, Jenny providing the appropriate response: she has ingested his advice thoroughly. Her characterization, not as an apostrophised reader but as a fictionalized auditor, creates a level of tangibility in the conduct book situation. Whereas Halifax's second-person address is channeled through the characterized reader to the intended reader, the *Tatler* presents the intended reader with a model of an auditor who not only listens but responds. Thus Jenny Distaff resembles to some extent a Theophrastian "character," for the text posits her as a model of a type of behavior. The implied audience of this sequence in the *Tatler* must identify with Jenny in order to respond appropriately to Bickerstaff's strictures.

When Jenny expresses fears that time will destroy her husband's passion for her, Isaac responds with a conduct book maxim: "Endeavor to please, and you must please; be always in the same disposition as you are when you ask for this secret, and, you may take my word, you will never want it. An inviolable fidelity, good humour, and complacency of temper outlive all the charms of a fine face, and make the decays of it invisible." Couching conduct book sentiments in a dramatic situation reinforces their impact by presenting them in a context, in this case provided by characters, a family relationship, a marriage. Jenny's response to Isaac's pronouncements convey to the reader the desirability (reinforced by Isaac's approbation) of behaving according to the standards he sets up. Furthermore, such a technique takes "advice" out of an abstract presentation of a system of rules (the approach taken by most conduct books) and places it in a concrete setting that possesses its own power to convince. The interaction of characters is compelling in itself: in short, Isaac's response (parental approbation) to Jenny's response (filial obedience) intensifies the authority of his advice. He pronounces, then judges her response. Implicitly, he also judges the response of the reader, who, through identification, is receiving the advice in concert with Jenny.

In the parental advice conduct book, the judgment of response is lacking: the direct address does not permit fictional characters, and the response to the text is a matter external to the text itself. However, in *Advice to a Daughter,* the father does pass judgment on one occasion, exercising parental sanctions on an extensively described set of character traits and series of actions. Adopting a form of the Theophrastian character—the "vain and affected woman"—he creates this figure through a lengthy description of her social conduct, private thoughts, dress, and appearance (e.g., "She cometh into a Room as if her Limbs were set on with ill-made Screws, which maketh the Company fear the pretty thing should leave some of its *artificial Person* upon the Floor").[14] Surrounding his description with words of disapproval, Halifax damns this woman both through explicit statement and through creation of a social context in which others damn her too. The reader must match herself to the picture, and ensure that she does not resemble it. Halifax finds this method of instruction particularly effective: "Let this *Picture* supply the place of any other *Rules* which might be given to prevent your *resemblance* to it, The *Deformity* of it, well considered, is *Instruction* enough; from the same reason, that the sight of a *Drunkard* is a better Sermon against that *Vice,* than the best that was ever preach'd upon that *Subject.*"[15] Replacing rules with a picture, Halifax renders them graphic, calling for identification (in this case negative) by the readers. The concrete is superior to the abstract, because an image carries a weight that words lack, allowing identification and transference to real people in the reader's experience who resemble it, and thus, in a sense, animating the picture. The character-type exists for the specific purpose of reader identification, a negative embodiment of the abstract rules of conduct, but also a negative embodiment of the reader (what the reader should not be). The negative character-type presupposes a "shadow," however: her opposite, constructed through implicit contrast with her.

The character-types of the *Tatler,* of course, are famous primarily as satiric pieces. But Steele and his coauthors also created types that serve a more simply didactic function, either as figures presented critically (similar to Halifax's version) or as figures presented as the embodiment of worth. Like Halifax, Steele presented these figures in a context, which was shaped both by Bickerstaff's direct commentary and by the reactions of others, but the *Tatler*'s "pictures" were much more elaborately conceived. For instance, a two-part sequence presents the character type of the "virtuous woman"—a counterpart to Halifax's vain woman—whose virtues are made apparent when Bickerstaff, an old family friend, pays a visit. In *Tatler* 95, painterly techniques join narrative ones to create a portrait of the "happy family"; one painterly scene vividly captures volumes of conduct book pronouncements. This portrayal of family life resembles closely the scenes of domestic felicity which were just emerging in eighteenth-century European painting; in France and England, artists like Greuze and Gainsborough replaced the formal, mannered style of seventeenth-century family portraits with the representation of warm, interfamilial relationships.[16] As part of a new ideology of "family bonding," eighteenth-century painting focused on women as the centers of family life. *Tatler* 95 made an early contribution to this genre of family portraits: the mother becomes the center of both narrative and descriptive concern.

Bickerstaff enters the home to the cheerful noise of children; the husband-father greets him warmly; the surroundings provide immediate de facto testimony to the harmony provided by the mother. Cheerful children, warm and comfortable surroundings, and a husband's loving praise testify to the shaping power of the virtuous woman. She is defined by and in relation to her context. The details of this domestic scene, both the physical details of well-being (the description of the house, food, warmth, etc.) and the verbal testimony to it, serve an iconographic function that surrounds, defines, and emphasizes the mother. The portrait is not iconographically static, but its enclosed space and limited duration emphasize its painterly qualities.

The discordant notes of sentimental tragedy which are suggested here (in the sequel to this scene, she dies) underscore the woman's worth. Her husband's first-person testimony, reinforced by Bikerstaff's agreement, clearly define his wife as an embodiment of conduct book precepts.

> Every moment of her life brings me fresh instances of her complacency of my inclinations, and her prudence in regard to my fortune. Her face is to me much more beautiful than when I first saw it; there is no decay in any feature which I cannot trace from the very instant it was occasioned by some anxious concern for my welfare and interests. . . . Oh! she is an inestimable jewel. In her examinations of her household affairs, she shows a certain fearfulness to find a fault, which makes her servants obey her like children; and the meanest we have, has an ingenuous shame for an offence, not always to be seen in children in other families.

Her virtues—complacency, kindness, lack of self-assertion, prudence, concern for others before herself, devotion to her husband's well-being—fit the conduct book requirements. Her character is compelling because of its specificity, its individuality, and yet she is representative of the qualities whose value is reinforced by everything around her, and they are imitable, not idiosyncratic, qualities. Thus this scene serves a didactic function: by surrounding virtue with desirable accoutrements, and clearly presenting those accoutrements as a result of that virtue, the *Tatler* invokes a reward system to underscore its conduct book lesson.

The husband, who serves as a complement to Bickerstaff here (a patriarchal figure whose approval contributes much to the lesson being presented), protests that during the fifteen years of their marriage his love for his wife has rather increased than diminished: "There is no decay in any feature which I cannot trace from the very instant it was occasioned by some anxious concern for my welfare and interests." This sentiment provides reinforcement for the answer Isaac later gives to Jenny's fears about the effect of time: "Endeavor to please and you must please." The "virtuous woman," whose husband still loves her, provides a "picture" of the conduct book maxims with which Isaac answers Jenny, and to the intended reader, this icon of virtue stands draped with the cloak of paternal approbation, just as the language of conduct book advice carries the nuances of paternal endorsement. The virtuous woman figure in the *Tatler* is an embodiment of Isaac's advice to Jenny and, thus, an embodiment of what Jenny *will be,* as she grows in conformity with Isaac's instructions.

To the extent to which Jenny Distaff as the characterized reader is a representative of the intended reader, the ideal wife, as the characterization of a future Jenny, becomes also a characterization of the potential in the readers, whose response must acknowledge the model. The paternal voice creates a wife to fit its standards (made all the more poignant and powerful by Isaac's momentary sadness that he is not married—implicitly, to her). Thus, this type serves a rhetorical purpose, which is constituted by paternal authority and conveys conduct book guidelines.

By translating abstract rules of conduct into a concrete characterization placed in a social context, the *Tatler* creates a socially dynamic setting for the exercise of parental authority, which constitutes and dominates the scene. An iconographically authoritative figure (the "virtuous woman") and a dramatically responsive auditor (Jenny Distaff) together provide the readers with a vehicle for identifying and absorbing conduct book instruction. The figure of Jenny Distaff demands identification with the role of auditor-reader itself, the image of the "virtuous woman" only with the representative of good behavior approved by the parental voice, but in both cases the relation of model to voice is the significant factor; as in Halifax's *Advice,* that paternal voice wields a powerful authority that is constituted by social endorsement of the patriarchal role. Prepared by their social and sexual backgrounds to "read" the text, female readers bring to the father-daughter conduct book and its offshoots a "competency" that is *social* rather than literary. The equipment required to "read" this didactic literature is not the apparatus of literary interpretation, but the apparatus of social reception and incorporation. Though in comparison to interpretation, reception seems to be a passive kind of reading, in actuality the two are both forms of active reading: one searches out meaning based on linguistic and literary training, and the other endows the readily available didactic (overt) meaning with a second (covert) level of complementary, yet individual or pathetic (i.e., audience generated), meaning.

By drawing on the virutally homogenous background of female social conditioning, and relying on the Aristotelian principle of the complementarity of ethos and pathos, the *Tatler* established within a single framework multiple contexts for addressing women. The superposition of Bickerstaff's various rhetorical modes (confidentiality, gallantry, and paternalism, to name the major three) allowed Steele to manipulate several primary categories of male-female interaction which, in his paper and in his society, were thoroughly interconnected. (The father, for instance, influences all of these categories, as the very embodiment of patriarchy.) Underlying the conscious rhetoric of Steele's reformist program, the social and historical determinants brought into play through the paternal voice create a covert rhetorical effect activated in the very process of reading. And that rhetoric carries a message of female subordination in a patriarchal culture.

Thus, Steele's address to women readers contains a double-edged significance. Behind the mock flattery of the paper's title lies a serious interest in women's concerns: "fair-sexing it," for Steele, represented a positive engagement in reformist issues such as the education of women, the need to provide female readers "instruction as well as entertainment" (a formula that Steele took seriously). And in his often-proclaimed dependence on his female readers, Steele joined an increasingly large group of his contemporaries who recognized the significance of women to literary culture—as a power within the marketplace. From this legitimization of women as readers it is only a small historical step to the legitimization of women as writers, as the emergence of published female novelists (and poets and translators) later in the century so powerfully demonstrates. On the other hand, the rhetorical impact of the *Tatler* was, in both its overt declarations and its covert effects, decidedly conservative, reinforcing the values of female subordination to patriarchal social structures, within the family and without. And at the same time that the history of the eighteenth century demonstrates increased female participation in literary culture on all levels, it also demonstrates the use of literature to maintain a restrictive status quo, of which the evolution into reactionary conservatism of the eighteenth-century "ladies' magazine" stands as one eloquent example. The *Tatler,* wielding its conscious and unconscious, overt and covert—and, according to contemporary accounts, highly effective—rhetorical strategies, provided a major impetus to both developments.

Notes

1. Ian Watt, *The Rise of the Novel* (Berkeley and Los Angeles: University of California Press, 1957), p. 50.

2. Rae Blanchard, "Richard Steele and the Status of Women," *Studies in Philology* 26 (1929): 329–55, esp. pp. 332–35.

3. I adopt these terms, which are simplified, because I want to clarify terminology and avoid confusion with other reader-response usages which would arise from the use of similar terms, like *primary/secondary* or *ethic/pathetic.* A distinction between *intended* and *implied* (in which the intended audience is the consciously designated authorial audience and the implied audience that embedded within the text) might be most appropriate, but the confusion already surrounding the use of these complicated terms would undoubtedly interfere with such an application of them. So I reserve the terms *overt* and *covert,* and I speak of the *intended* audience as that audience both overtly designated by the author and covertly affected by the rhetoric buried in the text.

4. I define the *intended audience* in a way similar to Wolfgang Iser's *implied audience:* the intended audience consists of the background and attitudes which the text demands of its readers in order to "read" (i.e., properly understand) it. When Bickerstaff adopts a voice, the text intends an audience appropriately responsive to that voice. (Presumably, different subaudiences could respond in different "appropriate" ways.) Wolfgang Iser, *The Act of Reading: A Theory of Aesthetic Response* (Baltimore: Johns Hopkins University Press, 1978).

W. Daniel Wilson (Readers in Texts," *PMLA* 96 [1981]: 852) comments on the similarities between the implied reader and the intended reader: "The implied reader differs from the intended reader only in name and to the degree that one attempts to push the author out of the picture." I do not wish to push the author out of the picture, so I reserve the term *intended reader.* Steele intended to address various components of his audience specifically; the point at which the question of intentionality becomes negligible is in the "deep structure," in a sense, of the audience's response. The audience is still the same as the one intended by Steele, but the deep response goes beyond that obviously solicited by the author (though it does not contradict it).

5. In addition to the work of Iser and Wilson, my discussion is indebted to the work of Stanley Fish on "the reading community" (see especially "Interpreting the Variorum," in *Reader-Response Criticism: From Formalism to Post-Structuralism,* ed. Jane P. Tompkins [Baltimore: Johns Hopkins University Press, 1980], pp. 164–84).

6. Richmond P. Bond, *The Tatler: The Making of a Literary Journal* (Cambridge: Cambridge University Press, 1971), p. 82.

7. John E. Mason, *Gentlefolk in the Making: Studies in the History of English Courtesy Literature and Related Topics from 1531 to 1774* (Philadelphia: University of Pennsylvania Press, 1935), p. 5.

8. I take this term from Wilson ("Readers in Texts," p. 848), who uses it to define a fictive reader. Although Elizabeth was a "real" reader, her presence in the text itself is literary or fictive, not "real."

9. George Savile, (Lord Halifax), *The Lady's New-Year's Gift: Or, Advice to a Daughter* (1688), in *The Complete Works of George Savile, First Marquess of Halifax*, ed. Walter Raleigh (Oxford: Clarendon, 1912), pp. 1–2.

10. Ibid., p. 19.

11. Bond, *The Tatler*, p. 172.

12. All quotations from the *Tatler* are taken from the edition by George Aitken (1898; reprint, New York: George Olms Verlag, 1970).

13. Although I am focusing here on female readers as the primary audience (the direct recipients of the text's didactic intention) which responds to Jenny's example, this conduct book interaction does not exclude male readers: in fact, it addresses them. Isaac Bickerstaff, as the paternal figure (and in his other female-oriented roles as the gallant or the confidant), provides a model of appropriate male behavior in various domestic or social situations involving women. The presence of intended male readers can in fact serve as a reinforcement or an intensification of the instruction to female readers by supplying the text with the tacit presence of other, corroborating, male figures who stand behind the voice of Isaac Bickerstaff. Thus the specific address to women-as-daughters does not dilute the *Tatler*'s readership but brings it together in a kind of "common cause."

14. Savile, *Advice to a Daughter*, p. 40.

15. Ibid., p. 42.

16. Cf. Carol Duncan, "Happy Mothers and Other New Ideas in French Art," *Art Bulletin* 55 (1973): 570–83, and Lawrence Stone, *The Family, Sex, and Marriage in England, 1500–1800* (London: Weidenfeld and Nicolson, 1977), p. 225.

Chapter 6
Malraux's Women: A Re-vision
Susan Rubin Suleiman

> Re-vision—the act of looking
> back, of seeing with fresh eyes, of
> entering an old text from a new
> critical direction.
>
> Adrienne Rich

The thought that it might be time to take another look at Malraux's novels first occurred to me a few years ago, while I was reading the passionate, angry pages that Annie Leclerc devoted to him in *Parole de femme.* "L'emphatique Malraux," she calls him—the repetitive proponent of conventional values, and first and foremost of the value of the hero: "Le héroes; c'est moi-je, le plus longtemps possible. *Ma* marque, *ma* mainmise, *ma* possession éternisée" ["The hero; it's me-me-me, for as long as possible. *My* mark, *my* takeover, *my* possession for eternity"]. Grandiose and ridiculous, ever the posturing male, Malraux's hero deserves all the scorn that a woman's word can heap on him.[1]

Leclerc exaggerates, of course; hers is not a critique but an attack, not a reading but a caricature. She bases her indictment on a few well-known quotations from *La Voie royale,* makes no distinction between Malraux and his character Perken, ignores the other novels, does away with ambiguities and contradictions. Malraux doesn't interest her; she merely uses him to make a point, then passes on.

And yet, her few acerb words prompted me to think once again, in a way I had not thought before, about Malraux's novels and their contemporary significance. I had first read the novels in graduate school, at Harvard in the early sixties. After finishing each one, I would read the corresponding chapter in Frohock's *André Malraux and the Tragic Imagination*—an excellent book, I thought then, and still do. Years later, I reread *L'Espoir* with some care, and wrote about it (in my book *Authoritarian Fictions*); but it was in a context that did not oblige me to rethink, only to expand and refine, my earlier reading. Malraux was, for me, a familiar and admired writer, exemplary in his concern for questions of the broadest human significance. Although the 1930s had receded into history, and Malraux himself had undergone a metamorphosis (perhaps more than one) since those impassioned days, his novels remained for me, like those of Sartre, Camus, and a few others, representative of a kind of fiction—serious, urgent, eloquent—which I regarded with what might be called historical nostalgia: they were not repeatable today, but they were definitely worth saving.

Now along came Annie Leclerc, telling me that he is not worth saving—not by, or for, women, in any case. And that made me pause. I, after all, had changed since the days in Widener Library when I reflected with a certain exaltation over the bitter defeat of Garine or Perken, the tragic victory-despite-defeat of Kyo and Katow, or the hard-won education of Manuel. Could it be that they, too, had changed over the years, or taken on a different meaning? I remembered the powerful conclusion of Frohock's chapter on *La Condition humaine:* "From their destinies [Clappique's, Ferral's, and Gisors'] we know the power of the Absurd. But at the same time we have also seen Katow go out to die, and we know that there inheres in man's fate, in spite of all the possibilities of defeat, the possibility of the power and glory of being a man."[2] Might I find, after so many years, that when Malraux speaks of the problematic glory of man's fate, he is not speaking to me? Might I discover, in his novels, what Judith Fetterley sees in the whole expanse of American fiction by male writers: "In such fictions the female reader is co-opted into participation in an experience from which she is explicitly excluded; she is asked to identify with a selfhood that defines itself in opposition to her; she is required to identify against herself"?[3]

Clearly, a re-reading—or, rather, a re-vision as Adrienne Rich defines it: rereading from a new critical perspective—was in order. A feminist perspective? Yes, to the extent that the whole enterprise was provoked by my reading of contemporary feminist writers and critics, and that its underlying question could not have been formulated outside a feminist problematic. At the same time, I was, and am, extremely wary of the temptation that besets any critic with a strong ideological allegiance: to transform commentary into polemics, and to start a critical investigation from foregone conclusions. I therefore decided to proceed as gingerly, and with as much "verifiability," as possible: rather than attacking head-on the question of Malraux's heroes, about whom in any case a great deal has been written, I would look instead at Malraux's . . . heroines? No, his women. Who are they? Where are they? What do they do? Who speaks to them, to whom do they speak? And what difference does it make?

The Name and Its Absence

My first observation brought with it a shock of discovery: in Malraux's six novels, with their total cast of hundreds of characters, only five women are named. Of these, two have only a first name and are evoked fleetingly: Perken, in *La Voie royale,* talks to Claude Vannec about the woman he once lived with, whose name was Sarah; Vincent Berger, in *Les Noyers de l'Altenburg,* had a servant named Jeanne. That leaves three women who have full names and who appear as more than mere evocations: May Gisors, Valérie Serge, Anna Kassner. I shall talk about them later.

And the others—those who appear without a name? The list is short enough to be mentioned in its entirety. In *Les Conquérants* (1928), the Genoese merchant Rebecci, mentor of the Chinese terrorist Hong, is married to "une indigène assez belle, devenue grasse" ["a quite beautiful native woman, gone to fat"]; she is later referred to, in a description by the first-person narrator, as "une grasse Chinoise" ["a fat Chinese woman"], and by another character as "sa [i.e., Rebecci's] Chinoise." The German revolutionary Klein, who is killed by the terrorists, has been living in Canton with "une Blanche" ["a white woman"]; when she comes to mourn over his mutilated body, she is referred to as "une femme," then "elle;" Garine and the narrator, who are present, do not speak to her. The dead wife of Nicolaieff, the Russian czarist agent turned revolutionary, is evoked: "terroriste sincère et respectée, qui mourut de facon singulière" ["a sincere and respected terrorist, whose death was a strange story"]. At one point, the narrator enters Garine's room and finds him buttoning his tunic while two naked women are lying on his bed: "deux jeunes Chinoises," "les femmes."

In *La Voie royale* (1930), Claude Vannec's mother and grandmother are evoked by the impersonal narrator; they are designated respectively as "sa mère" and "sa femme" (the grandfather's, old Vannec's, wife). There is also the evocation of Claude's and Perken's first meeting in a brothel in Djibouti, where Claude saw Perken "sous le bras tendu d'une grande négresse drapée de rouge et de noir" ["beneath the outstretched arm of a big Negro woman draped in red and black"]. Toward the end of the novel, Perken has two Laotian prostitutes brought for him and Claude: they are "deux femmes," "la petite" and "l'autre," who then becomes "elle"—she is the one Perken sleeps with. And all along, collectively, there are "les femmes"—the women who obsess Perken's memory and imagination, those in the Moi tribes, those whom his friend Grabot has himself flagellated by . . .

In *La Condition humaine* (1933), there is Hemmelrich's wife: "sa Chinoise" (as seen by Hemmelrich), who gets blown to bits by a grenade; there is an evocation of Katow's dead wife: "une petite ouvrière qui l'aimait" ["a little working girl who loved him"], "cette vague idiote" ["that vague idiot"]. The Japanese painter Kama talks about his wife and daughter, for love of whom he says he paints. Ferral, to vent his frustration after being bested by Valérie, picks up a Chinese courtesan whom he humiliates by treating her as a simple prostitute: "une courtisane chinoise," "une fille au visage gracieux et doux" ["a girl with a sweet, lovely face"], "cette Chinoise." Gisors at one point remembers his dead wife: "une Japonaise;" and there are the various women Clappique talks to: "la Philippine," "la Russe," "une solide servante blonde, libérée."

In *Le Temps du mépris* (1935), there is the old woman who speaks at an anti-Nazi demonstration about her dead son, killed by the Nazis: "une vieille silhouette maladroitement penchée sur le micro: chapeau de série, manteau noir" ["an old silhouette awkwardly bent over the microphone: mass-produced hat, black coat"]. In *L'Espoir,* there is a young *milicienne* who brings food to the men fighting with Barca and Manuel; a nurse in a military hospital; a woman hostage who escapes from the Alcazar in Toledo and gives information to the Republican Lopez; a woman who during the bombardment of Madrid asks Guernico and Garcia for advice about whether to stay or leave. Toward the end, Manuel speaks to Ximenez about a woman he had once loved passionately to no avail, and with whom he had slept the previous week with total indifference.

In *Les Noyers de l'Altenburg* (1943), a woman throws bread to the French prisoners at Chartres; Vincent Berger admires the women on the street in Marseilles after he returns from a six-year stay in the Middle East; the soldiers in young Berger's regiment show photographs of their wives or girlfriends: Leonard tells about the time he slept with an *étoile* at the Casino de Paris; Pradé talks to Berger about his son, who needs him to help him with schoolwork, and he also talks about his wife: "La femme, qu'est-ce qu'elle peut faire? C'est une fille de famille nombreuse. Elle n'est pas fine" ["The wife, what can she do? She's a girl from a large family. She's not intelligent"]. And there is the old peasant woman at the end, in whom Berger sees a symbol of humanity's eternal endurance.

Putting aside for the moment the three fully named women who appear in *La Condition humaine* and *Le Temps du mépris,* and allowing for a few unnamed ones that I may have missed, the above gallery constitutes just about the entire cast of female characters in Malraux's fictional universe. But *characters,* of course, is not the right word: taking up Roland Barthes's distinction in *S/Z,* we can call them, at most, *figures.* In order to have a character, Barthes remarks, there must be a proper name; it is the name that unites a series of dispersed traits, or semes, into a stable configuration, a character with a personality and a biography—and only a character, hence someone with a name, can be the "object of a destiny."[4] A figure is a different thing altogether: "It is not a combination of semes concentrated in a legal Name, nor can biography, psychology or time encompass it: it is a nonlegal, impersonal, nontemporal configuration of symbolic relationships."[5] Presumably, a named character can also function as a figure, "an impersonal network of symbols";[6] but a figure cannot become a character—not without a name.

If we call the women enumerated above figures, we must ask what they are figures of: What do they symbolize? Wives, prostitutes, mothers, providers of food or care, they are the eternal feminine as pictured by the male imagination. A chinese woman, a Japanese woman, a white woman, a woman: like the hat of the old mother at the demonstration, they are one in a series, interchangeable and anonymous. Shadowy presences or fleeting evocations, they exist as extensions of, in relation to, seen or imagined by, men who possess a name as well as a past and a future. We are given Rebecci's entire biography, but all we know of his *Chinoise* is that she was once beautiful and is now fat; Nicolaieff's life story is before us, but about his wife we know that she was a terrorist whose death was a "strange story." We know Gisors intimately; of his wife, we know only that she was not, like May, "à demi-virile," but she made possible for Gisors a love that was tender, serene, and sweet. Above all, we know that she is dead: there are a great many dead or absent wives in these novels, very few who are *there*. I would contend that their absence is not explicable only by the fact that Malraux wrote chiefly about war and revolution, two activities in which the presence of women is rare. That would certainly not account for the considerable number of dead wives and mothers, or for the apparently nonexistent ones, like Vincent Berger's wife (young Berger's mother) in *Les Noyers de l'Altenburg,* who is never mentioned. Whereas the father-son (or its variant, grandfather-grandson) relation is privileged in almost every novel—Claude and his grandfather in *La Voie royale,* Kyo and Gisors in *La Condition humaine,* Jaime Alvear and his father in *L'Espoir,* the three generations of Bergers in *Les Noyers,* not to mention the large number of "spiritual father–spiritual son" relations ranging from Rebecci-Hong or Gisors-Tchen to Ximenez-Manuel—Malraux's heroes seem to have experienced no affective ties at all to their mothers. The absence of women in their emotional lives is, thus, attributable to more than the mere circumstantial *données* of the fictions.[7]

Of the unnamed women who are present in the novels, it may be accurate to say that they are not so much figures as *figurantes:* they are "extras" on a stage where men are the objects of destiny.

Silence

The chief characteristic of a *figurant* is silence. Malraux's men are inveterate talkers, but they rarely address a word to a woman. Talking to a
woman would, of course, be difficult, because there are so few of them
around. But there is something else at stake here, too, a kind of fundamental incompatibility between what a man has to say and what a
woman can understand or cares about. "Avoir un coeur d'homme et ne
pas s'apercevoir qu'on explique cela à une femme qui s'en fout, c'est très
normal" ["To have a man's heart and not to notice that one is explaining
that to a woman who doesn't give a damn is quite normal"], says
Garine.[8] After sleeping with his "deux jeunes Chinoises," Garine but-
tons his officer's tunic and gives instructions to his *boy* to show them out
and pay them. He then tells the narrator: "Lorsqu' on est ici un certain
temps, les Chinoises énervent beaucoup, tu verras. Alors, pour s'oc-
cuper en paix de choses sérieuses, le mieux est de coucher avec elles et
de n'y plus penser" ["After you've been here for a while, the Chinese
women get on your nerves a lot, you'll see. The best thing is to sleep with
them and forget about it, so you can keep your mind on serious things"]
(*C*, p. 138). Oriental prostitutes are not people one talks to, especially if
one is a Garine or a Perken. But Garine doesn't talk to Klein's "white
woman," either: he watches her embrace Klein's mutilated body, then
tells the Chinese attendant: "Quand elle sera partie, tu les recouvriras
tous" ["When she's gone, you cover them all"] (*C*, p. 192). About Chen,
May says: "Je ne l'ai pas connu: il ne supportait pas les femmes" ["I
didn't really know him: he couldn't stand women"] (*CH,* p. 334). We
know, however, that Chen frequented prostitutes; what he evidently
could not stand was the *company* of women.

Quite a lot has been written about the eroticism of Malraux's "adventurer" or terrorist heroes: Garine, Perken, Ferral, Tchen. Eroticism is,
as the eroticists themselves explain it, first of all a need to dominate the
other, to use the other as a means of gaining possession of one's self.
Thus Ferral: "Son plaisir jaillissait de ce qu'il se mît à la place de l'autre,
c'était clair; de l'autre contrainte: contrainte par lui. En somme il ne
couchait jamais qu'avec lui-même, mais il ne pouvait y parvenir qu'à la
condition de ne pas être seul" ["He derived his pleasure from putting
himself in the place of the other, that was clear; of the other, compelled:
compelled by him. In reality he never went to bed with anyone but
himself, but he could do this only if he were not alone"] (*CH,* p. 232).
The woman in such a situation is obviously there to be negated, and she
must be silent. It is true, as Lucien Goldmann and others have noted,
that Malraux—or, if one prefers, the implied author of *La Condition*

humaine—does not endorse eroticism as a positive value;[9] it is clear in the novel that Ferral's drive to dominate women is merely the sexual side of a more general drive to impose his will on others, just as Perken's eroticism was the sexual counterpart of his desire to "leave a scar on the map." Significantly, in both instances the adventurer's project ends in failure.

The adventurer's scorn of women, his refusal to talk to them or allow them to speak—in other words, to consider them as fully human beings—is, thus, not attributable to the author of *La Condition humaine;* indeed, one can cite Valérie's letter to Ferral, in which she proclaims her refusal to be "only a body," as proof to the contrary. What seems to me more significant, however, is that even Malraux's revolutionaries, the men of goodwill like Kyo, Katow, Hemmelrich, Kassner, Garcia, or Manuel, find it extremely difficult to communicate with women. Leaving Kyo and Kassner aside for the moment, since theirs are the most fully developed relations with women (I discuss them in the next section), let us look at a few others.

Garcia and Guernico, walking on the street during the bombardment of Madrid, are stopped by a woman who tugs at Guernico's sleeve and asks whether he thinks she should leave the city. The dynamics of the brief scene that ensues are interesting enough to warrant reproducing it in full:

> Une femme prit le bras de Guernico et dit en francais:
> —Tu crois qu'il faut partir?
> —C'est une camarade allemande, dit Guernico à Garcia, sans répondre a la femme.
> —Il dit que je dois partir, reprit celle-ci. Il dit qu'il ne peut pas se battre bien si je suis là.
> —Il a sûrement raison, dit Garcia.
> —Mais moi je ne peux pas vivre si je sais qu'il se bat ici . . . si je ne sais même pas ce qui se passe . . .
> L'*Internationale* d'un second accordéon accompagnait les mots en sourdine; un autre aveugle, sa sébile devant lui, continuait la musique, là où le premier l'avait abandonnée.
> Toutes les mêmes, pensa Garcia. Si elle part, elle le supportera avec beaucoup d'agitation, mais elle le supportera; et si elle reste, il sera tué.
> —Pourquoi veux-tu rester? demanda amicalement Guernico.
> —Ca m'est égal de mourir. . . . Le malheur c'est qu'il faut que je me nourrisse bien et qu'ici on ne pourra plus; je suis enceinte . . .
> Garcia n'entendit pas la réponse de Guernico. La femme rejoignit un autre courant d'ombres. (*E,* 303)

A woman plucked Guernico's sleeve and addressed him in French. "Do you think I ought to leave?"

"She's a German comrade," Guernico explained to Garcia, but did not 'answer her.

"He says I ought to go," the woman went on. "He says he can't fight properly when I'm around."

"He is surely right," Garcia said.

"But I can't go on living if I know he's fighting here . . . if I don't even know what's happening . . ."

Another accordion playing the *International* droned an accompaniment to the words; a second blind man, begging-bowl on lap, was carrying on the tune from the point where the first had dropped it.

They're all alike, these women, Garcia thought to himself. If she goes, she'll take it hard at first, but she'll see it through; whereas, if she stays, he'll be killed. He could not see her face; she was much shorter than he and her face was screened by shadows of the passers-by.

"Why do you want to stay?" Guernico's voice was gentle.

"I don't mind dying. . . . The trouble is, I've got to eat well, and now that won't be possible. I'm pregnant. . ."

Garcia did not hear Guernico's reply. The woman drifted away on another stream of shadows.

Concentrating on the exchange between the woman and the two men, we note the following: she asks Guernico a question, to which he does not reply, turning instead to Garcia to explain who she is. The woman rephrases her question, and this time Garcia replies curtly that her husband is surely right (in asking her to leave). She responds by talking about her feelings, allowing her voice to trail off at the end of the sentence. Garcia's attention turns to the sound of the accordion in the background; then he thinks *to himself* that "They're all alike, these women," and that she might end up causing her husband's death. He does not tell her his thoughts, however; he clearly is scornful of her "typically feminine" ("they're all alike") lack of good sense, and, indeed, he does not address a word to her again. Guernico's question to her elicits a reply that shows courage (she is not afraid to die), but that also reinforces the impression that she is vacillating (note all the points of suspension), and that she lacks good sense: since she is pregnant, the answer to her own question should be evident. Garcia is no longer interested, however, and he doesn't even hear Guernico's rejoinder. After the woman disappears into the shadows, the two men resume their conversation, which is long and philosophical.

This is a minor incident in a lengthy novel, but it is not insignificant. It is one of the very rare scenes in *L'Espoir* where a woman speaks, or, what is even rarer, where a woman speaks to express her feelings. True, Garcia's indifference may not be due only to the fact that she is a woman—she is, after all, a total stranger, and he has many things on his mind—but there is no mistaking the scornful tone of the phrase "Toutes les mêmes," which explicitly marks her sexual difference. What is even more important, this difference represents, in his eyes, a potential threat of death for her husband: women can be dangerous; in any case, they hamper the serious activities of men.

In *La Condition humaine,* besides Kyo there are two other revolutionaries who either are or have been married: Hemmelrich and Katow. Hemmelrich lives with a Chinese woman and has a child by her; the child is seriously ill. After a first attempt to bomb Chang-Kai Shek's car, Tchen and his two friends seek shelter in Hemmelrich's store. He refuses to let them stay, fearing that if the police find them there with their bombs, they will kill the woman and the child. After the three leave, Hemmelrich goes upstairs to the bedroom where the sick child is, hating himself meanwhile for having let down his comrades: "Sa Chinoise était assise, le regard fixé sur le lit et ne se détourna pas" ["His Chinese woman was sitting, her eyes fixed on the bed; she did not turn around"] (*CH,* p. 179). Hemmelrich does not speak to her; he speaks to the child, then goes downstairs again. He thinks, with increasing fury and frustration, about the misery of his life, present and past. The only thing that keeps him from going out and joining the terrorists is the thought that his wife and child depend on him. A little later, Katow arrives, and Hemmelrich confides his sense of guilt and also his anger to him; his wretched life is somehow summed up by his wife, in whom he sees a poor humiliated creature like himself:

—Du dévouement, oui. Et tout ce qu'elle peut. Le reste, ce qu'elle n'a pas, elle, justement, c'est pour les riches. Quand je vois des gens qui ont l'air de s'aimer, j'ai envie de leur casser la gueule. (*CH,* p. 207)

"Devotion, yes. And everything she can. The rest—what she hasn't got—is all for the rich. When I see people who look as if they're in love, I feel like smashing them in the face."

Katow, who for reasons of his own understands only too well how Hemmelrich is feeling, tries to reassure him:

—. . . Si on ne croit à rien, *surtout* parce qu'on ne croit à rien, on est obligé de croire aux qualités du coeur quand on les rencontre, ça va de soil. Et c'est ce que tu fais. Sans la femme et le gosse tu serais parti, j'en suis sûr. Alors?
—Et comme on n'existe que pour ces qualités cardiaques, elles vous boulottent. Puisqu'il faut toujours être bouffé, autant elles . . . (*CH,* pp. 208–9)

". . . If you believe in nothing, *especially* because you believe in nothing, you're forced to believe in the virtues of the heart when you come across them, no doubt about it. And that's what you're doing. If it hadn't been for the woman and the kid you would have gone, I know you would. Well then?"

"And as we live only for those virtues of the heart, they gobble you up. Well, if you've always got to be eaten it might as well be them . . ."

It is not clear whether the "elles" in Hemmelrich's reply refers to "qualités cardiaques" or to women like his wife—devoted, alien, and mute—who are the immediate subject of the conversation. But it hardly matters, since the "qualités cardiaques" belong to those women. Hemmelrich is saying that he is tied down by his wife (or, rather, that he is "eaten up," and the choice of that image is not insignificant),[10] that he accepts his situation but is not happy about it. Katow, in the meantime, thinks but does not dare to say out loud: "La mort va te délivrer" ["Death will free you"] (*CH, p. 209). Hemmelrich is in fact "freed" shortly afterward, when the woman and the child are killed by a grenade attack on the store. He then throws himself into the battle:

Les épaules en avant, il avançait comme un haleur vers un pays confus dont il savait seulement qu'on y tuait, tirant des épaules et du cerveau le poids de tous ses morts qui, *enfin! ne l'empêchait plus d'avancer. (CH, p. 255; my emphasis)

His shoulders thrust forward, he pushed ahead like a tugboat towards a dim country of which he knew only that one killed there, pulling with his shoulders and his brain the weight of all his dead who, *at last! no longer prevented him from advancing.*

Later he escapes to the Soviet Union, where he finds happiness working in an electric plant.

As for Katow, he understands Hemmelrich's problem because he has experienced a similar one. He, too, was married once:

Revenu de Sibérie sans espoir, battu, ses études brisées, devenu ouvrier d'usine et assuré qu' ill mourrait avant de voir la révolution, il s'était tristement prouvé un reste d'existence en faisant souffrir une petite ouvrière qui l'aimait. Mais à peine avait-elle accepté les douleurs qu'il lui infligeait que, pris par ce qu'a de bouleversant la tendresse de l'être qui souffre pour celui qui le fait souffrir, il n'avait plus vécu que pour elle, continuant par habitude l'action révolutionnaire, mais y emportant l'obsession de la tendresse sans limites cachée au coeur de cette vague idiote: des heures il lui caressait les cheveux, et ils couchaient ensemble toute la journée. Elle était morte, et depuis . . . (*CH, pp. 209–10)

Having returned from Siberia without hope, beaten, his medical studies shattered, and having become a factory worker, convinced that he would die before seeing the Revolution, he had sadly proved to himself that he still possessed a remnant of life by treating a little working-girl who loved him with deliberate brutality. But hardly had she become resigned to the pains he inflicted on her than he had been suddenly overwhelmed by the tenderness of a creature who could share his suffering even as he made her suffer. From that moment he had lived only for her, continuing his revolutionary activity through habit, but carrying into it the obsession of the limitless tenderness hidden in the heart of that vague idiot: for hours he would caress her hair, and they would lie in bed together for days on end. She had died, and since then . . .

Katow will find his apotheosis in the gesture of self-sacrifice which links him to the two men for whom he gives up his cyanide pill and consents to be burned alive. For him as for Hemmelrich, it is the revolution that provides dignity and genuine communion with others— and those others are men, generically opposed to the "vague idiote" with whom he once spent his days. This opposition is, curiously, echoed and reinforced by one of Kassner's internal monologues while he is in the Nazi prison. Remembering his martyred comrades in China, Russia, and Germany, Kassner exclaims: "Vous, mes compagnons, . . . c'est ce qu'il y a entre nous que j'appelle amour" ["You, my companions, it is what exists between us that I call love"] (*TM,* p. 107).

Katow and Hemmelrich both choose (if that is the right word) women who are below them socially and intellectually, and whose death signifies liberation and the possibility of self-fulfillment for the revolutionary hero. Their humiliated companions bear at least some resemblance to the wordless prostitutes over whom Garine, Perken, and Ferral assert their manhood. Although the revolutionary is not an eroticist, his relations with women are not altogether different from those of the adventurer. As an older "Clappique" told Malraux in a conversation in Singapore (reported in the *Antimémoires*), the first characteristic of the adventurer is that he is unmarried: "D'abord, un aventurier est célibataire!"[11] Unhampered by a woman, free to act—that seems also to be the ideal state toward which the revolutionary hero tends.

When the narrator of *Les Conquérants* first meets Nicolaieff, he makes a remark that I find extremely illuminating in this context: "Le gros homme s'exprime en français avec un très léger accent. Le ton de la voix—on dirait, malgré lea netteté des réponses, qu'il parle à une femme ou qu'il va ajouter: mon cher—, le calme du visage, l'onction de l'attitude font songer à un ancien prêtre" ["The fat man speaks French with a very slight accent. His tone of voice—despite his clipped answers, you'd think he was speaking to a woman, or was about to add 'My dear fellow'—, his calm face, the unctuousness of his manner, make one think of an ex-priest"] (*C,* pp. 96–97). What not only is implied here, but is taken for granted, is that when men speak to women, they do not speak as they do among themselves. The "unctuous" intonation of a man speaking to a woman is enough to feminize him, make him appear less masculine (an "ex-priest"). Not speaking to women, or speaking to them in a "special" way, these are but two aspects of a single phenomenon: the fundamental scorn that Malraux's heroes feel toward women, and their deep-seated fear of them.[12]

Three Women

Not for nothing was Malraux a brilliant writer, however. If on some level he and all his heroes shared in "la misogynie fondamentale de presque tous les hommes" ["the fundamental misogyny of almost all men"] (*CH*, p. 54), he seems to have had the necessary lucidity to realize it, and—like his creature Kyo—to be ashamed of it. We can read his treatment of Valérie Serge, May Gisors, and Anna Kassner as a compensatory gesture, a way of righting the balance, as it were. At the same time, their stories—or rather, their episodes, for they ultimately play a small part in the two novels in which they appear—repeat, in different modes, the dominant theme of separation, of an inalterable and un-bridgeable difference between the sexes; they also repeat, rather unexpectedly, the valorization of the masculine that we have already encountered elsewhere.

Valérie's is the mode of irony. In this woman, in whom Ferral senses "un orgueil semblable au sien" ["a pride akin to his own"] (*CH*, p. 117), the eroticist adventurer meets an adversary to his own measure. Valérie is beautiful, rich, articulate—a woman who earns her own way and speaks her mind. During a conversation in his bedroom, shortly before they make love, Ferral tells her that a woman must of necessity give herself, and a man must of necessity possess her; to which she replies: "Ne croyez-vous pas, cher, que les femmes ne se donnent jamais (ou presque) et que les hommes ne possèdent rien? . . . Ce que je vais dire est très mal, mais croyez-vous que ce n'est pas l'histoire du bouchon qui se croyait tellement plus important que la bouteille?" ["Hasn't it occurred to you, dear, that women never give themselves (or hardly ever) and that men possess nothing? . . . Listen, I'm going to say something very wicked—but don't you think it's the story all over again of the cork which considered itself so much more important than the bottle?"] (*CH*, p. 120). By insisting on leaving the light on while they make love, so that he can watch her face as she reaches orgasm, Ferral seeks to assert the superiority of the "cork" over the "bottle." Valérie then retaliates with the famous scene of the canaries, in which Ferral plays the role of *dindon de la farce* while she plays that of director; whereupon Ferral does her one better and transforms her hotel room into an enchanted forest full of tropical birds: "Il aurait offert par haine à Valérie son plus joli cadeau" ["Through hatred he would have offered Valérie his handsomest gift"] (*CH,* p. 223). But the aim of the gift is clear: "Il fallait avant tout que, si Valérie racontait l'histoire des cages—elle n'y manquerait pas—il suffît qu'il en racontât la fin pour échapper au ridicule" ["It was necessary above all that, if Valérie told the story of the cages—she would not fail to do so—he would only have to tell the end in order to escape ridicule"] (*CH,* pp. 220–21).

It is in this context of a somewhat bitter drawing-room comedy, where what matters above all is the protagonists' image in the *salons,* that Ferral—and the reader of *La Condition humaine*—reads Valérie's letter:

> Vous savez beaucoup de choses, cher, mais peut-être mourrez-vous sans vous être aperçu qu'une femme est *aussi* un être humain. J'ai toujours rencontré (peut-être ne rencontrerai—je jamais que ceux-là, mais tant pis, vous ne pouvez savoir combien je dis tant pis!) des hommes qui m'ont trouvé du charme, qui se sont donné un mal si touchant pour mettre en valeur mes folies, mais qui savaient si bien rejoindre leurs amis dès qu'il s'agissait de vraies choses humaines (sauf naturellement pour être consolés). (*CH,* p. 217)

> You know a good many things, dear, but you will probably die without its ever having occurred to you that a woman is *also* a human being. I have always met (perhaps I shall never meet any who are different, but so much the worse—you can't know how thoroughly I mean 'so much the worse'!) men who have credited me with a certain amount of charm, who have gone to touching lengths to set off my follies, but who have never failed to go straight to their men-friends whenever it was a question of something really human (except of course to be consoled).

Valérie, in her mocking way, seems to be pointing her finger here not only at Ferral, but at all of Malraux's heroes; wasn't it a hero, after all, who said that to keep one's mind on "serious things," the best thing is to "sleep with them and forget about it"? Isn't it true that not a single one of Malraux's heroes—not an adventurer, not a revolutionary, not Gisors the philosopher, not Alvear the art historian, not even Kyo or Kassner— ever talks to a woman about any of the "truly human things" that preoccupy them all so persistently, and about which they talk to each other with such urgency and eloquence?

At the same time, it is worth noting that by humiliating Ferral, Valérie adopts a quasi-masculine stance: she will certainly not "convert" him to her point of view, she merely asserts her own power in a struggle where both self-respect and public image are at stake. Her gesture is a declaration of war, with all the aggressiveness that such declarations imply. If we admire her, as we are surely meant to do, it is because she is a woman with "masculine" pride and self-assertiveness. For that very reason, however, it seems clear that she can never have any but an adversary relationship with men.

May and Anna are quite different; they are the only two women in Malraux's novels who have what might be called an egalitarian love relationship with a man. Goldmann devotes some lyrical pages to his celebration of the love between Kyo and May; theirs is, in his words, "one of the purest and most beautiful love stories to have been described in the important works of the twentieth century."[13] According to Goldmann, the love that Kyo and Kassner feel for their wives is the counterpart to their feeling of authentic revolutionary community with their fellow men. The love between man and woman, in other words, is the private aspect of the more generalized love that unites men in "la fraternité virile." This is an attractive interpretation, one that allows Goldmann to explain why adventurers (for example) are not able to love women; what it fails to take account of are the very precarious nature of the love relationship as it is actually experienced by the two men in question (we never know exactly what the emotions of the women are, since Malraux maintains a strict internal focalization on the men when they are together), and the possibly problematic rather than integrative relation that exists, in Malraux's novels, between heterosexual love and "virile fraternity."

The love between Kyo and May is placed at the outset under the sign of ambiguity—of at least two ambiguities, in fact. First, there is the ambiguity of May's appearance: "Son manteau de cuir bleu, d'une coupe presque militaire, accentuait ce qu'il y avait de viril dans sa marche et même dans son visage. . . . Le front très dégagé, lui aussi avait quelque chose de masculin, mais depuis qu'elle avait cessé de parler elle se féminisait" ["Her blue leather coat, of an almost military cut, accentuated what was virile in her gait and even in her face. . . . Her very high forehead as well had something masculine about it, but since she had stopped speaking she was becoming more feminine"] (CH, pp. 48–49). When May speaks, she appears to Kyo like a man (here we find a familiar paradigm—to be fully feminine, the woman must be silent); at the same time, it is her sensual mouth, with its full lips ("le léger gonflement de ses lèvres"), that most clearly marks her as a woman.

The other ambiguity is more complex: it has to do with Kyo's sense of closeness to her and at the same time with his feeling of total separation from her. The alternation of these two feelings defines Kyo's relationship to May (and hers to him? We cannot be sure), which may be one reason why Gisors, after Kyo's death, thinks of their love as an "amour intellectuel et ravagé" (CH, p. 333).

Kyo's greatest feeling of alienation from May comes, understandably enough, after she tells him that she has finally slept with one of her colleagues at the hospital where she is a doctor. Although their marriage is not based on sexual exclusiveness and although he knows that her act

Susan Rubin Suleiman

had no more than passing significance for her, he cannot help feeling angry and jealous. What is more important in our context, however, is his discovery, after her "confession," that May had begun to recede from him way before—that it was not her infidelity, but time and habit, which would eventually separate her from him. The passage in which this realization hits Kyo must be quoted almost in full in order for its impact to be felt (significantly, Goldmann does not include it in the extensive quotations from the novel he uses in his discussion of Kyo and May):

> Il continuait pourtant à la regarder, à découvrir qu'elle pouvait le faire souffrir, mais que depuis des mois, qu'il la regardât ou non, *il ne la voyait plus;* quelques expressions, parfois. . . . Cet amour souvent crispé qui les unissait comme un enfant malade, ce sens commun de leur vie et de leur mort, cette entente charnelle entre eux, *rien de tout cela n'existait en face de la fatalité qui décolore les formes dont nos regards sont saturés.* "L'aimerais-je moins que je ne crois?" pensa-t-il. Non. Même en ce moment, il était sûr que si elle mourait, il ne servirait plus sa cause avec espoir, mais avec désespoir, comme un mort lui-même. *Rien, pourtant, ne prévalait contre la décoloration de ce visage* enseveli au fond de leur vie commune comme dans la brume, comme dans la terre. Il se souvint d'un ami qui avait vu mourir l'intelligence de la femme qu'il aimait, paralysée pendant des mois; *il lui semblait voir mourir May ainsi, voir disparaître absurdement, comme un nuage qui se ré- sorbe dans le ciel gris, la forme de son bonheur. Comme si elle fût morte deux fois, du temps, et de ce qu'elle lui disait.* (CH, p. 51; my emphasis)

> He continued nevertheless to look at her, to discover that she could make him suffer. For months, whether he looked at her or not, *he had ceased to see her;* certain expressions, at times. . . . Their love, so often hurt, uniting them like a sick child, the common meaning of their life and their death, the carnal understanding between them, *nothing of all that existed before the fatality which discolors the forms with which our eyes are satuarated.* "Do I love her less than I think I do?" he thought. No. Even at this moment he was sure that if she were to die he would no longer serve his cause with hope, but with despair, as though he himself were dead. *Nothing, however, prevailed against the discoloration of that face* buried in the depth of their common life as in mist, as in the earth. He remembered a friend who had had to watch the disintegration of the mind of the woman he loved, paralyzed for months; *it seemed to him that he was watching May die thus, watching the form of his happiness absurdly disappear like a cloud absorbed by the gray sky. As though she had died twice—from the effect of time, and from what she was telling him.*

Kyo's alienation from May, in other words, is not the temporary alienation of a husband who is angry at his wife; it is a much more deeply anchored thing, against which even his love for her is no protection.

138

And it is a thing that *kills* her—not once, but twice. May is also, in a sense, a "dead wife." Finally, as if this weren't enough, Kyo realizes that something else separates her from him: not anger or hatred, not jealousy, not even the destructive power of time, but a feeling without a name that suddenly transforms her into something incomprehensible: "Ce corps reprenait le mystère poignant de l'être connu transformé tout à coup,—du muet, de l'aveugle, du fou. *Et c'était une femme. Pas une espèce d'homme. Autre chose . . . Elle lui échappait complètement*" ["This body was being invested with the poignant mystery of a familiar person suddenly transformed—the mystery one feels before a mute, blind, or mad being. *And she was a woman. Not a kind of man. Something else . . .* She was getting away from him completely"] (*CH,* p. 54; my emphasis).

The fundamental alienation between men and women is here orchestrated in a tragic mode. Kyo's reaction, when he realizes his separation from May, is to want to clasp her to him: "coucher avec elle, se réfugier là contre ce vertige dans lequel il la perdait tout entière; ils n'avaient pas à se connaître quand ils employaient toutes leurs forces à serrer leurs bras sur leurs corps" ["To lie with her, to find refuge in her body against this frenzy in which he was losing her entirely; they did not have to know each other when they were using all their strength to clasp their arms around their bodies"] (*CH,* p. 55). Sexual union would be a way of escaping from the awareness of a more irremediable separateness. This union is prevented, however, for at that point the bell rings and Clappique enters; Kyo then goes out, and it is only later, while walking with Katow, that he is able to rediscover (or perhaps to reason himself into believing?) his sense of closeness to May: "Depuis que sa mère était morte, May était le seul être pour qui il ne fût pas Kyo Gisors, mais la plus étroite complicité" ["Since his mother had died, May was the only being for whom he was not Kyo Gisors, but the most intimate complicity"] (*CH,* p. 57).

The same alternation between alienation and communion (where, paradoxically, May's presence provokes the former, her absence the latter) occurs in the only other scene that Kyo shares with May, shortly before he is arrested and killed. His refusal to allow her to go with him to the meeting is in one sense a revenge for her earlier infidelity, and they both understand it as such; at the same time, it is an attempt on his part to protect her. After she finally lets him leave, he realizes that their kind of closeness does not allow for either revenge or protectiveness, and he returns to get her: "Avant d'ouvrir, il s'arrêta, écrasé par la fraternité de la mort, découvrant combien, devant cette communion, la chair restait dérisoire malgré son emportement. Il comprenait maintenant qu'accepter d'entraîner l'être qu' on aime dans la mort est peut-être la forme totale de l'amour, celle qui ne peut pas être dépassé" ["Before opening the door, he stopped, overwhelmed by the brotherhood of death, discovering how insignificant the flesh appeared next to this communion, in spite of its urgent appeal. He understood now that the willingness to lead the being one loves into death itself is perhaps the complete expression of love, that which cannot be surpassed"] (*CH*, p. 204).

Paradoxically, the love Kyo feels for May can find its ultimate expression only in death. Could their love story be a revolutionary version of *Tristan et Iseult?* That might explain why Lucien Goldmann found it so powerful and pure; but as readers of Denis de Rougemont know, the source of Tristan's love is narcissism . . .

It seems to me significant that Kyo's final, "fraternal," communion with May is explicitly contrasted, by Kyo himself, with the "dérisoire" quality of merely carnal love. One critic has remarked that Kyo's and May's marriage is a fraternal, rather than a conjugal, union.[14] I think it more exact to say that Kyo's heterosexual desire (which is mentioned in both of the scenes he has with May) is constantly deflected or sublimated toward a "higher goal," this higher goal being that of the homophilic (even if not homosexual in the usual sense) communion of revolutionary *brother*hood: *la fraternité virile.*[15]

The same sublimation, I would argue, occurs in the Kassner-Anna marriage in *Le Temps du mépris.* The revolutionary activist Kassner, after being imprisoned by the Nazis and thought dead by his wife, returns home, to her and their child. The couple's reunion is extremely awkward: "Il savait qu'il devait la prendre dans ses bras en silence, . . . mais il ne s'accordait pas aux vieux gestes de la tendresse, et il n'en existe pas d'autres" ["He knew that he should take her in his arms in silence, . . . but he felt uncomfortable with the old gestures of affection, and there are no others"] (*TM*, p. 173). Kassner realizes how much she has suffered in his absence, and how much she will continue to suffer (for his return is temporary, and he will have to leave again to be killed sooner or later), but that very realization separates him from her: "Cette souffrance qui la collait contre lui, de tout le poids de ce regard qui se voulait d'accord, qui se voulait gai, cette souffrance qu'il lui causait, l'éloignait atrocement d'elle" ["This suffering which made her cling to him with eyes full of desire for congeniality, for gaiety—yes, this suffering which he was causing her separated him from her atrociously"] (*TM*, p. 174). As they talk and as she has a chance to express her sadness even while affirming that she accepts the life she has chosen, he begins to feel closer to her. They caress each other gently as they talk; then, Kassner has a sudden "epiphany" as he thinks about the meaning of his life and of his approaching death—he must go out with Anna, walk with her in the street. The novel ends as he is waiting for her near the door.

Here, as in *La Condition humaine,* the revolutionary hero, already marked by death, subordinates the heterosexual drive (if that is still the right word—Kassner, unlike Kyo, doesn't seem to feel any physical *desire* for his wife) to a more mystical communion with his fellow men. Although he apparently includes Anna in this communion, it is striking how often in this novel we encounter what James Greenlee has called the "redundantly masculine" expression of *fraternité virile.*[16] At the demonstration where he goes to look for Anna, Kassner hears an old woman tell the crowd about the imprisonment of her son; he sees a number of women in the crowd whom he mistakes for Anna. Yet, when at the end of the episode he must sum up for himself the meaning of this experience (Malraux has told us in the preface that this is a novel with only two characters, "le héros et son sens de la vie" ["the hero and his sense of life"]), his way of expressing it is characteristically unisex: "Aucune parole humaine n'était aussi profonde que la cruauté, mais la *fraternité virile* la rejoignait jusqu'au plus profond du sang, jusqu'aux lieux interdits du coeur où sont accroupies la torture et la mort" ["No human speech went so deeply as cruelty. But *virile fraternity* could cope with it, could follow cruelty to the very depths of blood, to the forbidden places of the heart where torture and death are lurking"] (*TM,* p. 165, my emphasis). Earlier, in his prison, Kassner had already stated (in a sentence I quoted earlier) that genuine love was what existed between him and his (male) comrades. After he is released, he looks at the pilot who is flying him to safety and feels a strong bond with him: "L'action commune liait les deux hommes à la façon d'une vieille et *dure* amitié" ["Their common action joined the two men like an old and *firm* friendship"] (*TM,* p. 131, my emphasis).

After this, and despite Kassner's love for his wife, there seems little doubt that the word *homme* and its derivatives (e.g., *humain*) are to be understood, in this novel (perhaps in all of Malraux's novels?), in a gender-specific sense. What this means as far as women—even beloved women—are concerned is, of course, problematic. At one point during the demonstration, Kassner looks at the crowd and finds in it an expression of "les passions et les vérités qui ne sont données qu'aux hommes assemblés" ["the passions and the truths which are given only to men gathered together"] (*TM,* p. 164). In his mind, the exaltation of his communion with "les hommes assemblés" becomes joined with his "femme invisible," who is hidden from him by the crowd. But it is significant that the process is later repeated in reverse, when Kassner's reunion with Anna expands to become joined with the crowds of the street: individual—specifically, sexual—union with the beloved woman is rejected, or at least deferred, in favor of "les hommes assemblés." It is almost as if, in order to participate in Kassner's love, Anna had to become a man.

May, in her appearance and actions, was already *à demi-virile;* Valérie, in whom Ferral recognizes a pride similar to his own, chooses the male arena of contest and one-upsmanship in which to assert herself. Without wishing to indulge in paradox, one might well advance the proposition that the only women *characters* in Malraux's fictional universe—the only women deserving of a name and of either hateful or loving recognition by men—are men in disguise.

Conclusion

The foregoing raises a number of questions, and first of all this one: what difference does it make? What is the usefulness of rereadings such as the one I have been practicing, given that they only confirm what might seem by now to be an all-too-familiar fact: the literature of adventure and heroism, whether in the past or in our own time, has been overwhelmingly male—written by men, about men, for men, embodying male fantasies and founded on the most enduring male fantasy of all: the fantasy of a world without women.[17] Is there really a point in demonstrating, as if no one had noticed (even if they didn't talk about it) that Malraux's novels are exclusively "masculine" fictions? Yes, there is. It is one thing to notice something and leave it unexpressed, or cover it up like a guilty secret; it is quite another to examine it and attempt to state its significance. The fact that (to my knowledge, at least) none of the hundreds of articles, books, special issues of journals and commemorative pieces devoted to Malraux since his death—not to mention the thousands that appeared while he was still alive—has seriously questioned, or sought to explore the implications of, the status of women in his works is indicative of a certain critical blindness.

Or perhaps it is merely a sign of critical timidity: one does not wish to expose one's self to ridicule or to accusations of belaboring the obvious tilting at straw men. One therefore keeps still, or talks about Malraux and tragedy, Malraux and history, Malraux and revolution, Malraux and art, Malraux and the human condition, and the metamorphosis of the gods. It took an openly polemical, patently one-sided attack by a woman who was not afraid of ridicule to shake me out of my own complacency.

The usefulness, indeed the necessity, of such shake-ups for and by women readers and critics has been emphasized by recent works of feminist criticism. Judith Fetterley has called on women to become "resisting readers" in order to counteract a tradition in which, "as readers and teachers and scholars, women are taught to think as men, to identify with a male point of view, and to accept as normal and legitimate a male system of values, one of whose central principles is misogyny."[18] And this theme was sounded more than ten years ago by Elaine Showalter, in an essay devoted specifically to the question of "Women and the Literary Curriculum": "Women are estranged from their own experience and unable to perceive its shape and authenticity . . . they are expected to identify as readers with a masculine experience and perspective, which is presented as the human one.[19] Whence the need not only for the study of literary works by women writers, which present a different perspective—and the influence of books like Showalter's *A Literature of Their Own,* or Gilbert and Gubar's *The Madwoman in the Attic,* which aim to map a hitherto unexplored feminine territory in the literary landscape, indicates that such study is now well under way[20]—but also for a reappraisal of the "masculine experience . . . which is presented as the human one."

Does this mean that from now on, every time I teach Malraux, I will insist only on the "macho" or antifeminine aspect of his work? Not at all. Shortly after I finished writing the bulk of this essay, I lectured to an advanced undergraduate literature class at Harvard on *La Condition humaine.* With only two lectures scheduled for this complex novel, I could hardly devote more than a few minutes to the question of women. The nods of recognition I saw among the women students in the class, and the almost grateful looks with which they greeted my remarks on the absence of the name and on the women's silence in Malraux's novels, showed me that this was not merely an academic question. For these students it was important that it *not* be passed over in silence, or with an offhand observation.

At the same time, I would not wish to see such questions, or such rereadings, become territorialized as an exclusively feminist—or feminine—concern. Rather than denouncing Malraux, or any antifeminine writer, as the enemy (which Fetterley tends to do), we can analyze him as a symptom; and today that kind of analysis is as urgent, as important, for men as it is for women. What is it, in our culture and history—some would even claim in our biology—that has obliged men to prove their masculinity always and only through the repeated affirmation that they are "not female?" Why is misogyny a transcultural and transhistorical phenomenon, apparently as universal as the incest taboo? Is the need to negate woman—which is always, in the last instance, the need to negate one's mother—a permanent feature of male psychology? Questions such as these, which are prompted by, but go far beyond, the rereading of writers like Malraux, are being raised today increasingly not only by women or feminists or students of literature, but also by anthropologists, sociologists, psychologists, and cultural historians, male and female, who seek to understand our past and the direction of our future. If it is true, as Walter J. Ong (who is not a feminist) recently wrote in the conclusion of an important and thought-provoking book that "The entire history of consciousness can be plotted in relation to the always ongoing male-female dialectic,"[21] then it behooves all of us to attend to that dialectic. What is at stake is not only our words, but our world.

Notes

1. Annie Leclerc, *Parole de femme* (Paris: Livre de poche, 1974), p. 27. Unless otherwise noted, all translations from the French are my own.

2. W. M. Frohock, *André Malraux and the Tragic Imagination* (Stanford: Stanford University Press, 1952), p. 89.

3. Judith Fetterley, *The Resisting Reader: A Feminist Approach to American Fiction* (Bloomington: Indiana University Press, 1978), p. xii.

4. Roland Barthes, *S/Z,* trans. Richard Miller (New York: Hill and Wang, 1974), p. 68. Barthes goes on to note that the exception to the rule about the necessity of the name is a first-person narrator who does not name himself but says *I:* "To say *I* is inevitably to attribute signifieds to oneself; further, it gives one a biographical duration, it enables one to undergo, in one's imagination, an intelligible 'evolution,' to signify oneself as the object of a destiny." By that token, the narrator of *Les Conquérants* qualifies as a character, even though we don't know his name.

5. Ibid. Here, as in the previous quotation, I have modified Miller's translation somewhat.

6. Ibid., p. 94.

7. Malraux's biographer, Jean Lacouture, has expressed surprise at the fact that there are so few mothers in Malraux's novels. He hints at a psychoanalytic explanation ("We touch here on one of the most obscure aspects of the life and ethics of André Malraux"), but unfortunately there is not much concrete information on which to base one. We know that Malraux's parents separated when he was four years old, and that he grew up with three women: his mother, his aunt, and his grandmother. His relation to his mother was certainly not close, and his childhood does not correspond to that of the "mother's favorite son," which Freud suggested was typical for men of great achievement. Malraux himself stated that, unlike most writers, he hated his childhood; Lacouture comments that "to repudiate one's childhood is almost tantamount to insulting one's mother." See Jean Lacouture, *André Malraux: Une vie dans le siècle* (Paris: Seuil, collection "Folio," 1975), p. 12 and pp. 132–33.

8. *Les Conquérants* (Paris: Grasset Livre de poche edition, 1966), p. 65. In what follows, page numbers of the novels are given in parentheses in the text, using the following abbreviations: *C: Les Conquérants,* Livre de poche edition;

CH: La Condition humaine (Paris: Gallimard "Folio edition 1981); *E: L'Espoir* (Paris: Gallimard Livre de poche edition, 1963); *TM: Le Temps du mépris* (Paris: Gallimard, 1935). English translations (occasionally modified by me) are from the following: *The Conquerors,* trans. Stephen Becker (New York: Holt, Rinehart and Winston, 1976); *Man's Fate,* trans. Haakon M. Chevalier (New York: Vintage Books, 1968); *Man's Hope,* trans. Stuart Gilbert and Alastair Macdonald (New York: Grove Press, 1979; *Days of Wrath,* trans. Haakon M. Chevalier (New York: Random House, 1936). Some English translations (e.g., *Man's Fate*) omit certain passages I have quoted, and they often "erase" the effect of the original—as in the case where Hemmelrich speaks of his wife "gobbling him up," which Chevalier translated simply as her "getting the better of" him. In order to avoid overburdening the text with numbers, I have given page references only to the French editions.

9. See Lucien Goldmann, "Introduction à une étude structurale des romans de Malraux," in *Pour une sociologie du roman* (Paris: Gallimard, collection "Idées," 1964), pp. 175–78). According to James Greenlee, Malraux gives an "indictment of eroticism" not only in the character of Ferral, but as early as *La Voie royale* (Greenlee, *Malraux's Heroes and History* [DeKalb: Northern Illinois University Press, 1975], p. 53). Goldmann, more correctly, to my mind, claims that in the first two novels "eroticism and domination constituted precarious but positive values," and that it was only starting with *La Condition humaine* that eroticism became a negative value.

10. The psychoanalyst Wolfgang Lederer has documented, in an important book, the nearly universal fantasy of women as devouring females, ready to eat men alive. See his *The Fear of Women* (New York: Grune and Stratton, 1968), esp. the chapter entitled "The Snapping of Teeth."

11. *Antimémoires* (Paris: Gallimard, 1967), p. 378.

12. Lederer, through his extensive study of myth and folklore in both primitive and advanced societies, shows that misogyny, or scorn for women, is practically synonymous with *fear* of them. Malraux himself has been accused of misogyny by his first wife, Clara Malraux (*Nos vingt ans* [Paris: Grasset, 1966], pp. 99–103). If she may be considered a less than friendly witness, one can turn to Josette Clotis, who was Malraux's devoted companion until her death, and the mother of his two sons. In her private papers from the 1930s, quoted in a recent book that speaks admiringly of her passionate attachment to Malraux, Clotis noted about his attitude toward her: "He wants her to be discreet, serene, tactful: wants her to face him with admiring eyes, silent mouth, the brain of a happy, innocent bird. He says, 'You've understood nothing,' sometimes almost tenderly, sometimes with his hard voice, which can be so mean" (Suzanne Chantal, *Le Coeur battant: Josette Clotis–André Malraux* [Paris: Grasset, 1976], pp. 154–55).

13. Goldmann, "Introduction à une étude structurale des romans de Malraux," p. 177.

14. Greenlee, *Malraux's Heroes and History,* p. 66.

15. In fact, Malraux does not use the expression *fraternité virile* in *La Condition humaine.* He does, however, use the adjective *viril* twice in a single paragraph which describes precisely Kyo's feeling of communion with his fellow

(male) prisoners moments before his death: "Ce lieu de râles était sans doute le plus lourd d'amour viril. . . . Comment, déjà regardé par la mort, ne pas entendre ce murmure de sacrifice humain qui lui criait que le coeur viril des hommes est un refuge à morts qui vaut bien l'esprit?" ["This place of agony was no doubt the most weighted with virile love. . . . Already stared at by death, how could he not hear that murmur of human sacrifice which cried out to him that the virile heart of man is at least as strong a refuge against death as the mind?"] (*CH,* p. 304).

16. Greenlee, *Malraux's Heroes and History,* p. 66. Jacques Lacan, in an early article, pointed out that the "moral connotations" of the term *virilité* are a good indication of the "prevalence of the male principle" in our culture (article on "Famille" in *Encyclopédie française,* 1948; quoted in Catherine Clément, *Vies et légendes de Jacques Lacan* [Paris: Grasset, 1981], p. 99).

17. The fantasy of a world without women, where men would exist in peaceful harmony among themselves, is at least as old as the myth of Pandora, which sees woman as the source of all discord and unhappiness. See Lederer, *Fear of Women,* chap. 10; Catherine Clément, referring to the anthropological studies of Lévi-Strauss and Pierre Clastres, has remarked that "They both tell us how powerful, in every culture, is the dream of a world without women, where one could live together—that is, among men; an asexual world of warriors." Clément goes on to note that "in a culture where the male principle is predominant, androgyny is not an equal share of man and woman. It is male ["Elle est homme"]. See *Vies et légendes de Jacques Lacan,* pp. 99–100.

18. Fetterley, *Resisting Reader,* p. xx.

19. Elaine Showalter, "Women and the Literary Curriculum," *College English* 32 (1971), quoted in Fetterley, *Resisting Reader,* p. xxi.

20. Elaine Showalter, *A Literature of Their Own: British Women Novelists from Brontë to Lessing* (Princeton: Princeton University Press, 1977); Sandra Gilbert and Susan Gubar, *The Madwoman in the Attic: The Woman Writer and the Nineteenth-Century Literary Imagination* (New Haven: Yale University Press, 1979). Since my own essay was written (Fall 1981), feminist criticism in America has grown by astonishing leaps and bounds, both in the study of women writers and in the study of the representation of women or of "the feminine" in the works of male writers. For a generous sampling, see Elizabeth Abel, ed., *Writing and Sexual Difference* (Chicago: University of Chicago Press, 1983).

21. Walter J. Ong, *Fighting for Life: Contest, Sexuality, and Consciousness* (Ithaca: Cornell University Press, 1981), p. 208.

Chapter 7
Reading about Reading:
"A Jury of Her Peers,"
"The Murders in the Rue Morgue,"
and "The Yellow Wallpaper"

Judith Fetterley

As a student of American literature, I have long been struck by the degree to which American texts are self-reflexive. Our "classics" are filled with scenes of readers and readings. In *The Scarlet Letter,* for example, a climactic moment occurs when Chillingworth rips open Dimmesdale's shirt and finally reads the text he has for so long been trying to locate. What he sees we never learn, but for him his "reading" is complete and satisfying. Or, to take another example, in "Daisy Miller," Winterbourne's misreading of Daisy provides the central drama of the text. Indeed, for James, reading is the dominant metaphor for life, and his art is designed to teach us how to read well so that we may live somewhere other than Geneva. Yet even a writer as different from James as Mark Twain must learn to read his river if he wants to become a master pilot. And, of course, in *Moby Dick,* Melville gives us a brilliant instance of reader-response theory in action in the doubloon scene.

When I first read Susan Glaspell's "A Jury of Her Peers" in Mary Anne Ferguson's *Images of Women in Literature* (Boston: Houghton Mifflin, 1973, pp. 370–85) I found it very American, for it, too, is a story about reading. The story interested me particularly, however, because the theory of reading proposed in it is explicitly linked to the issue of gender. "A Jury of Her Peers" tells of a woman who has killed her husband; the men on the case can not solve the mystery of the murder; the women who accompany them can. The reason for this striking display of masculine incompetence in an arena where men are assumed to be competent derives from the fact that the men in question can not imagine the story behind the case. They enter the situation bound by a set of powerful assumptions. Prime among these is the equation of textuality with masculine subject and masculine point of view. Thus, it is not simply that the men can not read the text that is placed before them. Rather, they literally can not recognize it as a text because they can not imagine that women have stories. This preconception is so powerful that, even though, in effect, they know Minnie Wright has killed her husband, they spend their time trying to discover their own story, the story they are familiar with, can recognize as a text, and know how to read. They go out to the barn; they check for evidence of violent entry from the outside; they think about guns. In their story, men, not women, are violent, and men use guns: "There was a gun in the house. He says that's what he can't understand." Though Mrs. Hale thinks the men are "kind of *sneaking* . . . coming out here to get her own house to turn against her," in fact she needn't worry, for these men wouldn't know a clue if they came upon it. Minnie Foster Wright's kitchen is not a text to them, and so they cannot read it.

It is no doubt in part to escape the charge of "sneaking" that the men have brought the women with them in the first place, the presence of women legitimating male entry and clearing it of any hint of violence or violation. But Mrs. Hale recognizes the element of violence in the situation from the outset. In Sheriff Peters, she sees the law made flesh. "A heavy man with a big voice" who delights in distinguishing between criminals and noncriminals, his casual misogyny—"not much of a housekeeper"—indicates his predisposition to find women guilty. Mrs. Hale rejects the sheriff's invitation to join him in his definition and interpretation of Minnie Wright, to become in effect a male reader, and asserts instead her intention to read as a woman. Fortunately, perhaps, for Minnie, the idea of the woman reader as anything other than an adjunct validator of male texts and male interpretations ("a sheriff's wife is married to the law") is as incomprehensible to these men as is the idea of a woman's story. With a parting shot at the incompetence of women as readers—"But would the women know a clue if they did come upon it?"—the men leave the women alone with their "trifles."

Martha Hale has no trouble recognizing that she is faced with a text written by the woman whose presence she feels, despite her physical absence. She has no trouble recognizing Minnie Wright as an author whose work she is competent to read. Significantly enough, identification determines her competence. Capable of imagining herself as a writer who can produce a significant text, she is also capable of interpreting what she finds in Minnie Wright's kitchen. As she leaves her own house, Martha Hale makes "a scandalized sweep of her kitchen," and "what her eye took in was that her kitchen was in no shape for leaving." When she arrives at Minnie Wright's house and finds her kitchen in a similar state, she is prepared to look for something out of the ordinary to explain it—that is, she is in a position to discover the motive and the clue which the men miss. Identification also provides the key element in determining how Mrs. Peters reads. From the start, Martha Hale has been sizing up Mrs. Peters. Working from her perception that Mrs. Peters "didn't seem like a sheriff's wife," Martha subtly encourages her to read as a woman. But Mrs. Peters, more timid than Mrs. Hale and indeed married to the law, wavers in her allegiance: "'But Mrs. Hale,' said the sheriff's wife, 'the law is the law'." In a comment that ought to be as deeply embedded in our national folklore as are its masculinist counterparts—for example, "a woman is only a woman but a good cigar is a smoke"—Mrs. Hale draws on Mrs. Peters's potential for identification with Minnie Wright: "The law is the law—and a bad stove is a bad stove. How'd you like to cook on this?" At the crucial moment, when both motive and clue for the murder have been discovered and the fate of Minnie Wright rests in her hands, Mrs. Peters remembers her own potential for violence, its cause and its justification: "'When I was a girl,' said Mrs. Peters, under her breath, 'my kitten—there was a boy took a hatchet, and before my eyes—before I could get there—' She covered her face an instant. 'If they hadn't held me back I would have'—she caught herself, looked upstairs where footsteps were heard, and finished weakly—'hurt him'."

At the end of the story, Martha Hale articulates the theory of reading behind "A Jury of Her Peers": "We all go through the same things—it's all just a different kind of the same thing! If it weren't—why do you and I *understand?* Why do we *know*—what we know this minute?" Women can read women's texts because they live women's lives; men can not read women's texts because they don't lead women's lives. Yet, of course, the issues are more complicated than this formulation, however true it may be. A clue to our interpretation of Glaspell's text occurs in a passage dealing with Mrs. Peters's struggle to determine how she will read: "It was as if something within her not herself had spoken, and it found in Mrs. Peters something she did not know as herself. 'I know what stillness is,' she said, in a queer, monotonous voice." Obviously, nothing less than Mrs. Peters's concept of self is at stake in her decision. The self she does not recognize as "herself" is the self who knows what she knows because of the life she has lived. As she reads this life in the story of another woman, she contacts that self from which she has been systematically alienated by virtue of being married to the law and subsequently required to read as a man.

When I was in high school and first introduced to literature as a separate subject of study, I was told that one of the primary reasons people read, and, thus, one of the primary justifications for learning how to read, is to enlarge their frame of reference through encountering experiences that are foreign to them which are not likely to happen in their own lives and, thus, to enrich and complicate their perspective. Since as a young woman reader I was given to read primarily texts about young men, I had no reason to question the validity of this proposition. It was not until I got to college and graduate school and encountered an overwhelmingly male faculty intent on teaching me how to recognize great literature that I began to wonder about the homogeneity of the texts that got defined as "classic." But of course it took feminism to enable me finally to see and understand the extraordinary gap between theory and practice in the teaching of literature as I experienced it. If a white male middle-class literary establishment consistently chooses to identify as great and thus worth reading those texts that present as central the lives of white male middle-class characters, then obviously recognition and reiteration, not difference and expansion, provide the motivation for reading. Regardless of the theory offered in justification, as it is currently practiced within the academy, reading functions primarily to reinforce the identity and perspective which the male teacher/reader brings to the text. Presumably this function is itself a function of the sense of power derived from the experience of perceiving one's self as central, as subject, as literally because literarily the point of view from which the rest of the world is seen. Thus men, controlling the study of literature, define as great those texts that empower themselves and define reading as an activity that serves male interests, for regardless of how many actual readers may be women, within the academy the presumed reader is male.

Outside the academy, of course, women, operating perhaps instinctively on the same understanding of the potential of reading, have tended to find their way to women's texts. One of the most striking experiences of my own teaching career occurred recently, when I taught a graduate course designed to introduce students to the work of nineteenth-century American women writers. Though I had been working on these writers for three years and was engaged at the time in writing about them, I nevertheless arrived in the classroom full of anxiety, for I was still sufficiently a product of the system that had trained me to worry that my students might resent being asked to read literature that was not "classic." I was, however, completely mistaken in my apprehension, for in fact my women students (and the class was almost entirely women) loved the literature of nineteenth-century American women, and at the end of the course they indicated in a variety of ways their intention to keep on reading it. Many of them spoke movingly about the ratification and legitimization of self, indeed the sense of power, they derived from reading these texts and the relief they felt at finding within the academy an opportunity to read something other than texts by and about men. At one class session, however, an interesting phenomenon emerged. My students began describing the various methods they had developed for hiding from husbands, lovers, male professors, employers, and other male graduate students the nature of the texts they were reading. As we began to explore the reasons behind this behavior, we came to understand most immediately how politicized the act of reading is in a sexist culture. For it is not simply the case that men, in determining what is read, wish to provide a certain experience for themselves; it is equally the case that they do not want women to have this experience. Nothing else can explain the intensity and the persistence of male resistance to the inclusion of women writers on reading lists, examination lists, bibliographies, and so forth, where the concept of inclusion is almost always token and at best is an equal sharing of time and space. My students, in playing with the title of E.D.E.N. Southworth's popular novel of 1859 and describing themselves as reading with "a hidden hand," hit on the fact that women's reading of women's novels is not a culturally validated activity. Indeed, to the degree that such reading, by giving women the experience of seeing themselves as central, subject, and point of view, empowers the woman reader, and to the degree that such empowerment contravenes the design of patriarchal culture, women's reading of women's texts is literally treason against the state and of necessity must be a covert and hidden affair.

Our discussion led us to feel closer to nineteenth-century women readers as well as to women writers, for we began to think that we might understand in some essential way why nineteenth-century American women read with such passion, even avidity, the work of their contemporaries, despite the steady stream of warnings delivered to them on the abuses of novel reading. And, playing still further with the implications of "the hidden hand," we began to speculate on the degree to which the reading of women's texts by women might have been and might still be eroticized. For what else might one have to do with a hidden hand besides read? And might not the gratifications of masturbation and the gratifications of reading women's texts be similar for women? In a sexist culture, which has as one of its primary components institutionalized and enforced heterosexuality designed to serve the sexual interests of men, masturbation for women carries with it the potential of putting women in touch with their own bodies, of giving us a knowledge of our flesh which permissible sexual activity does not necessarily provide. Similarly, the reading of women's texts has the potential for giving women a knowledge of the self, for putting us in contact with our real selves, which the reading of male texts can not provide. Which, of course, brings us back to Mrs. Peters and "A Jury of Her Peers" and to a final question that the story raises.

Just as the women in the story have the capacity to read as men or as women, having learned of necessity how to recognize and interpret male texts, so are the men in the story presumably educable. Though initially they might not recognize a clue if they saw it, they could be taught its significance, they could be taught to recognize women's texts and to read as women. If this were not the case, the women in the story could leave the text as they find it; but they don't. Instead, they erase the text as they read it. Martha Hale undoes the threads of the quilt that, like the weaving of Philomel, tells the story of Minnie Wright's violation and thus provides the clue to her revenge; Mrs. Peters instinctively creates an alternate story to explain the missing bird and then further fabricates to explain the absent cat; and Mrs. Hale, with the approval of Mrs. Peters, finally hides the dead bird. Thus, we must revise somewhat our initial formulation of the story's point about reading: it is not simply the case that men can not recognize or read women's texts; it is, rather, that they will not. At the end of the story, the county attorney summarizes the situation "incisively": "It's all perfectly clear, except the reason for doing it. But you know juries when it comes to women. If there was some definite thing—something to show. Something to make a story about. A thing that would connect up with this clumsy way of doing it." But why, if it is all so perfectly clear to them, have the men made so little intelligent effort to find that "something" that would convince and convict? Why, in fact, has this same county attorney consistently deflected attention from those details that would provide the necessary clues: "Let's talk about that a little later, Mr. Hale"; "I'd like to talk to you about that a little later, Mrs. Hale." This is the question that "A Jury of Her Peers" propounds to its readers, making us ask in turn why it is more important for the men in this story to let one woman get away with murder than to learn to recognize and to read her story?

Part of the answer to this question has already been suggested in the previous discussion. The refusal to recognize women as having stories denies women the experience it ensures for men—namely, reading as a validation of one's reality and reinforcement of one's identity. But there is still more at issue here. Let us return for a moment to that gap between theory and practice which I mentioned in connection with my own introduction to reading. Certainly in theory there is nothing wrong with the idea that one might read to experience a reality different from one's own, to encounter the point of view of another who is other, and thus to broaden one's own perspective and understanding. Indeed, there is much to be said for it, for as Patsy Schweickart has cogently argued in her commentary on an earlier draft of this paper, the extreme anxiety raised by the issue of solipsism in masculine Western thought derives from that pattern of habitually effacing the other, of which the control of textuality is but one manifestation. However, it may well be the case that the gap between theory and practice at issue here has less to do with a need to efface the other than with a need to protect a certain concept of the self. In a sexist culture the interests of men and women are by definition oppositional—what is good for men is bad for women, and vice versa, given the nature of men's definition of their "good" in a sexist context. Inevitably, then, texts produced in a sexist culture will reflect this fact. Thus, texts written by men in such a context will frequently be inimical to women; and, while I would argue that there is no equivalent in the literature of women for the palpable misogyny of much of male literature, nevertheless, as the analysis of "A Jury of Her Peers" demonstrates, women's texts frequently present a radical challenge to the premises of men texts, premises that men rely on to maintain the fictions of their own identity. Thus, when men ask women to read men's texts under the guise of enlarging their experience and perspective, they are in fact asking women to undergo an experience that is potentially inimical to them; and when men insist that men's texts are the only ones worth reading, they are in fact protecting themselves against just such an experience. If we examine "A Jury of Her Peers" with this hypothesis in mind, we may find in the story an answer to the question that it propounds. For what is the content of the text that Minnie Wright has written and that the men are so unwilling to read? It is nothing less than the story of men's systematic, institutionalized, and culturally approved violence toward women, and of women's potential for retaliatory violence against men. For the men to find the clue that would convict Minnie Foster Wright, they would have to confront the figure of John Wright. And if they were to confront this figure, they would have to confront as well the limitations of their definition of a "good man," a phrase that encompasses a man's relation to drink, debt, and keeping his word with other men but leaves untouched his treatment of women. And if a man's treatment of women were to figure into the determination of his goodness, then most men would be found not good. Thus, for the men in the story to confront John Wright would mean confronting themselves. In addition, were they to read Minnie Wright's story, they would have to confront the fact that a woman married to a man is not necessarily married to his law, might not in fact see things "just that way," might indeed see things quite differently and even act on those perceptions. They might have to confront the fact that the women of whom they are so casually contemptuous are capable of turning on them. For, of course, in refusing to recognize the story of Minnie Wright, the men also avoid confrontation with the story of Mrs. Hale and Mrs. Peters—they never know what their wives have done alone in that kitchen.

Male violence against women and women's retaliatory violence against men constitute a story that a sexist culture is bent on repressing, for, of course, the refusal to tell this story is one of the major mechanisms for enabling the violence to continue. Within "A Jury of Her Peers," this story is once again suppressed. Mrs. Hale and Mrs. Peters save Minnie Foster Wright's life, but in the process they undo her story, ensuring that it will never have a public hearing. The men succeed in their refusal to recognize the woman's story because the women are willing to let the principle stand in order to protect the particular woman. Thus, if the men are willing to let one woman get away with murder in order to protect their control of textuality, the women are willing to let the men continue to control textuality in order to save the individual. The consequence of both decisions is the same: Minnie Wright is denied her story and hence her reality (What will her life be like if she does get off?), and the men are allowed to continue to assume that they are the only ones with stories. So haven't the men finally won?

Glaspell, of course, chooses differently from her characters, for "A Jury of Her Peers" does not suppress, but, rather, tells the woman's story. Thus, Glaspell's fiction is didactic in the sense that it is designed to educate the male reader in the recognition and interpretation of women's texts, while at the same time it provides the woman reader with the gratification of discovering, recovering, and validating her own experience. For "A Jury of Her Peers," I would argue, from my own experience in teaching the text and from my discussion with others who have taught it, is neither unintelligible to male readers nor susceptible to a masculinist interpretation. If you can get men to read it, they will recognize its point, for Glaspell chooses to make an issue of precisely the principle that her characters are willing to forgo. But, of course, it is not that easy to get men to read this story. It is surely no accident that "A Jury of Her Peers" did not make its way into the college classroom until the advent of academic feminism.

In the second story under discussion here, Edgar Allan Poe's "The Murders in the Rue Morgue," the very absence of any distinction between character and author, or, perhaps, between the experience of reading presented within the story and the experience of reading produced by the story, served as the generative fact in my developing reflections on gender and reading. I will never forget my first experience of teaching "The Murders in the Rue Morgue" as a feminist. When we had finished what I was then calling the "traditional" interpretation of the story, I asked my students a question I thought would inevitably open the way for a feminist analysis of the text. I asked them whether the sex of the victims played any part in the story's design or effect. Specifically, I asked them whether the story would be different, even imaginable, if the victims were male. In my naive assumption that the truths of feminism would be obvious once the right questions were asked, in my failure to recognize the significance of my own personal history, which included many readings of this story in which this question never occurred to me, I fully expected my students, in considering my question, to recognize what is to me now obvious—that is, that the sex of the victims was the hidden spring that has to be there to make the story work—and thus to commit themselves to a feminist interpretation of the text. Of course, my students did no such thing; they resolutely denied that gender had anything to do with the story and vehemently argued that it would work just the same if the victims were men.

At this point, the class went on to Hawthorne. But I went home to think, for here a version of the theory of reading proposed in "A Jury of Her Peers" was borne out in practice. Further, I was intrigued by the similarity between my students' behavior and that of the characters in the story. So I began to wonder if "The Murders in the Rue Morgue," like so many other American texts, was not another story about reading and, particularly, about the connections between reading and gender.

In this context, I remembered the analysis of "The Purloined Letter" by Daniel Hoffman in his brilliant book *Poe, Poe, Poe, Poe, Poe, Poe, Poe* (Garden City, N.Y.: Doubleday, 1972). Here Hoffman argues that Dupin can solve the crime of the purloined letter because he can imagine having committed it; in fact, as Hoffman points out, in order to resolve the situation Dupin exactly duplicates the initial event. The police, on the other hand, have been completely ineffective in the case because the strategy of the criminal does not coincide with the paradigm that they bring with them into the situation. The police assume that something stolen is something hidden, for that is how they would do it. Thus, though their labors at exploring every conceivable hiding place in the apartment of the Minister D——— are herculean in their thoroughness, they can not find the letter that has been left unconcealed. Like "A Jury of Her Peers," then, "The Purloined Letter" asserts that one is a competent reader only of texts that one has written or can imagine having written.

Now, what happens when we take this theory of reading and apply it to "The Murders in the Rue Morgue"? What are we to understand from Dupin's ability to solve this crime, to read this particular text? We can begin our reading by considering the nature of the crime/text at issue. Two women have been brutally murdered in a fashion that suggests the idea of sexual violation. They have been attacked in their bedroom late at night with only their night clothes on. One of the bodies has been forcibly thrust up a chimney, an image evocative of rape; hair, traditionally associated with feminine sexuality and allure, and described in the newspaper accounts of the event as "tresses," has been pulled from the head of one of the women, and strands of it lie about the hearth. If, as is the case in "The Purloined Letter," Dupin's ability to solve this crime depends on his ability to have committed it, then the beast who has done the deed becomes a metaphor for Dupin himself, and we are reading about a man who reveals his own tendency toward and capacity for violence against women, and, further, who reveals the connection between the violence and his idea of the erotic. But in contrast to the situation presented in "The Purloined Letter," Dupin's ability to solve this crime depends equally on his willingness to recognize this fact about himself, to recognize the existence of the beast in and as himself. For consider the behavior of other readers in the story. The depositions published in the newspapers contain some crucial features in common. All of the witnesses who try to identify the criminals are men; all of them agree that they heard two voices; all of them agree that one voice was that of a Frenchman; all of them agree that the other voice belonged to someone of a nationality not their own and someone with whose language they were unfamiliar; some of them think it was a man's voice, some think it was a woman's, but all of them agree that it was not their own voice that they heard in that room. In other words, each testifier is primarily determined to dissociate himself from the crime, to insist on his own innocence by attributing the crime to a "foreigner." With this as their agenda, these men will, of course, never solve the crime.

Dupin, as the master reader in the story, accords considerable significance to this particular feature of the collective male testimony. Like the women in "A Jury of Her Peers," Dupin is capable of more than one mode of reading. He understands how men usually read, since he can read them, and he understands the role that denial and projection play in facilitating the pleasure of recognition which is at the heart of the experience of reading. In "The Murders in the Rue Morgue," then, we have a story that at once dramatizes the intimate connection between "the creative and the resolvent," the writer and the reader, and also dramatizes the mechanisms for denying such a connection when it would interfere with the pleasure of reading. For "The Murders in the Rue Morgue" *facilitates as it exposes* the mechanisms of masculinist reading. The "criminal" in the case turns out, after all, to be a real, live, flesh and blood, orangoutang, not a metaphor and not a man, and this revelation clearly collaborates in maintaining the collective male position that they are innocent of such violence against women. The mutilation and death of the victims is random, accidental, and motiveless, and the point of the story is merely to demonstrate the extraordinary analytic intellect of Monsieur C. Auguste Dupin. But why, then, are the victims women? And why is the beast male? And why has the sailor wished to keep in his closet a "pet" of such "intractable ferocity" and "imitative propensities"? And why does Dupin choose this particular situation for the demonstration of his analytic powers?

At one point in his "resolution" of the case, Dupin discourses on the "invariably superficial" nature of truth, proclaiming that it will inevitably reside in the most obvious features of any situation. If we take Dupin as Poe's idea of the good reader and follow his direction, we are, I believe, brought back to the issue that I originally raised with my students. The sex assigned to victim and violator is so obvious as to pass almost entirely without comment. Yet to change the sex of either or both parties would produce a completely different story. Here, then, is truth on the mountaintop, not in the valley, the hidden spring which must be there if the story is to work. For Dupin's delight in the exercise of his analytic powers would not provide much pleasure for the reader were it merely demonstrated through the mind-reading sequence with which the story opens. Dupin recognizes the element of "amusement" in the affair—the pleasure of reenacting the crime in the process of resolving it. More obviously, perhaps, the reader of "The Murders in the Rue Morgue," under the cover of witnessing the wonders of Dupin's analytic intellect, gets a steady supply of vignettes of violence; the mutilated bodies of the female victims remain center stage, providing the crucial though unremarked source of interest. In this story, of course, the presumed reader is male. Poe gives us a striking picture of him: "A man entered. He was a sailor, evidently—a tall, stout, and muscular-looking person, with a certain daredevil expression of countenance, not altogether unprepossessing. His face, greatly sunburnt, was more than half hidden by whisker and mustachio. He had with him a huge oaken cudgel, but appeared to be otherwise unarmed." This handsome, rakish, cudgel-carrying sailor, like the reader of the story, gets to watch through the window the violent behavior of his "pet." Poor beast! His penchant for imitation began quite innocently with shaving, an operation that he has watched his master perform through the keyhole of his closet; it ends with his flourishing the razor as his master flourishes whip and cudgel, the production of terror in another providing him with a master-like pleasure. Seeing his master's face through the window, the beast reverts and tries to remove the evidence of his assumption of the master's role. But he has given his master a good show, as well as a good out.

Though Dupin steadily refers to the "murderers" in the case, he collaborates in the sailor's illusion of innocence. Le Bon is released, but the sailor is not punished. Indeed, he subsequently recovers the beast and obtains for it "a very large sum." Dupin may sneer at a police force that, when presented with two mutilated corpses, can still end its report wondering "if indeed a murder has been committed at all," but in his resolution of the affair, no *crime* has been committed at all. Is it possible, then, that gender provides the hidden spring for the resolvent as well as the creative faculty? Would such a resolution be tolerable to Dupin if the victims were male? In sum, then, though he comprehends the dishonesty of masculinist reading, Dupin chooses to collaborate in it and get his pleasure from it. Should I wonder that my students chose to do the same? For, unlike "A Jury of Her Peers," "The Murders in the Rue Morgue" is not didactic. As Dupin allows the sailor his illusion of innocence, so Poe allows the reader his. It is easy to miss the role gender plays in the story; Poe has made it so, thereby proving his point that one can only recover from a text what one already brings to it.

In her "Afterword" to the 1973 Feminist Press Edition of Charlotte Perkins Gilman's "The Yellow Wallpaper," Elaine Hedges claims that until recently "no one seems to have made the connection between the insanity and the sex, or sexual role, of the victim." Nevertheless, it seems likely, as she also suggests, that the content of the story has provided the reason for its negative reception, outright rejection, and eventual obliteration by a male-dominated literary establishment. Though not, I would argue, as determinedly instructive as "A Jury of Her Peers," neither, I would equally propose, is "The Yellow Wallpaper" susceptible of a masculinist reading as, for example, is "The Murders in the Rue Morgue." That it has taken a generation of feminist critics to make Gilman's story a "classic" bears out the truth of Glaspell's thesis.

Gilman opens her story with language evocative of Poe: "It is very seldom that mere ordinary people like John and myself secure ancestral halls for the summer." Here we have echoes of the "scenes of mere household events" which the narrator of "The Black Cat" wishes "to place before the world, plainly, succinctly, and without comment." Poe's ancestral halls serve as image and symbol of the mind of his narrator, and they serve as analogue for the texts men write and read. These halls/texts are haunted by the ghosts of women buried alive within them, hacked to death to produce their effect, killed by and in the service of the necessities of male art: "The death, then, of a beautiful woman is, unquestionably, the most poetical topic in the world—and equally is it beyond doubt that the lips best suited for such topic are those of a bereaved lover." Die, then, women must so that men may sing. If such self-knowledge ultimately drives Roderick Usher mad, nevertheless as he goes down he takes self and text and sister with him; no other voice is heard, no alternate text remains. No doubt the madness of Poe's narrators reflects that masculine anxiety mentioned earlier, the fear that solipsism, annihilation, nothingness, will be the inevitable result of habitually silencing the other. Yet apparently such anxiety is preferable to the loss of power and control which would accompany giving voice to that other.

Gilman's narrator recognizes that she is in a haunted house, despite the protestations of her John, who is far less up-front than Poe's Roderick. Writing from the point of view of a character trapped in that male text—as if the black cat or Madeline Usher should actually find words and speak—Gilman's narrator shifts the center of attention away from the male mind that has produced the text and directs it instead to the consequences for women's lives of men's control of textuality. For it is precisely at this point that "The Yellow Wallpaper" enters this discussion of the connections between gender and reading. In this text we find the analysis of why who gets to tell the story and what story one is required, allowed, or encouraged to read matter so much, and therefore why in a sexist culture the practice of reading follows the theory proposed by Glaspell. Gilman's story makes clear the connection between male control of textuality and male dominance in other areas, and in it we feel the fact of force behind what is usually passed off as a casual accident of personal preference or justified by invoking "absolute" standards of "universal" value: these are just books I happen to like and I want to share them with you; these are our great texts and you must read them if you want to be literate. As man, husband, and doctor, John controls the narrator's life. That he chooses to make such an issue out of what and how she reads tells us what we need to know about the politics of reading.

In "The Yellow Wallpaper," Gilman argues that male control of textuality constitutes one of the primary causes of women's madness in a patriarchal culture. Forced to read men's texts, women are forced to become characters in those texts. And since the stories men tell assert as fact what women know to be fiction, not only do women lose the power that comes from authoring; more significantly, they are forced to deny their own reality and to commit in effect a kind of psychic suicide. For Gilman works out in considerable detail the position implicit in "A Jury of Her Peers"—namely, that in a sexist culture the interests of men and women are antithetical, and, thus, the stories each has to tell are not simply alternate versions of reality, they are, rather, radically incompatible. The two stories cannot coexist; if one is accepted as true, then the other must be false, and vice versa. Thus, the struggle for control of textuality is nothing less than the struggle for control over the definition of reality and hence over the definition of sanity and madness. The nameless narrator of Gilman's story has two choices. She can accept her husband's definition of reality, the prime component of which is the proposition that for her to write her own text is "madness" and for her to read his text is "sanity"; that is, she can agree to become a character in his text, accept his definition of sanity, which is madness for her, and thus commit psychic suicide, killing herself into his text to serve his interests. Or she can refuse to read his text, refuse to become a character in it, and insist on writing her own, behavior for which John will define and treat her as mad. Though Gilman herself was able to choose a third alternative, that of writing "The Yellow Wallpaper," she implicitly recognizes that her escape from this dilemma is the exception, not the rule. Though the narrator chooses the second alternative, she does as a result go literally mad and, thus, ironically fulfills the script John has written for her. Nevertheless, in the process she manages to expose the fact of John's fiction and the implications of his insistence on asserting his fiction as fact. And she does, however briefly, force him to become a character in her text.

An appropriate title for the story the narrator writes, as distinct from the story Gilman writes, could well be "John Says." Though the narrator attempts to confide to "dead" paper her alternate view of reality, she is, at least initially, careful to present John's text as well. Thoroughly subject to his control, she writes with the distinct possibility of his discovering her text and consequently escalating her punishment for refusing to accept his text—punishment that includes, among other things, solitary confinement in an attic nursery. She rightly suspects that the treason of a resisting author is more serious than that of a resisting reader; for this reason, in part, she turns the wallpaper into her primary text: what she writes on this paper can not be read by John.

Gilman, however, structures the narrator's reporting of John's text so as to expose its madness. John's definition of sanity requires that his wife neither have nor tell her own story. Presumably the narrator would be released from her prison and even allowed to write again were John sure that she would tell only "true" stories and not "fancies"; "John has cautioned me not to give way to fancy in the least. He says that with my imaginative power and habit of story-making, a nervous weakness like mine is sure to lead to all manner of excited fancies, and that I ought to use my will and good sense to check the tendency. So I try." But, of course, what John labels "fancies" are the narrator's facts: "Still I will proudly declare that there is something queer about it. Else, why should it be let so cheaply? And why have stood so long untenanted? John laughs at me, of course, but one expects that in marriage. John is practical in the extreme"; "that spoils my ghostliness, I am afraid, but I don't care—there is something strange about the house—I can feel it." John's laughter, like that of the husbands in "A Jury of Her Peers," is designed to undermine the narrator's belief in the validity of her own perceptions and to prevent her from writing them down and thus claiming them as true. Indeed, John is "practical in the extreme."

Conversely, John's facts appear rather fanciful. In John's story, he "loves" his wife and everything he does is for her benefit: "He said we came here solely on my account, that I was to have perfect rest and all the air I could get." Yet he denies her request for a room on the first floor with access to the air outside, and confines her instead to the attic, where she can neither sleep nor rest. Later, when she asks to have the attic wallpaper changed, he "took me in his arms and called me a blessed little goose, and said he would go down to the cellar, if I wished, and have it whitewashed into the bargain." Yet while he may be willing to whitewash the cellar, he won't change the attic because "I don't care to renovate the house for a three months' rental." For a three months' confinement, though, John has been willing to rearrange the furniture so as to make her prison ugly: "The furniture in this room is no worse than inharmonious, however, for we had to bring it all from down-stairs." Though the narrator is under steady pressure to validate the fiction of John's concern for her— "He is very careful and loving . . . he takes all care from me, and so I feel basely ungrateful not to value it more"—she nevertheless intuits that his "love" is part of her problem: "It is so hard to talk with John about my case, because he is so wise, and because he loves me so." And, in fact, her narrative reveals John to be her enemy whose "love" will destroy her.

John's definition of sanity for the narrator, however, includes more than the requirement that she accept his fiction as fact and reject her facts as fancy. In effect, it requires nothing less than that she eliminate from herself the subjectivity capable of generating an alternate reality from his. Thus, "John says that the very worst thing I can do is think about my condition," and he designs a treatment calculated to pressure the narrator into concluding that her self not him is the enemy, and calculated also to force her to give her self up. She is denied activity, work, conversation, society, even the opportunity to observe the activity of others. She is to receive no stimulus that might lead to the development of subjectivity. Indeed, one might argue that the narrator overinterprets the wallpaper, the one stimulus in her immediate environment, as a reaction against this sensory deprivation. Nor is the narrator allowed access to her feelings: "I get unreasonably angry with John sometimes. . . . But John says if I feel so, I shall neglect proper self-control, so I take pains to control myself." By "proper self-control," John means control to the point of eliminating the self that tells a different story from his. If the narrator learns the exercise of this kind of self-control, John need no longer fear her writing.

The more the narrator "rests," the more exhausted she becomes. Her exhaustion testifies to the energy she devotes to repressing her subjectivity and to the resistance she offers to that effort. In this struggle, "dead" paper provides her with her only vital sign. It constitutes her sole link with her embattled self. Yet because she is imprisoned in John's house and text and because his text has infected her mind, she experiences anxiety, contradiction, and ambivalence in the act of writing. Forced to view her work from the perspective of his text, to see it not as *work* but "work"—the denigrating quotation marks reflecting John's point of view—she finds it increasingly difficult to put pen to paper. Blocked from expressing herself *on* paper, she seeks to express herself *through* paper. Literally, she converts the wall*paper* into her text. Initially the narrator identifies the wallpaper with her prison and reads the text as enemy. The wallpaper represents the condition she is not to think about as she is being driven into it. It is ugly, "one of those sprawling flamboyant patterns committing every artistic sin," disorderly, confusing, and full of contradictions. In struggling to organize the paper into a coherent text, the narrator establishes her artistic self and maintains her link with subjectivity and sanity. Yet the narrator at some level identifies with the wallpaper, as well. Just as she recognizes that John's definition of madness is her idea of sanity, so she recognizes in the wallpaper elements of her own resisting self. Sprawling, flamboyant, sinful, irritating, provoking, outrageous, unheard of—not only do these adjectives describe a female self intolerable to the patriarchy, they also code words that reflect the masculinist response to the perception of female subjectivity per se. In identifying with the wallpaper and in seeing herself in it, the narrator lets herself out; increasingly, her behavior becomes flamboyant and outrageous. Getting out through the text of the wallpaper, she not surprisingly gets in to the subtext within the text that presents the story of a woman trying to get out.

Possessed by the need to impose order on the "impertinence" of row after row of unmatched breadths and to retain, thus, a sense of the self as orderly and ordering, and at the same time identifying with the monstrously disruptive self implicit in the broken necks and bulbous eyes, the narrator continues to elaborate and revise her text. Her descriptions of the wallpaper become increasingly detailed and increasingly feminine, reflecting the intuition that her disintegration derives from the "condition" of being female: "Looked at in one way each breadth stands alone, the bloated curves and flourishes—a kind of 'debased Romanesque' with *delirium tremens*—go waddling up and down in isolated columns of fatuity." Yet the "delirium tremens" of "isolated columns of fatuity" can serve as a metaphor for the patterns conventionally assigned to women's lives and for the "sanity" conventionally prescribed for women. In the "pointless pattern," the narrator senses the patriarchal point. Thus, the narrator concentrates on her subtext, "a thing nobody seems to notice but myself," on the pattern behind the pattern, the woman who wants out.

At the end of "The Yellow Wallpaper," we witness a war between texts. The patriarchal text is a formidable foe; it has an enormous capacity for maintaining itself: "there are always new shoots on the fungus"; and its influence is pervasive: "I find it hovering in the dining-room, skulking in the parlor, hiding in the hall, lying in wait for me on the stairs. It gets into my hair. . . . I thought seriously of burning the house—to reach the smell." Its repressive power is equally large: "But nobody could climb through that pattern—it strangles so." Nevertheless, the narrator is sure that her woman "gets out in the daytime." And she is prepared to help her: "I pulled and she shook, I shook and she pulled, and before morning we had peeled off yards of that paper."

Despite the narrator's final claim that she has, like the woman in the paper, "got out at last," she does not in fact escape the patriarchal text. Her choice of literal madness may be as good as or better than the "sanity" prescribed for her by John, but in going mad she fulfills his script and becomes a character in his text. Still, going mad gives the narrator temporary sanity. It enables her to articulate her perception of reality and, in particular, to cut through the fiction of John's love: "He asked me all sorts of questions, too, and pretended to be very loving and kind. As if I couldn't see through him!" It also enables her to contact her feelings, the heart of the subjectivity that John seeks to eliminate. She no longer needs to project her rage onto the imaginary children who occupied her prison before her, gouging the floor, ripping the paper, gnawing the bedstead, for she is now herself "angry enough to do something desperate." Angry, she is energized; she has gotten through to and found her work. If the effort to be sane has made her sick, her madness makes her feel "ever so much better."

This relief, however, is only temporary, for the narrator's solution finally validates John's fiction. In his text, female madness results from work that engages the mind and will; from the recognition and ex-

163

pression of feelings, and particularly of anger; in a word, from the existence of a subjectivity capable of generating a different version of reality from his own. And, indeed, the onset of the narrator's literal madness coincides precisely with her expression of these behaviors. More insidious still, through her madness the narrator does not simply become the character John already imagines her to be as part of his definition of feminine nature; she becomes a version of John himself. Mad, the narrator is manipulative, secretive, dishonest; she learns to lie, obscure, and distort. Further, she masters the art of sinister definition; she claims normalcy for herself, labels John "queer," and determines that he needs watching. This desire to duplicate John's text but with the roles reversed determines the narrator's choice of an ending. Wishing to drive John mad, she selects a denouement that will reduce him to a woman seized by a hysterical fainting fit. Temporary success, however, exacts an enormous price, for when John recovers from his faint, he will put her in a prison from which there will be no escape. John has now got his story, the story, embedded in a text like *Jane Eyre,* of the victimized and suffering husband with a mad wife in the attic. John will tell his story, and there will be no alternate text to expose him.

Gilman, however, has exposed John. And in analyzing how men drive women mad through the control of textuality, Gilman has escaped the fate of her narrator and created a text that can help the woman reader to effect a similar escape. The struggle recorded in the text has its analogue in the struggle around and about the text, for nothing less than our sanity and survival is at stake in the issue of what we read.

Note

In conceptualizing this essay, I have been enormously helped by the work of Annette Kolodny, in particular her "A Map for Rereading: Or, Gender and the Interpretation of Literary Texts" (*New Literary History* 11 [1980]: 451–67), and of Jean E. Kennard in "Convention Coverage, or How to Read Your Own Life" (*New Literary History* 8 [1981]: 69–88). In writing, revising, and rewriting, I owe a large debt to the following readers and writers: Judith Barlow, Susan Kress, Margorie Pryse, Joan Schulz, Patsy Schweickart.

Chapter 8
"As the Twig Is Bent . . .":
Gender and Childhood Reading
Elizabeth Segel

One of the most obvious ways gender influences our experience as readers is when it determines what books are made available to us or are designated as appropriate or inappropriate for our reading. Nowhere is this fact so apparent or its implications so disturbing as in childhood reading. This is partly because the child does not have direct access to books, by and large, but receives them from adult hands. Adults decide what books are written, published, offered for sale, and, for the most part, purchased for children. And over the last century and a half, most adults have firmly believed that literary sauce for the goose is not at all sauce for the gander. The publisher commissioning paperback romances for girls and marketing science fiction for boys, as well as Aunt Lou selecting a fairy tale collection for Susie and a dinosaur book for Sam, are part of a powerful system that operates to channel books to or away from children according to their gender. Furthermore, because the individual's attitudes concerning appropriate gender-role behaviors are formed during the early years, the reader's choice of reading material may be governed by these early experiences long after she or he has theoretically gained direct access to books of all kinds.

To understand how gender operates on this level to condition the reading process, it is useful, first, to look at reading in childhood, ask how the reading lives of girls and of boys have typically differed, and seek out the origins of those differences.

Geoffrey Trease, distinguished British author of children's novels, tells us that in the early 1930s, when he began writing for children, "Books were labelled, as strictly as school lavatories, 'Books for Boys' or 'Books for Girls'."[1] This was also the situation in America, and it prevailed in the same rigid form at least until the 1960s, when the boundaries began to loosen a bit. 'Twas not ever thus, however.

In the few books intended for children's use that were published before the eighteenth century, no distinction seems to have been made between boy readers and girl readers. Manuals of conduct—the various volumes of "a father's counsel" or "a mother's legacy"—were apparently addressed in roughly equal numbers to sons or daughters, depending on the gender of the writer's own offspring. The Puritan tracts depicting godly children on their deathbeds which dominated seventeenth-century juvenile publishing seem to have dwelt with equal fervor on the uplifting spectacle of godly girls and godly boys going meekly to their reward.

The 1740s are generally viewed as marking the coming of age of children's books in England. In that decade, three London publisher-booksellers, Thomas Boreman, Mary Cooper, and John Newbery, began to provide children with books designed to delight as well as instruct them. Increasing middle-class literacy and prosperity set the stage for this development, along with the gradual popular dissemination of John Locke's educational philosophy, which advocated teaching children through play.

One of Newbery's most appealing early publications appears at first glance to herald the publishers' practice of dividing children's books into boys' books and girls' books. *A Little Pretty Pocket-Book* (1744), a miscellany of rhymes and fables in an elegant gilt and flowered binding, opens with two whimsical letters from Jack the Giant Killer to the child reader.[2] One is addressed to Master Tommy, and the other to Pretty Miss Polly. Furthermore, Newbery—canny merchandiser that he was—offered with the book for two pence additional a pincushion (for Pretty Miss Polly, of course) or a ball (for Master Tommy). On closer inspection, however, we see that the wording is exactly the same in each of the two letters, except that one speaks of being a good boy, the other a good girl; where one addresses "my dear Tommy," and the other speaks to "my dear Polly." Both letters praise the child for his or her "Nurse's report": you are, the letters say, "loving and kind to your Play-fellows, and obliging to every body; . . . you rise early in the Morning, keep yourself clean, and learn your Book; . . . when you have done a Fault you confess it, and are sorry for it." Including two letters instead of one was not, it would seem, a way of prescribing different conduct for girls and boys, but a way of personalizing the letter and the book itself in an engaging way.

The two letters also specify the use to which the ball and the pincushion are to be put, and our initial supposition—that Tommy will be gaily playing ball with his fellows while poor Polly sits laboring over her sampler—proves false. No, the objects are to serve the very same function, according to the Giant Killer. Both are red on one side and black on the other, and both come with ten pins. "For every good Action you do, a Pin shall be stuck on the Red Side, and for every bad Action a Pin shall be stuck on the Black Side." Jack rashly promises to send a penny when all the pins arrive on the red side, and a whipping should they all be found on the black. The virtues Newbery and his contemporaries were aiming to develop—obedience, industry, good temper—were evidently the same for both sexes. The reward for such virtues was the same, too, if we can judge from two of Newbery's most popular children's stories: both Goody Two-Shoes and Giles Gingerbread achieve by their goodness and application to studies "the love of all who know them" and the epitome of material success, a fine coach to ride in.

Neither the Puritan aim of saving the child's soul nor the characteristic Georgian aim of developing good character seemed to require a distinction between girl-child and boy-child. The domestic tales of the late eighteenth and early nineteenth centuries, such as Mrs. Trimmer's *The History of the Robins* (1786), the Edgeworths' *Harry and Lucy* stories (1801, 1825), and Mrs. Sherwood's *The Fairchild Family* (1818–1847), all featured children of both sexes as characters and were intended for readers of both sexes. All of these books clearly taught obedience, submission to authority, and selflessness as the cardinal virtues of both girls and boys. The few volumes produced solely for the child's entertainment in the early years of the nineteenth century, such as *The Comic Adventures of Old Mother Hubbard and Her Dog* (1805?) and *The Butterfly's Ball* (1807), also took no account of gender. The latter begins, "Come take up your Hats, and away let us haste / To the Butterfly's Ball, and the Grasshopper's feast," and the illustration shows both girls and boys among the fortunate children who are invited to the unusual party.

Early school stories were an exception. Because boarding schools were for boys or girls, not both, thinly disguised moral tracts with school settings were aimed at one sex or the other. Sarah Fielding's *The Governess; Or, Little Female Academy* specifies on the title page that it is "calculated for the entertainment and instruction of young ladies in their education."[3] Elizabeth Sandham wrote *The Boys' School; Or, Traits of Character in Early Life* (1800). Another of her productions was "an equally purposeful work about girls at school."[4] Mrs. Pilkington's two volumes, *Biography for Boys* (1805) and *Biography for Girls* (1806), suggest that then, as now, it was assumed that the child reader's emulation of the lives of the great would be more likely if girls read about famous women, boys about famous men.

While certain of the school stories and biographies for older children were targeted for boys or for girls, Samuel Pickering's study of eighteenth-century children's books bears out my conclusion that the first "significant differentiation made between books for little girls and for little boys" came with Mary Ann Kilner's *The Adventures of a Pincushion* (1783?) and *Memoirs of a Peg-Top* (1783).[5] These stories were among the best of the purported biographies of inanimate objects which were popular at the time. The pincushion and the peg-top both travel to boarding school and from one owner to another, in varying stations of life, all the while making improving comments on the scenes they observe. *The Adventures of a Pincushion* was "designed chiefly for the use of young ladies,"[6] *Memoirs of a Peg-Top* for boys. This distinction was apparently based on supposed different interests of girls and boys, rather than on different socializing aims for the two books—a specialization of vehicle rather than message. Indeed, Kilner asserted in her preface to *Memoirs of a Peg-Top* that "the laws of justice, probity, and truth" are "of *general* obligation." Her purpose in addressing the books to the "*different amusements . . .* in which each sex [was] more particularly concerned" was to make her books more interesting to children. It is worth noting that the chief difference between the companion volumes, besides the gender of the child characters, is that the peg-top book departs from the usual standard of gentility in approved children's fiction of the day. The top recounts an incident, for example, in which a blindfolded boy is fed a concoction of custard and cow dung.

Kilner's experiment seems to have had no imitators, and when Victoria came to the throne in 1837, the wholesale fencing off of children's books into books for boys and books for girls had not yet been effected. Elizabeth Rigby's very long article on children's books in the *Quarterly Review* (1844) makes no mention of boys' books or girls' books, either in her critical essay or in the annotations of recommended books which follow.[7] Even in discussing Marryat's *Masterman Ready* (1841), a book invariably referred to today as a boys' book, Rigby noted the danger that parents may "dispute with *their children*"—not with *their sons*—"the possession of it" (my italics).

Within a few years, however, the adventure fiction of Marryat, Ballantyne, Henty, and Kingston would be universally thought of as "boys' books," and domestic chronicles like Susan Warner's *The Wide, Wide World* (1850) and Charlotte Yonge's *The Daisy Chain* (1856) would set a transatlantic pattern for the "girls' book." By the last quarter of the century, articles like William Graham Sumner's "What Our Boys Are Reading"[8] and Edward G. Salmon's "What Girls Read"[9] had become commonplace on both sides of the Atlantic.

How to account for this extensive staking out of boys' and girls' claims on the previously common territory of children's books is the interesting question. Certainly a favorable economic climate was an important precondition. The market had to grow large before publishers would consider restricting sales by excluding potential readers. In 1808 Charles Lamb received a letter from his publisher, William Godwin, suggesting changes in his adaptation of Chapman's *Odyssey* for children, *The Adventures of Ulysses*. Godwin wrote:

> We live in squeamish days. Amid the beauties of your manuscript, of which no man can think more highly than I do, what will the squeamish say to . . . the giant's vomit, page 14, or to the minute & shocking description of the extinguishing the giant's eye, in the page following. You I dare say have no formed plan of excluding the female sex from among your readers, & I, as a bookseller, must consider that if you have, you exclude one half of the human species.[10]

Appropriate subject matter for boys might be judged too "strong" for girls, but for economic reasons publishers at this time preferred to dilute the material rather than limit the book's readers to one sex.

F. J. Harvey Darton, still the ultimate authority on the social history of English children's books, acknowledged the role of economics in making it possible to publish different types of books for boys and for girls by the mid-nineteenth century: "Mere numbers now made sub-division inevitable." Yet he went further, and suggested that this development was a positive step in the evolution of a true children's literature, one that hinged on "the discovery that *The* Child was *a* child, and, on top of that, that he was male and female, and was also different at five years of age and fourteen. . . . Hitherto the young readers had never been clearly defined. They were just 'children', and that meant anything from a baby lisping the alphabet to a young Miss or Master growing like the elder generation."[11]

"The young Miss . . . growing like the elder generation" presented a ticklish problem to her Victorian elders which provided further impetus to develop a distinctive literature for girls. "Girls' literature performs one very useful function," according to Salmon's important 1886 essay. "It enables girls to read something above mere baby tales, and yet keeps them from the influence of novels of a sort which should be read only by persons capable of forming a discreet judgment. It is a long jump from Aesop to 'Ouida', and to place Miss Sarah Doudney or Miss Anne Beale between Aesop and 'Ouida' may at least prevent a disastrous moral fall."[12] Mary Louisa Molesworth, also writing in 1886, cited *Mrs. Overtheway's Remembrances* (1866), by Mrs. Ewing, as a book "more particularly written for girls, and well adapted for that indefinite age, the despair of mothers and governesses, when maidens begin to look down upon 'regular children's stories', and novels are as yet forbidden."[13]

While this literature for older girls, clearly the forerunner of today's "junior novels" or young adult fiction, can legitimately be viewed as being responsive to children's needs (after all, children do need books that fall between Marguerite Henry and Margaret Drabble), Salmon's tone indicates that girls' literature "for that indefinite age" was part of a concerted effort to keep females pure and their imaginations unsullied by restricting their world, even within the home. "The chief end served by 'girls' literature' is that, whilst it advances beyond the nursery, it stops short of the full blaze of the drawing-room," Salmon concluded.[14] It was, by and large, a stopgap, watered-down fare, a part of the Victorians' Podsnappian attempt, so well described by Dickens, to proscribe whatever "would . . . bring a blush to the cheek of the young person."[15]

The evidence suggests that more than economic feasibility and increasing dominance of the middle-class made the middle class's definishment to develop distinctive girls' and boys' books. It was, above all, the sharp differentiation of male and female roles, well underway by the mid-nineteenth century, which mandated separate books for girls and boys.

The polarization of gender roles which accompanied the advance of industrialization and colonization has been well described elsewhere;[16] only the most salient features need be cited here. As work moved out of the home and female leisure became a sign of material success, middle-class women less and less were productive workers, becoming instead consumers confined to the domestic world. At the same time, the increasing dominance of the middle class made the middle class's definition of the role of women society's ideal of womanhood. Man's duties, in contrast, took him into the sordid and fiercely competitive world of industry and commerce and to the four corners of the world—to earn, to fight, and to rule the benighted subjects of empire. The home, under the aegis of the wife as "the angel in the house" was to be the refuge of moral and spiritual values. In place of her former active role of helpmate, the wife was offered the noble mission of influencing husband and children toward the good. This delegation to women of the responsibility for inculcating moral and religious values in men and children, and the generally enthusiastic acceptance of this function (even by women like Louisa May Alcott and George Eliot, who chafed at the restrictions this definition of women's role placed on them), had a profound impact on child-rearing practices and on the relations between the sexes.[17]

Its impact on children's books is unmistakable. For one thing, the women who dominated the ranks of juvenile authors viewed writing for children as the exercise of feminine moral "influence." The content of children's books naturally reflected the doctrine. As Salmon declared:

Boys' literature of a sound kind ought to help to build up men. Girls' literature ought to help to build up women. If in choosing the books that boys shall read it is necessary to remember that we are choosing mental food for the future chiefs of a great race, it is equally important not to forget in choosing books for girls that we are choosing mental food for the future wives and mothers of that race. When Mr. Ruskin says that man's work is public and woman's private, he seems for the moment insensible to the public work of women as exercised through their influence on their husbands, brothers, and fathers. Woman's work in the ordering, beautifying, and elevating of the commonweal is hardly second to man's; and it is this which ought to be borne in mind in rearing girls.[18]

Before the boys' book appeared on the scene, fiction for children typically had been domestic in setting, heavily didactic, and morally or spiritually uplifting, and this kind of earnest family story remained the staple of younger children's fiction. The boys' book was, above all, an escape from domesticity and from the female domination of the domestic world. The adventures of Tom and Huck, of Jim Hawkins and many lesser heroes of boys' books are the epitome of freedom in part because they are an escape from women, the chief agents of socialization in the culture. Though most boys' books entailed a simple code of honor, earnest introspection and difficult moral choices were taboo; these were books of action and adventure. As Gillian Avery puts it, "Long before girls were allowed amusing books, boys had their Marryat and Ballantyne—books of high adventure with the occasional pious sentiment slipped in as an afterthought, but with no continuous moral message."[19]

The authors of *these* books were not pious female pedagogues, but men of action! Of the British boys' book authors, Frederick Marryat had entered the Royal Navy at fourteen and had taken part in fifty naval engagements before he settled down to write books twenty-four years later. R. M. Ballantyne emigrated to Canada, where he worked for the Hudson Bay Company, often at remote outposts in the Far North. Thomas Mayne Reid, born in Ireland, came to America as a young man and became a trader on the western frontier, living among the native Americans. He fought in the thick of the Mexican War before returning to England to write boys' fiction. And G. A. Henty, chronicler of military history and celebrator of empire, was a war correspondent who had witnessed famous battles all over Europe and Africa for thirty years.

The liberation of nineteenth-century boys into the book worlds of sailors and pirates, forests and battles, left their sisters behind in the world of childhood—that is, the world of home and family. When publishers and writers saw the commercial possibilities of books for girls, it is interesting that they did not provide comparable escape reading for them (that came later, with the pulp series books), but instead developed books designed to persuade the young reader to accept the confinement and self-sacrifice inherent in the doctrine of feminine influence. This was accomplished by depicting the rewards of submission and the sacred joys of serving as "the angel in the house." Whereas in many boys' books, the happy ending is the adolescent "bad boy" successfully escaping socialization, holding out against the Widow Douglasses of the world, and thereby earning the admiration of all, in the girls' book, the protagonist who resists the dictates of genteel feminity must be "tamed," her will broken to accept a submissive and sedentary role. The so-called happy ending of such books is that she herself stops rebelling and chooses the approved role in order to gain or to retain the love and approval of those around her.[20]

The classic example of a girl who is "broken" to the conventional woman's role in a girls' book is the heroine of *What Katy Did,* by Susan Coolidge, which was published in 1872 and widely read in America and Britain for nearly a century.[21] It is a book that repays close attention for the illumination it sheds on the nature of the girls' book.

Katy Carr is the eldest of six motherless children in a well-to-do New England family. A lanky, impulsive, awkward, and passionate twelve year old, she darts from one scrape to another. As crabby Aunt Izzy rails about Katy's missing bonnet-string, torn dresses, and tardiness, the reader responds to Katy's generosity, creativity, and affectionate nature. Moved by the pleadings of her father and of the saintly invalid, Aunt Helen, Katy resolves to conquer her faults, but her resolutions are in vain. One particularly tempestuous day, she vents her frustrations by vigorously swinging, though Aunt Izzy has forbidden it. What Katy doesn't know is that the rope is not secure. Her punishment for this disobedience is a terrible fall and an injury to her back which keeps her in bed and in pain for four years.

In the first months she experiences a deep depression. Then Aunt Helen, beautiful and beloved by all (and an invalid herself, remember), talks to Katy about "God's school," the School of Pain, where the lessons are Patience, Hopefulness, and—believe it or not—Neatness.

The rest of the book chronicles how Katy grows in virtue and gains the love and approval of all. She learns to think of others, not herself, and to fill the place of the dead mother to the younger children. And, of course, being unable to walk for four years effectively cures her coltish exuberance.

The disturbing message that the ideal woman is an invalid is scarcely veiled. Aunt Helen tells Katy that after her own crippling accident she took pains to keep herself and her room looking attractive. It wasn't easy but, she says, "The pleasure it gave my dear father repaid for all. He had been proud of his active, healthy girl, but I think she was never such a comfort to him as his sick one, lying there in her bed" (p. 110). Katy is moved by this chilling vision to wish to "be nice and sweet and patient, and a comfort to people" (p. 111). She succeeds so well that the "happy ending" of the book is not so much the few tottering steps she manages in the last chapter as a compliment from Aunt Helen which ends the book: "You have won the place, which, you recollect, I once told you an invalid should try to gain, of being to everybody 'The Heart of the House' " (p. 166). Since this was the place to which all women were urged to aspire, we may well wonder what the book's effect was on young readers. The book's popularity with previous generations of girls may well be owing to the vivid embodiment in crippled, chastened Katy of the painful limitations that the all too familiar feminine role imposed on active, carefree children.

If one contrasts *What Katy Did* with a comparably popular and respected boys' book of the period—say, *Treasure Island*[22]—one is first struck by the difference in setting: the domestic confinement of one book as against the extended voyage to exotic lands in the other. Also notable is the solemn introspection and moral earnestness that the girls' book expects of its heroine and readers, in contrast to the carefree suspension of moral judgment allowed Jim Hawkins. Good and evil exist in *Treasure Island,* to be sure, but Jim never has to make difficult moral choices (he kills mutineer Israel Hands involuntarily; Long John Silver's escape means Jim doesn't have to turn him over to be executed, etc.). Another revealing contrast is the premium placed on obedience in *What Katy Did*—but not in *Treasure Island.*

Children's books until the mid-nineteenth century had without exception depicted obedience as the most important childhood virtue. Anne S. MacLeod's study of antebellum American juvenile fiction concluded that "no child character was seen to defy authority successfully."[23] There were fictional children who disobeyed, of course, but they were not approved of by their creators. Disobedient children reaping their just deserts abound in early children's fiction: consigned to hellfire, chased by bulls, run over by wagons, or merely left at home when others go on coveted excursions, they are a chastened lot.

The advent of the "good bad boy" in the evolving boys' book marked a radical change in what adults expected of children, or, put another way, in what adults defined as the ideal child—ideal boy-child, that is. Jim Hawkins, Tom Sawyer, and many other rascals disobey adults and get away with it. In fact, their defiance of adult authority constitutes a major part of their charm. Tom's resistance to Aunt Polly's civilizing efforts and his enjoyment of forbidden pleasures are what give him the edge in Aunt Polly's affections over the good boy, Sid. Jim Hawkins's defiance of actual or understood orders of the treasure expedition's adult leaders—going ashore with the mutineers, leaving the stockage, and so on—is what saves all their necks and brings the voyage to a triumphant end.

The reason for this cultural redefinition of the ideal boy is not difficult to deduce. When the man's role will take him into the great world to engage in fierce battles of commerce and empire, pluck and enterprise are the virtues to cultivate in male children, and those are precisely the qualities the boys' book heroes sport in abundance. Obedience was required of the child, but the young man was encouraged to leave that virtue behind him. Thus, we see that the boys' book was every bit as much a tool of socialization as the girls' book—albeit one with more child appeal.

The docile obedience required of adolescent girls in the girls' book stands in marked contrast to the autonomy of the boys' book pro-tagonist. The warning figures of Pandora and Eve seem to shadow many of these stories. To be sure, the appeal of many favorite girls' book heroines rested on their resistance to the confines of the feminine role, but nearly all of them capitulate in the end.[24] In many of these girls' books, the interest derives from the tension between the heroine's drive to activity and autonomy, and the pressure exerted by society to thwart these drives and clip her wings, so to speak. The obedience, self-sacri-fice, and docility expected of the young woman in this fiction are the virtues of a dependent. Since until late in the century nearly all women, married or single, were dependent on men, we can see that these books were in fact fulfilling their mission of preparing girls for womanhood (though we can hardly call it adulthood).

We have at bottom, then, not just a divergence of subject matter between boys' books and girls' books, but two forms of literature that were as polar as the ideal man and the ideal woman of the day were. The boys' book, even when entertaining and escapist, was essentially a Bildungsroman, a chronicle of growth to manhood. The approved girls' book depicted a curbing of autonomy in adolescence; while in form purporting to be a Bildungsroman, it is, in Annis Pratt's words, "a genre that pursues the opposite of its generic intent—it provides models for 'growing down' rather than for 'growing up'."[25]

The mass-marketed, syndicate-produced girls' series books that flourished in the late nineteenth and early twentieth centuries—from Elizabeth Champney Williams's Vassar Girls series (1883–1892), which emulated the popular travel adventure books for boys, to that perennial survivor, Nancy Drew—finally provided girls with an escape from domesticity and with active role models. Series titles like The Motor Girls, The Outdoor Girls, The Ranch Girls, The Moving Picture Girls, and The Khaki Girls indicate how far girls series books had roamed by 1920 from Susan Coolidge's bailiwick. But they were shallow, formulaic stories, for the most part, and Mary Thwaite is right when she judges that "the careful separation of stories into series, which publishers and librarians could complacently label 'Boys' or 'Girls', had in fact become a minor oppression of young readers in the later nineteenth century."[26]

This careful separation of books by gender did not affect children's reading as simply as the discussion thus far might suggest, however, for children's actual reading behavior could not be controlled as easily as the content of the books themselves.

For one thing, though girls when they reached "that certain age" could be prevented from joining boys' games and lively exploits, it was harder to keep them from accompanying their brothers on vicarious adventures through the reading of boys' books. And girls were avid readers of boys' books from the start. Amy Cruse, in her survey of reading in the Victorian era, mentioned numerous women, notable and unknown, who were brought up on Scott, the forerunner of the boys' book novelists (Mary Ann Evans began reading him at the age of seven!), Marryat and his cohorts.[27] Salmon quoted a female correspondent who confessed a childhood preference for Jules Verne and Ballantyne—along with *Little Women*.[28] Alice Jordan, writing on American children's reading, asserted that "girls read boys' books then [in the 1870s] as they do today [1947], and it was well that they did, for even when such books were poor they were more vigorous as a whole than stories for girls."[29] Laura Richards, accomplished and prolific writer of children's verse and girls' books, claimed that "all she knew of natural history she learned from Mayne Reid, whose dazzling heroes were her delight."[30] G. A. Henty reported that he received numerous letters from girl readers and that he valued them highly, "for where there is a girl in the same family the brothers' books are generally common stock, and are carefully read, appreciated, and judged. The author declares that girls write more intelligently and evince greater judgment in their criticism."[31]

Cruse suggested that the girl reading her brother's books "risked incurring a painful rebuke for her unladylike tastes,"[32] but Salmon's influential article on girls' reading was sympathetic:

> There are few girls who boast brothers who do not insist on reading every work of Ballantyne's or Kingston's or Henty's which may be brought into the house. . . . The explanation is that they can get in boys' books what they

cannot get in the majority of their own—a stirring plot and lively movement. . . . Nor is this liking for heroes rather than heroines to be deprecated.
It ought to impart a vigour and breadth to a girl's nature, and to give sisters a
sympathetic knowledge of the scenes wherein their brothers live and work.[33]

While it was assumed from the beginning of gender-typed children's
books that girls regularly raided their brothers' libraries, the universal
opinion was that boys did not and would not read girls' books. This was
certainly true of the tamer girls' stories, which were long on submission
and short on action—Charlotte Yonge's domestic novels, for instance.
As Edith Sichel wrote in 1901: "It is impossible to imagine many men
reading Miss Yonge. There is an intemperate tameness about her—at
once her charm and her defect—which forbids our associating mankind with her. It would be as if we dreamed of them taking high tea *in
perpetuo.*"[34] We must suppose that younger male readers would find
Yonge even less appealing.

Yet, a few published reminiscences indicate that an occasional boy
did cross the gulf from the male side to read a girls' book, and that he
enjoyed it. (The confessions are made from the safe distance of
adulthood and success.) Alexander Woollcott read *Little Women* and
reported it one of the handful of books which retained their appeal in
later life.[35] William Lyon Phelps, distinguished professor and critic,
read *Little Women* as a boy and confided to his journal that, like many
girls, "he thought the book spoiled by not having Jo marry Laurie."[36]

That boys ventured into the territory of girls' reading only with
considerable trepidation is clear from their accounts of the particular
circumstances. One boy who grew up in the 1870s described his acquaintance with the quintessential "girls' books" of Sophie May:

> It was a shameful thing for one who had recently enacted Deerslayer and the
> Young Engineer even to look at such books and I averted my eyes [from sets
> of Sophie May books at a neighbor's house]; but in the evening with home
> lessons done and time heavy I bribed my sister to go across the street and
> borrow *Little Prudy's Captain Horace*—the military title taking off some-
> thing of the curse. And once drawn in I read the whole lot . . . and I fell for
> them all, the heroines I mean—sedate Susie and patient Prudy and dashing
> Dotty Dimple—my first love.[37]

In our own day a similar confession was made by the novelist and
broadcaster Melvyn Bragg. He became "hooked" on Alcott after having
picked up at a seaside bookshop *Jo's Boys* (the title of which might well
have caught a young boy off guard). "I read it countless times," he
remembered,

and the pleasure I found in it must have been powerful, for it enabled me to hurdle the terrible barrier presented by *Little Women,* which I sought out at the library on the hunt for anything else by Louisa May Alcott. . . . For *Little Women,* Miss Alcott announced, firmly, on the title page was *A Story for Girls.* Yet I read it. And I think that this is a rare case of Miss Alcott being mistaken. As years went on I discovered that quite a few men had read it as boys—although most of them would qualify the admission by muttering on about sisters or cousins leaving it lying around . . . or the teacher "forcing" them to read it at school.[38]

Well, then, if most girls were devouring boys' books and a few brave boys were reading girls' books, the categorizing of books by gender in an attempt to enforce restrictive gender roles must have been a failure, right? Not necessarily. The crossing of the well-marked lines by child readers, unfortunately, did not render ineffective the messages of the books regarding the cult of manliness, the counsel of feminine subservience.

For one thing, the restrictiveness of the woman's role as prescribed by girls' books was also embodied in the female characters (when there were any) of boys' books. The docility and dependent fearfulness of Becky Thatcher or the selflessness of Tom Sawyer's Cousin Mary communicated cultural expectations as effectively as Katy Carr's reformation (maybe more effectively, since minor characters need not be as complex as successful protagonists). Furthermore, the restrictive fate of females which was spelled out in girls' books must have been sharpened and clarified by contrast with the plucky, cocky heroes of boys' wide-ranging fictional adventures.

The girl reader, no doubt, identified with these enviable heroes as she read, and, theoretically, she could have used them as role models in the dearth of fictional female alternatives to tamed tomboys and saintly sisters. Yet it seems likely that this would have entailed such a strong consciousness of inappropriateness that it would render boys' books little more than escapist fantasy for most girls, not much use in expanding the possibilities of their own lives.

Another ramification of the boys' books–girls' books division is that the phenomenon itself constituted a denigration of the female. The very fact that little onus was attached to girls reading boys' books, while boys reading girls' books was surreptitious and was experienced as somehow shameful, revealed to every child the existence of a hierarchy of value favoring the male. Every trespass onto masculine fictional terrain by girls must have reinforced the awareness of their own inferiority in society's view. As students of the still prevalent practice note, "Girls probably feel some internal pressure to adopt the male-typed choices on which society places such high value. One must assume that girls know the difference between first and second place, and have the same inherent desire for status boys have."[39]

Finally, the numbers of boys reading girls' books most likely has always been small. Salmon rejoiced that reading boys' books might "give sisters a sympathetic knowledge of the scenes wherein their brothers live and work." It appears that few boys over the years have gained a similar sympathetic knowledge of the scenes wherein their *sisters* live and work—a knowledge that fiction could have given them.

In recent years, publishers and librarians have been less likely to segregate books and label them "for boys" and "for girls" than the Victorians were, but the old assumptions about what constitutes appropriate reading for boys and for girls are still with us in the guise of attention paid to children's own reading interests. This would seem to be a step forward, since the many twentieth-century studies of children's reading interests appear to have as their goal ascertaining children's own preferences in reading material rather than using books as instruments to mold children to rigid gender-typed ideals.

And, indeed, an increase in sensitivity to children's reading experiences seems to have sparked the initial studies of children's reading interests in the 1920s. The most substantial study was conducted by George Norvell, an educator who collected data on the subject for over forty years, beginning in the early 1920s. His worthy objective was to promote voluntary reading by young people. To achieve this goal, he reasonably suggested that one needs to consider "(1) the reader's ability and interests and (2) the difficulty and attractiveness of the reading materials."[40]

In his attempt to discover what books students actually do enjoy, Norvell queried some fifty thousand subjects in grades seven through twelve concerning 4,993 selected titles. Students were asked to rate each selection they had read on a three-point scale: very interesting, fairly interesting, or uninteresting. Norvell's study admitted at the outset the questionable reliability of its design: "The plan chosen was to examine the reactions of boys and of girls toward a list of selections, each of which was dominated by a single factor, and to depend upon the minimizing of the potency of other factors through cancellation. Undoubtedly the method has pitfalls, since cancellation may not function as expected" (p. 48). In other words, the researcher may categorize a literary work by one characteristic, assuming that the reader's like or dislike of the work stems from that characteristic, when, in fact, the reader is responding to something quite different. For instance, a student may have rated *The Red Badge of Courage* as very interesting, not because its subject is war (as the researcher might assume) but because he was intrigued by Crane's use of symbol. Another student may have found it interesting only in comparison to other titles on the list and may have indicated a preference for it because it is a short novel.

Norvell's recognition of the method's pitfalls did not restrain him from using his accumulated data to draw sweeping conclusions about the dominance of sex as a determinant of young people's reading choices. "The data of this study indicate that sex is so dominant and ever-present a force in determining young people's reading choices that it must be carefully considered in planning any reading program for the schools" (p. 47). "If adolescents are to be provided with satisfactory materials, the reading interests of boys and of girls must receive separate consideration," and "for reading in common, only materials well liked by both boys and girls should be used" (p. 7). Since Norvell asserted elsewhere that "while boys will not tolerate books primarily about women, girls generally read books about men with satisfaction" (p. 51), this means that his recommendation was that no books about females be assigned or read aloud to mixed classes of girls and boys. It is not surprising that, when they were interviewed by a student of mine, a number of boys said that they had never read a book about a girl in their classes. And neither, of course, had their female classmates.

Yet this study, with all its faults, is one of the more sophisticated ones. Others have relied on forced-choice questionnaires, with questions like "Would you rather read a story about spacemen or one about elves?" One of the problems with this method is that the child has to select one, but might well never choose a book on either subject to read. Or the question might be "Which book do you like better, *Black Beauty* or *Alice in Wonderland*?" The researcher may assume that the child who picks the first prefers animal stories to fantasy, when the child actually enjoys books that make her cry.

Some researchers have described categories of books and asked children which of two types of books they prefer to read. But often the categories are arbitrarily defined. One study concluded that fantasy ranked significantly higher with fourth-grade girls than with their male classmates. Yet fantasy was described on the questionnaire as "a book that is a story of fairies, knights, or imaginary people."[41] This suggests the fairy tale and romance-oriented fantasy, but leaves out many other sorts of literary fantasy. The conclusion is, therefore, misleading.

Samuel Weintraub, whose critique of reading interest studies provides more detail than is possible here, noted that because categories change with each study or are used with different definitions, it has been impossible to synthesize the results of different studies.[42] He concluded:

> In general, the research into children's reading interests has suffered from, among other things, lack of clear definitions and lack of rigor in design, as well as from questionable data-gathering instruments. The instruments appear, for the most part, not to have been scrutinized for reliability or validity, except in the most superficial manner. Through the years the techniques that have been developed seem to have become established by repetition rather than by any careful consideration of their merits or shortcomings.[43]

Weak as the foundation they rest on is, the conclusions of these studies have had a powerful influence on the books boys and girls actually read today. Since it is not possible within the compass of this article to explore all the ways in which this influence has operated, I will focus on the striking effect of the "boys won't read about girls" conclusion of reading-interests researchers.

The following passages are taken from teacher education textbooks published in the last ten years:

> If forced to choose between a book appealing primarily to boys and one to girls, choose the boys' book. Girls might identify with and enjoy *Durango Street, Tuned Out,* or *Swiftwater,* but equally good books appealing chiefly to girls just won't fare equally well with boys.[44]

> The other major factor in reading interest [after age] is sex. Although children may be content to read the same books or have them read aloud, somewhere around the fourth grade, it is made clear to boys that they need special materials appealing to them. Unfair or not, after that time boys are not likely to enjoy girls' books, but girls will usually read and enjoy boys' books. Practically, that means the English teacher must choose common reading that will appeal to boys, ignoring *Jane Eyre, Rebecca, Mrs. Mike,* or *Pride and Prejudice. . . .* Getting boys to relate to literature is often a major problem, but it can become insoluble if the literature presented is incorrectly oriented.[45]

> It has been found that boys will not read "girl books," whereas girls will read "boy books." . . . Therefore, the ratio of "boy books" should be about two to one in the classroom library collection.[46]

The assumption has become a truism, one to which most teachers and librarians active today subscribe.

One effect of the resulting male domination of the literary curriculum in the schools was, of course, to assert the second-class status of the females as clearly as the boys' book phenomenon had ever done. The message to publishers of studies like Norvell's was to look for even more stories with male protagonists; they sold better. Scott O'Dell has related how his publisher asked him to change the sex of his protagonist in *Island of the Blue Dolphins,* a children's book based on an actual event, the survival for many years of a young Indian girl abandoned on a small Pacific island.[47] (Fortunately, O'Dell stood firm, and the story of Karana has become perhaps the most popular of all the books ever awarded the American Library Association's Newbery Medal.) Textbooks and early-reader trade books were particularly male dominated in the 1960s, since it had been noted with alarm that Johnny rather than Janey was likely to have trouble learning to read, and thus it seemed particularly important to offer at this level stories that appealed to boys.

The consciousness-raising that was at the heart of the women's movement began to awaken sociologists, educators, and literary critics to the staggering imbalance in the male-female ratio in picture books, textbooks, and others.[48] They objected to this practice as restricting the reading options of both boys and girls and negatively influencing the self-esteem of girls. Their protest fell on sympathetic ears, and because it was backed by the willingness of librarians and parents to purchase more balanced books as they became available, change was rapid. In the past ten years many fine books have been published with female characters who are much more varied in temperament and role. As early as 1976 a study of current trade books for children counted approximately equal numbers of male and female protagonists and an equal distribution of positive attributes between the two sexes.[49]

Girls now have numerous and varied feminine role models in the books published for children. Real progress has been made, as we can see when we compare the range of books about girls available today as compared to the books of even twenty-five years ago. In historical novels, contemporary fiction, biography, and fantasy, engaging, active heroines abound. Fairy tales featuring spry old ladies, female Paul Bunyans, and capable young girls of perilous quests have been resurrected and published to balance the passive princesses and wicked old witches of the most familiar tales.[50]

Yet what good is this wealth if in 1980 a textbook was telling prospective elementary school teachers that "boys will not read 'girl books' "? And however much we rejoice at the expansion of our daughters' literary horizons, we must recognize that the progress does not benefit our sons if most of them are as reluctant to read girls' books (defined as any book with a female protagonist) as boys were a century ago.

Granted, the appeal of certain books about girls has been strong enough to motivate boys to defy the taboo. Examples include O'Dell's *Island of the Blue Dolphins* (1960), mentioned above; Louise Fitzhugh's

Harriet the Spy (1964), a revolutionary book in its intrepid, eccentric heroine and its funny yet telling satire of adult mores; and *A Wrinkle in Time,* by Madeleine L'Engle (1962), a rare science-fiction novel for preadolescents in which the heroine's problem of being the homely, awkward daughter of a gorgeous, competent mother is entwined with her quest-mission through a hostile universe to rescue her father and save the world from the powers of darkness.

But the phenomenon of large numbers of boys reading these books is an exceptional event, much remarked on in library and publishing circles. It doesn't happen often, and most adults would never think of giving a boy a book about a girl. Parents often ask me to recommend books for family reading aloud. One of my suggestions, Laura Ingalls Wilder's *Little House* series, is greeted with surprise and skepticism by the parents of boys, though I assure them that my son and all his classmates, male and female, were enthralled by the adventures of Laura and Mary when a creative teacher defied expert opinion and chose it to read to her second-grade class. People who work with children can testify to the sad fact that reading a book about a girl is still cause for embarrassment for many young male readers. The student I mentioned earlier, who interviewed boys about their reading, asked one sixth grader: "Can you remember any books about girls that you enjoyed?" He replied, "No [pause], . . . except *A Wrinkle in Time.*" Then he quickly added, "But she wasn't really the main character." But Meg *is* the main character, of course; furthermore, the same boy had earlier named *A Wrinkle in Time* as his favorite book.

This makes clear what has been true all along—that the boys' book–girls' book division, while it depreciated the female experience and so extracted a heavy cost in feminine self-esteem, was at the same time more restrictive of boys' options, of their freedom to read (all the exotic voyages and bold explorations notwithstanding), than of girls'. The fact that girls could roam over the entire territory of children's books while most boys felt confined to boys' books didn't matter much when girls' books were for the most part tame, socializing tools geared to perfecting and indoctrinating young ladies, and virtually all the "good books" from a child's point of view were accessible to boys. But now that many girls' books (whether girls' books are defined as family stories and fairy tales or as all books featuring female characters) are enthralling and enriching stories, boys are the losers. The greater pressure on boys to confine themselves to male-typed reading and behavior, though stemming from the higher status of males, is revealed to be at heart a limitation—one obviously related to all the constraints that preserving the traditional male role impose. We can only speculate about the ramifications of this fact. In a society where many men and women are alienated from members of the other sex, one wonders whether males might be more comfortable with and understanding of women's needs and perspectives if they had imaginatively shared female experience through books, beginning in childhood. At the least, we must deplore the fact that many boys are missing out on one of fiction's greatest gifts, the chance to experience life from a perspective other than the one we were born to—in this case, from the female vantage point.

Patrick Lee and Nancy Gropper, in their article "Sex-Role Culture and Educational Practice," note that because girls experience less pressure than boys to assume same-sex-typed preferences, they tend to be more *bicultural* than boys.[51] (They are referring here to sex-role culture; the term more commonly used is *androgynous*.) They conclude that this biculturalism or androgyny is desirable, and that "boys and girls should be free to approach resources which are currently demarcated along sex-role lines, entirely in accord with individual differences in interests and aptitudes."[52]

If we agree, then an understanding of the subtle influence that restrictive nineteenth-century views on appropriate reading for girls and for boys still exerts on children's reading can help us to identify and challenge its hold.[53] Otherwise, unexamined adult assumptions about divergent reading interests of girls and boys will continue to perpetuate gender-role constraints we thought we had left behind.

Notes

1. Geoffrey Trease, "The Revolution in Children's Literature," in *The Thorny Paradise: Writers on Writing for Children,* ed. Edward Blishen (Harmondsworth, Middlesex: Kestrel, 1975), p. 14.

2. *A Little Pretty Pocket-Book* (London: John Newbery, 1744; 1767 ed. reprinted, London: Oxford University Press, 1966).

3. Sarah Fielding, *The Governess; Or, Little Female Academy,* 2d ed. (London: A. Millar, 1758).

4. Mary Thwaite, *From Primer to Pleasure in Reading,* 2d ed. (London: Library Association, 1972), p. 152.

5. Samuel F. Pickering, Jr., *John Locke and Children's Books in Eighteenth-Century England* (Knoxville: University of Tennessee Press, 1981), p. 244.

6. Mary Ann Kilner, *Memoirs of a Peg-Top* (London: John Marshall, 1783; reprinted, New York: Garland, 1976), p. vi.

7. [Elizabeth Rigby], *Quarterly Review* 74 (1844): 21. Excerpted in *Children and Literature,* ed. Virginia Haviland (Glenview, Ill.: Scott, Foresman, 1973), p. 15.

8. William Graham Sumner, "What Our Boys Are Reading," *Scribner's Monthly* 15 (1878): 681–85.

9. Edward G. Salmon, "What Girls Read," *Nineteenth Century* 20 (1886): 515–29.

10. Charles and Mary Anne Lamb, *The Letters of Charles and Mary Anne Lamb,* 3 vols., ed. Edwin W. Marrs, Jr. (Ithaca: Cornell University Press, 1976), 2: 278–79. Lamb responded: "Dear Godwin,—The Giant's vomit was perfectly nauseous, and I am glad that you pointed it out. I have removed the objection." But he declined to make other suggested changes (p. 279).

11. F. J. Harvey Darton, *Children's Books in England: Five Centuries of Social Life,* 3d ed., rev. Brian Alderson (Cambridge: Cambridge University Press, 1958), p. 217.

12. Salmon, "What Girls Read," p. 522. Sarah Doudney and Anne Beale wrote novels for girls which were noted for their piety and pathos. When Lucy Lyttelton's grandmother began reading aloud *Adam Bede,* "the new novel about which the world raves," it was "duly bowdlerized for our young minds," Lucy reported in her diary. She was eighteen at the time. "In most families George Eliot's works were absolutely forbidden to the young," according to Amy Cruse; those of Charlotte Yonge, on the other hand, were "always open to them" (*The Victorians and Their Reading* [Boston: Houghton Mifflin, 1936], p. 63).

13. Mrs. [Mary Louisa] Molesworth, "Juliana Horatia Ewing," *Contemporary Review* 49 (1886): 675–86; reprinted in *A Peculiar Gift: Nineteenth-Century Writings on Books for Children,* ed. Lance Salway (Harmondsworth, Middlesex: Kestrel, 1976), p. 506.

14. Salmon, "What Girls Read," p. 523.

15. Charles Dickens, *Our Mutual Friend* (Oxford: Oxford University Press, 1952), p. 129.

16. See Walter E. Houghton, *The Victorian Frame of Mind* (New Haven: Yale University Press, 1957), chap. 13; Anne S. MacLeod, *A Moral Tale: Children's Fiction and American Culture, 1820–1860* (Hamden, Conn.: Archon Books, 1975), chap. 1; and Ann Douglas, *The Feminization of American Culture* (New York: Alfred A. Knopf, 1977), chaps. 2 and 3.

17. The doctrine of feminine influence was articulated and embraced in both Britain and the United States, though the social and legal conditions of a frontier society made for interesting complications in America. See Helen Waite Papashvily, *All the Happy Endings* (New York: Harper, 1956), chap. 2; and Elizabeth Segel, "Laura Ingalls Wilder's America: An Unflinching Assessment," *Children's Literature in Education* 8 (1977): 63–70.

18. Salmon, "What Girls Read," p. 526.

19. Gillian Avery, *Childhood's Pattern: A Study of the Heroes and Heroines of Children's Fiction, 1770–1950* (London: Hodder and Stoughton, 1975), p. 166.

20. Papashvily argues persuasively that in popular romances written by women at this time the happy ending is a kind of wish-fulfilling fantasy wherein the woman is recognized as a heroic and noble survivor and her tyrannical or unfaithful husband is reduced to penitent beggary (*All the Happy Endings,* chap. 8). Though adolescent girls no doubt read some of these books, I do not find this compensating fantasy worked out in the books written by women specifically for girls.

21. Susan Coolidge [Sarah Chauncey Woolsey, pseud.], *What Katy Did*

(London: J. M. Dent, 1968). Subsequent references are cited parenthetically in the text.

22. Robert Louis Stevenson, *Treasure Island* (London: Cassell, 1883).

23. MacLeod, *Moral Tale,* p. 10.

24. Whether Jo March, in marrying Professor Bhaer and becoming a sort of Earth-mother, has capitulated is still being debated. My own opinion is that because the final image of Jo is of a strong and successful woman (and because readers, aware of the autobiographical element, consider that she grew up to be a famous writer), Alcott transcended the formula to a great extent, and it is for this reason that the book retained its popularity longer than other girls' books.

25. Annis Pratt, *Archetypal Patterns in Women's Fiction* (Bloomington: Indiana University Press, 1981), p. 14. Pratt notes that in the women's novels about adolescence, "at the same time that the authors . . . suggest psychic dwarfing as the inevitable destiny of young women in British and American society, they manage to introduce a considerable degree of protest into the genre through a vivid depiction of the feelings of its victims" (p. 35). Most girls' books of the nineteenth century, as we might expect, contain few traces of this protest. Women might hint at rebellious feelings to adult women readers, but the sacred duty of preparing girls to accept their assigned role apparently led them to suppress their reservations when writing for girls. The passage describes very well, however, several twentieth-century chronicles of girls' coming of age: Ruth Sawyer's *Roller Skates,* Carol Ryrie Brink's *Caddie Woodlawn,* and Laura Ingalls Wilder's *Little House* books.

26. Thwaite, *From Primer to Pleasure in Reading,* p. 171.

27. Cruse, *Victorians and Their Reading,* pp. 294–97.

28. Salmon, "What Girls Read," p. 524.

29. Alice M. Jordan, *From Rollo to Tom Sawyer and Other Papers* (Boston: Horn Book, 1948), p. 35.

30. Ibid., pp. 48–49.

31. G. Manville Fenn, *George Alfred Henty: The Story of an Active Life* (London: Blackie, 1907); reprinted in Salway, *Peculiar Gift,* p. 430.

32. Cruse, *Victorians and Their Reading,* p. 297.

33. Salmon, "What Girls Read," p. 524.

34. Edith Sichel, "Charlotte Yonge as a Chronicler," *Monthly Review* 3 (1901): 88–97; reprinted in Salway, *Peculiar Gift,* p. 488.

35. Ruth Hill Viguers, "Laura E. Richards, Joyous Companion," in *The Hewins Lectures 1947–1962,* ed. Siri Andrews (Boston: Horn Book, 1963), p. 188.

36. Jordan, *From Rollo to Tom Sawyer,* p. 38.

37. Ibid., p. 37.

38. Melvyn Bragg, "Little Women," *Children's Literature in Education* 9 (1978): 95.

39. Patrick C. Lee and Nancy B. Gropper, "Sex-Role Culture and Educational Practice," *Harvard Educational Review* 44 (1974): 398.

40. George Norvell, *The Reading Interests of Young People,* rev. ed. (Lansing: Michigan State University Press, 1973), p. 3. Subsequent references are cited parenthetically in the text.

41. Lian-Hwang Chiu, "Reading Preferences of Fourth-Grade Children Related to Sex and Reading Ability," *Journal of Educational Research* 66 (1973): 371.

42. Samuel Weintraub, "Two Significant Trends in Reading Research," in *Reading and Writing Instruction in the United States: Historical Trends,* ed. H. Alan Robinson (Urbana: IRA-ERIC, 1977), p. 61.

43. Ibid., p. 63.

44. Steven Dunning and Alan B. Howes, *Literature for Adolescents* (Glenview, Ill.: Scott, Foresman, 1975), p. 198.

45. Dwight L. Burton, et al., *Teaching English Today* (Boston: Houghton Mifflin, 1975), p. 173.

46. Dorothy Rubin, *Teaching Elementary Language Arts,* rev. ed. (New York: Holt, Rinehart, and Winston, 1980), p. 183.

47. Alleen Pace Nilsen, "Women in Children's Literature," *College English* 32 (1971), p. 918.

48. Elizabeth Fisher, "The Second Sex, Junior Division," *New York Times Book Review* (May 21, 1970), pp. 6–7; Nilsen, "Women in Children's Literature," pp. 918–26; Feminists on Children's Literature, "A Feminist Look at Children's Books," *School Library Journal* 17 (1971), pp. 19–24; and Lenore J. Weitzman et al., "Sex-Role Socialization in Picture Books for Preschool Children," *American Journal of Sociology* 77 (1972), pp. 1125–50.

49. Ruth M. Noyce, "Equality of the Sexes in New Children's Fiction," Report prepared at the University of Kansas, 1976. Educational Resources Information Center, ED no. 137/802.

50. Rosemary Minard, *Womenfolk and Fairy Tales* (Boston: Houghton Mifflin, 1975); Ethel Johnston Phelps, *Tatterhood and Other Tales* (Old Westbury, N.Y.: Feminist Press, 1978) and *The Maid of the North: Feminist Folk Tales from around the World* (New York: Holt, Rinehart and Winston, 1981); and Alison Lurie, *Clever Gretchen and Other Forgotten Folktales* (New York: Crowell, 1980).

51. Lee and Gropper, "Sex-Role Culture and Educational Practice," p. 398.

52. Ibid., p. 404.

53. See my article "Choices for Girls, for Boys: Keeping Options Open," *School Library Journal* 28 (1982), pp. 105–7, for practical suggestions for breaking down the gender-determined patterns of children's reading.

Chapter 9
Guaranteed to Please: Twentieth-Century American Women's Bestsellers
Madonne M. Miner

Mid-nineteenth-century America witnessed a remarkable change in the literary marketplace as novels began to sell in quantities previously unimaginable. In 1830, the sale of 6,500 copies of a single text would have been considered a feat; by 1860, publishers were boasting of sales in the hundreds of thousands.[1] Throughout the 1850s, for example, bookbuyers purchased more than 310,000 copies of *Uncle Tom's Cabin* (1852), more than 70,000 copies of *Fern Leaves from Fanny's Portfolio* (1853), and more than 90,000 copies of *The Lamplighter* (1854). The amazing escalation of sales during the mid-nineteenth century leads literary historians to assume the presence of a new group of book-buyers: a group of women.[2] Prior to the boom in women's novels, white middle- and upper-class men both produced and purchased the majority of American texts. But in the early and middle decades of the nineteenth century, white middle-class women came to enjoy what formerly had been the exclusive prerogatives of their brothers: education, leisure, and, perhaps, money for a few "luxury" purchases.[3] They moved into the literary marketplace, not only as writers, but also as readers, and readers with very specific demands.

The boom in women's texts indicates the beginning of a split between texts read by men and those read by women. Certainly, some men contributed to the popularity of Mrs. E.D.E.N. Southworth, Caroline Lee Hentz, Susan Warner et al., but evidence from the marketplace and from women writers themselves (who repeatedly addressed themselves to a female audience) suggests that for the most part men read texts by men, and women by women. In her study of nineteenth-century American novels written and read by women, Nina Baym observed that most male authors "assumed an audience of men as a matter of course, and reacted with distress and dismay as they discovered that to make a living by writing they would have to please female readers. Only three men before the Civil War enjoyed widespread success with women—Timothy Shay Arthur, Nathaniel P. Willis, and George Mitchell."[4] That male and female readers should have parted company when electing texts comes as no surprise; after all, they inhabited "separate spheres,"[5] and these spheres defined possibilities not only of experience, but also of imagination. Thus, the woman who is forbidden by social convention from setting foot on a whaling ship might be inclined to reject the whaling tale in favor of the domestic novel, whose imaginary kitchen floors she trod on, literally, every day.

Differences in men's and women's daily experiences contributed to the formation of a reading public split along sexual lines. But for a more complete understanding of gender-marked reading preferences, we first must ask about reading itself: Why did these nineteenth-century men and women choose to spend their time reading? In its magnitude, the question appears impossible. Recent psychoanalytic theories of the reading process, however, suggest an answer. Norman Holland argues that while *consciously* engaging a text for "social, biographical, political, philosophical, moral, [or] religious meaning," or for "escape, titillation, amusement," readers *unconsciously* engage this text for the sake of the pleasure of transforming "primitive wishes and fears into significance and coherence."[6] In other words, the fictional text provides a locus, a space, in which a reader might reexperience and rework unresolved fantasies and fears that date back to earliest infancy. According to this view, readers would be most attracted to texts that allow the most effective (and, hence, most pleasurable) engagement and transformation of the most primitive aspects of themselves.

This theory of reading suggests at least two corollary theories about textual preferences. First, since every individual adult reader will have experienced a range of childhood wishes and fears, s/he may enjoy a range of texts—but certain texts will answer more closely to her/his own particular psychic structure. For example, the child who could not fully resolve conflicts of desire experienced during the oral phase may be unconsciously drawn, as an adult, to those texts that re-present and, perhaps, resolve oral conflicts. Even when confronted with a text not of her/his own choosing, the reader engages in an individual selection and shaping process. According to Freud, the reader is " 'stimulated' only by those passages which [s/he] feels apply to [him/her]self. . . . Everything else leaves [him/her] cold."[7] We discover evidence of these response variations both in literature classrooms (one student finds paragraphs in Chopin's "Story of an Hour" riveting; another yawns with boredom) and in critical texts such as *Poems in Persons,* where Norman Holland describes various patterns of response characterizing individual readers and writers.[8]

That individuals have different psychic experiences, different needs, and, thus, different textual preferences should be obvious. Equally obvious (but not introduced as an issue by Freud or by most critics from the reader-response school) is a second corollary theory: Since a fundamental differential factor in psychic experience is sex (developmental experiences are *not* the same for girls and for boys), women, as a group, may choose texts different from those chosen by men to meet their different psychic needs. Interested primarily in male development, Freud never constructed an adequate model of female development, nor did he consider fully how sexual differences in development might lead to differences in psychic strategies (here, strategies enacted in writing and reading). Feminist theorists correct Freud on both counts. Responding to Freud's first omission, Nancy Chodorow suggested that as early as the preoedipal phase, girls and boys partake of different developmental and relational experiences, primarily because in our culture (and in that of the nineteenth century) children of both sexes most often are raised by a parent of the female sex. Because of her own psychic experiences, this female parent will "tend to treat infants of different sexes in different ways."[9] As articulated by Chodorow, this sex-specific treatment then produces sex-specific personality configurations (for example, women, nurtured by human beings of the same sex, may experience difficulties with individuation and separation).

Similarly, feminists with an interest in literary theory have begun to correct Freud's second omission. Originally concerned with differences in the writings of women and men, Annette Kolodny, Judith Gardiner, Nelly Furman, and others have recently extended their concern to include differences in reading and interpretation. All have noted the "crucial importance" of the *sex* of a reader or interpreter engaged in attributing "significance to formal signifiers."[10] This feature, previously ignored by critics Holland, Bloom, and Iser, may be a basic determinant in meaning construction. Combining the formulations of feminist psychoanalysts and literary theorists—all of whom are interested in the feminine personality and interpretation—we may deduce, first, that women and men, treated differently as girls and boys, quite probably will have recourse in later life to different treatments/different texts; and, second, that even when reading the same text, women and men quite probably will respond to, cathect with, and derive psychic satisfaction from different aspects of the text.[11]

With this understanding of reading processes and preferences in mind, we may return to the mid-nineteenth-century situation in America. On the one hand, middle-class women of this period had begun to enjoy the leisure and education requisite for reading. On the other hand, they also had begun to experience an attenuation of opportunity, a peculiar "disestablishment."[12] At the same time that women were being restricted more fully to roles within their homes, the home was losing its importance in communal production. Privatizing the home and feminizing the family led, of course, precisely to the sexually unbalanced situation described by Chodorow; as female parents assumed almost exclusive responsibility for early child care, they perpetuated sex-marked developmental differences. Given these features of the nineteenth-century middle-class situation, we should not be surprised that women were purchasing and reading texts in numbers previously unheard of, and that these texts differed in type from those read by men. Undoubtedly, this split in reading experiences produced yet further differences in the way women and men perceived themselves and the world. If we accept Leo Bersani's opinion that written language "doesn't merely describe identity but actually produces moral and perhaps even physical identity,"[13] we must conclude that "identities" produced during the nineteenth century through an immersion in literature split, quite often, along sexual lines.

Nina Baym and others have charted basic characteristics of "the story" repeated over and over in women's novels written and read during the mid-nineteenth century: "In essence, it is the story of a young girl who is deprived of the supports she had rightly or wrongly depended on to sustain her throughout life and is faced with the necessity of winning her own way in the world."[14] As Baym has explained, this story both responded to socioeconomic conditions and ministered to the "inherent psychic needs" of its audience.[15] By the 1870s, however, socioeconomic conditions and inherent psychic needs appear to have changed: "women's novels" of the type described by Baym failed to maintain popular interest. Looking at post–Civil War bestsellers, Baym suggested that "the feminine audience had become appreciative of a more androgynous literature. Works like *Ben Hur* and *In His Steps* . . . depict a community of men and women and imply general religious and social interests common to the sexes."[16] Although women readers undoubtedly helped put *Ben Hur* and *In His Steps* on the newly born bestseller charts, Baym shifted the terms of her argument somewhat by pointing to these texts. Earlier, Baym had restricted her consideration to bestselling texts by and about women; obviously, both Lew Wallace's *Ben Hur* and Charles Sheldon's *In His Steps* fall outside Baym's original category. Are we to assume, then, that after 1870, texts *by* and *about* women no longer engaged a popular following *among* women? Because the nineteenth-century story articulated by Baym falls into disfavor, are we to believe that a specifically female story ceased to appeal?

On the contrary: it is the contention of this essay that women and men, in great numbers, continue to read different texts (or to read the same texts differently), and that variations of a specific "women's story" continue to motivate the sales of texts sold primarily to women. For evidence of the first contention we only need examine the shelf arrangement of a popular bookstore (Westerns and adventure stories on one side, romances on the other) or to refer to the standard texts of popular culture: "The 'happy novels' satisfied one segment [read: women] of the popular market; the 'man story' appealed to another."[17] For evidence of the second contention, we must survey a range of twentieth-century "women's novels," paying attention to repeated plot structures, image patterns, and thematic concerns. The pages that follow provide a survey of specifically "female" aspects of three of the most famous twentieth-century American women's bestsellers: *Gone with the Wind, Forever Amber,* and *Valley of the Dolls.* Each of these novels was written by a woman, focused on a woman, and was addressed primarily to women.

Reading the texts carefully, we may construct a twentieth-century *white middle-class* American "woman's story"—a revision of Baym's nineteenth-century plot outline, more in keeping with twentieth-century psychic needs. On the most obvious level, these texts portray women and men caught in webs of desire; they make their appeal to women interested in heterosexual romance. Less obviously (more deviously, more powerfully), the texts portray women and *women* caught in webs of desire; they appeal to women similarly caught. Repeatedly, the texts portray daughters who, while seeking recourse in the arms of father-lovers, are bound to their mothers by intense physical and emotional appetites. Nancy Chodorow's comments about girls in our society hold true for girls in the novels: "Girls cannot and do not 'reject' their mother and women in favor of their father and men, but remain in a bisexual triangle throughout childhood and puberty."[18] Caught in this triangle, daughter-heroines voice complaints shared by daughter-readers: it is mothers who condemn daughters to inhabit bodies capable of mothering (an equivocal operation at best); it is mothers who leave, failing to provide adequate nourishment; it is mothers who remain, exacting compensation for nourishment not provided. The story told in the bestsellers, then, is built on a bisexual triangle, with tremendous psychic tension marking the relationship between mother and daughter. This particular story helps account for the bestsellers' success; *Gone with the Wind, Forever Amber,* and *Valley of the Dolls* allow a female reader to repeat the most ambivalent relationship of her child-hood, her relationship with the woman on whom she depended for sustenance and love, but from whom she eventually needed to distance herself. Despite the thirty years separating *Gone with the Wind* (1936) and *Valley of the Dolls* (1966), these bestsellers, as well as *Forever Amber* (1944), bear a marked resemblance to one another; each por-trays aspects of a daughter's relationship to her mother: desire, denial, fear, anger, compensation. Only by paying attention to these portraits can we hope to understand how the women's bestsellers appeal to their readership.

Before we do so, however, we must ask if the novels owe their success primarily to women readers. Unfortunately, prior to the computer age, booksellers rarely kept demographic statistics; we do not possess a precise breakdown of the book-buying public by sex. Thus, like Nina Baym working with nineteenth-century material, we must hypothesize an audience on the basis of advertising copy, review copy, and commen-tary from authors and their publishers. On all counts, evidence points to female consumers. Although the novels were advertised in magazines and newspapers which had a general appeal, advertisements also ap-peared with some frequency in magazines that were geared specifically to women. Review copy further supports the female-audience hypoth-esis. Many reviewers targeted women as the most appropriate or intended audience of the novel under review. For example, Robert Gutwilling, writing about the 1936 bestseller *Gone with the Wind,* commented: "It was a book written by a woman for women, and women embraced it."[19] Stephen Vincent Benet also posited a female audience for *Gone with the Wind,* noting that Mitchell consistently centers a reader's interest "not upon the armies and the battles, the flags and the famous names, but upon that other world of women who heard the storm, waited it out, succumbed to it or rebuilt after it, according to their nature."[20] Similarly, William Du Bois predicted on the basis of its heroine that *Forever Amber,* bestseller of 1944 and 1945, would be a "natural": "Anglo-Saxon booksellers, if they are honest, will confess that few characters in fiction are more beloved by female readers than the successful harlot."[21] Later reviewers continued to sing this refrain: Tom Nairn classified Susann's *Valley* as "a sick woman's book, through and through."[22]

Authors and publishers of the bestsellers seem to agree with their reviewers. Susann, possibly one of the best book marketers ever, began with the premise of a female audience: *Valley* "says something . . . and says it particularly to every woman";[23] she assumed that male readers would only be drawn in later: "Men buy mostly non-fiction, history, biography. But if a book has that extra thing, if it's a real story, if it's excitement, then men will buy it, if only to find out why their wives sat up with it all night."[24] Curious husbands, however, have not purchased sufficient copies of *Valley* to justify a reclassification of the novel. It remains a women's bestseller, at least according to its publisher, Bernard Geis, who estimated that the percentage of women readers of *Valley* ran as "high as 70 percent."[25] Thus, although men certainly read these texts, the texts owe their success to women, and they enjoy such a tremendous success with women because they present concerns most often ignored in texts by men.

Gone with the Wind

Generally, mention of Margaret Mitchell's *Gone with the Wind* calls forth images of Scarlett O'Hara and Rhett Butler, two very unforgettable characters engaged in one of the most famous romances in fiction. While granting the powerful appeal of this romance, I must discuss other, equally powerful, aspects of Mitchell's novel, a novel preoccupied with improvident mothers, hungry daughters, and empty houses. Signs of this preoccupation—which is bound to affect the female reader, who quite probably is similarly preoccupied—appear in the first two chapters of *Gone with the Wind*. These chapters, usually read as a leisurely introduction to the ways of southern belles and beaux, actually focus on physical and emotional appetites. In chapter 1, two minor characters, Stuart and Brent Tarleton, attempt to procure a good meal. Having been expelled from the University of Georgia, the Tarleton twins are afraid to return home to their hot-tempered mother, and they expect Scarlett O'Hara, who is seated on the porch of an obviously productive plantation, to invite them in for dinner. Despite the example of "good mothers" (Ellen O'Hara goes to the smokehouse to "ration out the food to the home-coming hands"[26] and Mammy orders Pork to lay out plates for the twins), Scarlett fails to fill these hungry children's stomachs. Certainly, Mitchell treats the Tarletons' quest in a light-hearted and humorous fashion, but as she draws on elements from basic childhood nightmares in structuring her account (to be hungry, to be denied food from the mother), she touches on primitive fears and frustrations. She elaborates on these frustrations in chapter 2, where, once more, a mother fails to meet her child's emotional needs. In this chapter Scarlett, in despair over the news that Ashley Wilkes is to marry Melanie Hamilton, returns to Tara for supper. Approaching the house, Scarlett meets her mother, who has been called away to nurse a neighbor. Ellen pats Scarlett's cheek and, in one of the remarkably few exchanges between mother and daughter to which we are privy, requests that Scarlett take her place at the table. Although Ellen, unlike Beatrice Tarleton, makes sure that the table is laden with food before she leaves, she *does* leave, thereby failing to supply daughter Scarlett with the emotional sustenance she so much desires at this point. Despite plentiful fried chicken, hot buttered biscuits, and yams, this meal is incomplete; Scarlett cannot fill Ellen O'Hara's place. Thus, on an emotional level, chapter 2 repeats the situation of chapter 1.

In the first two chapters of *Gone with the Wind,* Mitchell introduces image clusters that she will associate throughout the rest of her novel with a sense of maternal inadequacy. Although readers of either sex might respond to Mitchell's presentation of deprivation and inadequacy in these chapters, the image clusters work most effectively on female readers for two reasons. First, as a result of the psychodynamics of the American middle-class family, female children more than male feel themselves to be victims of maternal inadequacy. As Phyllis Chesler explains in *Women and Madness,* a mother's love for her daughter often is fraught with far more tension and anxiety than that for her son. Hence, the daughter receives equivocal, ambivalent messages from her mother, prompting feelings of confusion, anger, and despair from the daughter who wants so very much to be loved.[27] Second, Mitchell's clusters may exert an especially strong appeal to members of that sex which produces potentially inadequate mothers; identifying both with Scarlett and with Ellen, female readers may protest against the never-ending demands of ever-hungry children like the Tarleton twins or, in chapter 2, like Scarlett herself.

Undoubtedly the two most powerful representations of maternal inadequacy and female frustration occur in those chapters that depict Scarlett's attempts to return to Ellen and Mammy, to recapture an imagined "perfect union" between mother and child. The first of these attempts takes place after Scarlett functions as reluctant midwife to Melanie Hamilton. Knowing next to nothing about the delivery of children, Scarlett must rely on her wits and on the very abbreviated instructions of Dr. Meade: "There's nothing much to bringing a baby. Just tie up the cord" (p. 306). Almost immediately after the severing of Beau from his mother (Dr. Meade's "tying," of course, implied "cutting"), Scarlett determines on a return to *her* mother. Sitting on the porch trying to renew her strength, Scarlett sees flames, realizes that Atlanta is on fire, and panics: "She was a child mad with fright and she wanted to bury her head in her mother's lap and shut out this sight. If only she were home! Home with Mother" (p. 312). This desire—for enclosure within a protective maternal space—is expressed by Scarlett repeatedly in the novel. It is interesting that, while the longing "to bury her head in her mother's lap and shut out this sight" appears to be most directly provoked by the sight of Atlanta in flames, it emerges in close conjunction with the earlier vision of Beau being cut off from his mother. Scarlett's determination to return to Ellen immediately contradicts the fact—the "sight"—of this separation.

Psychoanalytic theory suggests that this "fact of separation" is more problematical for daughters, and, hence, more engaging as textual material for daughter readers. In order to assume her status as an individual, a child (of either sex) must disentangle herself from her primary love object: the mother. However, as Chodorow and others have pointed out, the femaleness of the mother induces a crucial asymmetry in the process of separation and individuation.[28] Because both parties belong to the same sex, the mother-daughter relationship offers identification possibilities that far exceed those offered by the mother-son relationship. As a result, the process by which a daughter disentangles herself from her mother is more complicated and longer lasting; in general, the conflicts implicit in this process are never unequivocally resolved. In light of such an analysis of the development of the female psyche, it is not surprising that *Gone with the Wind,* a bestseller among women, should manifest a preoccupation with such issues.

Acting on her desire to return to her mother, Scarlett, along with Melanie, Beau, Prissy and Wade, starts for Tara. As she strains to pilot these four children back to a maternal space, Scarlett is nearly overcome by darkness and fear. To prod herself forward, she calls on Ellen—for Scarlett, the embodiment of security and stability. As a child, Scarlett had confused her mother with the Virgin Mary, and she saw no reason to right this confusion as she grew older: "To her, Ellen represented the utter security that only Heaven or a mother can give" (p. 55). Now, working her way homeward, burdened with the knowledge of Ellen's sickness, Scarlett further obfuscates boundaries by pushing for an identification between Ellen and Ellen's house: Tara is the heaven/haven over which Ellen presides. With each weary step, Scarlett yokes person and place together more firmly: she wants to run to get "closer to Tara and to Mother," and she fears it will be hours "before she knew if Tara still stood and if Ellen were there" (p. 330).

Associating house and mother, Scarlett effects a merger that appears most often in gothic fiction, another genre that owes its popularity to women. Perhaps the association here appeals to some of the same psychic forces in female readers that the gothic does. One female reader of gothics explains that what draws her to the genre is its preoccupation with "the spectral presence of a dead-undead mother, archaic and all-encompassing, a ghost signifying the problematics of female identity which the heroine must confront."[29] This reader's comments suggest an explanation for a female reader's involvement in Scarlett's quest at this point in *Gone with the Wind;* along with Scarlett, the reader moves toward Tara, which here takes on the characteristics of a "forbidden center," a place where boundaries between life and death, mother and daughter, become confused.[30]

Insidiously, Scarlett's yoking of person and place undermines her faith in her mother's health, for as Scarlett draws near Tara, the landscape suggests that both this heaven/haven and its inhabitants have been destroyed: "The countryside lay as under some dread enchantment. Or worse still, thought Scarlett with a chill, like the familiar and dear face of *a mother,* beautiful and quiet at last, after death agonies" (p. 331; my italics). The simile is ominous, not so much because it forecasts Ellen's death, but because it intensifies associations between mothers and death; using the indefinite article *a,* Mitchell allows us to see this face as belonging not only to Ellen, Scarlett's mother, but to *any* mother, perhaps to our own mothers.

After a day and a night, Scarlett and her charges arrive at Tara. She peers up "the long tunnel of darkness" so as to discern whether or not Tara still stands: "The dear white walls, the windows with the fluttering curtains, the wide verandahs—were they all there ahead of her, in the gloom? Or did the darkness mercifully conceal such a horror as the MacIntosh house?" (p. 336). The passage expresses fear of the maternal body; what horrors confront the child who strains her eyes to peer up its "tunnel of darkness"? Recall that Scarlett had to do just this when she served as midwife for Melanie. As the shadowy outlines of her home grow more distinct, Scarlett, hoping to hug the walls themselves, starts to rush forward but then senses something is wrong: Tara is "shrouded with the same eerie quiet that hung over the whole stricken countryside" (p. 337). Gerald appears on the verandah, but he, too, is peculiarly silent. When Scarlett asks about her mother and sisters, Gerald replies, "The girls are recovering" (p. 338). Terrified, Scarlett cannot utter the question that must be asked, the question that might resolve "the frightening riddle of Tara's silence."

> As if answering the question in her mind, Gerald spoke.
> "Your mother—" he said and stopped.
> "And—Mother?"
> "Your mother died yesterday." (P. 338)

Occurring one-third of the way through the novel, this passage marks one of its climaxes. Suddenly, fears and premonitions from the past few days fall together, find a focus. For Scarlett, Tara is empty; the promise of maternal presence at the end of the tunnel has been betrayed. Looking for Ellen's arms, Scarlett finds only blank walls, dead ends. The child returns home to discover that there is no home, that the cord has been cut, that she is no longer a child. A female reader may readily participate in Scarlett's disappointment; like Scarlett, she must undergo some form of estrangement from her own mother if she is to assume an adult identity of her own.

The child Scarlett receives a further push toward adulthood when Dilcey informs her that as Ellen lay on her deathbed, she did not ask for any family members but, rather, cried for someone name Philippe. Unaware of a Philippe in Ellen's past, Scarlett sadly perceives the limitation of her perception of Ellen: rents appear in a formerly whole (if imaginary) fabric. These rents are realized graphically as Scarlett, leaving the sickroom in which her mother has died and her two sisters combat the raging fever of typhus, looks out the window of Tara. The plantation stretches before her, "negroes gone, acres desolate, barns ruined, *like a body bleeding under her eyes, like her own body, slowly bleeding*" (p. 349; my italics). Up to this point, Mitchell consistently called on maternal bodies to function as vehicle in land similes; she now requires that daughter Scarlett assume the position previously held by Ellen. In her movement from the generalized "a body" to the more specific attribution "her own body," Mitchell underscores Scarlett's reluctance to accept this burden. Also, in coloring this body with blood, Mitchell suggests that, on a purely physical level, Scarlett, possessed of a body that bleeds/menstruates, is as capable as Ellen of assuming maternal burdens.

Capable she is. Here we come to another extremely potent ingredient in Scarlett's character which is likely to prompt a strong response in a female audience. We are drawn to Scarlett not only because we share her desire to be cared for, to realize a perfectly stable relationship with an all-provident mother, but also because, once Scarlett's desire is denied, she shows herself capable of caring for herself. Surrounded by children ("Her father was old and stunned, her sisters ill, Melanie frail and weak, the children helpless, and the negroes looking up to her with childlike faith" [pp. 348–49]), Scarlett pursues the course of an adult— of a mother.[31] As mentioned earlier, one of the cardinal duties of mothers in *Gone with the Wind* is to provide food, and Scarlett, once informed of her mother's death, directs her first efforts to this end. Having eaten very little during the past two days, Scarlett asks Pork if there is food in the house, only to be told that the Yankees have taken everything. She then gives evidence of her abilities as provider; where

Pork assumes the entire plantation to be barren, Scarlett can suggest spots of fertility: the sweet potato hills and the scuppernong arbor may furnish immediate food and drink.

In the days that follow, Scarlett must forage further for supplies. Mitchell's depiction of Scarlett ravaging the slave quarter gardens at Twelve Oaks, biting into a dirty radish, vomiting, and then making her vow to heaven— " 'as God is my witness, I'm never going to be hungry again' " (p. 357)—affects us powerfully, as it presents us with a woman confronting an elementary fear of childhood: What happens when mother's cupboards are bare? Again, adults of both sexes may be drawn to a text that allows them to repeat and master this childhood fear, but because Mitchell depicts a hungry *female* heroine, identification will be far more pronounced in female readers (studies suggest that most men simply do not identify with female characters).[32] Of course, Mitchell's depiction of Scarlett in the slave quarter gardens is double-edged; it conveys the intensity both of Scarlett's hunger and of her will to live. As Scarlett lies prostrate in the dirt, she determines that there is no going back to the past (mother Ellen *is* dead), and that she must go forward. Propelled by this determination, Scarlett rises and settles her basket, heavy with turnips and cabbages, across her arm. This act is significant: Scarlett's willingness to bear the burden—food for the "children" at Tara—indicates her assumption of maternal responsibility. The basket cuts into her flesh, as does the responsibility. Although Scarlett manages to put apples, yams, peanuts, and milk on the table, she is ever preoccupied with the food problem: "The world outside receded before the demands of empty and half-empty stomachs and life resolved itself into two related thoughts, food and how to get it" (p. 357). As in the opening chapters of her novel, Mitchell here foregrounds an association between women and food, an association easily understood by women readers, who undoubtedly experience the demands signified by this association in their own lives.

Scarlett's second attempt to return home, to recuperate a sense of an all-provident mother, occurs after Melanie's second pregnancy, a pregnancy that takes Melanie's life and leaves Scarlett, once again, in charge of many orphans. As if to emphasize this pattern of maternal loss, Mitchell points out similarities in Scarlett's response to the deaths of Melanie and Ellen: "Suddenly it was as if Ellen were lying behind that closed door, leaving the world for the second time. Suddenly she was standing at Tara again with the world about her ears, desolate with the knowledge that she could not face life without the terrible strength of the weak, the gentle, the tender hearted" (p. 483). The scene recalls not only Ellen's death but also the culmination of Melanie's first pregnancy, where, as midwife attending a birth, Scarlett was compelled to confront the fact of separation. Here, again at the end of a pregnancy, we witness separation—this time, the separation of death.

Terrified, Scarlett seeks consolation in the arms of Ashley and Rhett, but the former proves to be a child himself, a fantasy created by the very young Scarlett. And Rhett? Rhett gives up the battle for the future and joins those who seek refuge in the past. When Scarlett flees to the "home" she shares with Rhett on Peach Tree Street, she discovers that he has withdrawn his love from her; he has excused himself from her life. Sure, as the small child is sure, that love is to be given on demand, she insists that Rhett open his arms to her, offer her a breast on which she may lay her head. Rhett's refusal reenacts a mother's refusal, finally, to indulge the child's wish to see her as a simple extension rather than a separate individual. Scarlett must accept the fact of Rhett's departure, but she cannot accept the fact of disconnection. Disappointed with Rhett, Scarlett vows to return once again to the maternal origins. Of course, Ellen is dead—but the process of generalization and obfuscation that identifies land and house with the maternal body sets up Tara as the site of reunification, nondifferentiation, and wholeness. When Scarlett, on the final page of the novel, resolves to go home, her destination is no longer Peach Tree Street, and the embrace she craves is not that of Rhett. This ever-unsatisfied child imagines that Mammy will be at Tara: "Suddenly she wanted Mammy desperately, as she had wanted her when she was a little girl, wanted the broad bosom on which to lay her head, the gnarled black hand on her hair. Mammy, the last link with the old days" (p. 862).[33]

Mammy may very well be at Tara, just as she was at Tara following Ellen's death, but now, as then, she cannot possibly meet Scarlett's expectations. Following Ellen's death, Scarlett laid her head on Mammy's broad sagging breasts and thought, "Here was something of stability . . . something of the old life that was unchanging" (p. 346). But Mammy's first words had to do with "weary loads," and Scarlett's illusions of stability were dispelled, just as they must be dispelled in her second return to Tara. By suggesting a repetition of previous scenes, Mitchell undermines belief in some past wholeness. Over and over again, Gone with the Wind shows us that Mammys have not always been at home, will not always be at home. We may desire Mammy as a stable presence, but Mitchell, from the first pages of her novel to the last, denies the possibility of realizing this desire: Ellen's absence at the dinner table presages later, more permanent, absence. Thus, the fantasy operating in Gone with the Wind—operating on both the novel's heroine and on us, its female readers—engages us in repeated cycles of desire and denial: desire for an all-provident mother, denial of her actual existence.

Forever Amber

Desire for and denial of the mother also operate powerfully in Kathleen Winsor's 1944 bestseller, *Forever Amber.* Although this novel, like Mitchell's, provides its readers with heterosexual romance (Amber marries four men, sleeps with many others, and bears various offspring), it also offers readers a clear representation of maternal omnipotence, as Winsor repeatedly depicts Amber in relation to men involved with women. From the first chapter of part 1 to the final chapter of part 6, Winsor's heroine doggedly directs her emotional energies to capturing the attention of a much-coveted male, but every such attempt propels Amber into some sort of relationship (mother, daughter, sister) with another female. Even more effective than Winsor's representation of these various bisexual triangles, however, is her representation of terrors associated with the female body. Like *Gone with the Wind, Forever Amber* allows a female reader to explore feelings of ambivalence toward the maternal body—that body belonging to her mother and, as she is a potential mother, to herself. As recent feminist psychoanalytic theory has pointed out, while accession to the maternal role enhances a woman's claim on paternal affections, it also precipitates the collapse of self into one's mother and the metamorphosis of one's body into something alien, something other. If identity boundaries are problematic for the female child, problems arise once again when the adult female bears a child. As the child has difficulty differentiating self from other, so, too, does the mother, who for nine months not only encompasses this other being but also loses control over the body she formerly identified as self.[34] Winsor conveys the dangers of the maternal position in a cluster of scenes that give a definite structure to the novel as they present and re-present a configuration of exclusively female characters caught in an exclusively female space: the body that may give birth.

We need not read far to arrive at the first of these scenes, as Winsor sets the prologue of her novel in a lying-in chamber. Her opening sentence, describing the chamber, obviously suggests a female space: "The small room was warm and moist."[35] As Winsor continues her description of the room and of the various women who occupy it, the space becomes increasingly ominous. A midwife works with her hands on a woman who has just given birth, while various village wives watch with "tense, anxious faces." The woman who has given birth, Judith Marsh, slips into a reverie but awakens to cramps and pain which do not abate. Raising her hand, Judith notes that it is smeared with blood. Only then do we understand, as Judith understands, the source of the chamber's tension and the meaning of its signs: Judith's body has betrayed her. She turns frantically to the midwife: "Sarah! Sarah, help me! I don't want to die!" (p. 16), but Sarah cannot stop the blood that flows from between Judith's legs.

Who could ask for more in an opening chapter? Winsor rivals Margaret Mitchell in her ability to convey the horrors of a birthing chamber, horrors stemming in large part from the pregnant woman's sense of confinement within her own body. Perhaps Winsor even surpasses Mitchell. When the barely pregnant Melanie Hamilton retreats into her narrow bedroom to die, she takes her unborn child with her. But Judith dies only after discovering that she has been doubly betrayed by her body; with unmistakable disappointment she learns she has given birth to a daughter rather than a son.

Of course, it is easy to see this mother as the first casualty in the ongoing struggle between mothers and daughters which *Forever Amber* documents. But of equal importance, surely, is an understanding of Judith's death as the first instance of a woman taken prisoner by her own body. This language is not too strong, as the text shows only a few chapters later, when Judith's daughter, now sixteen, learns that she, too, is to become a mother. At first the knowledge does not burden Amber St. Claire, for she hopes to use it to persuade the seafaring Bruce Carlton to remain in London with her. But Bruce abandons her for his ship, and as weeks pass, Amber feels increasingly "frightened and baffled by the knowledge that imprisoned within her body, growing with each day that passed, was proof of her guiltiness" (p. 85); Amber here figures her body as prison, the embryo as prisoner. Not long after, she refines this imagery. Riding back from The Royal Exchange, Amber and her new acquaintance, Mrs. Sally Goodman, witness the public whipping of a woman who has given birth to a bastard child. Amber cries out in horror as the whip slashes across the convict's shoulders, but Sally tells her not to waste her sympathy: "It's the common punishment, and no more than the wicked creatures deserve" (p. 91). Amber, however, cannot help but sympathize: " 'Oh, Gemini!' she thought in frantic despair. 'That might be me! That *will* be me!' " (p. 91). The prisoner-mother functions as a possible model for all mothers, and Amber is not far off in her prediction that she herself will follow in this woman's steps. Without a husband, she experiences her pregnancy "closing in on her, seeming to shut her into a room from which there was no escape" (p. 97); Winsor's articulation of Amber's fear allows a female reader to work through similar fears that she may have experienced (either conjecturally or actually): Will a fetus devour me? Will it leave me any space of my own? Terrified of this imagined room from which there is no escape, Amber accepts the marriage proposal of Sally's so-called nephew, Luke Channell. This, however, fails to bring lasting relief; in fact, it lands her literally in prison. When Luke and Sally cheat her of her money and make her responsible for their numerous bills, the pregnant Amber is taken to Newgate. With three other prisoners, Amber must await cell assignment in the Condemned Hold. A description of this room opens chapter 9: "The floor of the room was covered with rushes which smelt sour and old. . . . The walls were stone, moist and dripping and green with a mossy slime" (p. 105). Placing this description at the beginning of the chapter and insisting on details that generate a sense of constriction as well as an atmosphere of dread, Winsor links the Condemned Hold to the lying-in chamber of her prologue; these spaces—and the space of the maternal body—resemble one another in curious, ominous ways.

If the lying-in chamber of the prologue serves as prototype for the Condemned Hold of chapter 9, Moll Turner, a "morose slattern" chained to the wall across from Amber, serves as possible prototype for herself. Two other women, a young Quaker and a middle-aged house-wife, also sit chained in the hold, but it is to the "dirty slut with large open sores on her face and breasts" that Amber directs her inquiries about the prison. Through the conversation that ensues, Winsor suggests various affinities between the two superficially dissimilar females.[36] On learning that Amber is pregnant and cannot call on her family, Moll nods knowingly. "That's the way I began. He was captain in the King's army—a mighty handsome fellow in his uniform. But my dad didn't like to see his daughter bringin' a nameless brat into the family" (pp. 108–9). Like Amber, and like Amber's mother, Judith, this woman escapes her family with a man, only to find herself caught in another, no less binding, net. Amber stares at Moll "with fascinated horror, finding it almost impossible to believe that this ugly emaciated sick creature had once been young and in love with a handsome man, *just as she was*" (p. 109; my italics). While Amber sees herself, years hence, in Moll, Winsor adds one final bit of information about the latter, further enhancing the reflective possibilities of this mirror: Moll is thirty-two. If we add Amber's age (sixteen) to that of her mother at the time of her death (sixteen-seventeen), we see that Moll's birthdate must fall somewhere in the same year as Judith's: If the latter had lived, would she resemble her contemporary? In the process of becoming a mother herself, can Amber avoid becoming like either of these two mothers (one dead, the other nearly so)? Amber's stare of "fascinated horror," then, finds a parallel in the lives of many female readers: it is the gesture adopted by many daughters as they resolve to evade their mother's fate. Through Moll,

Winsor reminds readers of the mother out of nightmare, the mother from whom daughters must violently disengage themselves.

Of even more immediate concern to Amber than Moll's decay from pleasing young woman to repellent old hag is the physical meta-morphosis wrought on her own body by pregnancy. Winsor is no less concerned: while her description of Judith's ordeal during delivery may provoke sympathy and fear on the part of a female reader, her minutely detailed presentation of Amber, seven months pregnant, is likely to call forth feelings of revulsion and lead to serious questions about the desirability of motherhood:

> There was no doubt her appearance had suffered sad changes during the past five weeks. Now, at the end of her seventh month of pregnancy, she could no longer button her bodice, the once pert frills had wilted, and her smock was a dirty grey. Her gown was stained in the armpits, spotted with food, and her skirt hung inches shorter in front. She had long ago thrown away her silk stockings, for they had been streaked with runs, and her shoes were scuffed out at the toes. She had not seen a mirror since she had been there, nor taken off her clothes, and though she had scrubbed her teeth on her smock she could feel a slick film as she ran her tongue over them. Her face was grimy and her hair, which she had to comb with her long fingernails, snarled and greasy. (P. 116)

Eerily, the look of "fascinated horror" that Amber directed at Moll Turner, we now direct at her, the mother-to-be. Of course, one might argue that under ordinary circumstances pregnancy is not quite so miserable; after all, grease and dirt collect in Amber's hair not because she is pregnant but because she is in prison. But the text overrides this argument as it insists that maternity itself is a prison, a "growing, living net," a small room from which escape is possible only after nine months. Presenting pregnancy in such a consistently negative light, Winsor allows female readers the possibility of experiencing their own negative or ambivalent feelings about pregnancy without having to pay for these feelings in guilt (the usual price of ambivalence in "real life").

Amber leaves Newgate, gives birth to her child, and subsequently undergoes several more pregnancies. Although none of these is reported in as much detail as her first, Amber never fails to protest against the unwanted and apparently uncontrollable changes in her body/herself. At times her protest takes the form of a sharp admonition to the maid to lace her more tightly, to hold her burgeoning waist in as far as possible; at other times, so upset with the prospect of being "misshapen," Amber terminates the pregnancy early with an abortifacient. Winsor's most alarming example of pregnancy as a "looming monster" (p. 94), however, occurs in a scene depicting the Great London Fire. As Amber rides into the burning city, one of the sights to greet her, amid clouds of smoke and crowds of people, is that of pregnant women:

> There were a great many pregnant women, desperately trying to protect their awkward bellies, and several of the younger ones were crying, almost hysterical with terror. The sick were carried on the backs of sons or husbands or servants. A woman lying in a cart rolled slowly by; she was groaning and her face was contorted in the agony of childbirth; beside her knelt a midwife, working with her hands beneath the blankets, while the woman in her pain kept trying to throw them off. (P. 492)

Once more, Winsor uses setting as commentary on maternal situations; to be caught in the raging fire would seem to pose no more of a threat to these beings than to be caught in their expanding bodies. Also, once more, Winsor is unable to take her eyes off these terrified women; while touching on other members of the populace cursorily, she grants extended attention only to women with bulging bellies. Stripped to its essentials, the scene is reminiscent of Margaret Mitchell's famous Atlanta fire scene, during which Melanie, with Scarlett's help, gives birth to Beau. In both, a heroine must cope with the incessant demands of other female bodies that are trying to bring babies into a world that falls apart on all sides.

Valley Of the Dolls

Years before the feminist novels of the 1970s, Winsor and Mitchell produced novels that documented specifically female experience and addressed specifically female concerns, and they found a large female readership. The same readership made Jacqueline Susann's *Valley of the Dolls* a bestseller in the 1960s. On a most superficial level, we might read *Valley* as the "story of three girls who separately came to New York in search of romance and success in show business and social life but, in their ambitious climb, took to pill-popping and couldn't get out of the habit."[37] Certainly, Susann employed elements of romance and of melodrama so as to attract a certain type of bookbuyer. But beneath the romance and melodrama, we once more find a subtext centered on the mother-daughter relationship—most especially, on the way this relationship functions in a context of consumption (not only of "dolls," but also of food, affection, life itself). This subtext substantiates Susann's statement that *Valley* "says something . . . and says it particularly to every woman."[38]

Valley makes virtually no reference to fathers (they are beneficently absent), and very few references to mothers and sons,[39] but mothers and daughters abound: Susann suggests that her heroines—Anne Welles, Neely O'Hara, and Jennifer North—began their careers as consumers at the breasts of their mothers. Susann draws connections between mothers' nourishment and daughters' consumption most clearly in the case of Neely, orphaned at a very young age and, thus, according to the logic of the novel, craving substitutes for the maternal nourishment denied her. Early symptoms of Neely's tendency toward compensatory consumption occur in a scene between young Neely and Anne. As the latter leaves on a date, the former asks if Anne has any more of "those terrific chocolate marshmallow cookies left."[40] Anne offers the entire box, and Neely, "cradling the box," responds, "Oh marvelous! . . . I've got a library copy of *Gone with the Wind,* a quart of milk and all these cookies. Wow! What an orgy!" (p. 24). Never having been cradled, Neely cradles herself, surrounds herself with objects that she will consume and incorporate. The objects she selects associate reading with the gratification of childish appetites. The allusion to *Gone with the Wind* is a reflexive trope. Neely—greedily consuming a quart of milk, a box of cookies, and Mitchell's novel—prefigures the scene of reading, the orgy of consumption which, multiplied a millionfold, would be the measure of Susann's accomplishment.

By alluding to Mitchell's novel in her own, Susann encouraged comparison of the two bestsellers. *Gone with the Wind* is the only novel mentioned by name in *Valley;* further, when Neely, not long after reading Mitchell's novel, must choose a stage name for herself, she adopts Scarlett as ancestor, christening herself Neely O'Hara. Neely's choice is appropriate: both she and Scarlett live in the shadow of a large maternal figure; both experience intense pangs of hunger; both consume themselves in a frantic quest for nourishment. Neely's orgiastic ingestion of marshmallow cookies and Mitchell's novel serves as the first in a series of such scenes. As she grows older, her tastes become more expensive, but the motivation for this consumption remains the same. For example, when Neely feels abandoned by her husband, she tiptoes down to the kitchen, opens the refrigerator, and takes out a large jar of caviar: " 'Neely, we're gonna have a ball,' she cried aloud" (p. 306). After consuming the caviar, several pills, and a large quantity of liquor, Neely staggers to bed, leaving instructions with the butler: "I won't take any calls. I'm gonna sleep. And when I wake up tomorrow I want pancakes with butter and loads of syrup. I'm gonna have an orgy!" (p. 306). "To sleep and eat": this is the most infantile of orgies.[41] Despite or because of its regressive qualities, Neely's vision exerts a peculiarly strong force: to be asleep in a womblike state, to be fed on demand: What more could a hungry little girl ask for?

At times, Susann specifies the source of Neely's hunger. Neely tells her director, John Sykes, that her psychiatrist has pushed her to realize that she feels the need for "mass love" because she has never known a mother's love. John scoffs and chides Neely for accepting the verdict of one of those "fancy doctors who blame everything on the poor mothers of the world." He continues: "So your old lady kicked off early. Did she do it purposely just to get even with you?" (p. 301). John asks a reasonable question, a question we might ask; nonetheless, the novel insists that mothers *are* to blame. A few years after Neely's conversation with John, she finds herself in therapy with yet another "fancy doctor," and, sure enough, his very first question focuses on Neely's mother: "Tell me about your mother, Miss O'Hara" (p. 409). Neely may object that she has already spent too many years and too much money convincing her former psychiatrist that she doesn't remember her mother, but her objection merely compounds evidence against the woman who provided so little love that her daughter cannot even conjure up a memory.

If Neely's mother commits a mortal sin by dying, Jennifer's mother commits a sin of similar magnitude by living. She represents the mother who insists on reciprocity: having nourished her daughter, she now expects nourishment in return. Appropriately, Jen's mother regards Jen's breasts as the source of nourishment. She advises Jen to watch her weight, to keep her figure, and to make her breasts "pay while you have them" (p. 190). Of course, mama intends that money earned on these mammary glands will revert to her, the initial giver of milk. This intention pushes Jen even further into the role of consumer, purchasing and discarding closets of clothing so as to capture Tony Polar, and thereby meet the demands of her parent. Jennifer rebels, but in a rather surreptitious fashion; in a phone conversation between Jen and her mother, we learn that Jen has told Tony that her mother is dead. When Jen's very lively mother protests, Jen asks: "Mother, what should I tell him? That I have a mother and stepfather and a grandmother living in Cleveland who can't wait to move in with us?" (p. 190). The point here is that it makes no difference whether mothers are alive or dead, nutritive or nonnutritive; in either state they damn daughters to a condition of incessant consumption. Jen learns that, even in a state between life and death, mothers "louse you up." Just as she seems to have convinced Tony that he must marry her before he can enjoy her body, a telegram arrives, announcing the death of Anne's mother. This interruption ruins Jen's game (Tony forces himself on her), and all she can do is swear silently: "Damn, damn! What timing. Damn Anne's mother! Damn all mothers! Even in death they reached out and loused you up!" (p. 221). Jen's curse might serve as epigraph for Susann's novel because, in the final analysis, Susann damns mothers, damns them both for reaching out and for not reaching out. Like *Forever Amber, Valley* offers readers a fictional space in which they, too, may damn mothers, safely, without real-life repercussions.

Jen's curse is not the last levelled at the dead Mrs. Welles. Daughter Anne curses her mother in similar fashion following a weekend she and Lyon Burke spend together in Lawrenceville, during which Lyon proposes that he and Anne live in the maternal house. Anne's horrified response ("Before I came to New York I lived here, in this mausoleum. I was nothing. I was dead. When I came to New York it was like a veil lifting" [p. 243]) not only reminds us of the potential for gothic horror within so many women's texts, it also sends a silenced Lyon packing. Anne is left to damn the town of her birth: "Damn Lawrenceville! It was like an octopus, reaching out and trying to drag her down" (p. 243). Of course, it is Anne's mother who more accurately merits comparison to the octopus—the mother, who, in life, nearly smothers Anne in an exclusively female home, and, in death, reaches out tentacles to bind her once again. From the first pages of her novel on, Susann suggests that maternal body, maternal house, and maternal city fatally inhibit Anne's growth (the implication for a female reader, of course, is that mother is to blame for limitations daughter feels in her own life).[42] With Susann, we applaud Anne's initial escape to New York City. We are glad to see her run from the mother who insists that, although daughter might add a wing to the family house once she has married, she must live in this house, a house in which only women seem to survive. (Anne's father dies when she is twelve, leaving Anne to be brought up by mother and aunt, in grandmother's house.) The maternal body, so readily associated with the stifling maternal home, is an easy scapegoat for all ills in this novel, just as it so often is an easy scapegoat for the ills experienced by women readers.

Given that none of the "real mothers" in Susann's novel live up to expectations for a "good-enough mother," daughters turn elsewhere, to dolls. Susann's title, of course, plays on the multiple meanings of this word: Neely, Jen, and Anne are dolls; pills are dolls; dolls, for women who remain childless, are pills. In other words, just as a little girl is surrogate mother to or finds surrogate mothers in her dolls, the three women of *Valley* discover a substitute for mother/mothering in the pills that return them to a womblike state. Susann's description of the effect of the dolls/pills might well describe the experience of returning to a prenatal condition. Without exception, these descriptions are the most sensual in the novel—far more sensual than any description of lovemaking. When Jennifer, for example, takes her first pill, she reaches an all-time high: "Then she felt it! Oh God! It was glorious! Her whole body felt weightless . . . her head was heavy, yet light as air. She was going to sleep . . . sleep" (p. 216). Jen's bliss suggests a child in a cozy all-provident womb. Susann's description of what two pills could do reinforces this association: "One worked—but two! It was the most beautiful feeling in the world. She put her head on the pillow gently. The soft numbness began to slither through her body" (p. 227). If mothers will not supply daughters with "soft numbness," pills will. Thus begins a most fatal pattern of compensatory consumption.

What effect does knowledge of this fatal pattern of accelerating consumption have on a reader? Although we may feel sorry for this woman, surely a more general response is one of reassurance: "Yes, this is the way it is supposed to be; all women suffer emotional malnutrition; all women finally must turn to consumption for sustenance." "All": the product consumed by the reader guarantees an escape from a nightmarishly confusing "real world" landscape to a landscape of absolutes, where daughters are victims and mothers, victimizers. Anne turns to dolls for "a few hours of escape," and we turn to *Valley* for the same. Anne swallows capsules as we swallow pages. Susann suggests the analogy between character as consumer and reader as consumer when she describes the effect that Anne's first Seconal has on her. Anne takes the pill, and then: "She began to read. In ten minutes the print began to blur. It was fantastic" (p. 476). Here, locating the act of reading in close proximity to that of pill-popping, Susann blurs distinctions between the two acts and between their effects: the ingestion of both pills and print leads to a comfortable, if artificial, wholeness. While hungry daughters in *Valley* turn to various well-stocked shelves for sustenance, the female reader, also a hungry daughter, turns to the similarly well-stocked shelves of her bookstore. Having purchased a novel by Mitchell, Winsor, or Susann, this reader may retreat to her private reading space and indulge in a feast of pages. Under the guise of standard romance, these pages, unlike those of most bestsellers written by men and focused on men, provide the female reader with a meal guaranteed to appeal to her palate, a meal composed of dreams, nightmares, psychic and social structures affecting the lives of women—mothers and daughters—in twentieth-century American culture.

Notes

1. Susan Geary, "The Domestic Novel as a Commercial Commodity," *Bibliographical Society of America* (July 1976), pp. 369–70.

2. See especially James D. Hart, *The Popular Book* (Berkeley and Los Angeles: University of California Press, 1961), pp. 93–97; and Henry Nash Smith, *Democracy and the Novel* (New York: Oxford University Press, 1978), pp. 1–15.

3. Smith notes that, during the thirty years preceding the Civil War, "masculine and aristocratic values were supplanted by the leveling influences exerted by rapid increases in population and wealth, by the spread of free public schools, by the evangelical movement, and especially by the cultural influence of women, who for the first time were gaining enough leisure to have time to read, and enough education to enjoy and produce books" (*Democracy and the Novel,* p. 8).

4. Nina Baym, *Women's Fiction: A Guide to Novels by and about Women in America, 1820–1870* (Ithaca: Cornell University Press, 1978), p. 13.

5. For further discussion of "separate spheres," see Barbara Welter's "The Cult of True Womanhood, 1820–1860," *American Quarterly* 18, no. 2 (1966): 151–57; and Gerda Lerner's "The Lady and the Mill Girl," *Midcontinent American Studies Journal* 10, no. 1 (1969): 5–15.

6. Norman N. Holland, *The Dynamics of Literary Response* (New York: W. W. Norton, 1975), p. 30.

7. Sigmund Freud, "Analysis Terminable and Interminable," in *Moses and Monotheism: An Outline of Psycho-Analysis and Other Works,* vol. 23 of *The Complete Psychological Works of Sigmund Freud,* 24 vols., trans. James Strachey (London: Hogarth, 1964), p. 233.

8. Norman N. Holland, *Poems in Persons* (New York: W. W. Norton, 1973).

9. Nancy Chodorow, "Family Structure and Feminine Personality," in *Women, Culture, and Society,* ed. M. Rosaldo and L. Lamphere (Stanford: Stanford University Press, 1974), p. 47.

10. See especially Annette Kolodny, "A Map for Rereading: Or, Gender and the Interpretation of Literary Texts," *New Literary History* 11 (1980): 451–67; and Nelly Furman, "The Study of Women and Language: Comment on Vol. 3, No. 3," *Signs* 4 (1978); 182–85.

11. See Elizabeth A. Flynn's "Gender and Reading," *College English* 45 (1983); 236–53, for a discussion of ways in which male and female students in Flynn's freshman composition class enacted different reading strategies in responding to three short stories.

12. Ann Douglas introduced this term in her *The Feminization of American Culture* (New York: Avon, 1977). In her consideration of "The End of Mother Power" (pp. 55–64), she observed that as the home gave way to the factory as a site of financially productive endeavor, "the independent woman with a mind and life of her own slowly ceased to be considered of high value" (p. 59).

13. Leo Bersani, *A Future for Astyanax* (Boston: Little, Brown, 1976), p. 194.

14. Baym, *Women's Fiction,* p. 11.

15. Ibid., p. 40.

16. Ibid., p. 298.

17. Russell Nye, *The Unembarrassed Muse* (New York: Dial, 1970), p. 38. John Cawelti devotes somewhat more attention to the sexual split, but his conclusions are essentially the same as Nye's: "Appearing at all levels of culture [the adventure story] seems to appeal to all classes and types of person, though particularly to men. The feminine equivalent of the adventure story is the romance. This is not to say that women do not read adventure stories or that romances cannot be popular with men; there is no exclusive sexual property in

these archetypes of fantasy. Nonetheless, the fact that most adventure formulas have male protagonists while most romances have female central characters does suggest a basic affinity between the different sexes and these two story types (*Adventure, Mystery, and Romance* [Chicago: University of Chicago Press, 1976], p. 41).

18. Nancy Chodorow, *The Reproduction of Mothering: Psychoanalysis and the Sociology of Gender* (Berkeley and Los Angeles: University of California Press, (1978), p. 140.

19. Robert Gutwilling, "In History There's Never Been Anything Like It," *New York Times Book Review* (June 25, 1961), p. 6.

20. Stephen Vincent Benet, "Georgia Marches Through," *Saturday Review* 14 (July 4, 1936); 5.

21. William Du Bois, "Jumbo Romance of Restoration London," *New York Times Book Review* (Oct. 15, 1944), p. 7.

22. Tom Nairn, "Sex and Death," *New Statesman* (Mar. 8, 1968), p. 303.

23. Ken Purdy, "Valley of the Dollars," interview with Susann in *Saturday Evening Post* (Feb. 24, 1968), p. 76.

24. Ibid., quoting Susann, p. 78.

25. Bernard Geis to me, Sept. 14, 1982.

26. Margaret Mitchell, *Gone with the Wind* (New York: Pocket Books, 1965), p. 11. Subsequent references are cited parenthetically in the text.

27. Phyllis Chesler, *Women and Madness* (New York: Avon, 1972); see especially pp. 17–25.

28. See especially Chodorow's *Reproduction of Mothering*.

29. Claire Kahane, "Gothic Mirrors and Feminine Identity," *Centennial Review* 24 (1980); 47–48.

30. Ibid., pp. 49–50.

31. Interestingly, even before the war, women are presented as adults and men as children: "Ellen's life was not easy, nor was it happy, but she did not expect life to be easy, and, if it was not happy, that was woman's lot. . . . The man owned the property, and the woman managed it. The man took the credit for the management, and the woman praised his cleverness. The man roared like a bull when a splinter was in his finger and the woman muffled the moans of childbirth, lest she disturb him. Men were tough of speech and often drunk. Women ignored the lapses of speech and put the drunkards to bed without bitter words. Men were rude and outspoken, women were always kind, gracious and forgiving" (Mitchell, *Gone with the Wind*, p. 53).

32. In appendix A (p. 252) to her essay "Gender and Reading," Flynn cites some of the research on identification: Karen C. Beyard-Tyler and Howard J. Sullivan, "Adolescent Reading Preferences for Type of Theme and Sex of Character," *Reading Research Quarterly* 16 (1980); 104–20; Mary H. Beaven, "Responses of Adolescents to Feminine Characters in Literature," *Research in the Teaching of English* 6 (1972); 48–68.

33. It seems to me that there is a parallel to Scarlett's demands for mother/Mammy in the reading public's demand for a continuation of Scarlett's story. Readers simply did not want the novel to come to a close; they repeatedly

requested more pages. The novel, like a mother, becomes a love-object that we consume; we don't want it (her) to go away.

34. Winsor does not depict earlier body transformation in Amber's life: the onset of menstruation, breast development, and so on. Contemporary analysts, however, are quick to discuss identification problems attendant on these transformations—problems similar to those that attend the move into adulthood (see Maj-Britt Rosenbaum, "The Changing Body Image of the Adolescent Girl," in *Female Adolescent Development,* ed. Max Sugar [New York: Brunner/Mazel, 1979]).

35. Kathleen Winsor, *Forever Amber* (New York: Signet, n.d.), p. 7. Subsequent references are cited parenthetically in the text.

36. Given Moll's name and the setting in which Moll and Amber meet, there is a suggestion of affinities to yet a third female: Daniel Defoe's Moll Flanders. Surely one of the 365 books read by Winsor in researching *Amber* was *Moll,* a novel about a woman who "was Born in Newgate . . . was Twelve Years a Whore, Five Times a Wife," etc. Connections to Amber are obvious.

37. Thomas Whiteside, "Onward and Upward with the Arts: The Blockbuster Complex," *New Yorker* (Sept. 29, 1980), p. 72.

38. Purdy, "Valley of the Dollars," quoting Susann, p. 76.

39. The only exception to this generalized statement is Tony Polar, about whose mother we learn a considerable amount. Miriam, who plays mother to Tony after their real mother dies, blames this mother for Tony's mental illness: "It hadn't been the sins of the father, but their lousy tramp of a mother" (Jacqueline Susann, *Valley of the Dolls* [New York: Bantam, 1967], pp. 230–31.

40. Ibid., Subsequent references are cited parenthetically in the text.

41. In *Women and Madness* (p. 18), Phyllis Chesler notes: "Female children are quite literally starved for matrimony: not for marriage, but for physical nurturance and a legacy of power and humanity from adults of their own sex ('mothers'). . . . Most women are glassed into infancy, and perhaps into some forms of madness, by an unmet need for maternal nurturance."

42. See Adrienne Rich's discussion of "matrophobia" in *Of Woman Born* (New York: Bantam, 1977), pp. 237–43. She notes that matrophobia can be seen as "a womanly splitting of the self, in the desire to become purged once and for all of our mother's bondage, to become individuated and free. The mother stands for the victim in ourselves, the unfree woman, the martyr" (p. 238).

Part Three
Readers

Chapter 10
Gothic Possibilities

Norman N. Holland
Leona F. Sherman

The most immediate question in the psychology of literature is also the subtlest. The reader who stands before a paperback rack and does not know what s/he will enjoy, and the writer who wonders what phrase will work with that imagined reader, face the same problem as the psychologist of literary response. Each person's reading is different, yet there is enough recurrence among readings to make us think some lawfulness is at work. What, then, is the relation between the singularity and the regularity of literary response? How, for example, has a genre like the gothic maintained its popularity for two centuries? Why are the overwhelming majority of those who read gothics women?

Why, indeed, are there genres at all? The detective story, the Bildungsroman, science fiction, the regional novel, porn: we define these genres by their accidents—cops, youth, science, locale, genitals—but these are the mere *Stuff* of fiction. One cannot explain the extraordinary popularity of a genre, both as something to read and as something to write, by such superficials. Or can one?

The formula for the modern gothic, set by Daphne du Maurier's *Rebecca,* is, in the words of Emma Mai Ewing, "A story told by the heroine, often working as a governess companion [hence in a nurturing role] in a brooding castle or mansion. She is alternately attracted and repelled by the rakishly handsome man who plays the villain until almost the last page—and who then comes to her rescue."[1] The central image (in commercial terms, the illustration on the cover) shows "a fleeing girl in a flowing gown and a background structure—a castle, bamboo hut, Chas. Addams house, igloo—with a single light in the window." The image of woman-plus-habitation and the plot of mysterious sexual and supernatural threats in an atmosphere of dynastic mysteries within the habitation has changed little since the eighteenth century. Horace Walpole invented, so to speak, the gothic house in *The Castle of Otranto* (1764), and Ann Radcliffe brought all the elements of the genre together in *The Mysteries of Udolpho* (1794). To be sure, the modern Byronic lover combines the separated hero and villain of the eighteenth century, but that is about the only change.

Now, how simple it would be if we could say that the combination of castle, maiden-in-distress, family secrets, and seductive rake dictates response and so guarantees the gothic effect! Alas, the effect is not at all universal. Castles do not convey terror the way bottles pour wine. Fiction is not the cause but the means by which writers create and readers re-create an experience. Novels do not have emotions—people do.

They do, moreover, according to principles that can be stated in considerable detail. Observations of real readers reading (at the center where we both have worked) have led to the conclusion that each human being re-creates an experience from a fiction in terms of his or her particular style, character, or, to use the precise term, identity.

Identity we define as a way of grasping the mixture of sameness and difference which makes up a human life. We understand sameness in a person by seeing it persist through change, as when we say something like "That's *so* like Ralph!" Conversely, we understand change by seeing it against what has not changed: "That's not like Shoshana at all!" One way of formalizing this interplay of sameness and difference—there may be others, but our center has found this the most useful—is to think of identity as a theme embodying sameness plus variations embodying change. In this way, an identity theme becomes analogous to the theme one finds in a piece of music or literature. Such a theme is an attempt to state formally the constant core we recognize informally in sentences like "Wordsworth is the kind of person who . . ." This constant core we call, adapting ideas of Heinz Lichtenstein, an identity theme. It is our attempt to state what some individual brings to every new experience, the grammatical and actual "I" that we perceive as the subject of all the changes in that person. It is the theme against which we can understand new actions as variations playing a persistent theme in a new form. Reading and interpreting literature are such re-creations.

Within that one general principle, that reading re-creates the reader's identity, we can distinguish four modalities. We use the word *reader,* but *reader,* of course, is not quite accurate, since we sometimes hear literature or see it performed. We can take the *-ent* of *agent,* and speak of a *literent,* that is, someone who is actively responding to a literary work through any sensory mode. One can derive, in the same way, *novelent* or *dramatent* or, a term media people have begun to use, *mediants.* A literant brings to a literary work, just as to any external experience, a characteristic set of expectations, typically, pairs of hopes and fears. We want the text to be the kind of world we know how to deal with.

Therefore, as literents, we try to match from the literary work our characteristic strategies for achieving pleasure in the world and avoiding unpleasure. We bring to bear our whole system of defenses and adaptations, including all our skills, symbols, and values—the shorthand for all this is, simply, *defense.* We shape and change the text until, to the degree we need that certainty, it is the kind of setting in which we can gratify our wishes and defeat our fears.

By matching defense and expectation, literents can invest the work (as they have defensively shaped it) with characteristic clusters of wishes—fantasies. Finally, using the same adaptive strategies, they can transform those fantasies into the kind of significance they characteristically find meaningful: intellectual, social, moral, or aesthetic. A literent "makes sense" of the text, thus confirming the whole transaction.

In short, we match inner defenses and expectations to outer realities in order to project fantasies into them and then transform those fantasies into significance. Defense, expectation, fantasy, transformation, or, for short, DEFT. This model comes from the clinical experience of psychoanalysis, but it has a larger significance, as well. The idea of expectations places the literary work in time, in the ongoing sequence of our wishes and fears, while our transformation of the work toward significance attaches it to themes that transcend the immediate concerns of the moment. Fantasies are what we project from within onto the outer world. Defenses define what we let into ourselves from that outer world.

Thus, although DEFT is only the latest evolvement of Freud's early discoveries about dreams, jokes, and symptoms, it enables us to locate reading along two of the great axes of human experience: the line of time, and the boundary between self and other. At that intersection, each literent transacts the literary work for himself or herself. Response is lawful but completely individual.[2]

Can we extend these principles for understanding one individual's response to principles for understanding many? For example, responses to the gothic show one striking regularity. The *New York Times* of June 18, 1973, headed a feature article "Gothic Novels for Women Prove Bonanza for Publishers." One publisher complained that his "stable of writers" could not satisfy the female market's demand for "gothics." Another, Simon and Schuster, had doubled its sales of such "women's fiction." In all, gothics accounted for more than 5 percent of total paperback sales in the U.S.A., producing $1.4 million in profit. The *New York Times Book Review* headed its May 11, 1975, round-up "Gothic Mania," and reported that American paperback publishers in 1974 had issued about twenty-three million copies of 175 gothic titles by more than one hundred authors. The spring of 1975 saw 50 new titles. The writers are almost all women. One or two men write gothics, but they write under women's names. Similarly, although there are a few male readers, the overwhelming majority are women, mostly in their thirties and forties.

Why this extraordinarily long-lived popularity for a not-very-great literary form? And why is it preponderantly popular, both in the reading and in the writing, with women? The gothic and all such genres lead to the fundamental problem of literary causality. Each literent creates a uniquely individual experience from these gothic materials. Yet gothic novels offer the material for certain kinds of experience and not others. Each novelent has the human freedom to ignore the text, critics, common sense, and everything else in making a gothic experience. Yet psychological laws say that each literent creates an experience within his or her own identity or character. There are also regularities (but not laws) beyond the individual's psychology: gothic novels appeal strongly to some novelents (women of a certain age and society), and scarcely at all to others (adolescent boys of whatever culture).

In any popular genre, however, the principle must be the same: what many literents want to create dovetails with the possibilities the genre offers.[3] To understand how these novels make the gothic experience possible, then, to discover gothic possibilities, requires a double inquiry: into texts and into literents. That is why we decided to explore our own re-creations of the gothic.

The Castle

We can begin with the formula, maiden-plus-habitation, and the prototypical habitation in it, the castle. An older psychoanalytic criticism would have assumed a one-to-one equation: the castle symbolizes the body. Unfortunately, this kind of easy isomorphism does not stand up under experimental testing or even close introspection. Rather, each of us resymbolizes reality in our own terms.[4] A gothic novel combines the heroine's fantasies about the castle with her fears that her body will be violated. The novel, thus, makes it possible for literents to interpret body by means of castle and castle by means of body, but it does not force us to do so, nor does it fix the terms in which the two of us will do it.

Instead, the castle admits a variety of our projections. In particular, because it presents villains and dangers in an archaic language and mise en scène, it fits childish perceptions of adult threats. The castle is a nighttime house—it admits into it all we can imagine of the dark, frightening, and unknown. If, like Udolpho, it also has midnight revelry, violence, battles, confusing noises, and disturbances, it can express our childhood fears at the strange sounds of "struggle" between our parents in the night and the sexual violence children often imagine as a result. At the same time, the gothic novel usually says that the castle contains some family secret, so that the castle can also become the core for fantasies based on a childish desire that adulthood be an exactly defined secret one can discover and possess.

SHERMAN: When I think of a castle, I think of a house of heroic proportions, linked with dynastic histories, wars, and mysteries. I think of kings, queens, knights, and other heroes or villains of folklore who may have lived there. I find, in short, that I associate the castle not only with an idealized past epoch of social history (a nostalgia for romance, chivalry, Christian goodness, and divine order), but also with my own personal history of fantasies and fears. Perhaps it is the great size of the castle in relation to the heroine that reminds me of my childhood perception of adults and that permits me to project so readily my long-repressed fantasies that I will be a hero(ine) uniquely destined and renowned. I can easily associate the gothic hero(ine)'s hopes and fortunes with my own illusions of parental magnitude and personal grandeur and, in particular, with my own version of what Freud called the "family romance," the belief in my own secret greatness based on my descent from glorious and noble (and secret) parents, my ostensible father and mother being but the humble keepers of this illustrious foundling, me, Leona Sherman.

HOLLAND, SHERMAN: The castle delineates a physical space that will accept many different projections of unconscious material. De Sade makes this receptive function of the castle quite terrifyingly explicit: its chief attribute is an isolation in which the heroine is completely controlled by someone else while separated from those she loves. The castle threatens shame, agony, annihilation—and desire. From the torture chambers of, say, the monastery in *Justine,* we can create a magic realm, beyond all normative associations and experience, where the best anodyne one can hope for is catatonia. Given such an arena for sexual and sadistic games, we are free to use de Sade's satanic imaginings to structure our own wildest wishes and fears about loss and helplessness.

Poe, too, makes this receptive function of the habitation explicit, but in a different way: in "The Fall of the House of Usher," he uses the inset poem, "The Haunted Palace," to equate the house with the head. A palace stood "in the monarch Thought's dominion," with "Banners yellow, glorious, golden / On its roof." Wanderers "Through two luminous windows saw / Spirits move musically," while "all with pearl and ruby glowing / Was the fair palace door," and through it comes "Echoes" who sing "The wit and wisdom of their king." But after being assaulted by some unnamed horror, the windows are "red-litten," and through the door a throng rushes out like a river to laugh, but smile no more. Then, Poe's hero takes the place of the house, to be threatened with sensory penetration and madness.

The more usual gothic defines its heroine's anxieties as fears of nothingness, of vulnerability, and, above all, of sexual penetration. Here, clearly, the projections of men and women differ.

SHERMAN: For a woman in a sexist society, imagining being penetrated (an experience of being "filled") can be a pleasure but also a threat. Because my society demands my nonidentity, ego pain and social pleasure (and ego pleasure and social pain) combine to form the masochistic, schizophrenic feelings (yes, of pleasure) I get from gothic.

HOLLAND: For me, both identifying with a female and imagining being penetrated call into question my male identity. Both raise the threat posed by the castle and the gothic machinery to a pitch where I no longer wish them relevant to me, the male me, and I sense myself relegating gothic to an alienating category, "women's fiction." Perhaps this is why I am acutely aware of another property of the castle—its flinty hardness. I want those stones to be inert, neither hurt nor hurting, whatever threats and penetrations go on between villain and victim. *They* cannot be penetrated, and if not they, then not I.

SHERMAN: For me, the primary motivating fear in gothic is of nothingness or nonseparation. Thus the ambivalent importance of the castle in relation to the heroine: in the castle, you can have the merging and the otherness, along with the threat of annihilation. There life exists on the boundary. Holland's and my responses highlight both aspects of this issue and locate an axis of fear and desire common to both our experiences. For me, the nothingness and the vulnerability are crucial; they make the sexuality so threatening. Traditionally, for women, nonseparateness and dependency have been real issues. Confronting them brings selfhood into question and feels dangerous, while successfully confirming one's feminine identity feels exciting and pleasurable.

HOLLAND, SHERMAN: Thus, the castle admits a variety of relationships between itself and the novelent and between itself and the characters of the novel. It becomes all the possibilities of a parent or a body. It can threaten, resist, love, or confine, but in all these actions, it stands as a total environment in one-to-one relation with the victim, like the all-powerful mother of earliest childhood. The castle becomes the entire world of possible relationships for its prisoner. The two of us feel in it a recapitulation of that earliest stage in human development, when the boundaries between inner and outer, me and not-me, are still not sharply drawn, and self cannot distinguish itself from the mother, who is the outside world. It is a "potential space" in the term of D. W. Winnicott, a space *between:* "The potential space between baby and mother, between child and family, between individual and society or the world, depends on experience which leads to trust. . . . It is here that the individual experiences creative living. . . . By contrast, exploitation of this area leads to a pathological condition in which the individual is cluttered up with persecutory elements of which he has no means of ridding himself."[5] Like the gothic heroine.

Because the castle presents a markedly untrustworthy Other that encompasses the entire not-me, physical escape becomes the only way of meeting its threats. From this logic comes the paradigmatic pattern of the gothic: persecution followed by flight, flight being the outward turn from threatened sexual penetration or intrusive parental care. "I will not let the castle force itself into me—I will put myself outside it." The gothic thus offers for our re-creation a dialectic in its geometry, both that of the castle and that of the exterior landscape, which is the escape from the castle. Radcliffe's description of Udolpho is typical: "The towers were united by a curtain, pierced and embattled also, below which appeared the pointed arch of an huge portcullis, surmounting the gates: from these, the walls of the ramparts extended to other towers, overlooking the precipice, whose shattered outline, appearing on a gleam, that lingered in the west, told of the ravages of war—Beyond these all was lost in the obscurity of evening."[6]

HOLLAND: The passage offers me a trail to follow back and forth and up and down: from the towers down to the arch, up the walls to the towers, down and out from them to a precipice, out and beyond to "obscurity." Given such a perceptual trail, I find I can play it like a piece of music, moving my feelings up and down, in and out of, these vectors and dimensions. "United," "below which," "surmounting," "from these," "overlooking," "told of," "Beyond these"—everything seems to me related. In these words animating an inanimate landscape, I get an almost paranoid feeling of a world linked and united against me, "embattled," "huge," "shattered," "ravages." Thus, I can use all this geometry of relationship to structure my own projections, working into it such basic psychic issues as the boundary between the me and not-me, between outer and inner, or such themes as the dependency of my comfort in physical space on a feeling of repose and security in inner space. In gothic, I can structure my feelings by means of both the outer landscape, provided for escape, and the inner landscape of the castle, with its threats of or flights from penetration.

HOLLAND, SHERMAN: We return to the castle—one always does, after all. Like our first homes in real life, it is under the sway of parental figures, and, thus, in another way, the castle allows the two of us to re-create the trust and dependency of childhood. It offers a parental en-vironment, the castle itself as a parent (as above), but also the parents-in-the-castle. They come in sharply different flavors. Udolpho will have the evil Montoni and Mme. Cheron, and Otranto the menacing Man-fred, but poised against them the generous Hippolita and the noble (but, alas, dead) Alfonso or the "good father," St. Aubert. In other words, the older characters offer a reader a moral polarity. We two invest them with negative feelings toward our parents (or positive ones for the idealized versions). The good are very good and the bad are very bad (or mysterious), and this dualism is defined in a child's morality: who is good and who is bad depends on how they treat the child-heroine. They recapitulate the all-powerful evil tyrant and the "wicked stepmother" of fairy tales. Further, the very fact they are so sharply and easily distinguished gratifies deep and early wishes for a life that is clear and simple. Gothic measures out its complexities in discrete issues.

Typically, the bad father-figure will have sexual designs on the hero-ine; often the bad mother-figure will aid him. As in the child's world, sex is "bad." In the same way, a castle like Udolpho shares both the good motherly qualities of a shelter and the threatening sexuality of its pro-prietor. Yet, to the extent one fuses with the castle as the child in earliest infancy feels inseparable from its mother, its ambiguity poses a deep ontological threat: if I and the mother on whom I depend for nurture and life itself are both agents of aggression, sexuality, and (perhaps therefore deserved) punishment, then I call my very existence into question by my own sexual desires. At the same time, the gothic plot stresses the difference between the sexes and introduces a variety of occasions for sexual desire. Thus, it enables the two of us to lose identity one way, by fusing with the parents (or castle) as in earliest childhood, but to assert it in another, sexually. In effect, a literent can make his or her sexual identity (based on difference from the other) the defense against the loss of his or her deeper, human identity (based on sepa-rateness from the other). And this special pattern may be another reason gothic appeals so differently to the sexes.

In gothic, it is the male villain who usually represents sexual desire. As Leslie Fiedler has suggested, the villain makes available to literents a dark, asocial world of fantasy, dream, and the unconscious, a subversive attack on the bourgeois values embodied in the heroine.[7] He seems, compared to her, more mythic and timeless, a creature of all the ages. If he does not physically penetrate the heroine, he has (like Montoni in *Udolpho*) eye contact—piercing and controlling glances. He, thus, may express what she dare not, her sexual desires, perhaps even sadomasochistic desires, in the gothic paradigm of young heroine and middle-aged, sexual villain. At the same time, because she fears him and suffers from his machinations, she gives us the possibility of using fear to justify wish and wish to provoke fear. She pays in anxiety for whatever guilt-ridden sexual or parricidal wishes she expresses for her readers toward this "bad father."

The good female, thus, plays very much the opposite role from that played by the bad male. The villain is more ancient and alien, while she tends to be an idealized contemporary portrait. Probably the respectable woman novelist identified more consciously with her than with any other characters. Nevertheless, the heroine can play a double part. She can assume an active, questing, intruding role, as she tries to find out the secret of the castle, at the same time that she plays the passive, inceptive victim.

SHERMAN: I feel "truthful" and socialized woman come together in this longing to have both the active, penetrating role usually taken by males in our society (and in the gothic novel) and the traditional receptivity assigned to my sex. As I follow, say, Emily in *The Mysteries of Udolpho,* her intrusive, aggressive mode elicits threats of violence, rape, and murder. I can feel relief—my guilt prevailing—as Emily does not achieve a mature realization of active, female sexuality; but finally I am distinctly unhappy with the even more restricted, passive attitude toward her sexual role with which she finds safety in the nonsexuality, really, of romance and La Vallée. I feel in the duality of her position the tension between the solutions I seek as an adult woman and the solutions I once accepted from society in childhood.

Finally, for heroines like Emily, the basic role is resistance. In the fictional as in the real world of the eighteenth and nineteenth centuries, a young woman had to resist objectionable marriages, seduction, jealousy, and rape. Men dominated their world with these tactics. Women had few means with which to defend themselves, and defeat meant ruin. Gothic novels enabled literents, especially women, to experience these conditions in the gothic castle at the hands of gothic mothers, fathers, and lovers (and, of course, *gothick* meant "barbarous, rude, savage"). The genre's romance and its conventional ending in marriage allowed a woman to use romantic love as a defense against the male, sexual forces that menaced her at the same time that she could enjoy those forces (either as actor or victim) in fantasy. The woman could be—and not be—passive and resistant during the body of the novel. Then the ending provided her a way to arrive at the right psychological solution for that society and that time.

HOLLAND, SHERMAN: Thus, no matter what wishes its literent might indulge in the beginning and middle, the genre proves deeply conservative in the end. To the two of us, other people or objects never seem in gothic to be quite other. Rather, they are intimately connected to, part of, dependent on, and controlled by the heroine or the parent-figures around her. Such nonseparateness characterizes childhood generally, and in particular the earliest relationship of child to mother before one is aware of self or time. To us, this style also accounts for the pervasive "status quo" feeling we have in reading gothic. Characters and events repeat from one generation to the next, enabling the reader to deny changes in time. The supernatural provides a rationale for doom and determinism. Inherited riches mean the characters never work, never, that is, construct distinctive identities for themselves apart from parental inheritance.

The gothic novel itself is a set piece, unchanged in two hundred years, much like its dominant image, the gothic castle, cathedral, or abbey, which stands aloof from ordinary human life and change. It says, in its own way, victims endure. It imitates death, too: cold, still, silent, overwhelmingly oppressive. The literent who enjoys the genre and image can identify with the aggressor, Montoni, or with the inquisitive Emily, yield to the destroyer, and once again find a simplifying peace in social conservatism.

Until that familiar resolution in marriage, however, the gothic revels in unfamiliarity: the *topos* of the mysterious family secret. Again, the genre offers us opposites, the known and the unknown, and again, the castle provides a symbol for them. As the gothic convention par excellence, its very structure exemplifies the stout, external form, yet it conceals some hidden secret, knowledge of which will ultimately prove more important than the strength of stone and iron. The secret allows us to project into the castle the deepest mysteries of life, its origins, continuance, and destiny.

SHERMAN: Whenever I think of an object of mystery and concealment, I find myself harking back to the ultimate mystery, the maternal body with its related secrets of birth and sexuality. Again, I re-create in the gothic a mingling of my very early relationship with my mother, mother as environment, with my present sense of her as a sexual, procreating being. Then I use the mysteries and concealments of gothic the same way. It is as though my mother and I were probing here and there in this house or castle or head or body. I know she knows, but she won't tell me. I know I know, but I doubt because she won't tell me. She says one thing, but I see another on her face. I feel we can't really talk about what we know, because she would be calling her whole past life into question and endangering her present. She thinks the concealment necessary for my survival, and finally, she loves me and wants to protect me above all. The mysteries are the issues of sex and birth and death and, too, the necessity of concealing them.

HOLLAND: In many ways, the element of mystery seems the point at which writers find the limits of the genre. *Northanger Abbey* is not a gallery of delicious mystery, but a burlesque of gothic. The mysterious manuscript found by Catherine Morland hides no grim secrets, only laundry bills and expense accounts. Radcliffe's "explained super-natural" makes it easy for us—sometimes too easy—to relax from the tense quest for the secret into the conventional ending of romance. In effect, rationality is the "countergothic." The absence or removal of mystery, if slow, provides the stock happy resolution; if fast, parody. Thus, Poe's use of rational explanation, so important in shoring up his own precarious character structure, makes it possible for us to balance off and limit the horror of his various buryings alive. De Sade, on the other hand, becomes the "ultra-gothic." He goes beyond the suspense and mystery to carry out those terrible mysterious urges in full view of the literent.

Finally, then, mystery defines the mystery with which we began: the potential of the gothic, given what we know about the complex way in which appeal begins with literents before literature. A genre such as the gothic creates certain possibilities, but whether or not those possibilities or others become actual experiences depends on the individual literent, his or her identity, literary acumen, and immediate motivation.

HOLLAND, SHERMAN: Thus, although we are a man and a woman looking at a "feminine" genre, we cannot assume that our responses are representative of male and female literents generally. Having taken in gothic materials in certain gender-related ways, we can guess that other men and women might similarly divide—but we can only know they do when different individuals in fact respond differently.

In looking at the gothic through our own reactions, we two are articulating the "potential space" between the gothic novel and its literent *as we actualize it*.[8] In its plot, the novel permits the two of us to hover between radical exploration and a familiar, conservative ending. In its characters, it permits us to enter the interplay between an asocial, timeless, penetrating villain and a contemporary, "correct," and resis-tant virgin. The structure of the novel permits us to perceive the other characters, besides the virgin-heroine, as mother- and father-figures, sharply divided into good and bad, with the bad including the mys-terious and the sexual. Finally, the gothic gives us a central image: the maiden inside and outside the habitation, that recurring castle. It may be:

A maternal space	or	A hardness
—nurturing		
—and/or sexual		
—expressed in a geometrical dialectic		
An idealized past	or	The reader's present
—big in size		
—a family romance		
An inside		
—a secret		
—to be penetrated	or	—a hardness
—enclosing	or	—to be escaped

In all these possibilities, it seems to us, inside and outside form the essential tension. The castle does not simply "stand for" the body of the heroine (as a psychoanalytic critic might have said in 1915). Nevertheless, just as a child of either sex might interpret its psychosocial surroundings by means of the inner and outer space of its own body, so the gothic novel provides a polarizing of inside and outside with which an adult woman, particularly in a sexist society, might symbolize a common psychosocial experience: an invaded life within her mind, her body, her home, bounded by a social structure that marks off economic and political life as "outside."

SHERMAN: As I see it, escapist fiction, especially gothic, makes sense for women in their thirties and forties. Romance has been the only arena available to women in my culture for the projection of fantasies of personal glory. Women have largely defined themselves and their aspirations through a love relationship with a man. If that be the ultimate experience, other forms of escapist fiction simply do not offer what gothic does, for gothic allows one to complicate that fantasy of personal glory by fear and violence. It allows anger, ambivalence, and resistance in the very realizing of the fantasy.

HOLLAND: Our colleague Claire Kahane made an interesting suggestion: that gothic creates, in both the labyrinthine castle and the interactive landscape, an inner, relational space. There, woman, not man, wins, despite—or precisely because of—being in the position of a victim. Finally, it is Emily who controls this novel.

SHERMAN: There's power in resistance—passive aggression—and that's another resource gothic offers. It says receiving, sexually and otherwise, can be a power position as well.

HOLLAND, SHERMAN: This is what we mean by "gothic possibilities." *Udolpho* does not "cause" a gothic experience. It does, however, make the resources for such an experience available to those novelents whose identities can create gothic and who have social, political, gender-linked, or characteristic reasons for wanting it. The "text" itself embodies no more than the possibility of a certain kind of relationship between its words and its literents.

Thus, to talk about "the appeal" of gothic leads to an insoluble problem: the prediction of human choices. Literary critics, however, would like to be able to say that a certain text causes a certain reaction, with all the comfortable simplifications of a stimulus-response model. No one, however, has been able to locate anything "in" a gothic novel or, for that matter, "in" *Hamlet* or any other masterpiece, which causes any predictable pattern of favorable or unfavorable reading. There simply is no way we can get from the possibilities offered by a gothic to the relations novelents actually establish with the novel, although we can go the other way, to discover the possibilities in the text from the actualities of responses. Starting from the text, however, we can apparently say no more than that a certain text makes a certain response possible or unlikely or difficult. Yet that amounts to more than one might think.

The Shape of Appeal

HOLLAND: With my characteristically geometric imagination, I can visualize the relationship of literent to text as combining two movements. The first runs from the literent to the text: s/he trusts the text, bestowing or investing a part of her/himself in it. In order to do so, s/he must have been able to establish her/his characteristic defenses by means of the text (as in the DEFT principles of reading). The second movement feeds back from text to literent. It involves more of a turn or pivot, whereby the literent shapes her/his relation to the work as a whole by means of her/his sequential experience of the work in time. The first, frontal relation is the more familiar, and it fits some of our traditional ideas of appeal.

First, the more the materials of gothic admit the projection of universal psychological issues, the more people are likely to so project. This is not quite the same as saying that materials general in themselves ("birth, and copulation, and death," to use the Eliotic phrase) will arouse general interest. To be sure, initiations, marriages, and ceremonies about death would not occur generally among humans if they did not provide symbolisms for expressing general human concerns. Many other things, however, that are not themselves universal, admit the projection of universal themes in literature.

Castles are not universal, yet the two of us have been able to find in them: a body, a head, a mind, unchanging hardness, undifferentiated parents, parents differentiated into hard father and yielding mother or sexual father and idealized mother. Above all, we have found in the castle mother—mother as nurturer, as sexual being, as body, as harboring a secret, as an indifferent hardness, and so on. The castle has an immense structure of—possibility. It is not an old-fashioned "Freudian symbol." Rather, the novel makes it possible for each of us to relate to the castle in his or her own style, using and not using various items of plot, character, and language. This way, projection is one "possibility" of gothic, and indeed, of all fiction and all reality. To the extent that we actualize it, we might translate it into an aesthetic judgment of intensity.

Second, to the extent ambivalence pervades all human feeling, literary works achieve part of their success by permitting us to work out both the wishing and the fearing of a given event.

SHERMAN: In the gothic, I believe much of this dual potentiality comes from the symbolization of sexuality, overtly feared but covertly wished. Similarly, one may wish to solve the mystery yet fear what will be revealed. If the Rochester, the villainous, sexual, older man, turns out to be a rescuer, the female novelent can find two ways of submitting to him, one permitted, one taboo. Further, her fear of the villain may assuage any guilt for hidden sexual wishes toward this potential lover, who may in turn bring out her feelings toward a father. Similarly, one might find in the gothic two versions of mother: a nurturing mother who should be trusted and a sexual mother who should not. In literents' pairings of wish and fear, we may be seeing the psychological sense of the aesthetician's "unity in diversity."

HOLLAND, SHERMAN: It is particularly important that the *language* of literature have this potential for admitting ambivalent impulses. The two of us, for example, find we can endow the passage we quoted from *Udolpho* with a whole series of contrasts and tensions between up and down, out and back, or near and far. Like the "pure form" of music, they provide a structure on which to work out one's feelings. By contrast, the inversions of Poe's poetry, which might have provided a linguistic tension to readers in the last century, seem flat and stale to us in this one. We might translate the openness of language to people's ambivalences as the familiar aesthetic criterion, complexity.

All such projections into details are possible only because the two of us have matched defenses in more general ways. We brought to the gothic the characteristic balance of wish and defense each of us carries about all the time. We approach the world with expectations like "They will take something away"; "They will come nearer"; "I will gain something." We cope with such feelings by seeking a giver, distancing ourselves, looking for reassurance, and the like. When we encounter a new situation by opening a gothic novel, we understand it at first in the most general of terms: "book," "novel," "popular," "gothic." We generate expectations from our general balance of defense and fantasy and test the new novel against them: "pleasing terror," "bland language," "suspense," "penetration," "women's writing," or other expressions that mix wish and fear.

A novelent proceeds to make the book more precise as s/he reads—this heroine in this particular castle with these particular terrors and adjectives—but shaping it by her/his characteristic defenses. S/he overlooks some things but invests others with details from personal experience. Ideally, this process will come, not to an exact match—that would seem dull—but to a feeling of accord sufficient to sustain a sense of trust. We need to feel that the novel will do the kinds of things for us that are appropriate for this novel to do. As we achieve this trust, we "match" defenses and expectations by means of the novel.

HOLLAND: As a gothic's literent has established trust, s/he projects into the novel her/his particular private fantasies about penetration, the suspect hero, corridors, rooms, beds, and so on. S/he can transform those fantasies toward meaningfulness, using the plot, characters, setting, and language (as s/he has taken the novel in) and all her/his cognitive and literary skills. The process has the same shape as the creation of a dream: my day-residues (analogous to textual details) drop down and assimilate my deeper wishes, which rise to consciousness in secondary and rational elaboration.

The interaction between text and novelent begins in personal expectations about books, novels, genres, or heroes and heroines. It ends in a general feeling of significance. In between, I think, the relationship narrows like an hourglass to precise points of matching particular details taken from the text to particular expectations generated by the literent, both sets of details being shaped and selected through the literent's system of defenses.

It is in the neck of that hourglass that the second, turning movement becomes crucial, for this feedback from the text is necessary to sustain that original cognitive and emotional matching. A novelent uses her/his response to the events "inside" the novel to fuel her/his response to the novel from outside it, and vice versa. I compose the villain's wish to penetrate the heroine from my own wish to penetrate the mystery of the book or castle, and vice versa. From each I derive feelings with which to create the other: the more suspense I feel in the reading transaction, the more threatening the villain can become. So with the *topos* of the mysterious secret. Out of Emily's wish to find the truth about the world in which she is caught, I shape my own wish to find how the story comes out.

Conversely, I can shape from my ambivalent feelings about the penetration *in* the novel an ambivalence toward my penetration *of* the novel. I want to penetrate its mysteries, yes, but I do not want to be penetrated by the book—I do not want to relax and let this kind of book happen to me like other novels. In the same way, my ambivalent absorption in the book, my feeling that *Udolpho* creates a stereotyped and artificial reality with which I am nevertheless involved to the exclusion of the real world, can let me imagine an ambivalent wish to escape in the plot. From my own mixed feelings toward the novel, I generate the heroine's mixture of eagerness to get out of danger and hesitation to enter the unknown outside. Out of Mrs. Radcliffe's failure to provide enough human aggression for me in the character of Emily, I supply it: Why doesn't she face up to Montoni? Out of the aggression I have supplied to the sequence of events, I shape my dissatisfaction with the novel: Why doesn't *it* give me a firm resistance to Montoni?

In having this second movement, this pivot, in response, my reading the novel at large resembles my interpreting the sentence in little. That is, as the psycholinguists following Chomsky have shown, we interpret sentences by some kind of transformation from deep to surface structure. We also, however, interpret sentences from left to right. And somehow—no one knows quite how—these two directions, left to right and deep to surface, interact.[9]

This pivotal use of the sequence of events in the novel also corresponds to the way we identify with a character. The word *identify*, however, does not do justice to the precision of the transaction. We make for ourselves drives and defenses out of a character ostensibly "there" in the text and so shape a relationship between the text and ourselves. The making is the relating.[10]

It is all like sailing a boat: I shape from the relation to wind and wave "out there" a direction I define "in here" but achieve in the outward interaction of boat, wind, and water, which in turn changes the original relation to wind and water. Neither boat nor wind, water nor sailor, can be understood in isolation. My sailing is not "in here" or "out there"— it is the relationship between the two. It is the turning and heading between "in here" and "out there."

A psychoanalytic approach shows that we interpret fiction, as a whole, the same way. The left-to-right, "out there," sequence of events in a novel provides resources with which we can build a relation to the total novel which embraces the book in another movement of mind from deeper to higher levels and back again. Critics would like this model to predict literary responses, but as is true in the social sciences generally, one cannot predict human behavior, except by arbitrarily limiting it through questionnaires or elections that permit only a few choices. Such limits cannot possibly reach the fineness with which we re-create the novel as a whole or as an action in time. What this left-to-right and lower-to-higher model of our relation to a text does let us do is understand responses after they occur.

SHERMAN: Thus, I use the mysteries of gothic to articulate feelings about my mother, a nurturing environment now become also a woman with a sexuality I must treat as her secret. The mysteries are the issues of sex and birth and death and, too, the necessity of knowledge and concealment in a tension between known truths and feelings within and conventions and lies required from without. The castle with its family secret is the embodiment of this, the gothic denial.

HOLLAND: I find in my ambivalence toward the spatial and cognitive penetrations of gothic a reason why I dismiss these novels as "women's fiction" (and the very term reveals a deep issue for me, Is "it" there or fictional?).

HOLLAND, SHERMAN: In other words, we discover how gothic possibilities have become gothic actualities, but only *after* and *because* we have made them actual. We can understand the relation between the text and us through a general psychoanalytic principle. We re-create the text to make it an expression of our own personal style or identity, matching defenses and expectations to the text so as to project fantasies into it and transform them and it toward significance.

Within that DEFTing, we shape two movements, the second a feedback to sustain the first. In the first, we compare our expectations and defenses with the text and invest it with fantasy and meaning: we move from self as a whole to text as a whole. This one-to-one movement relates to such traditional categories of aesthetic judgment as intensity (if we think solely of projection) or unity-in-complexity (if we think of the balance of dualities like wish and fear, sex and aggression, or drive and defense).

In the other movement, we feed a sequence of events in our ongoing relation with the text back into ourselves so as to shape that first, total relation between text and self. It is in that turning toward ourselves that we most exactly match our personal defenses and expectations with those we derive from the resources of the text. We use our detailed expectations about what is going to happen in the text and the way we deal with what then happens to shape the further expectations and defenses we bring to the text as a whole.

In the movement from each of us as a whole toward the text as a whole, we are relatively flexible, particularly as regards fantasy and transformation. The pivotal movement is far more chancy, quite subject to the vagaries of mood and the variables of identity. It is, however, this matching between the left-to-right events in the text and the deeper-to higher transformations of the literent that is pivotal—in both senses of the word.

HOLLAND: I bring to *The Mysteries of Udolpho* positive and negative expectations about novels, literary language, the eighteenth century, gothics, or "women's fiction." Then, as I read, I find I can not shape from this heroine, this villain, this castle, or these descriptions satisfying structures (defenses) to cope with the theme or fantasy of penetration that I find intriguing but doubly threatening.

SHERMAN: I, however, find that the same literary materials express for me a sexist society's thwarting of woman's quest for self-knowledge and authenticity. The castle situation provides a model for my suppressed feelings about dependency and separateness, the trust I feel toward my mother coupled with the frustration and even terror I also feel, knowing that what I know must be suppressed at the expense of my own sense of self. In what sexual attraction I share between heroine and villain, I confront my own participation in a masochistic mythology that equates sexuality with brutality. The pursuit in the castle allows me both to be open to these issues and to resist them. I find myself re-creating from gothic my ambivalence toward a femaleness that is my mother in me: nurturing and sexuality, mother and woman and child, conflicted between her and me and therefore in me as me.

HOLLAND, SHERMAN: Since our maleness and femaleness are so important in our respective responses, it could be that we are demonstrating prototypically male and female responses, but we will never know by simply assuming we are. One cannot learn about actual responses except by studying actual responses. We cannot learn about them by starting with the text, for texts do not determine responses—it would be closer to the truth to say that experiences determine texts. For the same reason we can learn nothing about the actual popularity of gothics from imagined readers, be they Holland and Sherman writ large, the "implicit reader" of Wolfgang Iser or Harald Weinrich, the "informed reader" of Stanley Fish, or even the "superreader" of Michael Riffaterre.

We can, however, learn how unique experiences combine to make the gender-linked "appeal" of gothics by considering the ways we and others convert gothic possibilities into human actualities—in other words, by listening (with the proverbial third ear) to the authentic experiences of real people.

Notes

1. *New York Times Book Review,* May 11, 1975, pp. 10, 12.

2. Norman N. Holland's *Poems in Persons* (New York: W. W. Norton, 1973) and *5 Readers Reading* (New Haven: Yale University Press, 1975) fully develop these principles and the evidence on which they are based. Shorter statements appear in his " 'English' and Identities," *CEA Critic* 35 (1973): 4–11; "A Touching of Literary and Psychiatric Education," *Seminars on Psychiatry* 5 (1973): 287–99; and "Unity Identity Text Self," *PMLA* 90 (1975): 813–22. A refutation of the usual assumption that a text defines or controls a certain range of response which individuals then vary appears in Holland's "A Letter to Leonard," *Hartford Studies in Literature* 5 (1973): 9–30.

3. David Bleich, in "Robert Frost and Cultural Popularity" (*Sphinx* 38 [1975]: 21–40), explores this principle, but the logic of the paper seems doubtful. "Over one hundred associative responses" treat "Stopping By Woods" as a decision to renounce death, but on the strength of one person's responses, Bleich claims "that the poem evokes various kinds of love fantasies which the death-interpretation overlays."

4. See, in particular, Charles Rycroft, "Symbolism and Its Relationship to the Primary and Secondary Processes," and "An Enquiry into the Function of Words in the Psycho-Analytical Situation," in his *Imagination and Reality* (New York: International Universities Press, 1968). See also idem, "Is Freudian Symbolism a Myth?" *New York Review of Books,* Jan. 24, 1974.

5. D. W. Winnicott, *Playing and Reality* (London: Tavistock, 1971), p. 103.

6. Ann Radcliffe, *The Mysteries of Udolpho* (1794; reprint, London: Oxford University Press, 1970), p. 227.

7. Leslie Fiedler, *Love and Death in the American Novel,* rev. ed. (New York: Stein and Day, 1966), pp. 115, 121.

8. See Murray M. Schwartz, "Where Is Literature?" *College English* 36 (1975): 756–63, which applies Winnicott's developmental concept to the literary transaction.

9. See, for example, Jerry A. Fodor and Merrill F. Garrett, "Some Syntactic Determinants of Sentential Complexity," *Perception and Psychophysics* 2 (1967): 289–96; or Jerry A. Fodor, Merrill F. Garrett, and Thomas G. Bever, "Some Syntactic Determinants of Sentential Complexity, II: Verb Structure," *Perception and Psychophysics* 3 (1968): 453–61. A useful summary of research in this field is Judith Greene's *Psycholinguistics: Chomsky and Psychology* (Baltimore: Penguin Books, 1972) and, more recently, Jerry A. Fodor, Thomas G. Bever, and Merrill F. Garrett, *The Psychology of Language: An Introduction to Psycholinguistics and Generative Grammar* (New York: McGraw-Hill, 1974). An important contribution from the generative semanticists is George Lakoff and Henry Thompson, "Introducing Cognitive Grammar," Proceedings of the First Annual Meeting of the Berkeley Linguistics Society, 1975 (Mimeographed).

10. See Norman N. Holland, *The Dynamics of Literary Response* (New York: W. W. Norton, 1975), pp. 279–80.

Chapter 11
Gender Interests in Reading and Language
David Bleich

Those familiar with the scholarly literature on "reading" will know how unstable a concept "reading" is. Sometimes it refers to the physical-sensory process of registering in one's mind the words on the page, and sometimes it refers to the ability to understand a text. Some make distinctions in the concept according to what is read, and some according to who is doing the reading. And some just assume that the concept is self-explanatory and then reflect on it. For everyone, however, the concept has a certain assured sense that permits some deeper discussion to proceed. Once we associate the idea of "gender" with reading, though, we are obliged to understand our perspective in much more specific ways. We are raising the issue of who is reading, and we are saying that the readers are in some generic sense biologically defined. We are then wondering if biological boundaries of people have an effect on an activity that seems to be unbound by biological constraints: both sexes learn to read under the same circumstances and with the same expectations of success. Furthermore, the question is closely tied to the problem of gender and language. People learn their native language fluently regardless of their gender, and it seems almost too obvious to mention that men and women speak to one another in the "same" language. By introducing the idea of gender to reading and language, we are reflecting on whether this apparent sameness is really a viable assumption.

I pose the question in the following way: How far do generic biological differences reach into the mental functioning of each gender? This is a problem in the light of several considerations. Most immediately, the change in the political relationship of men and women over the past century has raised questions of whether men and women actually understand one another. Since many believe there has been a widespread culturally rooted failure of understanding, solutions to this failure are being sought. On a purely physiological level, certain findings about the chemical and structural character of the brain have also suggested a basis for gender differences in cognitive processes. It is definitely plausible that different hormonal balances affect the overall directions of thought and language in each sex. And, psychologically, men and women often show different "needs," different predispositions, and, usually, different tastes: On what basis can we make sense of such differences?

Reasoning about the biological basis of both mental and physical phenomena has never been a straightforward matter. For example, certain diseases are gender related or race related; yet, members of the other gender or another race also get the disease. Or, while baldness occurs primarily in men, some women get bald also. At a certain age, women can no longer bear children, but men can continue to beget them, in principle, into their old age. Certain antibiotics work on most people, but not on some others. Does this mean that there is no real understanding of how antibiotics work? And what is the basis of homosexuality, a phenomenon that seems to be as old as recorded history? Many now believe that this has a biological basis. It is customary to say that our biological understanding of such things is incomplete. But it is nevertheless reasonable to suppose that *two* sorts of understanding are needed to deal with any single "case": the knowledge of a generic trend and the knowledge of an individual's biological idiosyncrasies. Medical advice has traditionally been given on these two bases.

I believe that the problem of gender differences in reading and language requires this less than certain, nonpredictive sort of understanding. When I teach a class, I notice that men speak differently from women about the same works of literature, but in no universal way: there are significant patterns, but there are also significant exceptions. In the material that Robin Lakoff discusses, the situation is similar: there are strong gender differences in usage, but one gender can still use the other's language and remain in its own idiom. We are, thus, looking for a contingent regularity: one that exists in large numbers of people, but that is also regulated by individual factors of growth, taste, and culture. In medicine, "influenza" is generic. But "new strains" pop up, and new manifestations of the old strain look different in different people. In the study of reading and language the case is similar, but even less certain. Because of the strong influence of culture on language use, it is even harder to separate the biologically generic from the culturally individuated features of language.

Psychoanalysis has confronted this sort of problem from its beginnings. For example, in diseases like hysteria and neurosis, the first guess was that they had a "sexual" origin. But this guess proved somewhat too simple. As psychoanalysis moved from hypnosis to the conscious use of language as its technique, it was the ability of the patient to articulate the circumstances and the history of the illness which created a new perspective on the illness (not in every point sexual) which, often, ameliorated it. At the same time, this action did not always work, and the illness remained and sometimes even worsened. But as with other medical situations, these failures did not mean that the successes were fraudulent or ascribable to chance. It is only that some people are more amenable to this treatment than others. I will understand psychoanalytic treatment, therefore, as a variation of medical treatment in the direction of language. The therapeutic use of language is highly individuated, and less generic, than the therapeutic use of penicillin. But there is nevertheless something generic about the fact that, sometimes, the right articulation of one's personal history permanently ameliorates neurotic suffering.

The generic element is the presupposition that, for each person, there is a path from the biological body, through the psychology, to the language that each person uses in consequence of that psychology. In particular, biology creates the circumstance of there being two parents for each child. In all human societies the child of these parents develops psychologically through interaction with them. This situation "mixes" the biological with the psychological so that it is difficult to distinguish one influence from the other. The development of language not only combines the biological and psychological factors held in common among child and parents, but also rapidly takes on features from the culture at large as soon as the child enters a peer group, and probably even sooner. But as later influences make themselves felt, the earlier influences remain; even though, as adults, we feel relatively independent of our parents, we nevertheless remain "their child." For this reason, it is a plausible strategy to reflect on how the transition from the biological to the psychological to the social affects the language of each person. At each stage of development, language plays a central role in stabilizing the stage-specific crises. Each stage requires a certain advance or an incremental growth in language in order for a person to retain his or her psychosocial stability. Thus, there are grounds for *expecting* a person's language to reflect, to one degree or another, the underlying biological influences as they appear through psychosocial development. With regard to the present issue of gender, we should expect that one's sense of one's gender (the psychology of gender identity) follows from the fact of biological gender, and as this sense is brought into society through growing up, one's language will be a function of both the fact of gender and one's sense of it. (If one is homosexual, for example, the sense of one's gender will be different from the analogous sense in the nonhomosexual person.)

The foregoing considerations were implied to me, in part, by Leo Stone's 1961 monograph *The Psychoanalytic Situation* (New York: International Universities Press). It is a study of the interpersonal circumstance of psychoanalysis and of what role language may be playing in it. Stone's own aim was relatively modest. He investigated the classical psychoanalytic issue of transference and its co-concept, countertransference, for the purpose of justifying a more flexible and negotiable posture for the orthodox psychoanalyst. He identifies his study as "a brief critique of the principle of unmodified 'anonymity'," and he presents his "conviction that some experimental relaxation of stringency in this sphere can be carried out . . . with appreciably heightened effectiveness for the psychoanalytic situation" (pp. 110–11).

The basis of his argument is his reflection on the traditional role of the physician, particularly his or her unique privilege of having intimate access to the patient's body. He argues that it is reasonable to understand the patient's view of this special access as an analogue to the patient's mother's similar access in childhood. Before a child even gets to a doctor, he or she makes his or her body fully available to the parents, more often the mother, for examination. When the child grows up, his or her doctor retains this parental privilege. The psychoanalytic doctor, Stone now observes, changed this practice in an interesting way: the analyst declared a strict taboo on bodily contact and demanded instead that the same level of intimacy be exercised on a purely verbal level. Stone's main insight is that, although this shift occurred because of the needed change from hypnosis to free association, the new conversational situation actually alludes to a basic event in infantile development—the child's change in conception of the mother from the "mother of intimate bodily care" to the "mother of separation." Stone's proposal for psychoanalysis is that the analyst would do well to be both sorts of doctors to the patient. This does not mean that the analyst ought physically to examine the patient, but that he or she ought to *present himself* or *herself* as the more open figure as well as the purely detached listener. If the analyst is both sorts of "mother" for the patient, the latter's transference neurosis, which is what the analyst actually works with, is given much wider play: the patient finds a more palpable "mother of intimate care" from which to separate through his or her own cultivation of a purely verbal intimacy.

We may think further about the role of language in this situation. The maternal role of the analyst is created by the verbal intimacy of the analytic relationship. The verbal "conventions" of psychoanalysis—the speaking rules as explained by the analyst to the patient—show the patient the maternal situation. The process of "cure"—the separation and individuation as described above—is actually a process of "language acquisition" very similar to the original acquisition of language in infancy: the patient creates a new language, so to speak, for his or her present sense of self, by individuating relative to the analyst, in the same way that individuation took place through language in infancy relative to the mother. In infancy, syntax appears as the way to create potential access to the mother who may not be present. The child can *conceive* of the mother or *talk about* her or *call* her or *call for* her. Because in infancy syntactical language is the machinery for the onset of self-awareness, the "new" language created by the therapeutic "maternal" situation uses the well-rooted schematism of infancy to create the new sense of self which ameliorates neurosis (which is here understood as a paralysis of the growth of the sense of self). The familiar characteristic "moment of insight" in psychoanalysis is the patient's new symbolization of the otherness of the analyst, which coincides with the perception of the "otherness" of the "old" self and the construction of the "new" self. In principle, this process is the same regardless of the genders of patient and analyst.

The analyst is, therefore, a generic symbolic mother in all cases. In life, every individual speaks the "mother tongue," which is an idiomatic reflection of the fact that the overwhelming majority of human beings are brought into language (not "taught" in any simple sense) by the first relationship with the mother. Just as both sexes are born of mothers, the language foundation of both sexes is maternal. The highly differentiated and socially shaped styles of language we find in adulthood are responses to, and developments of and from, the universal verbal intimacy of the mother-infant relationship. Psychoanalysis uses for its work not simply language, but language within relationship, which repeats the language acquisition circumstance in infancy.

Gender consciousness appears in the developmental phase that follows the phase of language acquisition and uses the schematism of language acquisition in the following way. The child takes the ability to objectify others as well as himself or herself and makes it work in a new context. With the beginning of bodily sexual consciousness in the middle of the third year, the child perceives men and women as different categories—there are two *kinds* of otherness, masculine and feminine—and the child perceives himself or herself as a "member" of one of those categories in addition to being a separate person altogether. There are two kinds of otherness, a general kind applying to all other people, and a sexual kind applying to only the other sex. There are also two senses of self, as someone different from all others and someone different from the others of the other sex. This formulation prepares us for the present inquiry, which asks if we can detect a change in language that reflects the change in psychology wrought by the gender-consciousness developmental stage. I will now, therefore, present the material that led me to say, provisionally, that we can detect features of adult language that are consistent with the acquisition of gender identity in early childhood. I will then continue this theoretical argument in the light of this material.

In a recent seminar at Indiana University, seven students and I studied what I called "comparative literary response patterns of men and women." We had no guesses as to what would be the outcome, but we tried to create circumstances that, we thought, might or could show differences according to gender. We read works by Emily Brontë, Emily Dickinson, Herman Melville, and William Wordsworth, and we collected, from each of us, the kind of "response statements" I described in *Subjective Criticism* and other essays of mine. We thus "asked" if reading or literary perception varies according to the gender of the author as well as of the reader, and if perception varies as a function of literary genre, in this case fiction and lyric poetry. After collecting five response statements from each of the four men and four women, we found a significant gender-related difference in response only with regard to literary genre. We did not see that response varied significantly with the gender of the author, and we did not find any obvious differences in the respondents' sheer use of language. What we did notice and generally agreed was the case was that men read prose fiction differently from the way women did, and that both sexes read lyric poetry similarly. The salient parameter was the perception of the "voice" in the literature. Men and women both perceived a strong lyric voice in the poetry, usually seeing it as the author's voice, while in the narrative, men perceived a strong narrative voice, but women experienced the narrative as a "world," without a particularly strong sense that this world was narrated into existence. Perhaps another way of articulating the difference would be that women *enter* the world of the novel, take it as something "there" for that purpose; men *see* the novel as a result of someone's action and construe its meaning or logic in those terms.

In presenting these differences in reading, I will make certain adjustments in my usual way of discussing responses. I will not, first, present the work of all eight seminar members, but only that of four, myself included. It will not serve the theoretical point to account for each member's response in a full way at this time. Second, and perhaps more importantly, I will cite only part of the response statements of each of our readers. Each statement is very long, and enough can be said about parts of the responses to make it clear to others how to proceed in order to test my claims. Third, I will forego a description of the character and atmopshere of the seminar experience and of the attitudes brought into it by the members; this factor itself requires long reflection, but I omit it with the understanding that it is a salient factor that ultimately bears on the results I am claiming. All of these adjustments appear only because this is an essay and not a book.

Masculine response to fiction: Mr. C

Here is the opening of Mr. C's response to *Wuthering Heights*.

> Before re-reading *WH* for this response statement, I read a biography of Emily Brontë by Winifred Gérin, and looked forward to applying that new knowledge of the author in the attempt to understand precisely what emotional significance each part of the narrative held for Emily herself. This attempt to discover and to re-enact through my own emotions the configuration of emotions that Emily probably felt in composing *WH* reminds me of similar attempts of mine to "fully" understand and master the viewpoints and emotional responses of real-life friends and lovers. One girlfriend of mine in particular, R, continually awed me with her ferocious energy and baffled me with her kaleidoscopic changed of mood; quite often I felt uncomfortably off-balance in her presence, particularly when she attacked deep-seated traits of mine (e.g., fear of communicating) as instances of male chauvinism, when I had had no inkling that, nor could persuade her to explain to me how, those traits were typically sexist and not mutually shared by both men and women. . . . The single person in my life with whom I most strongly identified the fantasy-figure of Emily Brontë was R; both of them possess a great strength of character and highly original minds. . . .
>
> Several of my responses to *WH*, then, proceed, I think, from this identification of Emily Brontë with R. I was both awed and irritated by several instances of Emily's behavior as documented in the Gérin biography: her outraged refusal to speak to her sister Charlotte for weeks after Charlotte's discovery of Emily's hidden cache of poetry, her willful, perhaps even willed, death after brother Branwell's funeral, her outbursts of rude unsociability. I can remember a three-day stretch when R would not speak to me while she nursed her anger, and several times when she picked a fight in public.

While Mr. C does not concentrate on the author throughout his response, his sense of her is a point of orientation, a perspective that defines his attitude and his sense of the reading. Mr. C prepares himself for his reading of the fiction by reading a biography. This is partially connected with Mr. C's own aspirations at the time of the response of becoming an author himself. The contact with the fiction for him is also a contact with his own vocational plans. He sees Brontë as being in the same *class* with himself—one who creates fictions—but still, clearly, as a different person.

By identifying Brontë with a former girlfriend, he marks the author as a well-defined other person: in this case, one who poses a serious challenge, emotionally and intellectually, to his responsive capacities, mainly through her unpredictable outbursts of hostility. In the rest of his statement, Mr. C portrays his reading in this reactive way: there is a strong force in the text, and he is reacting to *it*, seeing *it*, and reflecting on *it*. A characteristic statement is, "At the moment she [Catherine Earnshaw] fakes a fit in order to upset Edgar, I lose any approval I felt before for her love relationship with Heathcliff and never give that approval again throughout the rest of the novel." A similar statement appears about Nelly Dean: "I strongly disapprove of her continuous lying and her withholding of information which could allow the people around her to carry out their responsibilities toward family members, kin, and friends." At this point, Mr. C does blame the author directly for the kind of characters she presents: he feels "irritated with Emily Brontë for her contradictory treatment of Edgar Linton," who at one time is portrayed as a "poor soft thing" and another as the " 'captain' who does not abandon his ship." Mr. C's acts of "approval" apply not simply to the characters by themselves, but to them as products of the author's initiative. His presupposition must be that the author presented her figures to him (for some reason), and his role as the reader is to approve of/disapprove of the *author's* presentation.

Even though there may be a certain animus against what he perceives to be the feminine accent in Brontë, this animus is not behind Mr. C's objectification of the author, only, perhaps, on the *value* he places on that objectification. His isolation of Melville as an author is just as pronounced, but the value he places on him may be higher:

> Melville is one of the few authors for whom I feel a detailed affinity. . . . If you have read my other responses this semester, you will no doubt recognize the recapitulation of concerns in this fantasy portrait of Melville: the identification with old age, the concern for financial responsibility, the feeling of being an underground man, etc. . . .
>
> I resolved to go underground, as I imagine Melville also did in his mid-thirties, from which vantage point I could scrutinize the possibility of receptiveness in others or launch an unexpected assault that would strike dismay and fear in others (identification with Babo in *Benito Cereno,* and partially with Claggart in *Billy Budd*). For all these reasons, I feel a fellowship with Melville, and sympathize with his sorrows, burdens, self-irony, scorn, and suppressed rage.

It did not make so much of a difference to the strength of his objectification of the author whether he felt affinities with her or him: the level of objectification, or otherness, is the same for Mr. C for either author.

A student in this seminar, Ms. D, also studied Mr. C's responses and came to the following conclusion about his response to *Wuthering Heights:*

> Mr. C seems to respond more strongly to the author than to the actual novel, or to put it differently, the response to the text is only secondary as it is mainly determined by his image of what he self-consciously calls "the fantasy-figure of Emily Brontë" which he arrived at from reading Winifred Gérin's biography. He responds to the novel as to something Brontë thinks and says and which he objects to. Thus he is more involved in his comprehension of Emily Brontë's personality and constantly differentiates himself from the male figures in the novel. . . .
>
> In objectifying the author he seems to enter into a dialogue, a controversy with her which allows him to present his own point of view, to define himself in his own terms, and thus assert a strength which would have been denied to him in a close identification with the male figures.

Of particular interest in Ms. D's remarks is her characterizing Mr. C's involvement with Brontë as a "dialogue." She thus calls attention to the sense in which Mr. C's reading is a language act in a wider sense. Reading the novel *is* a conversation of sorts, which I think occurs spontaneously, but which is permitted more literal disclosure by the particular sort of response that was solicited. The same idea of dialogue would accurately describe his response to Melville, with the difference that there is no controversy. The dialogue with Melville does the same thing as the dialogue with Brontë, that is, permits him "to define himself in his own terms." Melville's terms are more sympathetic to him than Brontë's, but the act of self-definition through dialogue is the language act that I think emerges in both readings as they objectify the author.

Masculine Response to Fiction: Mr. Bleich

Ms. D analyzed my responses to the fiction, and here is a passage from my response to *Wuthering Heights* which I think bears out her observations:

> An especially striking scene for me was when Hindley finally decides to kill Heathcliff but is prevented by Isabella, who also wishes him dead. Instead of allowing the murder, she gets in the choice remark, "Heathcliff, if I were you, I'd go stretch myself over her grave and die like a faithful dog." This is more or less what he does. He did what his wife told him to do. All the dogs that appeared at the onset of the novel annoying the hapless Lockwood began to make a little more sense, and they made even more sense as I read of Emily Brontë's fond attachment to her bulldog, "Keeper." These dogs are men— wild, hungry, and incomprehensibly loyal to their master—woman. The author of the tale is a woman, as is its principal narrator, Nell, presumably an

effigy of a real servant in the Brontës' home. Lockwood is an inconsequential and peripheral listener, a mere foil, a contrivance so that the female principle can have its say.

This perception of the novel is placed between a whole series of my associations with my mother and her family, which, I report, was ruled by a "tough, caustic, and money-hoarding woman," my grandmother. These associations emerge as I notice that "there are no mothers in this tale—just motherless men and passionate women." The missing "mother," therefore, is the author, my association with whom appears in response to the "especially striking scene." From the beginning and throughout, I "know" this is a novel presenting feminine thoughts. When I say that Lockwood is a "contrivance," I mean that Brontë contrived him into her work. While, in reading, I identify with Heathcliff in several salient ways, particularly when he says, "So much the worse for me, that I am strong," my identification flags when I decide that "Heathcliff is swallowed up by the female principle and fritters away his own life acting it out." I perceive, in other words, Brontë as an external figure, one who controls the novel and who works by the "female principle" that stimulates my own feelings about the "paradoxical character of relations between the sexes." Ms. D notices rightly that I try to escape from these feelings, as she observes,

> In this objectification of Heathcliff Mr. Bleich defines his present perception of himself. Through the power of reason he has found a way of dealing with his dependency on women which was threatening only in its inexplicability. He has come to accept the relation between mother and son as "the strongest of all" and thinks that only in the case of a motherless man the attachment of man and wife can attain a similar strength.
>
> In respect to *Wuthering Heights,* Mr. Bleich observes that "there are no mothers because the Catherines are the mothers and Heathcliff and Hareton the sons." I infer here that he perceives the power of women as the power of mothers as every woman is potentially a mother. In responding to the novel Mr. Bleich seems to assert the power of his reason in opposition to the female power of procreation which, though strong in its unavailability to him, is not a faculty of intellect and reason. The author Emily Brontë is thus the symbolical mother of her creation, the fiction. Her power as author is the power of the mother. Identifying with Heathcliff therefore means not only with a man dominated by women in the fictional context but also by the author, a woman. In objectifying the author, Mr. Bleich related to her as a woman telling a story whose mode and content confirm his comprehension of the typical feminine.

In principle, I agree with Ms. D's analysis of my response. Although I don't elaborate as much as Mr. C does about Brontë (nor do I think of her as "Emily"), my underlying sense of the author is just about as great as Mr. C's. My seeing her so prominently is the enabling logic of my reading: it all makes sense to me in a certain familiar way, and I feel released, so to speak, to respond freely; at the same time the response articulates the enabling logic, especially through my various associations with my mother and grandmother.

In my response to Melville's three stories ("Cock-a-doodle-doo," "Bartleby the Scrivener," and "Billy Budd") my focus on the author is just as strong:

> This reading was a surprise to me, since I hadn't read Melville in many years at which time I remembered only the power of the stories, rather than the power of the language. . . . I became aware that the way things were said were as if I had said them after long deliberation . . . I looked at the picture of Melville at the front of the book and was glad to find, instead of a wise, grey-haired old man, a young man with a Mona Lisa–like expression telling of a faint sneer behind the thoughtful pose.
>
> I am beginning to suspect old Melville of hating himself for his very solution of becoming a writer, for standing by and observing, for joining the multitude of those with "rational" solutions to the undertow of natural depravity served by the structures of civilization. . . .
>
> Is the man who cannot speak also the cock who can write? Like Bartleby, Billy, and the cock, all rolled into one? Does homographicus hate homoloquitus? I begin to read the narrators as men, and the objects of their attention as women. I begin to think that, whether cultural or biological, this silent element is the woman in Melville—either a real woman, or a part of himself he associates with women that he considers unavailable even to himself.

Here again, my abiding sense of the author as having a comprehensible psychology is the enabling logic of my responses. The figure of the author is a reassurance, a password that unlocks any inhibitions I may have to spontaneous response to the work. There is a kind of human framework I "see" in the fiction, and it makes my "human framework" answer the propositions of the author. As a psychological structure of my reading, it is no different from the one that saw Brontë, though I obviously identify more with Melville. As with Mr. C, identification with the author is secondary, or is contingent on factors other than the deeper or more basic impulse to see the author as "other."

Feminine Response to Fiction: Ms. B

Ms. B goes through a complete response to *Wuthering Heights* without mentioning the name of the author. Her primary attention seems to be on the heroine, Catherine, but as an effigy of her (Ms. B's) mother, who died prematurely when Ms. B was in her teens. Ms. D explains the relation of this fact to Ms. B's response as follows:

> The closeness to her mother was based on her identification which in its completeness approached self-obliteration. In identifying with her mother she could never be like her mother—strong and the main protagonist—but remained a helpless, dependent child.

In her response, Ms. B does not report that she actually identifies with her mother, but only that she admired her, particularly her "magnetic" personality and her physical beauty. The response shows that she sees Catherine in just these terms, and then she identifies with those who also long for her, like Heathcliff, and one who longs for someone else— Isabella, in her longing for Heathcliff.

> Because my father had a personality similar to Linton's, mother never knew a man like Heathcliff. Yet, I gathered from my reading that Heathcliff and Catherine were so close that they possessed the same identity. Although I didn't possess Heathcliff's strength, as a child, I was at times so close to my mother that I felt an extension of her identity. It took a few years after her death before I could distinguish my own opinions and feelings from hers. Like Catherine, my mother was a forceful and enigmatic woman. . . .
>
> Isabella's infatuation for Heathcliff resembles a crush that I had on a professor of English at another college. I idolized him to the point of idiocy. Like Isabella, I was shy and greatly embarrassed around the object of my misguided affections. When I discovered to my horror that he was marrying someone else, I cried for days and bitterly cursed the bitch he had chosen. Like Isabella viewed Heathcliff, I considered that jerk a real "monster."

Ms. B's identifications are not clearly demarcated. In part, she identified with Catherine through Heathcliff because of his longing for her and his "identity" with her. At the same time, Catherine is an object of infatuation not unlike the English professor, but also like her mother. Another way of describing the identifications is that they are fluid or flexible. It is true that Ms. B's association of her admired mother is a strong one in the response, but it translates not into the single perception of a single character, but into the tendency to feel affinities with several figures in the novel, and several relationship situations.

In this excerpt, we should also consider its nonjudgmental style. Her last sentence says that she considered her English professor a "monster." She does not render her similar judgment of Heathcliff but shows instead the analogy between her feelings and Isabella's. This is in contrast to the "approval" Mr. C gives or withholds from the characters, or to the interpretations I place on the narrators in Melville. Ms. B's response is able to articulate the analogy of feeling without interpolating a judgment of the characters. Such moves also appear in her response to Melville's stories:

> The character of Bartleby reminds me of my friend J. She used to sit in the secretarial lounge and constantly study. Her entire life was concerned with Russian linguistics. She rarely went out drinking . . . I have tried to understand her odd personality for six years. . . .
>
> I remember that as a child on Good Friday we would attend religious services at school. The preacher would exclaim that everyone should feel a sense of guilt because of Christ's crucifixion. We, depraved beings, were responsible for his death. (We weren't relieved of our guilt until his resurrection on Sunday.) While reading "Billy Budd" I felt a sense of guilt and futility. The guilt was derived from my religious indoctrination and the futility from my relationship with J. Although I could not change the events leading to Billy's execution and Christ's crucifixion, I felt a sense of guilt and responsibility. It's stupid to feel guilty for an act that you did not commit.

Here Ms. B does give two judgments, but each is about a real person— J's "odd personality," and her own stupidity for feeling guilty under the influence of preaching. There is no judgment of Bartleby directly, and it may not be correct to infer that her judgment of J applies to Bartleby, since in another part of the response, Ms. B explains what a valuable friend and influence J had been. In the second paragraph here, Ms. B's strong judgment is against religious doctrine for influencing her to feel guilty while reading this story, and against J for giving her the occasion to experience futility. What we see here is the exact opposite of what occurred in Mr. C's and my response: the story seems not to have borne on how Ms. B felt in response to it. Ms. B remarks: "Probably because I read the novella on Good Friday and had talked to J I responded to the religious aspects." Her explanation of her response is almost entirely situational: the circumstances of her reading made her see the work in a certain way.

Ms. D used the term *self-obliteration* to characterize Ms. B's response to Catherine and her (Ms. B's) mother. In writing the second paragraph here, Ms. B reports feeling "guilt and futility" reading "Billy Budd." The last sentence of the paragraph says, "It's stupid to feel guilty for an act that you did not commit." When juxtaposed to one another, I think Ms. B's two sentences suggest a process of involvement and separation from the story. The separation is the judgment about herself that it is "stupid" to feel guilty. The involvement may be described (perhaps too severely) as "self-obliteration." But this process of "going in" and "coming out" of the story appears in both of Ms. B's responses to the fiction, and it describes Ms. B's relationships with her mother and J *as presented in the responses.* Ms. B, the reader, develops, in a way, through the response process. The orientation of this development is her own growth, or her own sense of participation in certain relationships. The masculine readers' point of orientation was the author, and whether he or she is contributing to the readers' known, preexisting values.

Feminine Response to Fiction: Ms. D

Reflecting on her response, Ms. D observes,

> My response is concerned exclusively with Catherine's life and death; it is her fate that I responded to most and that in the selective process of writing the response I chose to negotiate with the class. In identifying with Catherine I have to confront the ambivalence I feel about myself. I sympathize with Cathy's power, her uncontrollable temper, yet aware of the unacceptability of her extreme behavior, I feel that "I would not like to be together with a woman like Cathy." . . . In identifying, I too become the object of disapprobation and disrespect. Though troubled by my ambivalence toward Cathy I am more disconcerted by the criticism of her person and begin fervently to "take her part."

Like Ms. B, Ms. D's attention is on Catherine in a way that calls up in her conflicting values and feelings: the problem of self-definition is the orienting factor. Also, there is no mention at all of the author. Instead, Ms. D begins her response with the following thoughts:

> The first time I read *Wuthering Heights* . . . I found the book in my father's room on his desk. What made me finally want to read it was a handwritten dedication to my father by an acquaintance of my parents—the wife of a colleague of my father's about the same age as my mother—which I read with curiosity because of its personal character. It had been one of those days when I was hunting around for something to read to get completely absorbed in and many times ended up reading a detective story or the like. I still remember being kind of frustrated by the novel because none of the women were agreeable to identify with.

The keynote is the reader's own family, in particular, the family issue raised by the fact that a woman "about the same age as my mother" gave her father a book with a personal dedication. Ms. D suggests that she was in a mood to find things out—perhaps by reading a detective story—but reading the novel did not seem to answer this mood because of the difficulty of identifying with the women. It looks as if her curiosity about the book and about her father were combined, but that neither "question" was answered by the reading experience. The uncertainty of the external circumstances of the reading was continued in the actual experience of reading (with the author playing no role in this drama). Notice now in the following remarks how the earlier material seems pertinent:

> Catherine kisses her father good night and discovers that he is dead. I've
> never witnessed a death yet and the idea of only very suddenly noticing the
> death of a close person is really frightening—also very repelling. The only
> funeral I ever attended yet was the one of my aunt last summer. I had not seen
> her for at least ten years; my father avoided seeing her because of a serious
> controversy they had concerning the inheritance from my grandmother, but
> that's not the reason why I didn't see her any more. She was the mother of my
> favorite cousin but he had so much trouble with her and his stepfather and I
> never felt easy at their place. As I never met her on family meetings I just
> stopped seeing her. I never felt close to her yet I couldn't help crying during
> the funeral; to my embarrassment I could not hide it from the astonished
> eyes of my brother. I feared that he thought me ridiculous just doing what
> everybody else did.

I think the idea of an ambivalent identification with Catherine will put
at least some light on the problems in this paragraph. In responding to
Catherine suddenly seeing her father dead, Ms. D shifts the attention to
her own father's sister whose *son* was her favorite cousin. Instead of
surprise at seeing this aunt dead, there was surprise at her own response
to the death—the crying during the funeral in spite of her distance from
this aunt; that is, Ms. D is surprised at *her own response* rather than at
seeing anyone else dead. If we think back to the implications of the
earlier paragraph, the nature of the ambivalent identification with
Catherine seems clearer. The antagonism toward her father which the
inscription may have brought out in her is balanced by the identification
with that woman "about the same age as my mother," an identification
with the aunt as being close to the favorite cousin, *and* the natural
identification of a young woman with her mother. I suggest this relatively complex explanation only because it seems consistent with how
Ms. D presents her ambivalent identification with Catherine: one that
reflects partial stakes in several relationships in her (Ms. D's) real life
and is pointedly devoid of any consciousness of the author. It is as if the
reading itself began with the family, rather than the text or the author; at
the beginning of the response, she alludes to her school experience, but
only to say that she was already out of school when she read it the first
time. Her sense of place in her interpersonal environment, and not the
awareness of the author, is the basis of her responses to and perception
of *Wuthering Heights*.

Ms. D's response to the Melville stories alludes to the author in her
first paragraph and then drops the subject. However, the purpose and
style of the allusion is markedly different from mine and Mr. C's:

> Knowing that my roommate and friend N likes Melville a lot I felt that our
> recently frequent fights only added to my dislike of Melville. I read "Billy

Budd" about one year ago in a course I liked a lot. And it is also due to this course that I started associating Melville with one of these "major writers" forever concerned with a universal truth, with mysterious mysticism, all so much more highly evaluated than the "trivial" occupation of so-called minor writers with domestic and regional concerns. In his admiration for Melville N seemed to be as impressed as other men by what I like to call Melville's pretentious universal significance.

In the remainder of the response, the topic of N continues to occupy Ms. D, and it is more him than Melville who is the topic of the foregoing paragraph. In particular, Ms. D announces that her attitude toward the stories is partially determined by the admiration for Melville of sexist men. But if we go through the whole response, we would not be able to identify Ms. D's strong feelings on this issue, or not as some kind of prejudice against the stories, in any case. As she reports it, first a friend and then a course—two social experiences in real life—explain her sense of the author. But this sense does not remain a rigid perspective on the reading. Rather, N's attitude, and other attitudes like his she finds in her experience, appear as part of the reading response. She returns, in other words, to the interpersonal context of her sense of the author, rather than to that sense itself. The masculine readers rely on their sense of the author itself.

In the responses to lyric poetry, the sense of the author seems more or less similar for both men and women. Each gender saw the author as the governing intelligence of the various works. While each respondent also reacted in significant detail to various parts of the poems—thoughts, lines, images, and so on—at one or more points in every response the readers showed a direct concern for the historical figure of the author, and they usually presupposed that this figure is the speaker of the poems, or that the speaker is a direct "representative" of the poets. The three works by Wordsworth read were "Resolution and Independence," "Intimations of Immortality," and "Mutability." Some poems by Dickinson were suggested, but respondents were free to choose others and respond to them.

Masculine Response to Lyric Poetry: Mr. C

About the Wordsworth readings, Mr. C observes,

> In general, I am left cold by Wordsworth's idealization of childhood and boyhood in "Resolution" and "Intimations." Perhaps that is because I did not enjoy the unusual freedom Wordsworth seems to have been allowed while a boy at Hawkshead Grammar School. . . .

> I rarely envision the future as a less happy time of life because, like the
> narrator of "Intimations" I celebrate the "falling from us" and find hope
> in the "blank misgivings of a Creature / Moving about in worlds not
> realized." . . .
>
> I often tend to share Wordsworth's fear that the inevitable end of poets is
> "despondency and madness," poverty, solitude, pain of heart, and distress.
> My knowledge of biographical facts seems to bear out the idea that poverty is
> a major care of great artists (look at Mozart, Beethoven, Schubert, Melville,
> Faulkner, and company.) . . . I fear that my life as an artist will involve a
> parasitism on others as unfortunate as my parents' vicarious satisfactions in
> the careers of their children and will confirm that status of a child to which
> my parents have tried to confine me all my life.

Mr. C aspires to be a writer. He takes in very seriously Wordsworth's
reflection on the fate of poets and translates them into the terms that he
thinks will likely be in his life if he follows his aspiration. In spite of the
fact that he sees real differences between himself and Wordsworth—
that is, his identification with Wordsworth is not thoughtless or vain—
the reading of the poetry seems to be for him a positive occasion for
utilizing this identification in his own growth and development. Mr. C's
is therefore a very active sense of the author, even to the point of
conscious appropriation of his sense of the historical poet, and it goes
beyond simple identification with the speakers.

About Emily Dickinson, Mr. C writes,

> I realize that I sometimes feel like a father to Emily, although in a majority of
> the poems in our selection I usually feel the older brother's indulgence
> toward a tomboy sister (e.g., in the poem "I never told the buried gold"). In
> "I never lost as much but twice" (49), I intermittently identify with Burglar-
> Banker-Father-God, looking through my door at the endearing little urchin
> on my doorstep. Again, in the poem "My life had stood—a Loaded Gun—"
> (754), I see Emily as a young girl fantasizing that she is a boy child who is
> allowed to accompany his father on a hunting trip, although at times she
> reverts to the role of the devoted daughter: "And when at night—Our good
> day done— / I guard My Master's Head—." There is a slightly uncomfort-
> able feeling about identifying with the Master in this poem, however, be-
> cause I read into the scene at night after the hunt the possibility that Emily is
> incestuously attracted to me, and that I am not repelled, though made
> uneasy, by that knowledge. . . .
>
> I admire Emily's self-objectivity in being able to notate a variety of re-
> sponses to this sense of rejection and to the integrity of the Other. ["A Bird
> came down the Walk" (328)]

Although "Emily" becomes a relatively clear "other" for Mr. C, the level
of attention to her is similar to what he pays Wordsworth. Mr. C's sense
of the poetry uses a specific image of Dickinson which is self-con-

sciously assimilated to the mode of satisfaction he may derive from the reading: he imagines Dickinson wishing to be a boy, and he imagines her "incestuous attraction" to him as Master/Father. But the psychology of such an involvement is less pertinent to our main point than is the fact that Mr. C does consider *Dickinson* as the poems' speakers, and sees himself as reader, in this personal communication with the author, just as he did with Wordsworth.

Masculine Response to Lyric Poetry: Mr. Bleich

Here is a sample of my response to the Wordsworth poems.

> Reading Wordsworth makes me understand why he is a source of great fascination for people I respect. I first "understood" Wordsworth when I heard his poetry read by his descendent, Jonathan Wordsworth, some years ago. He had suitable British tones, the general atmosphere of understatement, and the overall enactment of the term "emotion recollected in tranquility." I understood at that time this characteristic action of mine—to rethink a feeling over a long perspective on the past and to come to terms with it by providing the memory with just the right vocabulary.

Most of the rest of my response goes through a series of identifications with the various speakers, and I compare my ways of coping with their ways. My comparison is motivated by my underlying sense that I am listening to and learning from the real Wordsworth, in a manner very like my finally understanding Wordsworth when I heard his poetry through the voice of his actual descendent. The need for, and sense of, the historical figure is heightened in me by the elliptical character of the lyric language: I do not merely confront interesting language; rather, the language underscores ever more sharply the person originating it.

Here is one of my comments on Dickinson:

> Emily Dickinson is one of my favorite authors of all. Her words, I have found, repeatedly express feelings I have and always seem to present new slants on things I habitually think about. She represents what I consider a quintessentially womanly intelligence, of a kind I often seek and expect but rarely find. She seems to have an extraordinary power not just to say things but to think without a trace of baloney. Her economy of expression is seductive, leaving "pregnant" "gaps" in my perception of the thought, that gives me the feeling of being thus "loaded."

My sense of Dickinson regarding how her language is directed toward me is the same as my sense of Wordsworth. The language "means" the person, so to speak; it means that the "quintessential womanly intelligence" is meaning the language. The gender perceptions, for both poets and both Mr. C and myself, are subordinate to the perception we

251

have in common—the otherness of the poets who are speaking to us. Since I identify with both poets, I infer that the gender is not a serious factor in my perception of the poets' otherness. So I should note that ultimately the effect of my response to Dickinson is that I assimilate her language—I cite it in conversations and in classrooms as something brought into my own language. I make her language my own. While I will return to this action of mine in the concluding theoretical commentary, we are only showing now that the *poet's* language and not the language by itself is the main object of my perception.

Feminine Response to Lyric Poetry: Ms. B

About halfway through her response to Wordsworth, Ms. B offers the following:

> Lionel Trilling's article "The Immortality Ode" considers the lines "Whither is fled the visionary gleam? / Where is it now, the glory and the dream?" Trilling discusses Wordsworth's fear of his decline as a poet. His article helps me to apply other meanings. I remember when I belonged to a poetry group in my home town. We went around town reading our poetry. I remember thinking that I was the next great female poet, but when I came to Bloomington I began losing that "visionary gleam." Classes began to consume all my time and I began to suffer from writer's paranoia. Other poets past and present were better and their poetic vision greater. My fears caused me to lose that creative motivation. Now, for me to write a line or verse is almost impossible.

Although the idiom of Ms. B's thoughts is somewhat less direct than Mr. C's or mine, this passage shows clearly that Ms. B also "sees" the poet in the poetry. Ms. B does say that she understands the lines in terms of Wordsworth's fear of his declining talent (I assume this because she does not dispute Trilling, but seems to see him as an explicator of the poetry). Her description of her "decline" as a poet in Bloomington presupposes an identification with Wordsworth: "I began losing that 'visionary gleam'." While this is not a deep or complex identification, it is enough to show that her perception of the poetry rests on her imaginary perception of the poet, similarly to the way Mr. C and I have such an imaginary perception.

While Ms. B continues to see the poet behind the poems in her response to Dickinson, her response is more complex in this case.

> "This world is not conclusion / A sequel stands behind / Invisible, as music. . . . " I can envision many of my Lutheran teachers or ministers saying these words. It reminds me of all the optimistic garbage I was told to believe in. The words "positive as sound" greatly irritate me, because I could never

be positive about the next world. I was and still am naturally skeptical about everything, including religion. Perhaps I am one of those puzzled "scholars" Dickinson refers to.

Poem 448: "This was a Poet—it is that / Distills amazing sense / From ordinary meanings." I remember two poetry readings I attended at IU. Two years ago I listened to Borges give a public reading of his poetry and last year I attended a reading given by a Russian poet. In both instances they read their poetry in their native language and then a local academic translated. I was usually disappointed when the individual poem was translated, because the academic lacked the fervor and insight of the poet. . . . The Russian poet was always greatly applauded, while the academic was given mild appreciation by the audience. I became bored by the academic.

These passages show, first, an implied critique of Dickinson, but also a strong identification with her. In the light of what she writes in response to poem 448, the tone of the earlier paragraph seems somewhat less certain: Ms. B seems to make a pejorative comparison of Dickinson's certainty with that of the "garbage" given by ministers, but when Dickinson's thoughts are then taken as the poet's thoughts, the scholars and academics are the boring figures. We might wish to guess that Dickinson's "native" language, poetry, has the "fervor and insight" that both the minister and the academic lack. Also, in the light of Ms. B's own admiration for the "visionary gleam" given in her response to Wordsworth, the faint note of ambivalence toward Dickinson could be reflecting Ms. B's feelings about the loss of her own poetic initiatives. In any event, we need not go more deeply into Ms. B's psychology to see that her perception of the poet governs her response.

Feminine Response to Lyric Poetry: Ms. D

At the beginning of her response to Wordsworth, Ms. D remarks that his poetry "reminds me of my first semester in English" in college. The course was given in an old building where "the professors seemed old and the poets dealt with in a lecture course on Romantic poetry seemed to be as old and dusty as the instructors." This remark is the keynote for a "distance from Wordsworth" sentiment that marks the rest of the response. The end of the response includes the following observations:

At this point I feel it would have been good to know something more about Wordsworth, some biographical information in order to get close to him as a person and to create a picture of him with which I could establish some kind of contact.

In "Intimations of Immortality" I imagined the speaker to be a child; or, to put it another way, I could "understand" the childhood he looked back upon because I partly identified it with my brother's. In both other poems I lacked this contact, especially in "Mutability." The opening lines remind me of a physics laboratory: scales and numbers, dissolutions and chemical processes. The words of the poem only seem to disguise pure theory and the voice remains unsubstantial and impersonal to me.

If Ms. D felt this distance from Wordsworth which only biographical information might reduce, why was the situation not similar with Brontë and Melville? There was a definite antagonism toward Melville which was precipitated by her sense of his values. But she did not seek biographical information to ameliorate the situation. With Wordsworth, she is similarly influenced by a prereading "atmosphere" of the old and obsolete, but in this case she thinks biographical information might help. In fact, some sort of "contact" with him "as a person" is what she calls for. I believe the difference lies in the way she approaches each genre, and not with the values she thinks each author stands for. It also may be that the "personal" nature of lyric poetry, to her, gives the opportunity for authorial contact, through biography, that the narrative character of the fiction does not.

Her response to Emily Dickinson also bears comparison to the Melville response. Near the beginning of the Dickinson response Ms. D observes:

> Dickinson's name had been familiar to me for quite a while but I had never read her poetry. About half a year ago a student mentioned her to me saying that she was crazy and hypersensitive and told me the story about her sitting in a separate room when visitors came and conversing with them through the scarcely opened door. The small book of her poetry I borrowed from the library . . . was edited by Ted Hughes, the husband of Sylvia Plath, which added another particle to an evolving picture—Emily Dickinson as one of those women always on the verge of suicide. Cody's biography (first chapter) only completed an image I had thought of already before; a depressed and egocentric woman hard to understand and to love.

A friend of Ms. D's is also associated with her acquaintance with Melville. In the Melville response, the relationship with N helped to motivate her dislike of Melville's work. Here, the nature of the relationship with the friend is unimportant, emotionally, to her view of Dickinson, or at least she *sees* the relationship as thus unimportant. In any event, the emphasis here is similar to the emphasis in Wordsworth—the "evolving picture" of the author helped along considerably by a formal biography. Even if the relationship in this response was significant (as it was in the Melville response) why is the biography sought here, but not for Melville?

Toward the middle of her response Ms. D further observes:

Emily Dickinson's secluded life in the house of her family, her anxiety to meet people, this all seems like a nightmare which I have left behind; it reminds me of thoughts and anxieties I had when I was sixteen years old— the fear of never being able and never wanting to grow up and getting away from my parents.

Unambiguously, Ms. D sees the poems in terms of themes she attributes to the poet herself, rather than to the body of the work or even to the works that she, Ms. D, read. Responding to poem 285 ("Because I see— New Englandly") Ms. D writes, "She conceives of herself as the product of the landscape of her birth, of its nature and climate. I feel the same about me, at least, I'm inclined to sentimentalize a part of my native city, a suburb where I spent my first four years." No comparable level of involvement with the authors appears in her responses to the fiction.

The foregoing eight instances portraying a gender difference in reading based on the study of four people are not enough to be understood as definitive. On the other hand, it is not likely that chance alone is responsible for these differences. What we do have is a preliminary indication of a possibly deep difference in the *perception* of language according to gender, with reading being one area where this difference can be studied. Because I am saying that there appears to be a difference in the perception of narrative, I would like to bring attention to the perception of narrative in another way: how a narrative is retold by men and women. I think that the kind of gender difference we see in the retelling of narrative will confirm and enlarge what we earlier found regarding the perception, or lack thereof, of the author.

The instance I will discuss uses William Faulkner's short story "Barn Burning." From a class of freshmen at Indiana University, I collected about one hundred and twenty retellings and picked, at random, one hundred—fifty from men and fifty from women—for use in this inquiry. The assignment was "Retell, as fully and as accurately as you can, Faulkner's 'Barn Burning'." The essays were written in about thirty minutes in a large lecture hall and ranged in length from 200 to 600 words. The original purpose of this exercise was the study of reading differences among individuals, and most instructors treated the essays with this purpose in mind. However, the students also knew that gender differences were part of our class's general interest, and some instructors raised the issue with these essays after they were written. However, the finding that I am reporting here did not develop until after the course was completed. In the following discussion, I will first give a general sense of the gender differences in the retellings and then give instances of specific items in support of this general sense. As with the previous set of responses, I will now only cite pertinent passages, not the complete essays.

The men retold the story as if the purpose was to deliver a clear, simple structure or chain of information: these are the main characters; this is the main action; this is how it turned out. Details were included by many men, but as contributions toward this primary informational end—the end of getting the "facts" of the story straight. The women presented the narrative as if it were an atmosphere or an experience. They generally felt freer to reflect on the story material with adjectival judgments, and even larger sorts of judgments, and they were more ready to draw inferences without strict regard for the literal warrant of the text, but with more regard for the affective sense of the human relationships in the story. Here are the first paragraphs of retelling by two men; the second is my own.

Mr. J:

> The story begins as the boy and his father are in the courthouse of a small town where the father has been thrown out of town for allegedly burning down his boss's barn. The motive he had for burning the barn was that he and his boss had a disagreement over how much he owed him for the corn his pig had eaten while he roamed around unpenned. The family left town as they had so many times before.

Mr. B:

> Sarty was in a courtroom when his father Abner was accused of burning a barn. Abner, it was testified, had sent his black servant to tell that the barn was flammable, and this testimony made it seem that Abner was guilty. Sarty, who seemed to know that Abner was guilty, did not testify against his father and so it was not proven that Abner burned the barn. The judge, however, told Abner to get out of town, which he did.

I cite these together because in spite of the fact that I am about twice Mr. J's age, the paragraphs seem similar in narrative tone. The detail of the pig enters for Mr. J as the dispute that brought them to court, while my detail of the black servant enters to explain why Abner was accused. I consider these to be details because other readers omitted them without seeming to distort the story. In both our cases, the use of detail was to explain rather than to characterize or to give a judgment of our own. Neither of us introduced at this time the issue of loyalty or "blood," which was also a part of the story's first paragraph. Here, now, is a first paragraph by Ms. S:

> "Barn Burning" by William Faulkner was a story about a family, two daughters, two sons, a mother, father, and aunt. The story was based during the time when plantation owners owned farmers to work on their land. The father was a poor man and was obsessed with burning barns when he dis-

liked the plantation owner. Burning barns was the only way the father could show retaliation.

In this paragraph there are several instances of tendencies found much more frequently in women than in men. Ms. S sees the story as something that happened to a family, not just to the "main character." At least seventeen of the fifty women actually took a sentence to enumerate all the family members, whereas only three or four of the fifty men did. When men alluded to the family, it was usually of the form, "Abner took his family to another place," or, in one case, "The story begins with Abner, the father and head of the family." Mr. J's paragraph shows something like this when he writes, "The family left town as they had so many times before." My own opening paragraph says nothing about the family. Ms. S's second sentence was something not many readers alluded to at all—the sociohistorical circumstances of the story—but there were perhaps six women and only one or two men who did this. For Ms. S, this fact seems to be an important part of her sense of the story. Snopes's poverty was also a factor more for the women than for the men. Notice that Ms. S gives an interpolated judgment in this connection: because the family was poor, Abner developed an obsession as his way of "showing retaliation." This issue is not named as such in the story, but because Ms. S mentioned it, it suggests that she sees her tacit inferences as part of the story, a mode of perception much less common in men. I know I made such inferences as Ms. S describes, but I did not think of them as part of the story.

The distribution of comments regarding the mental health and moral intention of Abner is significant. Only two of the fifty men seemed to bring in these factors. One said that Abner had "poor character," while another said he had "no sense and fewer patience." Similarly, the idea of revenge was virtually unmentioned among the men, although some did say he was "angry" or "defiant." At least eight women, however, wrote that Abner was "mentally unstable" or showed "a lot of emotional problems"; the women give these judgments as part of their presentation of his behavior: "The father was crazy or had some kind of mental problem. He never told the famly exactly where they were going." The latter fact is in the story; the former "fact" is this reader's judgment as to why the story's fact existed. By and large, the women who mentioned mental problems said they were the cause of Abner's desire for revenge:

The story, "Barn Burning," dealt mainly with one man's struggles with society and the effect it has on his son and their relationship. The father is an outcast, which is established fairly clearly at the beginning. He has a disposition that possibly is mentally unstable and consists of revenge in the form of burning down the property of other people.

Notice here also that Ms. C brings in the idea of "society" and the fact that Abner is an "outcast." The mention of the relationship between father and son—as opposed to the discussion of each individual figure—is also more usually found in women's retellings.

Whatever negative comments the men had about Abner, they were not associated with his habit of taking vengeance, while the women saw the vengeance as related to a psychological obsession. We might pause here to reflect on whether we would, in our culture, understand the idea of vengeance as more masculine than feminine. We regularly see "Mafia" stories, Westerns, police dramas, and the barely concealed ethic of vengeance among "tough" men is considered a folk value. We might guess on these cultural grounds alone that the men would "see" the vengeance in this story more often than the women did. Yet, just the opposite happened. I don't believe enough men are sufficiently embarrassed about this ethic to want to censor it in their work. I believe, rather, that the men are being more literal in their renditions of the story; the story does not announce that Abner is seeking vengeance. One must infer vengeance from the narration of events. Because the women feel freer to include their inferences—both about the vengeance and about Abner's mental health—such inferences appear fluently in their renditions of the story. Even though cultural values are definitely at work in the readings of both men and women, I think this is an instance where the stronger psychological tendency to render other language in a certain way overrides the effect of cultural values on the retellings.

A similar case came up in my experience in the perception of Hemingway's story "Hills Like White Elephants." I have asked various groups—mostly freshmen, but also one group of adults over thirty—what the "operation" in that story is. Even though all readers were old enough and experienced enough to know about abortions, women regularly "see" an abortion much more quickly and with much more certainty than men do. If you argue that, culturally, they see it because they are women, this would be only partly true: that is, it is only partly true that women see it because they are "closer" to thoughts of abortion than men are. Men are frequently involved in conversations such as the one in the story, and they know as much about abortions from their own self-interest as women do from theirs. I believe, therefore, that because the word *abortion* does not appear in the story, men don't want to "put it in." Men are cautious about "accuracy," and they thus inhibit themselves from saying things that may not be literally documented. It may be that the literal absence of the word *abortion* from this story by a masculine author combines with the masculine wish to be detached from such problems to cause the nonperception in the men. But also, because inference is more regularly considered part of women's perception, women achieve certainty about this particular inference much sooner than men do.

Because of their greater fluency of inference, women "see" feelings in the story more quickly than men do. In retelling "Barn Burning," both men and women gave most of their attention to Sarty, but we may discern differences in the *kinds* of attention each gender gave to him. As we recall, the opening of the story introduces Sarty through his response to the cheese smell in the courtroom:

> The store in which the Justice of the Peace's court was sitting smelled of cheese. The boy, crouched on his nail keg at the back of the crowded room, knew he smelled cheese, and more: from where he sat he could see the ranked shelves close-packed with the solid, squat dynamic shapes of tin cans whose labels his stomach read, not from the lettering which meant nothing to his mind but from the scarlet devils and silver curve of fish—this, the cheese which he knew he smelled and the hermetic meat which his intestines believed he smelled coming in intermittent gusts momentary and brief between the other constant one, the smell and sense just a little of fear because mostly of despair and grief, the old fierce pull of blood.

As retold by Mr. B, this passage comes out as:

> The "Barn Burning" starts out in a courtroom that at one time, by my guess, was a store or something. It smelled of cheese and meat to the boy whose father was on trial for allegedly burning down someone's barn.

And Mr. D writes:

> As the boy stood there watching, at a distance, his nose began to pick up the scent of cheese and fish.

Ms. A offers the following:

> In the beginning there is a general store filled with people and a trial is going on. The author focuses on the little boy. The boy's father is on trial for burning a man's barn down. The boy must be hungry because the smell of cheese and some kind of fish are capturing his attention.

The "facts" for Mr. B are that the boy who was awaiting the trial smelled cheese; for Mr. D they are that the boy's "nose" began to pick up the smell. This latter is a plausible change, since the text reports that the boy's stomach and intestines sensed the smells of cheese. But both of these contrast to Ms. A's observation that the "boy must be hungry" because the smells "are capturing his attention." This is a much more complex statement, since it aims to portray what is in Sarty's mind (rather than in his nose). Also, if we contrast this to Mr. B's statement,

Ms. A describes the smell as "capturing his attention," while Mr. B says that the courtroom smelled of cheese. In one sense, Ms. A's inference that the boy "must be hungry" seems obvious; yet she was the only reader to draw this conclusion from this paragraph. I think it happened because Ms. A sees the language as *aiming* to create (in the reader) the sense of his or her feelings and motives. To understand the language at all *means* to draw such inferences about feelings and motives from the metaphors in the original text. For the men, however, to understand the language *means* to repeat the "facts" it presents and to avoid drawing "extra" inferences. Mr. B can only "guess" that "at one time" the courtroom was a store. If he took the risk of drawing an inference, however, he would have to say that the courtroom actually was a store, which he would infer from the simple presence of the food. His reading had overlooked the second word of the story and then could not compensate by making the inference from less literal language; so he had to guess. As we see, Ms. A also guessed at something, but her guess tries to construct the affective situation of the boy.

In general, the women's retellings showed a more complex expression of the emotional condition of the boy. One woman wrote that Sarty was "fearfully awaiting to hear of his father's outcome." Another said that the boy was "sitting in quiet fear," and a third that the "boy was glad" to learn he won't have to speak in court. In the passage from the story quoted above, it is not syntactically clear that "just a little of fear" that Sarty "senses" should be translated as "sitting in quiet fear." Yet the women try to render this affective circumstance simply. The men, however, do not render it at all: they do not try to describe Sarty's feelings as he sat there. The following contrast is also pertinent. One woman describes Sarty as "thinking to himself that he had to lie about what his father had done." A man reporting the same idea wrote of Sarty's "uncertainty of whether to tell the truth or lie." Compare "thinking to himself" to "uncertainty"; "whether to tell the truth or to lie" with "he had to lie." The woman describes an active subject feeling coerced; the man describes a person reflecting on *which* action to take. Although the men undoubtedly felt fear, force, and pain in response to the story, such feelings stay out of the retellings, and this is just as true in my own retelling. Here is another pair of descriptions of Sarty which both use the word *torn* to name his situation. The man writes that the story is "about a small boy torn between lying and telling the truth." The woman writes, "A young boy is torn between what he knows is right and his ties with his father." The man's description centers entirely on the boy and presents the problem as between two abstract courses of action, lying and telling the truth. The woman's description emphasizes the active subject—"what he knows is right"—as well as the demands of the relationship with the father—"his ties with his father." I claim that because the men are more instinctively distant from the reading, abstractions emerge in their retelling more readily. Because the women enter into the human relationship situations in the story more readily, they retell the story more in terms of interpersonal motives, allegiances, and conflicts, and less in terms of the perspective of a single character or the author.

Elizabeth Flynn suggests in "Gender and Reading" that men are generally more frustrated by the failure to understand the reading than are women. This tendency emerged in the present inquiry also; I attribute it to the proposition that the need for literal comprehension is an essential part of the distancing impulse. Because women distance themselves less, comprehension, while nevertheless important, is not as urgent a factor in the response process, and so they will construe a general affective logic for the fiction even if they are not quite sure of what is "going on." In my samples, men will more often interrupt their retelling by saying that the story was "written in a confusing way" or that it had "many ambiguous parts to it." Only one woman wrote that the story was "somewhat confusing," and this, she wrote, was because "it was not totally clear in where exactly it took place." One woman expressed no doubt at all in reporting that the story is about a "Negro man and his family who are constantly moving from one place to another." This error may be due to the following judgment she also made: "The father, presumably out of hatred for whites, has an obsession for burning their barns." It made so much sense to her that Abner's violence was racially motivated that she thought nothing more of it. She obviously already had an intuitive conception of the political situation in the South which supplied her with the *affective* logic that overrode details of her reading which may not have borne out *her sense of what would* lead someone to burn barns. To her, that is, the only underdog in the South is the Black, and she would have to be explicitly told that there are other underdogs in that society. Rather than take such risks as this woman did (she acknowledges it is a risk by using the word *presumably*), the men would sooner announce that they just don't know or can't tell, thus, in a sense, keeping their distance.

One may wish to review some of the received aesthetic theories—Wordsworth's "emotion recollected in tranquility," the concept of the "aesthetic emotion" in the nineteenth century, or Bullough's popular notion of "psychical distance"—in this light. These could very well be understood as typically masculine viewpoints, ways in which men relate to works of art by virtue of the gender component in their psychology.

We need not reject these viewpoints for this reason or even reject the possibility of their being true of women readers in certain cases. We do need to question seriously if the universal language of these views— Must *all* aesthetic readings "have" psychical distance, for example?— prevents us from noticing how thoroughly masculine values and psychology have created "objective" standards of reading. It may well enhance their importance to reunderstand traditional theories as interest bound, especially when such interests are gender related.

Bearing in mind that such questions about the history of criticism and literary values could be reunderstood with gender interests in mind, let me now pick up the theoretical thread I suspended early in this chapter. In particular, the fact that both men and women perceive the "voice" of lyric poetry similarly and that each gender perceives narrative fiction differently should be understood as adult language features traceable to the acquisition of gender identity in early childhood. Thus, the biology of the child, combined with his or her psychological relationship with the parents, creates a psychosocial gender interest that may be detected in that person's language throughout the life cycle.

The lyric trope is self-reflexive: I sing of myself, I speak of my experience. The lyric trope thus acts out the psychological schemata of self-objectification. The poet's/speaker's objectification of himself or herself causes the reader, in the act of reading, to perform this same action, the action of self-objectification, and the reader perceives his or her own action as "the same" as the poet's/speaker's. This trope, therefore, recalls the action of language acquisition which renders the child capable of objectifying both self and (undifferentiated with respect to gender) other. Men and women, as a result, read the lyric poetry in the same way, that is, with the same high level of awareness of the poet/speaker. Self/other objectification occurs without respect to gender awareness. It is the psychological achievement that makes language possible in both sexes—as each acquires language in the relationship with the same figure, the mother. The self-reflexive *convention* of lyric poetry recalls the self-reflexive psychological action of language acquisition in both sexes.

Lyric language is autonomous and/or expressive speech. It is meant less to be spoken *to* someone than to be spoken *in the presence of* someone. It is most fully and most originally a "speech act"—speech that is important because it was performed as much or more than because of what it says. This is very similar to infantile speech, whose development is encouraged by the mother's enthusiasm at its sheer performance. The infantile exercise of self-reflexivity is a cause for celebration, since it is taken by both mother and child as a shared accomplishment, a common cause. Take Dickinson's line, "I heard a fly buzz when I died." This is a performance to be registered rather than a communication from which knowledge is to be extracted. Its self-reflexivity is not narcissistic, but invitational, just as the mother's use of language is always also an invitation for the child to "use language" and not just "say what I say." Although the child first does imitate the mother, he or she eventually "uses language" by *answering, responding,* or *reacting.* In Dickinson's line, the false phrase "I died" calls attention to the pure performance of the speech. But the autonomy of such speech is meant to be shared as mother and infant share language. Each performance is an invitation to the other, which lays the groundwork for all subsequent use of language in dialogue situations. This psychology is common to boys and girls and thus renders plausible the fact that both men and women focus on the voice of the poet/speaker in lyric poetry.

The adult reader of lyric poetry is not unlike the adult patient in psychoanalysis in the situation envisioned by Leo Stone, where, regardless of the actual gender of the analyst, he or she is a psychological mother to the patient, who becomes verbally infantile by being verbally intimate. In salutary cases, the patient will "separate" from the mother-analyst and "individuate"—become a "new" person, autonomous and independent. All the readers of lyric poetry, by noticing the author, by expressing concern for this author, by wanting to know about him or her, are going through the process of "separating" themselves from the maternal voice of the singer. Each reader of either gender tries to objectify this voice in the conventional ways—first by seeing its historical separateness, and then by inquiring after biographical information. This, of course, is not a clinical process, but a natural one. We readers naturally focus on the poet's "voice" and catch that singleness of its source in much the same way that we define the singleness of the original maternal voice—spontaneously. Since we are adults, however, reflective processes go to work immediately to restore our adult autonomy by finding a way to affirm that "this is the poet's voice" and "this is my reading voice," to affirm our otherness and the poet's otherness, thus returning us from imagination and memory to the real context of the reading experience. The responses that we all wrote perform this "return" for us. This is why we see the uniform interest in the author for each gender.

The narrative voice, like the lyric voice, is still the voice of the mother (tongue), but instead of the characteristic trope being "I speak" or "I speak of myself," it is "I speak of this other item, this object, this 'third' person." The narrative voice brings into the "conversation" this third person, the he, she, or they. If we think of the first and second persons being the mother and infant, then the third person is the "father." Affectively, a child becomes a third person when he or she makes the gender distinction between the two other people. The child grasps at once the belonging to one of the two gender categories and the non-belonging to the adult category. Because gender identity is achieved relative to *two* different parents, we would expect that the path toward this achievement is different for each gender. This difference in path is reflected in the different ways each gender perceives the narrative trope.

When little girls identify with their mothers (with regard to gender), they will have the greater tendency to *sense that* "my language is mother's language," or that "mother and I, because we are the same sex, speak the 'same' language." The little boy, seeing his similarity to father with respect to gender, will have the greater tendency to *sense that* "my language is other than mother's language" (even though it may actually be similar in many respects). The little boy has the psychological grounds for seeing an otherness in the mother's language that is more radical than what the little girl sees. Because the narrator's voice remains the "mother tongue," and because this voice now invokes a "third person," the narrative action thus recalls the childhood action of gender identification. (Bear in mind that I am *not* claiming that the child first learns to use the third person at this stage, but rather that he or she first grasps these sociogrammatical categories in a gender-affective way at this time.) Thus, for the little boy, the speaker herself becomes an other in a way she was not, to him, in the language acquisition stage. Put another way, not only does the narra*tive* point outward, to something or someone else, but the "narrator" herself is someone else in a different sense. For the boy, both the content of the narrative and the source of the narrative are other.

For little girls, this is obviously not the case. In an important way, the narrator herself remains the "same" figure she was in the language acquisition stage—just an other, but now somewhat *less* of an other by virtue of her being the same gender as the little girl. Otherness in general for the little girl becomes less other than it does for the little boy. This condition of "less otherness" explains why the women perceived the narratives as they did. With regard to the narrator, first of all, the women, in a sense, automatically blended in with him or her (as we think of the narrator as "the speaker of the mother tongue") and/or they automatically blended in with the author. The women "become" the tellers of the tales that they are reading, and they therefore do not notice or demand to notice the author. For women entering the "world" of the tale, furthermore, the "world" of the tale, too, loses its distinct otherness. The women tend to identify with more than one figure in narratives, even to identify with feelings and situations, and to experience the reading as a variety of social emotions. Neither the teller nor the tale is radically other for the women.

The men, however, draw boundaries much more decisively. For them to "see" the author is as fluent as it is for the women not to see him or her. Being aware that an author is behind a narrative seems to be a gender-specific form of self-orientation toward narrative for the men. Regardless of which gender the author is, the author's status of being "behind" the narrative activates the men's schema of seeing a referential user of the mother tongue as "other." Similarly, the tale itself is more other for the men. The novels were more self-consciously *appropriated* by the men than by the women, who tended more to "enter" the tale. Also, to retell a story, one must recreate "it" as it "is." The women seemed more ready to retell it as it was *experienced*. This would account for the women's greater fluency in interpolating their judgments into their retellings. In the responses to the novels, however, the men were more prone to judge the individual characters while identifying with only one or two. The women were less likely to offer a judgment of individual figures and more likely to describe differential allegiances to various figures and situations.

The general psychological difference between men and women that was suggested by these various responses is that otherness, or objectivity, for women is a much more provisional mental act. Both men and women regularly objectify things, even symbolic things like stories and ideas. But it does not seem as urgent an act for women as it does for men. With this in mind, let me take a last step back to biology. Both men and women are born of women. Women, therefore, probably perceive men as "less other" than men perceive women. For a man to come into his own involves a more radical separation from the mother than it does for a woman to come into her own, even though both genders do require a decisive separation at the infantile stage of language acquisition. What makes it less decisive for women is that the acquisition of the sense of gender identity takes them "back" in a sense to the mother from whom they just separated. What makes the separation more decisive for men is that the acquisition of the sense of gender identity moves them further away from the "other" who gave birth to them.

Why should it be, finally, that responses to literature suggest such a conclusion? If we understand literature as the cultural record of accumulated language tropes that are used in the various developmental phases of the life cycle, literature must "work" by reactivating these tropes, to one degree or another, in each person's reading experience. There was never a phase of civilization when there were no lyrics and no stories; there were only different forms of lyrics and stories. Because literature serves language by recording its history and use, it must be capable of restimulating, in each new generation, the abiding human interests in language. Many of these interests are political, cultural, or ethical. But some, such as gender, are biological and psychological. It seems appropriate to allow at this time that alongside the many common interests men and women have in language and literature they also have interests that are permanently tied to the biological fact that they are of different genders.

Chapter 12
Gender and Reading
Elizabeth A. Flynn

Recent scholarship on the relationship between gender and reading has arisen primarily from two different sources: reading research that examines the behavior of elementary and high school students, and feminist literary criticism that analyzes literary texts from a reader-oriented perspective. Reading researchers have contributed empirical data on gender-related similarities and differences among developing readers, and feminist literary critics have contributed descriptive studies of the ways in which texts shape responses along gender lines. We know very little, though, about the reading patterns of relatively mature male and female readers. In an attempt to extend the studies of reading researchers to include college-age students and to bring an empirical orientation to the reader-oriented work of feminist critics, I conducted an exploratory study designed to examine the interpretive strategies of college freshmen in their responses to three frequently anthologized short stories, James Joyce's "Araby," Ernest Hemingway's "Hills Like White Elephants," and Virginia Woolf's "Kew Gardens."[1] The twenty-six women and twenty-six men who comprised my sample were enrolled in a freshman composition course taught at Michigan Technological University in 1980. Students in seven sections of composition wrote responses to the stories during three different class sessions. They were told that a wide range of responses was possible, including summarizing the stories, analyzing them, or relating them to their own experiences. (See the Appendix for a description of the course, the students, and the assignments.)

My analysis of the data was informed by a conception of the reading process which assumes that reading involves a confrontation between self and "other." The self, the reader, encounters the "other," the text, and the nature of that confrontation depends on the background of the reader as well as on the text. Text and reader are necessarily foreign to each other in some ways, and so the exchange between them involves an imbalance, what Wolfgang Iser calls "asymmetry" or "contingency." Georges Poulet emphasizes this imbalance in his description of the reading process. He writes, "Since every thought must have a subject to think it, this thought, which is alien to me and yet in me, must also have a subject which is alien to me. It all happens, then, as though reading were the act by which a thought managed to bestow itself within me with a subject not myself."[2] The reader allows the foreign object to "bestow itself" within his or her mind, and so self and other coexist, for a time.

What Poulet does not emphasize is that the coexistence of reader and text can take a number of different forms. The reader can resist the alien thought or subject and so remain essentially unchanged by the reading experience. In this case the reader dominates the text. Or the reader can allow the alien thought to become such a powerful presence that the self is replaced by the other and so is effaced. In this case the text dominates the reader. Either the reader resists the text and so deprives it of its force, or the text overpowers the reader and so eliminates the reader's powers of discernment. A third possibility, however, is that self and other, reader and text, interact in such a way that the reader learns from the experience without losing critical distance; reader and text interact with a degree of mutuality. Foreignness is reduced, though not eliminated. Self and other remain distinct and so create a kind of dialogue.[3]

The dominant pole is characterized by detachment, observation from a distance. The reader imposes a previously established structure on the text and in so doing silences it. Memory dominates over experience, past over present. Readers who dominate texts become complacent or bored because the possibility for learning has been greatly reduced. Judgment is based on previously established norms rather than on empathetic engagement with and critical evaluation of the new material encountered. The reader absents the text. A response to Joyce's "Araby" illustrates this strategy of domination. The student wrote enthusiastically about his encounter with the text, but there is little evidence that a pattern of meaning was created as a result of that encounter.

> The beauty that one comes away with from reading "Araby" is the feeling. When I read this story I could almost say I was there. I was able to relate some of my past experiences with what James Joyce used for setting. The general feeling of the street, and the buildings gazing at one another are all related to past experiences. I am able to say that, "Hey, I was on a street just like that." And when I can put my personal experiences to work the story becomes loaded with color.
>
> The adjectives that are used throughout the story are very descriptive. The garden was not just a garden, but it was a wild garden. I am able to picture a

wild garden; however, a wild garden may be one thing to you and another to me, but it makes no difference to the net effect.[4]

The student's positive attitude toward the reading experience suggests that subsequent readings of the story will result in meaningful interaction. This first reading, however, has not moved the student very far beyond himself. The text activated his imagination, and so he remembered streets and gardens from his own past. He has not yet put those images to use in comprehending the story, however. He makes no reference to the plot of "Araby" or even to its protagonist.

The submissive pole, in contrast, is characterized by too much involvement. The reader is entangled in the events of the story and is unable to step back, to observe with a critical eye. Instead of boredom the reader experiences anxiety. The text is overwhelming, unwilling to yield a consistent pattern of meaning. A response to "Araby" written by another student illustrates this submissive stance.

> "Araby" is another story that has great inner meaning. Each paragraph has some meaning; for example, the first paragraph has some deep inner meaning about what the houses represent. The second paragraph is the same way, in the deep meaning sense, but talks about some dead priest's home and what was found in the back yard. And every paragraph in between, right up to the last one, has something to be interpreted. I would start to interpret them if I could, but I can't make much sense out of the whole thing.
>
> In describing the story, it starts out with a street description of some old homes. The story then goes to some boys playing in the street, and then to a specific boy and what is happening to him as he, apparently, falls in love with a neighbor girl. The narrator tells about all the little things the boy is doing when falling in love like gazing under the window blind until she comes out and walking behind her when she is walking to school. And then his first time talking to her.

This student was so close to the textual details that he could make no sense of them; he brought little of his past experiences to bear on the text and so could gain no critical distance from it. He summarized the plot of the story in hope that some meaning would emerge. For him the text is a reservoir of hidden meanings rather than a system of signs to be acted on. Like the author of the previous response, this student will no doubt interact with the text more meaningfully in subsequent readings of the story. Right now, however, he is so overwhelmed by the text that he is unable to assign meaning to it.

These two responses are potentially interactive but are so far from revealing meaningful engagement with the text that they represent minimal communication. Productive interaction involves the active participation of the reader in the construction of meaning. Readers formulate hypotheses as they encounter the signs of the text, and those hypotheses are constantly being altered as new information is processed. Iser in *The Act of Reading* explains the process as follows: "The reader's communication with the text is a dynamic process of self-correction, as he formulates signifieds which he must then continually modify" (p. 67). As the reader's perspective shifts, so do the signs in the text, so that they are constantly taking on different patterns of significance. The reader's energies are expended attempting to find a consistent pattern of meaning from among the seemingly incompatible stimuli, and meaning is finally achieved only when tensions are resolved. Iser calls this resolution a closed gestalt. Signs no longer appear unrelated or contradictory but, rather, form a meaningful whole.

Within the category of interaction, then, we have levels of engagement with the text. A reader may be at an early stage of the interactive process and so unable to resolve the conflicting patterns that phantasmagorically emerge and recede during the act of reading. Characters, images, events, take on importance and then shrink into insignificance as the reader gropes toward meaning. Evaluations of textual details shift until the reader reconciles conflicting elements and achieves a balance between detachment and involvement.

Productive interaction, then, necessitates the stance of a detached observer who is empathetic but who does not identify with the characters or the situation depicted in a literary work. Comprehension is attained when the reader achieves a balance between empathy and judgment by maintaining a balance of detachment and involvement. Too much detachment often results in too much judgment and hence in domination of the text; too much involvement often results in too much sympathy and hence in domination by the text. However, when the reader is able to integrate past experience with the experience created by the text through critical evaluation of the interwoven signs encountered in the process of reading, comprehension is achieved and learning takes place. Iser describes the effect of productive interaction as follows:

> The new experience emerges from the restructuring of the one we have stored, and this restructuring is what gives the new experience its form. But what actually happens during this process can again only be experienced when past feelings, views, and values have been evoked and then made to merge with the new experience. The old conditions the form of the new, and the new selectively restructures the old. The reader's reception of the text is not based on identifying two different experiences (old versus new), but on the interaction between the two. (P. 132)

Past and present are synthesized into a new experience. The reader is transformed, renewed.

The following response statement reveals features of the interactive process. The discussion of "Araby" is clearly an initial reaction, but it nevertheless suggests that the student achieved a balance of detachment and involvement in reading the story.

> "Araby" by James Joyce is a very complicated story for as short as it is. He uses many symbols in this story. Religion is mentioned several times and through his use of this, it seems that the boy in the story imagines himself to be a crusader. He has a very high opinion of himself. When Mangan's sister asks him to buy her something at the bazaar he feels as if he is on a crusade for her. Joyce mentions a chalice and speaks of prayers and praises all concerned with this girl. The boy in the story treats the girl as an idol or a god. I think he fears touching her not only because he admires her so but also because it will make her appear more human. She might not appear so glorious in his eyes.
>
> The boy places entirely too much importance on going to the bazaar. He can hardly wait until Saturday comes and when it does he is even more impatient waiting for his uncle. It's like he's living his life to do this one thing, buy the girl something at the bazaar (Araby). When he gets to Araby he rushes in and soon realizes everything is above his price range. He becomes angry and disappointed, realizing that all along he had been fooling himself. He was too filled with self-importance and his sense of purpose to realize what might happen.

This student interacted with the text in the sense that she not only described the plot of the story, she also assessed the character of the boy and evaluated his behavior. She took the stance of an understanding and yet detached observer who seemed to understand what motivated the boy's behavior yet did not judge him overharshly. Like the narrator of the story—the young man who reflected on his childhood experiences—the student observed the boy from a distance and so came to understand him and hence to understand the text. She created a consistent pattern of meaning and resolved the tension between the unselfconscious and deluded young boy and the more knowing, more judgmental narrator.

My analysis of the responses to "Araby," "Hills Like White Elephants," and "Kew Gardens" revealed, not surprisingly, that the preponderance of responses by both women and men were submissive. Because students were encountering the stories for the first time, they had difficulty stepping back from the texts in order to interpret them. Response statements contained attempts at interaction with the stories—partial explanations of characters or events, questions, tentative hypotheses. But they also contained expressions of frustration, uncertainty, puzzlement. Most students struggled to move from entanglement in the text to interaction with it. They wanted to comprehend the stories but had not yet been successful in doing so. A response written by a woman student is typical of the majority of the responses in the sample.

> This story ["Araby"] left me in the fog. Even though I read it over and over it still seems like I missed something in it.
>
> It starts off describing a street then it tells of a house. In this house lives a boy and his aunt and uncle. The author goes on and tells you about the street the children play on and also about a girl the boy likes.
>
> The boy sort of worships her; he never talks to her, he just admires her from a distance. One day she finally does talk to him. He was so shocked he didn't know what he said to her. She asked him if he was going to Araby (bazaar). He said he would try to go, and if he did he'd bring something back for her.
>
> When he got home he asked if he could go. His aunt and uncle said yes (in a way, but they really didn't give their final approval). So the day of the bazaar he waited all day for his uncle (work?), who didn't get home until late; finally when he did get home his uncle said he could go.
>
> At the end he goes to the bazaar and the English girl asked if she could help him in a rude manner.
>
> All I know is that he was Irish Catholic.

The reliance on plot summary, the expression of frustration, and the uncertainty are characteristic of statements written by students who have not yet arrived at a satisfying interpretation of a text. Actions are related but not evaluated. Events are retold but not deciphered.

On the periphery of these seemingly amorphous and indistinguishable responses to the three short stories, though, were statements that revealed distinct patterns of response along gender lines. Some differences between the responses of some women and men students did emerge. A pattern of dominance was evident in some of the men's responses, especially in statements based on "Araby" and "Hills Like White Elephants," but no such pattern was evident in responses written by women. Also, more women than men were able to resolve the tensions in the stories and form a consistent pattern of meaning.

Differences between the men's and women's statements were most pronounced in "Araby." The predicament of a young boy losing his sense of perspective because of his infatuation with his friend's older sister seemed to evoke extremes of rejection or identification in some of the men students, responses that interfered with their understanding of the story.

With the exception of the dominant response quoted above and the response of a male student who effaced the text by fragmenting it into disconnected examples of metaphoric personification, the male students who displayed a tendency toward domination of the text did so because they judged characters without empathizing with them or because they detached themselves from the emotional content of the text. One male student, for instance, rejected the text in its entirety and in so doing dominated it.

> This story seemed to be about a deranged person that is in love with a degradable woman. The author seems to fill in the story with descriptive words, because he realizes the events of the story are boring.
>   The story was written in such a way that no one would know what was happening, so that he could be thought of as a good writer. . . . In this case, since no one knows what he's talking about many ideas about what is hidden in the story will be made up and therefore he will be thought of as a good writer (even though he thought of B.S. in the first place).

This student's way of dealing with the difficulty of the text was to dismiss it. The response is characteristically dominant in that it defends one-way projection as an appropriate reading strategy and thereby renders the text voiceless.

Four other male students were overly judgmental in their treatment of Mangan's sister, a response that distracted them from a central concern of the story, the boy's solipsistic infatuation. Three male students saw the girl as manipulating the boy for her own ends. One described the boy as having been "used" by the girl. Another described the girl as "just using him." Another remarked that the girl was "just playing him along." The fourth male student described the girl as "ignoring" the boy and equated her with the woman at the bazaar who was abrupt with him. The student wrote, "He had been ignored by the lady in the booth just like he had been ignored by the girl he was in love with, or were they the same people?"

The dominant reader is often a detached reader; the text is not engaged, and so the reader feels little empathy for the central characters. In three of the responses written by male students, the protagonist was treated with detachment, and so his experience was kept at a safe distance. One male student called the protagonist a "little guy"; another described the events portrayed in the story as "some guy's fantasy"; still another endowed the narrator with the name "Jack" and referred to him as a "young kid." If the boy is simply a "little guy," then his experiences are insignificant, and the conflict described in the story need not be taken seriously. The tone of the response statement written by the student who named the protagonist "Jack" is complacent, matter-of-fact.

> This is a story about a young kid who is in love with his friend's sister. The boy and his friend love to tease his sister by hiding in the shadows at night when she would call her brother in for tea.
>
> Jack was madly in love with this girl and went totally out of his way just to see her but not speak to her. He used to peep out the window and watch for her to leave for school and would chase after her. He would always walk behind her until it came time to part in different ways and then he would speed up and pass her.
>
> Jack would never hardly speak to her until she spoke to him first. She asked him if he was going to the bazaar Araby because it was going to be excellent. He went completely out of his way to see Araby because he said if he went he would bring her something.
>
> He was at the bazaar and was looking for something to buy her but this crabby lady drove him away and that made him very mad.

The response trivializes the boy's situation. The student's account suggests that the boy's frustration is externally induced, and it omits mention of the discovery the boy makes about himself.

These dominant responses suggest that these male readers were uncomfortable with "Araby," either because they found it too difficult or because its focus on male infatuation disturbed them. These responses account for fewer than half of the men's responses, however. An even greater number of male students had difficulty comprehending the story because they were too involved in the text, sometimes because they identified with the protagonist too strongly and were unable to distance themselves from him. These submissive responses almost always revealed an inability on the part of the reader to deal with the ending of the story. The conclusion of "Araby" brings together the narrator's perspective and the young boy's perspective so that the reader will recognize the extent to which the boy's fantasies isolated him from his family and peers. Very few male students responded to the resonating finale, though, often because they were unable to recognize the boy's limitations.

A few male students expressed dissatisfaction with the ending of the story. One wrote, "In judging this story, I really didn't think it was very good. I didn't like the way the author ended the story." Another responded, "The story just ended." A third suggested changing the ending to a happier one. The one male student who gave a fairly full account of the conclusion nevertheless failed to recognize the significance of the boy's judgment upon himself, partially because he identified with the boy too strongly. His response reads:

James Joyce uses imagery and symbolism to illustrate the feelings which a young boy goes through when he is infatuated with a girl. Joyce says that the boy would sleep at her door waiting to see her. He would follow her to school thinking about her as he walked behind her. "Her name was like a summons to all his foolish blood."

The young boy's feelings were not understood by the older generation who were callous to his words. They considered the bazaar to be a small happening, when it was actually a big event in the boy's eyes.

The boy finally does arrive at the bazaar but does not find things as he wanted them to be. He is shaken from the fantasy world by the absence of the girl. This anguish he feels because of the loss of the fantasy world is illustrated by the symbolistic sentence, "Gazing up into the darkness I saw myself as a creature driven and derided by vanity, and my eyes burned with anguish and anger." The protective coating was lifted and the bright light shown into his unprepared eyes causing them to burn and redden.

Joyce tells the story of a young boy's growing up through these imaginative symbols and images. These images tell the story in a vivid, alive manner.

The student clearly identified with the boy's experience and sympathized with him. He also recognized that the boy is "shaken from his fantasy world" and that the experience at the bazaar removes him of his "protective coating." His focus on the girl's absence, however, interfered with his comprehension of the boy's final judgment on himself. According to this student's account, the boy's epiphany results from a feeling of loss rather than a recognition of his own self-delusion.

That other male students identified with the boy is evident in their response statements. One, for instance, wrote, "It was easy to relate to the narrator's boyish infatuation with an older girl, since I can recall having similar experiences." His identification was not accompanied by comprehension of the story, however. He admitted, "I couldn't grasp the central thought in the story." Since a resolution of the tensions in "Araby" necessitates some understanding of the ending of the story and thus some detachment from the boy's situation, such close identification no doubt interfered with the student's ability to create a consistent pattern of meaning. Four other male students mentioned that they could relate to the boy's experience, and they, too, had difficulty interpreting the story. Only two women students mentioned that they could relate to the boy's experience. Their responses suggest that their identification with the boy was also a distraction, though not to the extent that it was for the men. Both mentioned that the boy felt anger or humiliation at the end of the story, but neither gave a full explanation for the boy's feelings.

The women students in the sample were, for the most part, better able to achieve a balance between detachment and involvement in reading "Araby." No women students judged Mangan's sister over-harshly, and none referred to the protagonist as a "little guy" or a "young kid." Many recognized the boy's limitations and yet regarded his experience as significant. And although the majority of responses by women students were submissive in that they revealed entanglement in the text, eleven women were successful in making sense of the story, usually because they came to a satisfying interpretation of its ending. One female student wrote, "After being tempted many times the boy finally realizes that he cannot survive in the world of vanity, and that he must return to the real world. The world that is filled with illusions that people put forward to make everything look nicer." Another woman observed, "He realized here that he had been driven there by his vain love for this girl as stated in the last paragraph." Another accounted for the ending as follows: "I think he had come to realize how foolishly he had acted. This realization embarrassed him, so he turned it to anger at himself." Another female student described the boy's unsuccessful visit to the bazaar and concluded, "He gave up and left; thinking of himself as a person driven by vanity." Another wrote, "In the end, I think he realizes how foolish his feelings have been. In the darkness of the bazaar, he sees things in a new way. He realizes he just has a crush on this girl and she will never feel anything for him." Most of these accounts employ the word *vanity* and make specific reference to the last line of the text.

The concerns in "Hills Like White Elephants" are quite different from those of "Araby," and yet the students' responses followed a pattern similar to that found in the responses to Joyce's story. Some men dominated the text, though this strategy was not evident in the responses of the women. The majority of responses were submissive, but more women students were able to resolve the tensions in the story than were men students. Once again, men students were often closer to the extremes of domination or submission, and the women were often closer to the interactive center.

"Hills Like White Elephants" focuses on a conversation between an American man and a young woman called Jig as they await a train that will take them to Madrid, where Jig will have an abortion. The conversation is tense because Jig is being pressured into going through with the operation yet is resistant because she feels the child would bring some stability and meaning to the couple's relationship. The conflict is resolved through the young woman's denial of her feelings and the man's assertion of his will. This is a story, then, about female vulnerability and defeat. The imagery suggests that the woman's position is life-affirming and that renewal is possible only through her victory over the man. The ending of the story, though, suggests that she is powerless to change the nature of the relationship.

Surprisingly, only one student, a male, was overly judgmental in his reaction to the story. We might expect that college freshmen would be moralistic in their responses to an unmarried couple contemplating an abortion. He wrote, "In the story the man wants the girl to get an abortion. This man seems to know an awful lot about the operation so it must not be the first time he did it to a girl. The fact that he had so many hotel tags on his luggage indicates that he has only one thing on his mind." Other indications of domination by male students suggested rejection of the text because of its difficulty, or detachment from it rather than harsh judgment of the characters. The male student who found the protagonists of "Araby" to be "deranged" and "degradable" also rejected "Hills Like White Elephants," but his response suggests that he was bothered not by the immorality of the protagonists but by the difficulty of the text.

> The story stank. It was boring and didn't end with any main idea. It ended like a dream; it exists and has a hidden reason for happening. The hidden reason isn't worth finding out because it is small in comparison to the time it takes to search for it. A dream is enjoyable, but after being known it is thrown in the trash and forgotten forever.

This student seems once again to be reacting so strongly because he was unable to comprehend the text. He didn't understand the ending of the story, and he experienced the text as dreamlike because it seemed to defy coherent analysis. The student emphasized the imbalance between the value of the message contained in the story and the amount of energy required to extract that message. Perhaps he did not understand the nature of the conflict well enough to come to some evaluation of it.

Another dominant response by another male student also emphasized the difficulty of the story. He wrote:

> My impression of the story was that it wasn't a story at all. It was just a short conversation between two people. The story consisted of just a couple of pages filled with quotes.
>
> Another reason I didn't like it was it left the reader blind. The story just starts right up and doesn't tell anything about who the people are or about what is going on. I had to read through the story a couple of times just to figure out what they were talking about. Nothing was said right out in the open about getting an abortion.
>
> All I have to say [is] it was short and different.

This student, too, rejected the story because he could not understand it.

The text, for him, was "just a couple of pages filled with quotes."

The student who referred to the narrator of "Araby" as "Jack" and who detached himself from the boy's plight responded in a similar way to "Hills Like White Elephants." Once again he revealed an inability to empathize with the protagonists, and once again he trivialized the conflict being described. In the concluding paragraph of his response he wrote, "Finally after a lot of nagging she asked if he would do anything for her and he said yes. She then gave him the pretty please bit with a dozen pleases and asked him to quit bugging her and finish his drink." The student's use of slang expressions suggests that he did not take the interchange between the two seriously.

The male students, on the whole, revealed less self-involvement in "Hills Like White Elephants" than they did in "Araby." Fewer felt the need to dominate it, and there is less evidence of identification with the male protagonist. None of the male students, understandably, indicated that they had had a comparable experience to the one described in the story. They nevertheless had difficulty resolving its seemingly discordant elements, often because they were unable to make connections between the setting and the conversation between the man and the young woman.

Five of the twenty-six men in the sample discussed the relationship between setting and theme in analyzing the story. The remaining male students either ignored the setting or expressed frustration in attempting to interpret it. One male student wrote, "The 'Hills Like White Elephants' could find little meaning in my interpretation of the story. I know that this symbol holds the key to the understanding of the conflict in the story but my imagination didn't quite cut through the story so I could see the meaning." Another responded, "I'm having a hard time trying to figure out what the hills represent." These male students, and numerous female students as well, were unable to recognize that the setting establishes a dichotomy between fertility and infertility, which provides an indirect commentary on the man's desire for the abortion and the woman's reluctance to go through with it, so the students were unable to recognize the significance of the man's defeat of the woman at the end of the story. The effect of this inability to make sense of the ending was an inability to evaluate the conversation between the man and the woman and so to recognize that the woman has been defeated. One male student, for instance, accounted for the ending as follows: "She says she's fine. She seems to be scared because of the unwanted operation. The heat and tension have caused them to argue. When the entire event is over, the relationship will be much better." Another male student said, "The story just seems to be about two people who travel a lot, are in love, and are now troubled with a pregnancy." In neither response is there an evaluation of the respective positions of the two protagonists. The students are too close to the events of the story to see that two different approaches to life are being displayed and judged.

One male student successfully integrated setting and characterization in his response.

> Hemingway's "Hills Like White Elephants" relates the conversation between an American couple in Spain as they await a train to ride to the city for an abortion operation. The girl is hesitant about having the abortion, and comments on various aspects of their present surroundings and their past relationship to convey this to the man. She sees the cool white hills, trees, and river across the valley as symbolizing the beauty and meaning a child could bring to their life, whereas the treeless landscape, the rail station, and the bar equate with the barren, transient life they have known to this point.
>
> The man loves the girl, but tries to convince her that their life is happiest when they are alone together; the prospect of a child has brought unhappiness. He does not want to assume fatherhood and its responsibilities; he does not want to share her.

Another male student made reference to the sterility/fertility dichotomy in the setting and concluded, "The girl gazes longingly at the hills almost as if she wishes she was surrounded by this fertile, rather than the dry, sterile area." His response statement made no reference, however, to the conflict between the two characters or to the man's final domination. One male student saw a connection between the phrase "hills like white elephants" and an abortion, since a "white elephant" refers to something gotten rid of, as does an abortion. He also wrote, "The part of the skin of the hills may have something to do with the skin of the child after the abortion." Neither association, however, led him toward a satisfying interpretation of the story, and he concluded his response with a digression: "Something that just occurred to me is that the sun was shining brightly on the hills, giving them an appearance of being white. Could this possibly have meant the son of God shining down on the dead child and taking its soul to heaven? The white being the brilliance of Jesus on the child?" Another male student made a connection between the white hills and the abortion but did not use the insight to evaluate the characters or their conflict, but found instead that "the story is trying to make us aware of the complex problem and feelings about abortion." This student concluded that "the argument between the two main characters is unresolved at the end of the story." Another male student referred to a different aspect of the setting, the train station, and decided, "The significance of the train station is that this whole ordeal can be carried right out of their lives afterwards and forgotten. The easy way out!" This account minimizes the significance of the resonating decision made at the end and implies that the choice will have few emotional ramifications.

These responses are typical of other submissive responses by male students in that they demonstrate a lack of critical distance. Often the male students in the sample portrayed the conflict as an argument between two equals which remains unresolved at the end of the story. Or the men's responses indicated that they were unaware of the man's domination or the woman's powerlessness. The women's responses were also predominantly submissive and also demonstrated a lack of critical distance. More women than men related setting to theme, however, and more women seemed able to gain enough distance from the two characters to judge their situation.

Although we might expect that women students would react to "Hills Like White Elephants" the way some men reacted to "Araby"— by identifying with the same-sex protagonist and thereby losing critical perspective—this tendency was present but not pronounced in the response statements. A woman student who digressed in her response about the problems of "pregnancy before marriage" and who mentioned the example of a close friend who consulted her for advice did not come to a very precise critical assessment of the couple. She wrote, "Something had changed their lives. They were no longer happy; they had fallen into a rut." And another woman student who projected onto Jig her own delight in the purity and innocence of babies made no reference to the conflict between the two characters and said nothing of Jig's defeat at the end of the story. In both cases, it would seem, a preoccupation with the pregnancy distracted the students from the central focus of the story, the interaction between the characters.

More frequently, however, sympathy for Jig was accompanied by discernment of the limitations of the two characters. One woman student, for instance, empathized with the female character and yet revealed an awareness of her weakness.

> Ernest Hemingway's "Hills Like White Elephants" is a unique story. In it, there is a conflict going on between what may be man and wife or may be two lovers. The story takes place in a train station located near a river with mountains in the background. The mountains are a representative of the conflict. The girl believes that together they can have everything; however he disagrees. The actual conflict in the story is whether she should have an abortion or not. She is unsure but is willing to do it because of her love. He wants her to have the abortion because all he needs is her.
>
> This story could have been written today. Abortion often causes conflicts. The men like represented in the story don't always realize the many side

effects which the woman experiences. They try to say that there are none, physical or mental, but there are. In the story, the girl doesn't care much about herself. She cares more for her lover/husband.

Typically, in the end, the male's dominant views have come through. She agrees to have the abortion and says that there is nothing wrong. Unfortunately this relationship will probably end because conflicts are not resolved. To have a meaningful relationship, they must be more open.

Although the student clearly sympathized with the female character, she was able to gain enough distance to see that Jig is incapable of asserting herself and of making her wishes known. The student was also aware of the man's domination of the woman and of the lack of communication between the two. And unlike a number of students who made no evaluation of the positions of the two characters, this student recognized that Jig's defeat is unfortunate. Another woman student was even more emphatic in her assessment of the two characters. She observed, "The woman is childlike and submissive wanting what the man wants and on the whole the relationship suggests shallowness and a sense of being naive (especially the woman seems to be naive)." A third woman student expressed a similar attitude. She wrote, "I get the distinct feeling that the girl is young and doesn't have too much mind of her own. She is very undecided in her decision of keeping the baby or not. The man is pressuring her to have the operation and gives reasons for it."

Other women students used the setting as a touchstone for evaluating the characters in the story. One woman, for instance, saw the couple's discussion of the hills as a commentary on their approaches to life. She responded, "When the girl says the hills are like white elephants, the man says he never saw a white elephant. This seems to be saying that the man has no imagination. He just goes through life drinking beer and talking." Another woman took Jig's attitude toward the hills to be a reflection of her attitude toward her child.

During the course of the story her feelings change about the child. She states that the hills no longer remind her of white elephants, which leads you to believe that she is no longer sure about the abortion. It is obvious that the man is pressuring her to get the operation because he says that he will love her more if she gets it. She is torn both ways because she wants the baby, but if she keeps it she'll probably lose the man; and in order to keep the man she must give up the baby.

Another student mentioned Jig's looking across the field and seeing a cloud drift past. This gesture, and Jig's comment, "And we could have everything and every day we make it more impossible," revealed to the

281

student that Jig wants to have the child and that the man's resistance to her desire is a reflection of his unwillingness to take on the responsibilities of fatherhood. Another woman student discussed Jig's confusion in terms of the title of the story. She said, "In my opinion the girl didn't know what to do at first so the baby was the white elephant but toward the end it seems she felt the operation was the white elephant. But she was still all confused not knowing which way to go." Another woman student used the setting to determine the author's attitude toward the abortion. She said, "The sombre tone and lifeless setting help to convey the type of operation. For example, the countryside is described as treeless and extremely hot. From this we can infer that the operation was not a pleasant one, but rather sad and unwanted. This idea is supported even more by the tone of the conversation." Two other women students used the setting to decipher character and theme. One thought Jig's reference to the hills looking like white elephants revealed her preoccupation with her unborn child. Another interpreted her comment that the hills look like skin to mean "although they look perfect and pure on the surface, there is something beneath the skin, some substance. This is how she imagines her relationship is: perhaps once clean and pure on the top, but underneath it all there seems to be nothing to bind them together."

The responses to "Kew Gardens" did not follow the pattern of the responses to the other two stories in that there was little evidence of domination of the text. Although both men and women students had difficulty comprehending the story, their frustrations did not take the form of aggression. It was as if the text, which deals explicitly with the rejuvenating powers of nature, had had the effect on the students that the garden had on the individuals who passed through it: it soothed and calmed otherwise anxious souls. The male student who found both "Araby" and "Hills Like White Elephants" to be boring and meaningless seemed to be pacified by "Kew Gardens."

> The story was slow-moving, about a park. The people in the park were all going about their business while the insects were going about theirs, in their own world. It was like going to a park and resting on the ground, relaxing and seeing an ant just walking on the ground. The park itself was completely peaceful to you, and you see the ant and he seems without a worry, but then you remember he is in his own world and doesn't even know you exist.

Instead of resisting the text, the student placed himself within it. Domination became acceptance. Other male students who rejected or resisted the other stories seemed to be similarly drawn into the world of "Kew Gardens." The student who trivialized both "Araby" and "Hills

Like White Elephants" took the events in "Kew Gardens" much more seriously. The student who reduced "Araby" to a series of unrelated figures of speech made an attempt to interpret "Kew Gardens" by identifying a common characteristic of the people who passed through the garden, their tendency to reflect on their past.

The preponderance of responses to "Kew Gardens," like the responses to the other two stories, were submissive in that students had difficulty stepping back from the events of the story and finding a pattern of meaning. Responses included unassimilated plot summaries, hypotheses about the meaning of the text which accounted for only a fragment of the textual details, and expressions of frustration or confusion. As in the responses to the other two stories, however, more women were able to evaluate the disparate elements in the text and shape them into a meaningful pattern, one that involved empathetic judgment. Four male students and nine female students formulated statements that revealed a consistent pattern of meaning. The women's responses, however, tended to be more sharply focused.

One male student interpreted the story as follows:

> In the short story, "Kew Gardens," Virginia Woolf contrasts the unity and orderliness of nature with the apparent aimlessness of humanity. She describes the beauty of a flower bed, with all the different colored flowers joining together to produce a sense of unity and purpose, and then describes various persons as they stroll through the garden, each with his or her own thoughts and meaningless actions.
>
> Virginia Woolf shows how humans are wrapped up in their own world. We hurry about, busily attending to our own seemingly important affairs, and show little thought or concern for others around us. Instead of unity we practice individuality. We see, but we are blind to anyone and anything around us that does not directly benefit us.

Three other male students recognized that Woolf contrasts the human order with the natural order. One student wrote, "Woolf seems to be telling us that nature is actually a controlling force on man, not the other way around as usually is thought." Another wrote, "The human values weren't worth much compared to the easy-going life found in the garden. Descriptions of the people were vague and they all seemed to fade away into the hot atmosphere. This seemed to show they were fading away from nature back to the world of work." Another student wrote, "Through the detailed description of nature, the author relates nature's ingredients to human experiences. It seems throughout the essay that these human experiences are just another breeze, meaning that although many have gone by, many more are to come, and that many of these experiences aren't as important as the people think they are."

Nine women students expressed similar themes, often focusing, however, more sharply on the limitations of the people described in the story. One student wrote: "We listen to the human voices and see how ridiculous the conversations are. If the garden is left in silence it seems to live. But as soon as some person starts talking the garden is silent. The snail doesn't move. The voices cause everything to freeze. Once the people are gone the garden comes to life." Another observed, "It seems the author, Virginia Woolf, feels that nature is above mankind in the story. She gives the insects the ability to think and to possess goals. The humans walk about aimlessly and searching for something. What they are searching for I get the feeling they don't really know." Another wrote:

> Now the people themselves seemed to have influence over what takes place in (the) garden, but it was as if the garden had some sort of control over their past lives. It was as if the garden seemed to hide important mistakes that the people who came through the garden had made. The lives of the people seemed to change after they left the garden, almost as if they had just reached a turning point in their lives. It seems as if the flowers and the insects are an audience for the players: the players being all of the people that come into the garden, and they all seem to be putting an act on for each other.

These four male students and nine female students focused on the constancy of nature in contrast with the inconstancy of humanity. The women students, however, were more critical of the characters in the story: their conversations are "ridiculous"; they are searching for something but do not know what; the people are "putting on an act" for each other. Other responses by women students also indicated critical detachment. One woman wrote, "The garden, which all the people pass, is a symbol of nature's stability. The people who pass represent the unpredictable human race. The first couple that passes shows how people are never really satisfied with what they have. The small family seemed disjointed and unhappy. When the disoriented old man went by, the reader was aware of the kind of self-destruction one can induce." Another wrote, "Man's separation is shown through the disjointed conversation of the characters. They all have their own thoughts and show little concern for anyone else's thoughts. This is true of all three groups that pass the flower bed." Another wrote, "The people didn't seem to really relate to their surroundings; instead they allowed their thoughts to take them elsewhere. They chose to dive into the past and just leave the garden behind."

The conclusions that can be drawn from the analysis of the responses to the three stories must necessarily be tentative because of the size and nature of the sample. In order to make conclusive assertions about the relationship between gender and reading we need to look at a large number of response statements, at the responses of women and men readers from a variety of backgrounds, and at responses to numerous kinds of texts at various stages in the reading process. The study does suggest, however, that male students sometimes react to disturbing stories by rejecting them or by dominating them, a strategy, it seems, that women do not often employ. The study also suggests that women more often arrive at meaningful interpretations of stories because they more frequently break free of the submissive entanglement in a text and evaluate characters and events with critical detachment. My own informal observations of student readers bear out these contentions. I have noticed, for instance, that some male students react unempathetically to literature about vulnerable women characters such as Sylvia Plath's *The Bell Jar* and Margaret Atwood's *Surfacing,* and judge the protagonists "insane" or "crazy." I have also observed that women are often receptive to texts in that they attempt to understand them before making a judgment on them.

If further research supports my central contention, then we may find that women are considerably more confident and competent readers than they are speakers. Research on the relationship between gender and speaking indicates that men are assertive speakers who dominate conversations but that women are hesitant and deferential in speaking to others. Robin Lakoff in *Language and Women's Place,* for instance, argues that women are tentative and cautious in their speech; men are authoritative, coercive. She observed that men more frequently use forceful intensifiers such as the superlative *very,* whereas women use less forceful intensifiers such as *so* and *such.* She also found that women tend to use questions when declaratives would be more appropriate and to use modals and hedges to express uncertainty more than men do.[5]

Pamela Fishman's research essentially supports Lakoff's contention that women lack power in speech settings. In order to determine how women and men interact in conversation, Fishman placed tape recorders in the homes of three couples and then analyzed their topics of conversation. Fishman found that men dominated the conversations, either by ignoring topics initiated by their partner or by developing topics they themselves initiated. Fishman writes:

> We have seen that, at least among intimates in their homes, women raise many more topics than men. They do so because their topics often fail. They fail because the men don't work interactionally to develop them, whereas the women usually do work at developing topics raised by men. Thus, the definition of what are appropriate or inappropriate topics for a conversation are the man's choice. What part of the world a couple orients to is in his

control, not hers. Men control topics as much, if not more, by veto as by a positive effort.[6]

Reading is a silent, private activity and so perhaps affords women a degree of protection not present when they speak. Quite possibly the hedging and tentativeness of women's speech are transformed into useful interpretive strategies—receptivity and yet critical assessment of the text—in the act of reading. A willingness to listen, a sensitivity to emotional nuance, an ability to empathize with and yet judge, may be disadvantages in speech but advantages in reading. We may come to discover that women have interpretive powers that have not been sufficiently appreciated.

Appendix

The twenty-six women and twenty-six men were enrolled in one of seven sections of freshman composition taught by two male colleagues and myself in the spring quarter, 1980. Students wrote responses to the three stories during the first twenty minutes of the first class period in which the story was to be discussed. This structure insured that responses would be relatively free of the influence of the instructor or other classmates. Eleven women and eleven men in the sample who were enrolled in sections taught by one of the instructors read "Hills Like White Elephants" during week two, "Kew Gardens" during week three, and "Araby" during week ten of a ten-week quarter. The remaining fifteen women and fifteen men studied "Hills Like White Elephants" in week five, "Araby" in week eight, and "Kew Gardens" in week nine. Students knew that response statements would count toward their grade (responses to nine stories would constitute 15 percent of their grade) and that they would receive full credit if their responses indicated they had read the stories carefully. Instructors provided little feedback on the responses, and students did not know their statements would be used for research purposes until the end of the term.

Students had the benefit of study questions that followed each story in the Norton anthology. They sometimes made reference to the questions in their responses, especially in discussing "Hills Like White Elephants," since a question indicated to them that Jig and the man were discussing an abortion.

Students who comprised the sample were fairly representative of the 1979–80 freshman class as a whole. The women in the sample had a mean score of 20.5 on their ACT composite score, compared to a mean score of 21.7 for all freshman women at Michigan Tech who entered the university in 1979. The men in the sample had a mean score of 19.04 on the English ACT, compared to a mean score for all freshman men at Michigan Tech of 19.8. (Mean scores for the sample were based on ACT scores of only 24 women and 24 men, as scores were not available for two women and two men.) These scores indicate that both in the sample and in the freshman class as a whole, women had somewhat higher verbal abilities, at least as measured by the ACT. Students in the sample were representative of Michigan Tech freshmen in other ways, as well. All but two men and one woman were 18 or 19 years old. Twenty-four of the twenty-six men were majoring in a field related to science, engineering, or math; the remaining two were majoring in business administration. Eighteen of the women were majoring in a field related to science, engineering, or math; the remaining eight were majoring in nursing (three), business administration (four), or social sciences (one). None of the students was majoring in humanities.

The selection of students was complicated by the fact that Michigan Tech is a predominantly male institution: in 1979–80, men outnumbered women 4 to 1. The ratio of men to women in the 1979–80 freshman class was 3 to 1, but the ratio in the seven sections of composition which served as a source for the sample was even higher (3.5 to 1), since a number of women students generally place into honors sections. I had originally intended to include forty women and forty men in the sample, but found I had responses to the three stories from only twenty-six women after I eliminated students not taking the course in sequence. The twenty-six men were selected from the data pool at random.

Notes

Professor Tzvetan Todorov provided valuable feedback on a draft of this chapter. I also received very helpful criticism from John F. Flynn on subsequent drafts of the article. Preliminary research was made possible by a Faculty Research Grant from Michigan Technological University. John F. Flynn and Jim Hefling contributed response statements from their freshman composition sections.

1. The anthology used in the course was R. V. Cassill, ed., *The Norton Anthology of Short Fiction,* shorter ed. (New York: W. W. Norton, 1978).

2. Wolfgang Iser, *The Act of Reading: A Theory of Aesthetic Response* (Baltimore: Johns Hopkins University Press, 1978), p. 167; Georges Poulet, "Criticism and the Experience of Interiority," trans. Catherine and Richard Macksey, in *Reader-Response Criticism: From Formalism to Post-Structuralism,* ed. Jane P. Tompkins (Baltimore: Johns Hopkins University Press, 1980), p. 44.

3. These categories were also suggested by Tzvetan Todorov's discussion of the Spanish conquest of the Indians in his course "The Conquest of America," taught at the School of Criticism and Theory, Northwestern University, June/July 1981. Professor Todorov argued that individual Spaniards assimi-

lated Indian culture into their own and in so doing destroyed it, identified so strongly with Indian culture that they lost their European identity, or engaged in dialogical interaction with the Indians.

4. Distracting errors in punctuation and spelling have been corrected in this and other response statements.

5. Robin Lakoff, *Language and Women's Place* (New York: Harper and Row, 1975), pp. 142–43.

6. Pamela Fishman, "What Do Couples Talk about When They're Alone?" in *Women's Language and Style,* ed. Douglass Butturff and Edmund L. Epstein (Akron, Ohio: E. L. Epstein, 1978), p. 21.

A Selected Annotated Bibliography

Elizabeth A. Flynn and
Patrocinio P. Schweickart,
with Carol A. Brown

This bibliography is a list of scholarly works on the relationship between gender and reading. In compiling the list, we have drawn from several fields: feminist literary criticism and theory, reader-response criticism, and reading research. The list is meant to be reasonably inclusive but not exhaustive, especially in the areas of feminist criticism and theory and reading research. We have selected works that make connections between gender and reading in an explicit way. Annotations attempt to highlight these connections.

Feminist Criticism and Theory

Archer, Jane; Sally Ann Drucker; Marilyn E. Matis; Donna Meek; Karen Peterson; and Marcella Sherman. "Initiating a Context: A Collective Approach to Feminist Critical Theory." *Radical Teacher* 18 (1980): 33–39.

Describes a course in feminist literary criticism that explored relationships between feminist criticism and Marxist, psychoanalytic, and post-structuralist approaches. Found useful Norman Holland's "transactive criticism."

Booth, Wayne C. "Freedom of Interpretation: Bakhtin and the Challenge of Feminist Criticism." *Critical Inquiry* 9 (1982): 45–76.

Culler, Jonathan D. *On Deconstruction: Theory and Criticism after Structuralism*. Ithaca: Cornell University Press, 1982.

Theories of reading, including treatment of "reading as a woman."

Deutelbaum, Wendy. "Introduction." *Reader,* no. 8 (1980), pp. 4–5.

One of the first calls for a "feminist reader criticism."

Diehl, Joanne Feit. "Come Slowly Eden: An Exploration of Women Writers and Their Muse." *Signs* 3 (1978): 572–87.

Any theory of influence must account for the sex of the poet.

Donovan, Josephine. "Feminism and Aesthetics." *Critical Inquiry* 3 (1977): 605–8.

The traditional formalist assumption has been that the reader should "give in" to the vision imposed by the work. Feminist criticism suggests, rather, that one should enter into the fictional world only if it seems that the characters and situations depicted therein are authentic and just.

Ellmann, Mary. "Phallic Criticism." In *Thinking about Women*, 28–54. New York: Harcourt Brace Jovanovich, 1968.

Books by women are treated by male critics as though they themselves were women, and criticism embarks, at its happiest, upon an intellectual measuring of busts and hips.

Evans, Nancy Burr. "The Value and Peril for Women of Reading Women Writers." In *Images of Women in Fiction: Feminist Perspectives,* edited by Susan Koppelman Cornillon, 308–14. Bowling Green, Ohio: Bowling Green University Popular Press, 1972.

Reading women writers is perilous for women readers because they may identify with female protagonists too readily. Literature written by women is valuable for women readers when they learn from the experiences of female heroes.

Fetterley, Judith. *The Resisting Reader: A Feminist Approach to American Fiction.* Bloomington: Indiana University Press, 1978.

To read the canon of what is currently considered classic American literature is to identify as male. The female reader is co-opted into participation in an experience from which she is explicitly excluded; she is asked to identify against herself.

Flynn, Elizabeth A. "Women as Reader-Response Critics." *New Orleans Review* 10 (1983): 20–25.

Finds commonalities in the positions of three female reader-response critics: Jane Tompkins, Louise Rosenblatt, and Susan Suleiman.

Friedan, Betty. "The Happy Housewife Heroine." In *The Feminine Mystique,* 28–61. New York: Dell, 1963.

Describes the power of the "feminine mystique," the image of women as housewives-mothers portrayed in women's magazines in the fifties.

Furman, Nelly. "The Study of Women and Language: Comment on Vol. 3, No. 3." *Signs* 4 (1978): 182–85.

Interpreting language is no more sexually neutral than language use or the language system itself.

———. "Textual Feminism." In *Women and Language in Literature and Society,* edited by Sally McConnell-Ginet, Ruth Borker, and Nelly Furman, 45–54. New York: Praeger, 1980.

By examining women in the reading process, we could begin to elaborate a feminist poetics and see how literary works become meaningful for women.

Gardiner, Judith Kegan. "On Female Identity and Writing by Women." *Critical Inquiry* 8 (1981): 347–61.

Many women critics tell women readers how to read women writers; and they tell women writers how to write for women readers. The implied relationship between the self and what one reads is personal and intense.

Gaudin, Colette, et al. Introduction to "Feminist Readings: French Texts/American Contexts." *Yale French Studies,* no. 62 (1981), pp. 2–18.

Essays in this volume posit: that both the production and reception of the text, be it literary, critical, or theoretical, is grounded in gender; that when women speak, either within or about texts, the very fact of their participation undermines tradition and calls for its redefinition; that feminist readings of cultural as well as literary texts promise to invent new configurations within which women may act as subjects.

Gilbert, Sandra. "Life Studies, or Speech after Long Silence: Feminist Critics Today." *College English* 40 (1979): 849–63.

Feminist critics feel a need to locate themselves—their literal selves rather than their literary personae—somewhere in their critical work. Women's studies research is the work of impassioned rereading.

———. "Patriarchal Poetry and Women Readers: Reflections on Milton's Bogey." *PMLA* 93 (1978): 368–82.

Literary women, readers and writers alike, have long been confused and intimidated by the patriarchal etiology that defines a solitary Father God as the only creator of all things for such a fiercely masculine cosmic Author would appear to be the sole legitimate model for all earthly authors.

Greenberg, Caren. "Reading Reading: Echo's Abduction of Language." In *Women and Language in Literature and Society,* edited by Sally McConnell-Ginet, Ruth Borker, and Nelly Furman, 300–309. New York: Praeger, 1980.

If the text can come to be seen as a locus of processes, as speaking itself, then it can cease being represented by and occupying the political position of dead women. It will no longer be open to critical or creative dominance. Domination or mastery of the text must disappear as a political necessity of criticism.

Gubar, Susan. "The Blank Page and the Issue of Female Creativity." *Critical Inquiry* 8 (1981): 347–61.

Contemporary critics not infrequently write about the act of reading in sexual terms.

Jacobus, Mary. "The Difference of View." In *Women Writing and Writing about Women,* edited by Mary Jacobus, 10–21. New York: Harper and Row, 1979.

All attempts to inscribe female difference within writing are a matter of inscribing women within fictions of one kind or another, necessitating a rewriting of these fictions. This work of revision makes female difference of view a question rather than an answer, and a question to be asked not simply of women, but of writing too.

———. "Is There a Woman in This Text?" *New Literary History* 14 (1982): 117–41.

Finds problematic the insistence of American feminist critics on "women's experience" as the ground of difference in writing and reading.

Jardine, Alice. "Pre-Texts for the Transatlantic Feminist." *Yale French Studies,* no. 62 (1981), pp. 220–36.

Finds promising the elaboration of a feminist strategy of reading/writing that reaches beyond while in dialogue with the tradition of purifying male topoi.

Juhasz, Suzanne. "The Critic as Feminist: Reflections on Women's Poetry, Feminism, and the Art of Criticism." *Women's Studies* 5 (1977): 113–27.

An important early attempt to characterize feminist readings—in particular, feminist readings of women's poetry. Juhasz privileges "the personal, the individual, and the subjective within the act of criticism," the "engagement of the critic herself as an active participant and identifiable voice in her work."

Kamuf, Peggy. "Writing Like a Woman." In *Women and Language in Literature and Society,* edited by Sally McConnell-Ginet, Ruth Borker, and Nelly Furman, 284–99. New York: Praeger, 1980.

Reading a text written by a woman will be reading it *as if* it had no determined father, no patriarchal heritage.

Kennard, Jean E. "Convention Coverage, or How to Read Your Own Life." *New Literary History* 8 (1981): 69–88.

Demonstrates that an alliance between feminist criticism and reader-response criticism is an especially fruitful one.

———. "Personally Speaking: Feminist Critics and the Community of Readers." *College English* 43 (1981): 140–45.

Posits the existence of a community of feminist readers who read feminist criticism in a personal way.

Kolodny, Annette. "A Map for Rereading: Or, Gender and the Interpretation of Literary Texts." *New Literary History* 11 (1980): 451–67.

Feminist appeals to revisionary rereading offer a potential enhancing of our capacity to read the world, our literary texts, and even one another, anew.

———. "Dancing through the Minefield: Some Observations on the Theory, Practice, and Politics of a Feminist Literary Criticism." *Feminist Studies* 6 (1980): 1–25.

Identifies three crucial propositions that underlie feminist criticism: (1) literary history is a fiction; (2) insofar as we are taught how to read, what we engage are not texts but paradigms; (3) since the grounds upon which we assign aesthetic value to texts are never infallible, unchangeable, or universal, we must reexamine not only our aesthetics but, as well, the inherent biases and assumptions informing the critical methods which (in part) shape our aesthetic responses.

———. "Some Notes on Defining a 'Feminist Literary Criticism.'" *Critical Inquiry* 2 (1975): 75–92.

Feminist critics must develop not only new critical methodologies but also new and different critical voices.

———. "Turning the Lens on 'The Panther Captivity': A Feminist Exercise in Practical Criticism." *Critical Inquiry* 8 (1981): 329–45.

A distinguishing characteristic of the feminist critic is the habit of consciously, purposely, and consistently seeking out the significance of the presence of women as readers, writers, and social participants in speaking of the historical context for any given literary text.

Miller, Nancy K. "Women's Autobiography in France: For a Dialectics of Identification." In *Women and Language in Literature and Society,* edited by Sally McConnell-Ginet, Ruth Borker, and Nelly Furman, 258–73. New York: Praeger, 1980.

Proposes a dialectical practice of reading which involves reading women's autobiographical writings along with their fiction. Such "double reading" provides an apparatus for deciphering the female self.

Millett, Kate. *Sexual Politics.* New York: Avon Books, 1970.

Calls for a form of literary criticism that takes into account the larger cultural context in which literature is conceived and produced. This larger context is a culture that supports masculine authority in all areas of life.

Mulvey, Laura. "Feminism, Film, and the *Avant-garde.*" In *Women Writing and Writing about Women,* edited by Mary Jacobus, 177–95. New York: Harper and Row, 1979.

A formalist feminist film criticism foregrounds the process itself, privileging the signifier, necessarily disrupting aesthetic unity and forcing the spectator's attention on to the means of production of meaning.

Ohmann, Carol. "Emily Brontë in the Hands of the Male Critics." *College English* 32 (1971): 906–13.

There is a considerable correlation between what readers assume or know the sex of the writer to be and what they actually see, or neglect to see, in his or her work.

Rich, Adrienne. "When We Dead Awaken: Writing as Re-Vision." *College English* 34 (1972): 18–30.

A radical critique of literature, feminist in its impulse, necessitates knowing the writing of the past, knowing it differently than we have ever known it, not to pass on a tradition but to break its hold over us.

Schor, Naomi. "Fiction as Interpretation/Interpretation as Fiction." In *The Reader in the Text: Essays on Audience and Interpretation,* edited by Susan R. Suleiman and Inge Crosman, 165–82. Princeton: Princeton University Press, 1980.

Calls for a recognition that interpretation is a fiction and that the interpreter is not omnipotent. The commentator's humility is bound up with his (or her) femininity.

Schumacher, Dorin. "Subjectivities: A Theory of the Critical Process." In *Feminist Literary Criticism: Explorations in Theory,* edited by Josephine Donovan, 29–37. Lexington: University Press of Kentucky, 1975.

Feminist critics' self-conscious awareness, their open struggle with the problems of outlining their own critical method, their new understanding of the sex-linked ideas that critics apply to texts are, while not new to criticism, a challenge to many other critics to examine their own sex-linked ideas.

Showalter, Elaine. "Feminist Criticism in the Wilderness." *Critical Inquiry* 8 (1981): 179–205.

A cultural model of women's writing can help us read women's texts.

Spector, Judith. "Gender Studies: New Directions for Feminist Criticism." *College English* 43 (1981): 374–78.

Sees women's studies as a vital part of a larger enterprise, gender studies. The study of male authors is wholly legitimate for the feminist scholar.

Spivak, Gayatri Chakravorty. "Displacement and the Discourse of Woman." In *Displacement: Derrida and After,* edited by Mark Krupnick. Bloomington: Indiana University Press, 1983.

The collective project of feminist critics must always be to rewrite the *social* text so that the historical and sexual differentials operate together.

———. "French Feminism in an International Frame." *Yale French Studies,* no. 62 (1981), pp. 154–84.

The French feminist critical practice of "symptomatic" reading isolates seemingly marginal moments to demonstrate the ethico-political agenda. Such an approach, when applied to discourses that spell out and establish the power of the patriarchy, is an excellent strategy for undermining the masculinist vanguard.

Thiebaux, Marcelle. "Foucault's Fantasia for Feminists: The Woman Reading." In *Theory and Practice of Feminist Literary Criticism,* edited by Gabriela Mora and Karen S. Van Hooft, 44–61. Ypsilanti, Mich.: Bilingual, 1982.

The only possible library for a woman is one invented by herself, writing herself or her own discourse into it.

Zimmerman, Bonnie. "What Has Never Been: An Overview of Lesbian Feminist Literary Criticism." *Feminist Studies* 7 (1981): 451–75.

Discusses the development and the current state of lesbian feminist criticism and surveys the essential texts.

Readers and Texts

Baym, Nina. "Melodramas of Beset Manhood: How Theories of American Fiction Exclude Women Authors." *American Quarterly* 33 (1981): 123–39.

An illustration of the symbiotic relationship between an androcentric canon and androcentric reading strategies.

———. *Novels, Readers, and Reviewers: Responses to Fiction in Antebellum America.* Ithaca: Cornell University Press, 1984.

Classifies readers on the basis of education, class, age, gender, and family membership.

———. *Woman's Fiction: A Guide to Novels by and about Women in America, 1820–1870.* Ithaca: Cornell University Press, 1978.

Most male writers in nineteenth-century America assumed an audience of men as a matter of course and reacted with distress and dismay as they discovered that to make a living by writing they would have to please female readers. Women's experience seems to be outside the interests and sympathies of the male critics whose judgments have largely determined the canon of classic American literature.

Bell, Barbara Currier, and Carol Ohmann. "Virginia Woolf's Criticism: A Polemical Preface." In *Feminist Literary Criticism: Explorations in Theory,* edited by Josephine Donovan, 48–60. Lexington: University Press of Kentucky, 1975.

Berg, Elizabeth. "Impossible Representation: A Reading of *Phèdre.*" *Romanic Review* 73 (1982): 421–37.

Brownstein, Rachel M. *Becoming a Heroine: Reading about Women in Novels.* New York: Viking, 1982.

Female readers of classic English novels find easy transference, in realms such as "essence of character," to the fictional heroine. Men are more likely to respond to the fantasy of action. Classic heroine-centered novels do not offer a blueprint for a feminist utopia; to enjoy them is to experience the pull of a seductive, reactionary dream.

Carpenter, Carol. "Exercises to Combat Sexist Reading and Writing." *College English* 43 (1981): 293–300.

Through active inquiry students recognize the powerful sexist conventions in thought and language and, by developing their language skills, are in a position to question, perhaps even change, the culture that has shaped them.

Cota-Cárdenas, Margarita. "A New Kind of Reader: The Chicano Feminist." *Reader,* no. 8 (1980), pp. 23–28.

Drotner, Kristen. "Schoolgirls, Madcaps, and Air Aces: English Girls and Their Magazine Reading between the Wars." *Feminist Studies* 9 (1983): 33–52.

Traces the development of the "first truly mass-produced leisure reading to reach virtually all pre-adolescent girls" in England—the girls' magazines that flourished from 1919 to 1945. Drotner describes the changes in the form and content of the stories in the magazines and relates them to the changing socioeconomic situation of middle- and working-class school-girls and to the ideological function required by this situation.

Felman, Shoshana. "Rereading Femininity." *Yale French Studies,* no. 62 (1981), pp. 19–44.

Balzac's novel *The Girl with the Golden Eyes* dramatized the "riddle of femininity" as the double question of the reading of sexual difference and of the intervention of sexual difference in the very act of reading.

Flynn, Elizabeth A. "Women Reading: A Phenomenological Approach." *Reader,* no. 8 (1980), pp. 16–22.

Furman, Nelly. "A Room of One's Own: Reading Absence." In *Women's Language and Style,* edited by Douglas Butturff and Edmund L. Epstein, 99–105. Akron, Ohio: University of Akron Press, 1978.

Applies the reading method of the narrator of *A Room of One's Own* to the text itself.

Gardiner, Judith Kegan. "Psychoanalytic Criticism and the Female Reader." *Literature and Psychology* 26 (1976): 100–107.

Critique of the masculine bias in Norman Holland's *5 Readers Reading* and *Poems in Persons.*

Higonnet, Margaret. Introduction. In *The Representation of Women in Fiction: Selected Papers from the English Institute, 1981,* edited by Carolyn G. Heilbrun and Margaret R. Higonnet. Baltimore: Johns Hopkins University Press, 1983.

A focus on the topic of women leads us beyond texts to questions about our processes of interpretation and representation.

Hirsch, Marianne. "Gender, Reading, and Desire in *Moderato Cantabile.*" *Twentieth Century Literature* 28 (1982), 69–85.

Holland, Norman N. "Transactive Teaching: Cordelia's Death." *College English* 39 (1977): 276–85.

Examines responses of five women and four men to *King Lear.* The men brought to the play a need, typical of men in our society, to feel powerfully in control of events. The women brought the problem of coping with patriarchal culture.

Homans, Margaret. "Eliot, Wordsworth, and the Scenes of the Sister's Instruction." *Critical Inquiry* 8 (1981): 223–41.

Maggie Tulliver starts out as an accurate reader who distinguishes easily between elucidating a text foreign to her and inventing her own stories. As Maggie grows up and becomes more feminine she becomes an overly literal reader—a docile reader.

————. *Women Writers and Poetic Identity: Dorothy Wordsworth, Emily Brontë, and Emily Dickinson.* Princeton: Princeton University Press, 1980.

This book tests the hypothesis that it should be possible to read the poetical words of women writers primarily as literary texts and in a literary context, while at the same time finding a language for evaluating the literary effects of the author's femininity.

Jacobus, Mary. "The Buried Letter: Feminism and Romanticism in *Villette.*" In *Women Writing and Writing about Women,* edited by Mary Jacobus, 42–60. New York: Harper and Row, 1979.

The feminist critic must produce an ex-centric text, a displacement into criticism of ruptures and expressions of women's discourse. Feminist critical strategy should include the unfolding of literature whose very repressions become an eloquent testimony to imaginative freedom, whose ruptures provide access to a double text, and whose doubles animate, as well as haunt, the fiction they trouble.

————. "The Question of Language: Men of Maxims and *The Mill on the Floss.*" *Critical Inquiry* 8 (1981): 207–22.

Undertakes a "symptomatic" reading of a thematically relevant chapter from Eliot's *The Mill on the Floss* in the hope that this quintessentially critical activity will bring to light if not "a possible operation of the feminine language" at least one mode of its recovery—language itself.

Johnson, Catherine. "The 'Spectator' and the 'Viewer.'" *Reader,* no. 8 (1980), pp. 28–32.

Kahane, Claire. "Gothic Mirrors and Feminine Identity." *Centennial Review* 24 (1980): 43–64.

Kaplan, Cora. "The Indefinite Disclosed: Christina Rossetti and Emily Dickinson." In *Women Writing and Writing about Women,* edited by Mary Jacobus, 61–79. New York: Harper and Row, 1979.

The compacted lyrics of Emily Dickinson and Christina Rossetti, which form a sub-genre of their work, employ atypical forms of imagery. The poems are shapes like ink-blots, from which casual readers and critical theorists alike decipher related images in their own experience.

Lanser, Susan Snieder, and Evelyn Torton Beck. "[Why] Are There No Great Women Critics? And What Difference Does It Make?" In *The Prism of Sex: Essays in the Sociology of Knowledge,* edited by Evelyn Torton Beck and Julia A. Sherman, 79–91. Madison: University of Wisconsin Press, 1979.

Not only the conception of criticism but critical theories themselves have been seriously distorted by the omission of women's thought. Patriarchal culture continues to resist, denigrate, and mistrust woman as critic, theory-builder, or judge.

Larsson, Lisbeth. "Women's Reading." *Women's Studies International Quarterly* 3 (1980): 227–83.

Discusses popular women's literature in Sweden.

McCrindle, Jean. "Reading *The Golden Notebook* in 1962." In *Notebooks/Memoirs/Archives: Reading and Rereading Doris Lessing,* edited by Jenny Taylor, 43–56. Boston: Routledge and Kegan Paul, 1982.

Describes the powerful effect *The Golden Notebook* had on her when she read it in 1962.

Mann, Peter H. "The Romantic Novel and Its Readers." *Journal of Popular Culture* 15 (1981): 9–18.

Suggests that romantic fiction is popular because it reassures women that there is such a thing as love.

Marsden, Madonna. "Gentle Truths for Gentler Readers: The Fiction of Elizabeth Goudge." In *Images of Women in Fiction: Feminist Perspectives,* edited by Susan Koppelman Cornillon, 68–78. Bowling Green, Ohio: Bowling Green University Popular Press, 1972.

Miner, Madonne M. *Insatiable Appetites: Twentieth-Century American Women's Bestsellers.* Westport, Conn.: Greenwood Press, 1984.

Modelski, Tania. *Loving with a Vengeance: Mass-Produced Fantasies for Women.* New York: Methuen, 1982.

Audience-centered critique of three genres of popular art forms that appeal to women—harlequin romances, gothic romances, and soap operas.

Orloff, Kossia. "A Feminist Reading of *Can You Forgive Her?* and *Portrait of a Lady.*" *Reader,* no. 8 (1980), pp. 32–36.

Radway, Janice A. *Reading the Romance: Women, Patriarchy, and Popular Literature.* Chapel Hill: University of North Carolina Press, 1984.

Provides a comprehensive explanation of why the women in Radway's study find romance reading not only practically feasible and generally enjoyable but also emotionally necessary as well.

———. "Women Read the Romance: The Interaction of Text and Context." *Feminist Studies* 9 (1983): 53–78.

An analysis of data consisting of interviews with 16 avid female readers of popular romance novels and of a lengthy questionnaire completed by 42 such readers suggests that some contemporary romances actually attempt to reconcile changing attitudes about gender behavior with more traditional sexual arrangements.

Shapiro, Ann R. "The Woman Reader and the Male Critical Establishment." *Reader,* no. 8 (1980), pp. 5–11.

Showalter, Elaine. "Women and the Literary Curriculum." *College English* 32 (1971): 855–62.

Silver, Brenda. *Virginia Woolf's Reading Notebooks.* Princeton: Princeton University Press, 1983.

Taylor, Jenny. "Introduction: Situating Reading." In *Notebooks/Memoirs/Archives: Reading and Rereading Doris Lessing,* edited by Jenny Taylor, 1–42. Boston: Routledge and Kegan Paul, 1982.

Provides an overview of critics' responses to Lessing's novels.

U'Ren, Marjorie. "The Image of Women in Textbooks." In *Women in Sexist Society: Studies in Power and Powerlessness,* edited by Vivian Gornick and Barbara K. Moran, 318–28. New York: Basic Books, 1971.

Wilson, Elizabeth. "Yesterday's Heroines: On Rereading Lessing and de Beauvoir." In *Notebooks/Memoirs/Archives: Reading and Rereading Doris Lessing,* edited by Jenny Taylor, 57–74. Boston: Routledge and Kegan Paul, 1982.

Wilson charts her different reactions to Lessing and de Beauvoir as a young woman and at the present. The process leads to discoveries about contemporary feminism and about her own development as a feminist.

Research on the Reading of Children and Adolescents

Asher, Steven R., and Richard A. Markell. "Sex Differences in Comprehension of High- and Low-Interest Reading Material." *Journal of Educational Psychology* 66 (1974): 614–19.

Boys' reading comprehension was facilitated by high-interest materials, while girls were relatively unaffected by interest level of material.

Beaven, Mary H. "Responses of Adolescents to Feminine Characters in Literature." *Research in the Teaching of English* 6 (1972): 48–68.

Girls identify with male characters whereas boys do not identify with female characters.

Bernstein, Joanne. "The Changing Roles of Females in Books for Young Children." *Reading Teacher* 27 (1974): 545–49.

Beyard-Tyler, Karen C., and Howard J. Sullivan. "Adolescent Reading Preferences for Type of Theme and Sex of Character." *Reading Research Quarterly* 16 (1980): 104–20.

Boys preferred story synopses with male protagonists and girls preferred synopses with female protagonists. Boys' preferences for male protagonists became significantly stronger as grade level increased, whereas girls' preferences for female protagonists decreased significantly as grade level increased.

Chansky, Norman M.; Joanne Czernik; James Duffy; and Lillian Finnell. "Sex Differences and Initial Reading Performance." *Psychological Reports* 46 (1980): 523–26.

Girls' performance in first grade was slightly higher than that of boys in the samples surveyed.

Assesses the reading interests of fourth graders using a questionnaire technique. Boys indicated a preference for sports, biography, mystery, social studies, science, humor, animal stories, adventure, fantasy, and poetry, in that order. Girls showed a preference for mystery, humor, adventure, biography, animal stories, poetry, fantasy, social studies, science, and sports. There were significant sex differences in all categories except animal stories and mystery.

Chiu, Lian-Hwang. "Reading Preferences of Fourth-Grade Children Related to Sex and Reading Ability." *Journal of Educational Research* 66 (1973): 369–73.

Downing, John, Richard B. May, and Lloyd O. Ollila. "Sex Differences and Cultural Expectations in Reading." In *Sex Stereotypes and Reading: Research and Strategies,* edited by E. Marcia Sheridan, 17–34. Newark: International Reading Association, 1983.

The differences noted between sexes in reading are generally small in comparison to the range of differences within a sex and have proved to be difficult to measure conclusively.

Duncan, Patricia H. "Sex Roles and Reading Instruction: A Critique of Related Research." *National Reading Conference Yearbook* 25 (1976): 52–62.

Dwyer, Carol Anne. "Comparative Aspects of Sex Differences in Reading." In *Reading, What of the Future?* Proceedings of the Eleventh Annual Conference, 267–73. London: Ward Lock, 1975.

Where reading is seen as an activity appropriate to females, girls should read better than boys. In cultures where reading is seen as an activity appropriate to the male role, boys should read better than girls.

———. "Sex Differences in Reading: An Evaluation and a Critique of Current Theories." *Review of Educational Research* 43 (1973): 455–67.

Fillmer, H. Thompson. "Research on Language Differences between Males and Females." In *Sex Stereotypes and Reading: Research and Strategies,* edited by E. Marcia Sheridan, 80–90. Newark: International Reading Association, 1983.

Publishers must follow guidelines designed to reduce the stereotypes of women as sex objects and passive observers of life. School textbooks should include an equal number of references to women and men.

Frasher, Ramona S. "A Feminist Look at Literature for Children: Ten Years Later." In *Sex Stereotypes and Reading: Research and Strategies,* edited by E. Marcia Sheridan, 64–79. Newark: International Reading Association, 1983.

Progress has been made in the area of fiction for children in terms of increasing the number of females in main character roles and in protraying them with more positive and varied personality characteristics and in a greater variety of behaviors. Special purpose books designed to compensate for the absence of women in varied occupational roles have appeared in increasing numbers.

Gates, A. I. "Sex Differences in Reading Ability." *Elementary School Journal* 61 (1961): 431–34.

Girls' reading scores are higher than boys' from third through eighth grade. Data support an environmental rather than a physical explanation of sex differences in reading achievement.

Graebner, D. "A Decade of Sexism in Readers." *The Reading Teacher* 26 (1972): 58.

Greenbaum, Gloria R. "High School Seniors Read with a Purpose: To Spot Sex Stereotypes." In *Sex Stereotypes and Reading: Research and Strategies,* edited by E. Marcia Sheridan, 108–12. Newark: International Reading Association, 1983.

Describes a class project designed to create awareness among high school students of the impact sex stereotyping has had on them and on youngsters in their formative years.

Hamlin, Talbot. "American Reading Materials: A Selective Reflector." In *Sex Stereotypes and Reading: Research and Strategies,* edited by E. Marcia Sheridan, 49–63. Newark: International Reading Association, 1983.

Reading materials today present a broader, more comprehensive view of society than that presented in earlier readers. They are less sexist and more humane.

Hoover, Nora Lee. "Multicultural Nonsexist Education: A Two-Edged Sword." In *Sex Stereotypes and Reading: Research and Strategies,* edited by E. Marcia Sheridan, 102–7. Newark: International Reading Association, 1983.

The classroom teacher who attempts to promote cultural pluralism within the context of a truly nonsexist classroom may find the mesh somewhat more difficult to achieve in practice than in theory.

Johnson, Carole Schulte, and Gloria R. Greenbaum. "Girls' and Boys' Reading Interests: A Review of the Research." In *Sex Stereotypes and Reading: Research and Strategies,* edited by E. Marcia Sheridan, 35–48. Newark: International Reading Association, 1983.

The voluminous studies which found interest differences based on sex can be criticized on the basis of data collection procedures and instruments used. Boys tend to reject both female and male characters when the content is not appealing to them. Girls and boys have many overlapping reading interests, although girls tend to have a wider variety of interests.

Johnson, Dale D. "Sex Differences in Reading across Cultures." *Reading Research Quarterly* 9 (1973–74): 67–86.

Sex differences in reading ability as measured by tests may be related to cultural influences.

Johnson, E. G.; L. Gibbons; H. Kepsi; and R. Parker. "Differential Effects of Sex-Oriented Reading Material on Children's Reading Performance." *Australian Journal of Education* 23 (1979): 297–98.

Sex-oriented reading material was found to have a differential effect on the recall scores of boys and girls ages 9–10. A similar trend was found for the comprehension scores based on the cloze procedure. The sex of the tester had no significant effect on performance.

Kingston, Albert J., and Terry Lovelace. "Sexism and Reading: A Critical Review of the Literature." *Reading Research Quarterly* 13 (1977–78): 133–61.

Reviews 78 articles which investigate sexism in basal readers, texts, and children's literature.

Lehr, Fran. "Cultural Influences and Sex Differences in Reading." *The Reading Teacher* 35 (1982): 744–46.

May, Richard B., and Lloyd O. Ollila. "Reading Sex-Role Attitudes in Preschoolers." *Reading Research Quarterly* 16 (1981): 583–95.

Nilsen, Alleen Pace. "Sexism in Children's Books and Elementary Teaching Materials." In *Sexism and Language,* edited by Alleen Pace Nilsen, Haig Bosmajian, H. Lee Gershuny, and Julia P. Stanley, 161–79. Urbana, Ill.: National Council of Teachers of English, 1977.

Children's books are a male-oriented medium characterized by subtle and unsubtle stereotypes and sexist language.

———. "Women in Children's Literature." *College English* 37 (1971): 918–26.

Porro, Barbara. "The Nonsexist Classroom: A Process Approach." In *Sex Stereotypes and Reading: Research and Strategies,* edited by E. Marcia Sheridan, 91–101. Newark: International Reading Association, 1983.

In order to combat sexism in the classroom the teacher must be committed to develop an awareness of sexism and to confront whatever sexist attitudes and behaviors that awareness reveals.

Sheridan, E. Marcia. *Sex Differences and Reading: An Annotated Bibliography.* Newark: International Reading Association, 1976.

Reviews literature on sex differences and reading. Categories include "Sex Differences in Reading," "Sex Differences Based on Reading Methods," "Sex Differences in Interest and Attitude," "Cognitive and Psychological Sex Differences."

———. "Sex Stereotypes in a Sociocognitive Model of Reading." In *Sex Stereotypes and Reading: Research and Strategies,* edited by E. Marcia Sheridan, 1–16. Newark: International Reading Association, 1983.

By presenting only persons in traditional roles in reading materials, we limit the role models to those acceptable to people who espouse a particular value system. In so doing, we contribute to children's misconceptions by presenting them with incomplete information regarding their conception of people.

Squire, James R. *The Responses of Adolescents while Reading Four Short Stories.* Champaign, Ill.: National Council of Teachers of English, 1964.

Taylor, Marjorie, E. "Sex-Role Stereotypes in Children's Readers." *Elementary English* 50 (1973): 1045–47.

Textbooks fail to help prepare girls for future realities and contribute subtly and significantly to the formation of negative self images.

Tibbetts, Sylvia-Lee. "Sex Differences in Children's Reading Preferences." *The Reading Teacher* 28 (1974): 279–81.

Social pressure or training may be the most significant factor behind observed sex differences.

———. "Wanted: Data to Prove that Sexist Reading Material Has an Impact on the Reader." *Reading Teacher* 32 (1978): 165–69.

We have been alerted to the possible damage done by the overwhelming preponderance of sexist reading material. The next step is to find some valid reliable method of measuring it.

Townes, B. D.; E. W. Trupin; D. C. Martin; and D. Goldstein. "Neuropsychological Correlates of Academic Success among Elementary School Children." *Journal of Consulting and Clinical Psychology* 48 (1980): 675–84.

Girls were found to be superior to boys in verbal reasoning, language skills, and serial perceptual matching skills, whereas boys were superior on tests of spatial memory and motor skills. These age and sex differences were related to differences in academic achievement and discussed in terms of implications of findings for curriculum planning.

Women on Words and Images. *Dick and Jane as Victims: Sex Stereotyping in Children's Readers.* (Expanded 1975 ed.) Princeton: Women on Words and Images, 1975.

Extends a 1972 study that found that boys and men were present in children's readers in overwhelmingly larger numbers than were girls and women. Further, the study found that male characters generally had positive traits such as ingenuity and adventurousness while female characters had negative traits such as dependency and passivity.

The 1975 study found that the overall imbalance described in the earlier study still exists, but some females were found who were clever, competent, and initiating, and a few males were found who expressed emotion.

Contributors

DAVID BLEICH is professor of English at Indiana University. He is the author of *Readings and Feelings* and *Subjective Criticism* (Johns Hopkins), as well as numerous articles on readers' responses to texts.

ROGER CHAFFIN is assistant professor in the Department of Psychology at Trenton State College. He has published articles in the *Journal of Verbal Learning and Verbal Behavior*, the *Journal of General Psychology*, the *Journal of Applied Psychology*, the *Journal of Experimental Psychology*, *Cognitive Science*, *Psychological Bulletin*, and the *Journal of Psycholinguistic Research*.

MARY CRAWFORD is associate professor of psychology and women's studies at West Chester University. She has published articles in *Psychonomic Science*, *Learning and Motivation*, the *Journal of Experimental Psychology*, the *International Journal of Women's Studies*, and elsewhere.

JUDITH FETTERLEY is associate professor of English at the State University of New York at Albany. She is the author of *The Resisting Reader: A Feminist Approach to American Fiction* and of numerous articles, including essays on Hemingway, Chopin, Wharton, Alcott, and Twain.

ELIZABETH A. FLYNN is associate professor in the Department of Humanities at Michigan Technological University. She is the editor of *Reader: Essays in Reader-Oriented Theory, Criticism, and Pedagogy*, and has published articles in *College English*, *College Composition and Communication*, *New Orleans Review*, *Writing Instructor*, and elsewhere.

NORMAN N. HOLLAND is Milbauer Eminent Scholar at the University of Florida, where he directs the Institute for Psychological Study of the Arts. His publications include *The Dynamics of Literary Response, Poems in Persons, 5 Readers Reading, Laughing: A Psychology of Humor*, and *The I*, and numerous articles and reviews.

JEAN E. KENNARD is professor of English and women's studies at the University of New Hampshire, where she teaches couses in nineteenth-century fiction, modern British and American literature, and women writers. She is the author of *Number and Nightmare: Forms of Fantasy in Contemporary Fiction* and *A*

Study of the Two-Suitor Convention in Victorian Fiction. Her articles on feminist critical theory have appeared in *College English, New Literary History* and *Signs.*

MADONNE M. MINER, assistant professor of English at the University of Wyoming, is the author of *Insatiable Appetites: Twentieth-Century American Women's Bestsellers* and of various essays on women writers, characters, and readers. She is currently working on a book-length study of the reader's role in feminist fiction of the 1970s.

SUSAN SCHIBANOFF is associate professor of English and women's studies at the University of New Hampshire. Her studies of Chaucer and medieval literature have appeared in *ELH,* the *Journal of English and Germanic Philology, Modern Philology,* and *Speculum.* Her work on early women writers has been published in *Signs, Women's Studies International Quarterly,* and *Tulsa Studies in Women's Literature.* Currently she is working on a study of early audience reception of the Wife of Bath's Prologue and Tale.

PATROCINIO P. SCHWEICKART is associate professor of English at the University of New Hampshire, specializing in criticism and theory, and women and literature. She has published articles in *Reader, Modern Fiction Studies, Signs,* and the *Canadian Journal of Social and Political Theory.* She received the 1984 Florence Howe Award for Outstanding Feminist Scholarship for "Reading Ourselves," the essay included in this volume.

ELIZABETH SEGEL is a lecturer in the English Department and a member of the core faculty in Women's Studies at the University of Pittsburgh. A frequent contributor to children's literature journals, she serves on the editorial boards of *Children's Literature in Education* and the *Advocate.* Segel is coauthor (with M. M. Kimmel) of *For Reading Out Loud! A Guide to Sharing Books with Children.*

LEONA F. SHERMAN worked with Norman Holland at the Center for the Psychological Study of the Arts, SUNY, Buffalo.

KATHRYN SHEVELOW is assistant professor of Eighteenth-Century English Literature at the University of California, San Diego. She is at work on a book on the early English periodical, its social context, and its readership. She specializes in early-eighteenth-century literature and culture.

SUSAN RUBIN SULEIMAN is John L. Loeb associate professor of the Humanities at Harvard University. She is the author of *Authoritarian Fictions: The Ideological Novel as a Literary Genre* and co-editor of *The Reader in the Text: Essays on Audience and Interpretation,* and she has published numerous articles on modern French literature and literary theory. Her current research is on problems of avant-garde writing and on feminist theory.